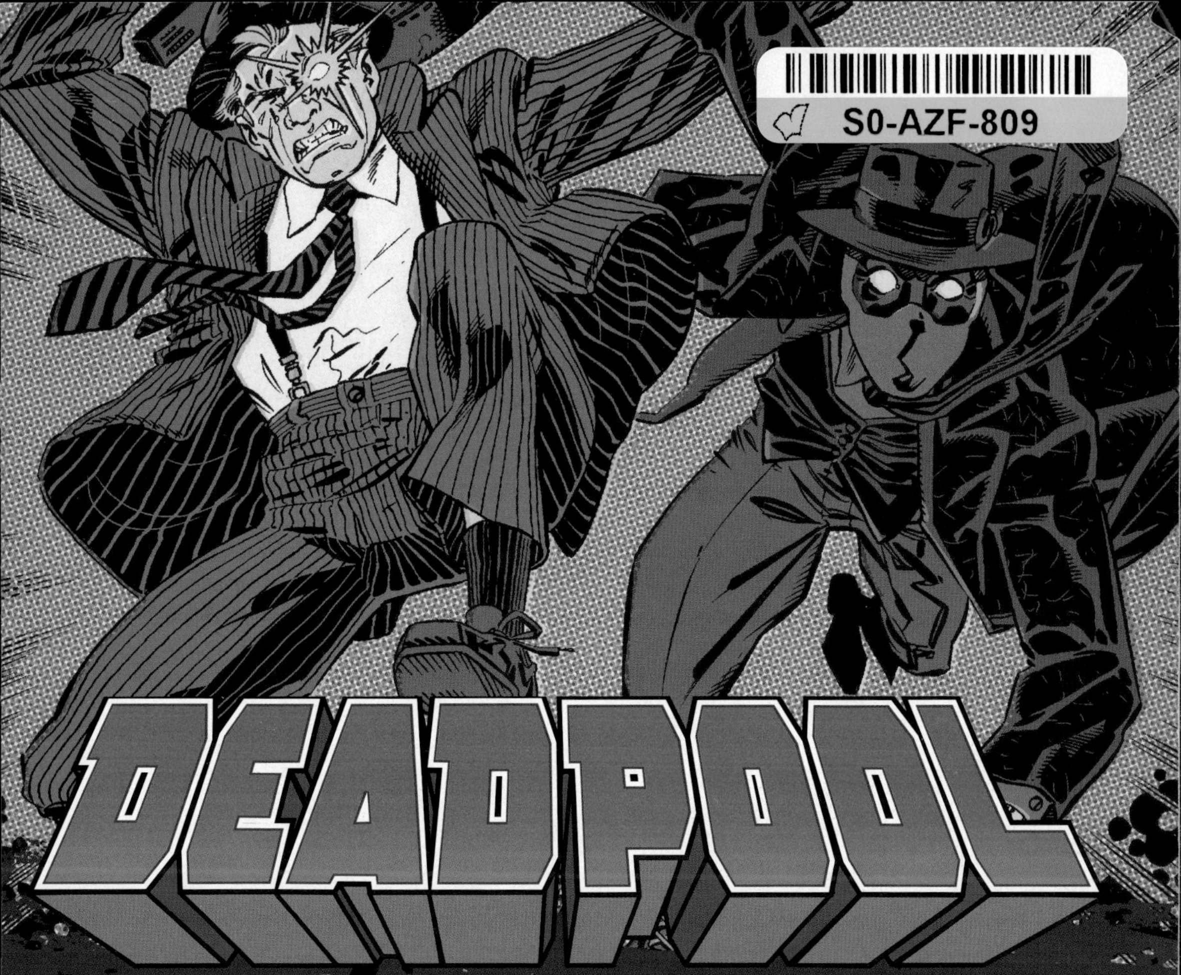

DEADPOOL

WRITERS

GERRY DUGGAN & BRIAN POSEHN

ARTIST

SCOTT KOBLISH

COLORIST

VAL STAPLES

LETTERER

VC'S JOE SABINO

COVER ART

PHIL NOTO (#26), TOM SCIOLI & VAL STAPLES (#20), KRIS ANKA (#13), SCOTT KOBLISH & VAL STAPLES (#27), KEVIN MAGUIRE & ROSEMARY CHEETHAM (#7), SCOTT KOBLISH & RUTH REDMOND (#45), MARK BROOKS (#34) AND SCOTT KOBLISH & JAMES CAMPBELL (#40)

ASSISTANT EDITORS

FRANKIE JOHNSON, HEATHER ANTOS & CHARLES BEACHAM

EDITOR

JORDAN D. WHITE

SPECIAL THANKS TO DAVID MANDELL

DEADPOOL CREATED BY ROB LIEFELD & FABIAN NICIEZA

Collection Editor: Alex Starbuck • Assistant Editor: Sarah Brunstad • Editors, Special Projects: Jennifer Grünwald & Mark D. Beazley
Senior Editor, Special Projects: Jeff Youngquist • Layout: Jeph York • Book Designer: Joe Frontirre • SVP Print, Sales & Marketing: David Gabriel

Editor in Chief: Axel Alonso • Chief Creative Officer: Joe Quesada • Publisher: Dan Buckley • Executive Producer: Alan Fine

DEADPOOL: FLASHBACKS. Contains material originally published in magazine form as DEADPOOL #7, #13, #20, #26, #27, #34, #40 and #45. First printing 2016. ISBN# 978-0-7851-9748-5. Published by MARVEL WORLDWIDE, INC., a subsidiary of MARVEL ENTERTAINMENT, LLC. OFFICE OF PUBLICATION: 135 West 50th Street, New York, NY 10020. Copyright © 2016 MARVEL No similarity between any of the names, characters, persons, and/or institutions in this magazine with those of any living or dead person or institution is intended, and any such similarity which may exist is purely coincidental. **Printed in the U.S.A.** ALAN FINE, President, Marvel Entertainment; DAN BUCKLEY, President, TV, Publishing and Brand Management; JOE QUESADA, Chief Creative Officer; TOM BREVOORT, SVP of Publishing; DAVID BOGART, SVP of Operations & Procurement, Publishing; C.B. CEBULSKI, VP of International Development & Brand Management; DAVID GABRIEL, SVP Print, Sales & Marketing; JIM O'KEEFE, VP of Operations & Logistics; DAN CARR, Executive Director of Publishing Technology; SUSAN CRESPI, Editorial Operations Manager; ALEX MORALES, Publishing Operations Manager; STAN LEE, Chairman Emeritus. For information regarding advertising in Marvel Comics or on Marvel.com, please contact Jonathan Rheingold, VP of Custom Solutions & Ad Sales, at jrheingold@marvel.com. For Marvel subscription inquiries, please call 800-217-9158. **Manufactured between 11/20/2015 and 12/28/2015 by R.R. DONNELLEY, INC., SALEM, VA, USA.**

10 9 8 7 6 5 4 3 2 1

Welcome, good reader, to this very special collection of Deadpool stories. As a comic book aficionado, I am sure you know that the issues contained within were very nearly lost to the ages, and only sheer luck has brought them to light. These lost issues, now found and published, each represent a gem from a bygone era and an enlightening look into the state of comics in general and Deadpool in specific.

While each lost issue was published upon its discovery in recent years, for this collection, we present them in chronological order for historical context.

The oldest issue in this volume was actually not originally produced as a Deadpool book—it was a rejected *Sgt. Fury and His Howling Commandos* tale from sometime in the '50s, but it's unclear what year precisely. The issue actually pre-dates *Deadpool #1* by some five to ten years, but the pages were infamous at the Marvel offices in those days, with mimeographs of the insane issue circulating as a cautionary tale to the Bullpen not to make their stories too "out there." Experts have long theorized that when the time came to revamp the lead character of the long-running but in-decline *Wade Wilson, Mountie with a Mouth* series as a super hero, the creators took their inspiration from the mysterious red-faced man from the rejected tale. The rest, as they say...is a combination of actual published history and a bit of retconning.

Next up, we have the first actual shelved issue from the *Deadpool* series—a tale from sometime around 1965 or 1966. It's rumored that the issue was actually plotted for Jack Kirby to draw, but that he came down with a cold and was in bed for the six hours he'd scheduled to draw the issue. Regardless of the veracity of that rumor, it is known for sure that the editors were so enraged that the plot of the issue depended on the production of —and you'll pardon the mention of it—*fecal matter* that they pledged the issue would never see the light of day. Now, for your pleasure, we've made liars of them.

It's unclear why the next issue was shelved. It looks to be from the mid-to-late 1970s, and the notes regarding it are unclear. Regardless, the issue itself delves deep into the cultural milieu of the era, and perhaps some of the hot-button issues raised were more excessively heated than the buttons the company was comfortable pressing. And perhaps it is a bit of a conspiracy theory, but one wonders why the villain from the issue was never reused, considering that his was a name on many a lip at the time. Perhaps "The Man" was uncomfortable with him. We may never know.

The next issue is an interesting one as it represents an attempt by the Deadpool team to tie in with a large storyline going on in another series. *Iron Man*'s Tony Stark famously dealt with alcohol abuse issues in the classic "Demon in a Bottle" storyline, but many metaphorically ignorant readers have long wondered why the titular "demon" never makes an appearance in the story. It turns out, the answer was to be found in this lost Deadpool crossover issue. It's believed that this story was legitimately lost, having slipped between the drawers of the filing cabinet, denying Deadpool his rightful legacy as the man who finally helped Tony clean up his act—a wrong righted at last.

The one story in this volume that we are NOT able to print as it was originally intended is the shelved backup created for 1982's *Deadpool Annual #17*. A short story of a "team-up" between Deadpool and Ms. Marvel, the design for the alien invaders was deemed inappropriate due to its resemblance to...something not approved by the Comics Code. Unfortunately, upon unearthing the story, modern editors could not help but agree—those aliens are ENTIRELY inappropriate. We were, however, able to present the story in a slightly censored form.

It's no secret that the '90s is the era Deadpool is most associated with—and no wonder! It's the decade when one of Marvel's oldest and steadiest-selling D-listers finally exploded in a big way and received the recognition that his small but loyal fanbase knew he so rightfully deserved. So it's no surprise that we have TWO stories from the '90s featuring the Merc-Mouthed one, and both from that early period just BEFORE Deadpool's start making guest-appearance in *New Mutants #98*. The first is a discarded tie-in to 1991's "Infinity Gauntlet" crossover. Its rejection resulted in a near-historic event—the month of August 1991 featured NO comic books with Wade Wilson in them, the first time that ever happened since his first appearance in 1943.

The second '90s appearance is a dark one, and one wonders if Deadpool would have ever become as popular had this issue been printed as intended. The editors at the time felt it made the character irredeemable, had him cross a line he could never un-cross, dotting i's that, like Little Orphan Annie's, should have remained dotless. Were they right? It's up to you to decide, fair reader, to answer the question, "How do you like Wade now?"

Finally, as a bonus, we present a more modern tale, but one that's not quite your conventional Deadpool fare. Marvel sometimes will make customized comic books as advertising for other companies. So it was with this issue, which Roxxon commissioned as a coloring book in which Deadpool would teach children about the wonders of their new energy-producing technology, Gamma Fracturing. In the end, Roxxon refused to have the book distributed, destroying every available issue. The only surviving copy we could locate was a used one, already colored in by a child...but a relatively talented child, so we present that version of the book here.

This brings us to the end of this journey through the lost history of Deadpool...a history that was undiscovered for far too long, but which, now published, is 100 percent canonical and should be considered factual by any and all Handbook or Wikipedia writers. We hope you find it enlightening.

Jordan D. White
Comic Book Historian
11/25/2015

26

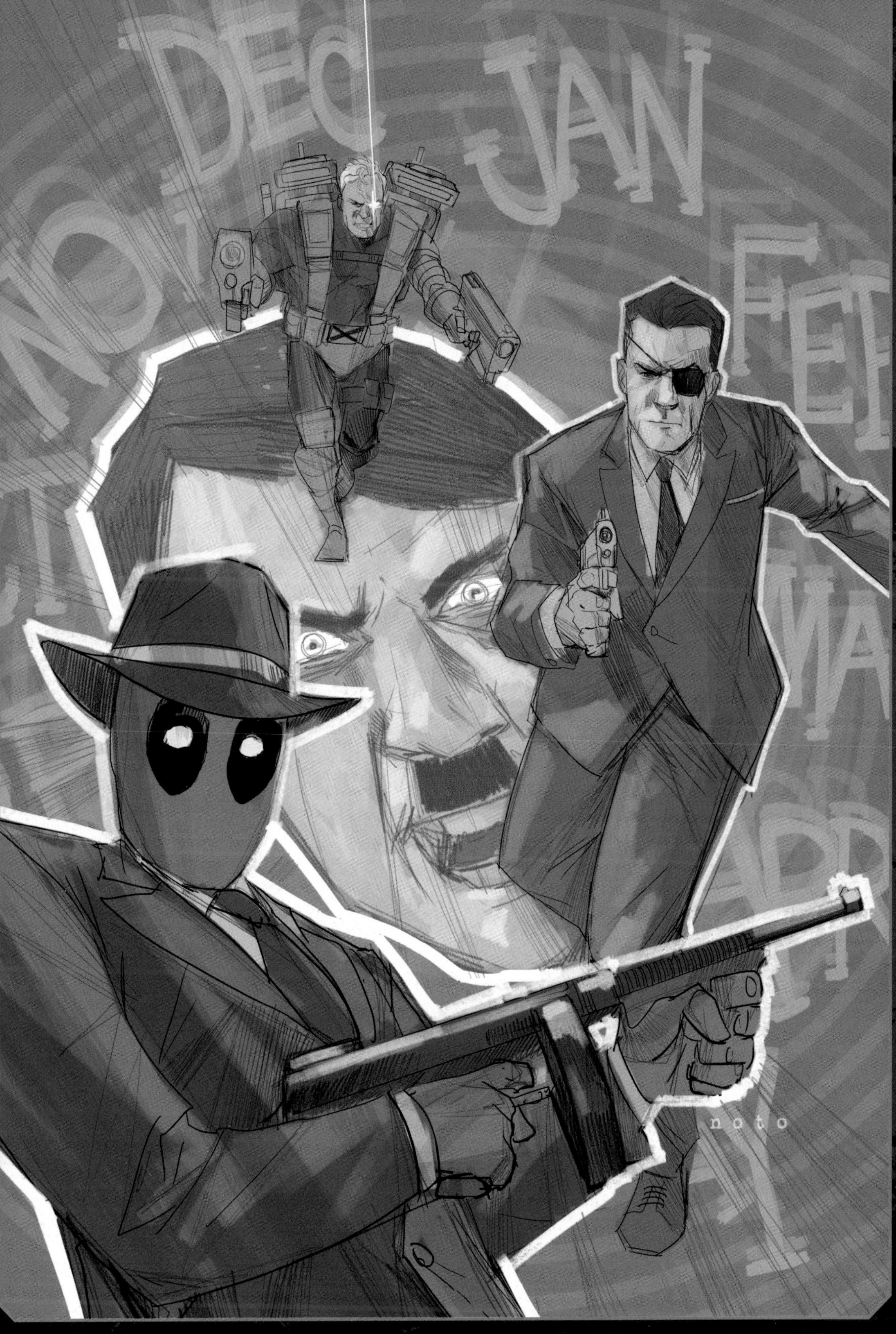
DEC
JAN
noto

DEATH COMES TO TINSELTOWN (OR THE LAST HITLER)

Possibly the world's most skilled mercenary, definitely the world's most annoying, Wade Wilson was chosen for a top-secret government program that gave him a healing factor allowing him to heal from any wound. Now, Wade makes his way as a gun for hire, shooting his prey's faces off while talking his friends' ears off. Call him the Merc with the Mouth...call him the Regeneratin' Degenerate...call him...DEADPOOL.

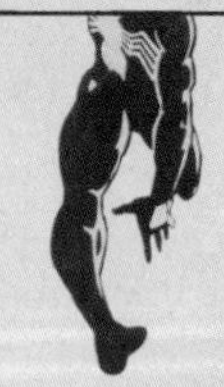

OK, this is a weird one.

Just when I thought we had completely run out of old inventory issues of Deadpool we could run, we stumbled upon this crazy gem.

It was intended to be an issue of SERGEANT FURY AND HIS HOWLING COMMANDOS. The notes from the editor at the time seem to suggest the two writers were stinking drunk when they came up with the idea for the issue, and in his opinion, it showed. He couldn't make heads or tails of the mess, fired the pair of them on the spot, and slipped the pages into a file marked "Last resort—run only in the direst of deadline crunches."

As you might have heard, we've got a pretty massive issue planned for issue 27. I don't want to spoil it for you...but suffice to say there are HUGE developments in Wade's life, in addition to there just being a MASSIVE amount of story jam-packed into the issue. It should come as no surprise to you that that means Gerry, Brian, and artist Mike Hawthorne have all fallen WAY behind. I think they got so caught up in celebrating what a great idea issue 27 was that they never got around to actually MAKING the epic, record breaking masterpiece.

I'd say that qualifies as the direst of deadline crunches.

Don't think of it as having a terrible, old, rejected story foisted-off on you...think of it as giving the creative team that little bit of extra time to REALLY knock your socks off next issue.

Be seeing you!

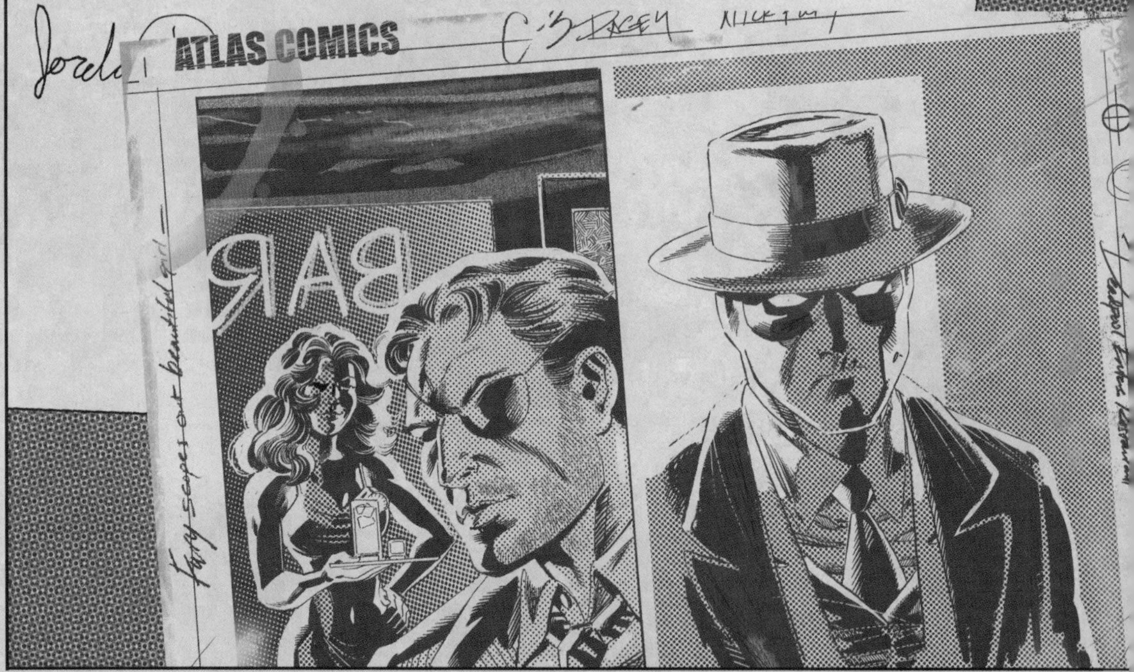
ATLAS COMICS

DEATH COMES TO TINSELTOWN (OR THE LAST HITLER)

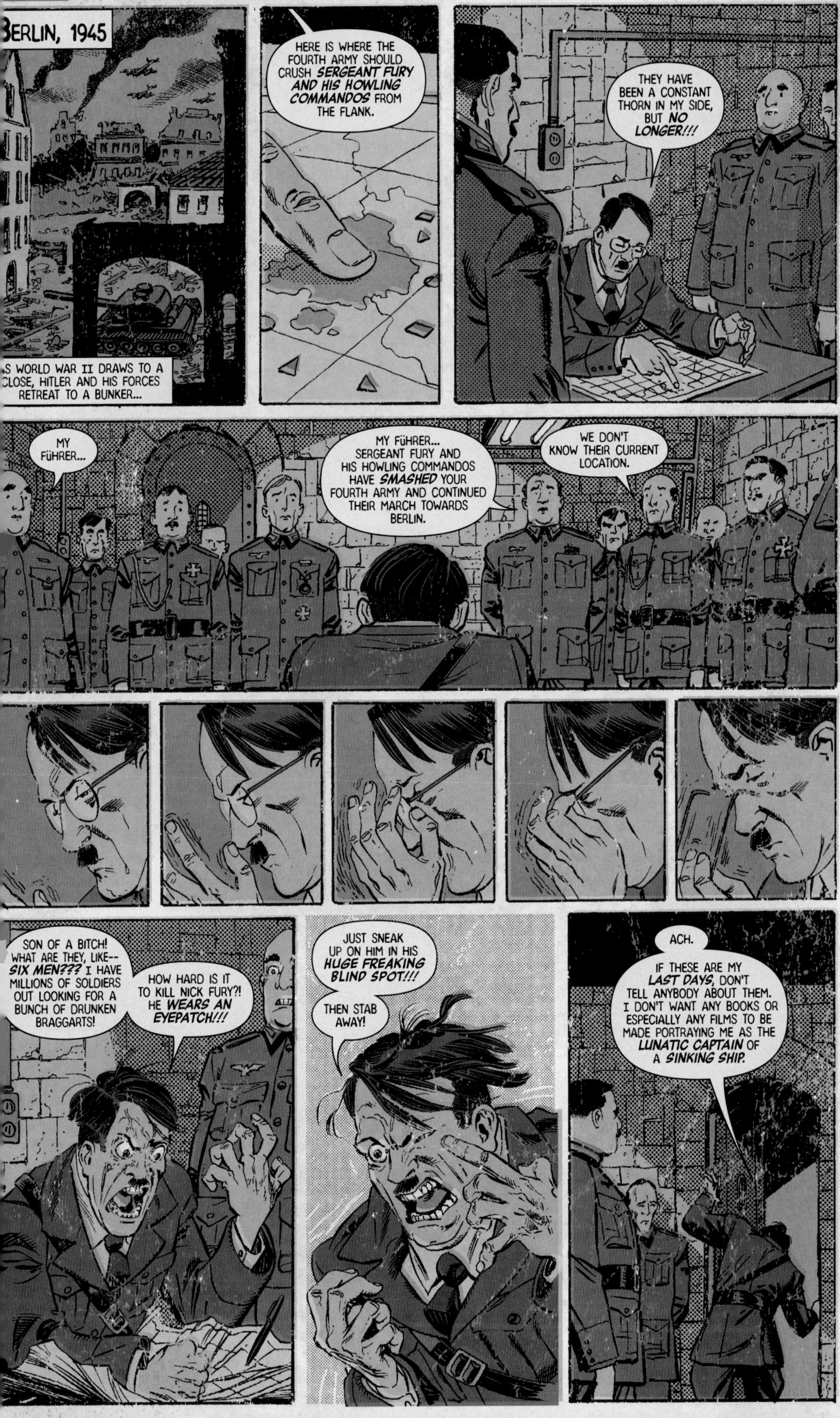
BERLIN, 1945
S WORLD WAR II DRAWS TO A CLOSE, HITLER AND HIS FORCES RETREAT TO A BUNKER...
HERE IS WHERE THE FOURTH ARMY SHOULD CRUSH SERGEANT FURY AND HIS HOWLING COMMANDOS FROM THE FLANK.
THEY HAVE BEEN A CONSTANT THORN IN MY SIDE, BUT NO LONGER!!!
MY FÜHRER...
MY FÜHRER... SERGEANT FURY AND HIS HOWLING COMMANDOS HAVE SMASHED YOUR FOURTH ARMY AND CONTINUED THEIR MARCH TOWARDS BERLIN.
WE DON'T KNOW THEIR CURRENT LOCATION.
SON OF A BITCH! WHAT ARE THEY, LIKE-- SIX MEN??? I HAVE MILLIONS OF SOLDIERS OUT LOOKING FOR A BUNCH OF DRUNKEN BRAGGARTS!
HOW HARD IS IT TO KILL NICK FURY?! HE WEARS AN EYEPATCH!!!
JUST SNEAK UP ON HIM IN HIS HUGE FREAKING BLIND SPOT!!!
THEN STAB AWAY!
ACH.
IF THESE ARE MY LAST DAYS, DON'T TELL ANYBODY ABOUT THEM. I DON'T WANT ANY BOOKS OR ESPECIALLY ANY FILMS TO BE MADE PORTRAYING ME AS THE LUNATIC CAPTAIN OF A SINKING SHIP.

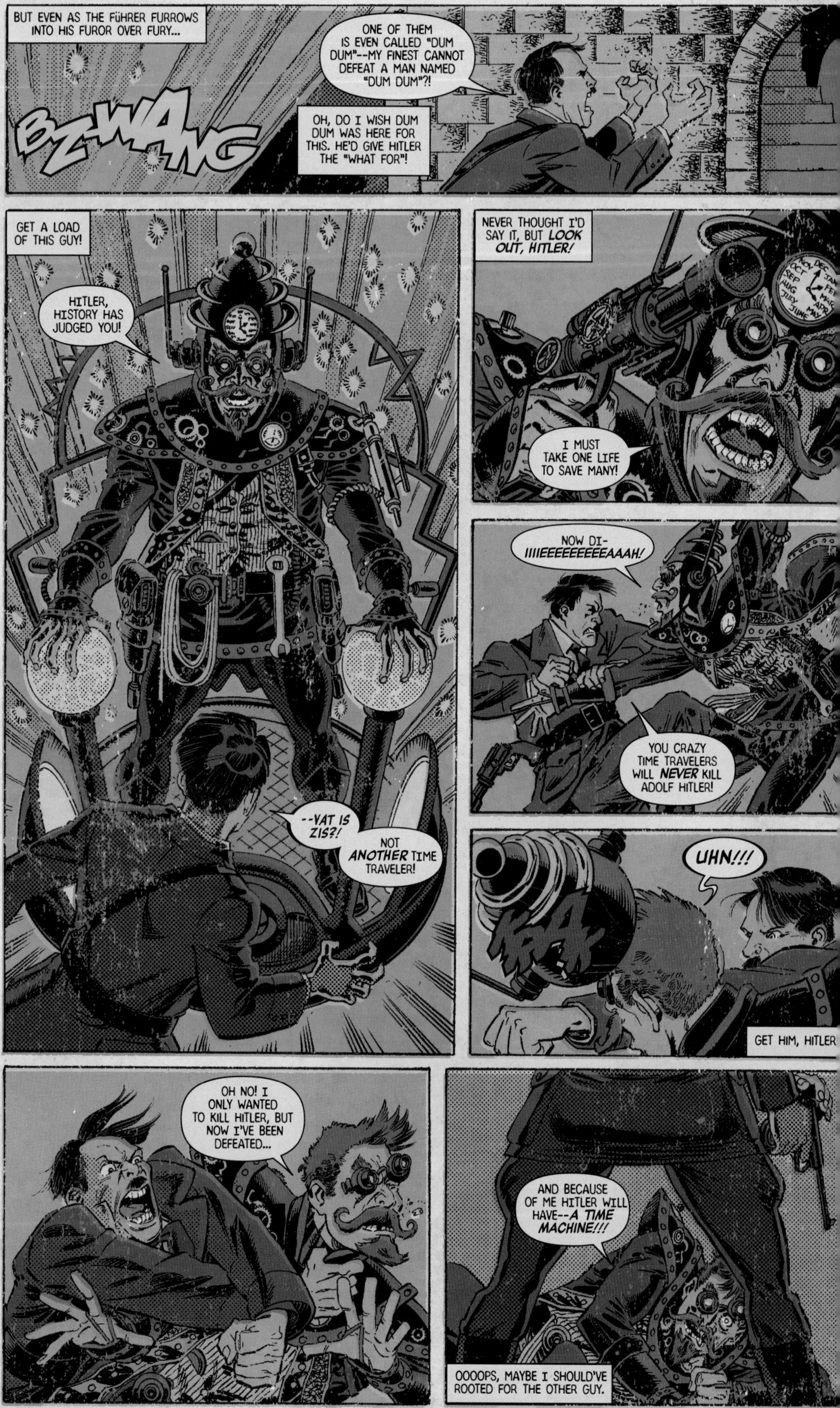

BUT EVEN AS THE FüHRER FURROWS INTO HIS FUROR OVER FURY...
ONE OF THEM IS EVEN CALLED "DUM DUM"--MY FINEST CANNOT DEFEAT A MAN NAMED "DUM DUM"?!
OH, DO I WISH DUM DUM WAS HERE FOR THIS. HE'D GIVE HITLER THE "WHAT FOR"!
BZ-WANG
GET A LOAD OF THIS GUY!
HITLER, HISTORY HAS JUDGED YOU!
--VAT IS ZIS?!
NOT ANOTHER TIME TRAVELER!
NEVER THOUGHT I'D SAY IT, BUT LOOK OUT, HITLER!
I MUST TAKE ONE LIFE TO SAVE MANY!
NOW DI-IIIIEEEEEEEEEEAAAH!
YOU CRAZY TIME TRAVELERS WILL NEVER KILL ADOLF HITLER!
UHN!!!
GET HIM, HITLER
OH NO! I ONLY WANTED TO KILL HITLER, BUT NOW I'VE BEEN DEFEATED...
AND BECAUSE OF ME HITLER WILL HAVE--A TIME MACHINE!!!
OOOOPS, MAYBE I SHOULD'VE ROOTED FOR THE OTHER GUY.

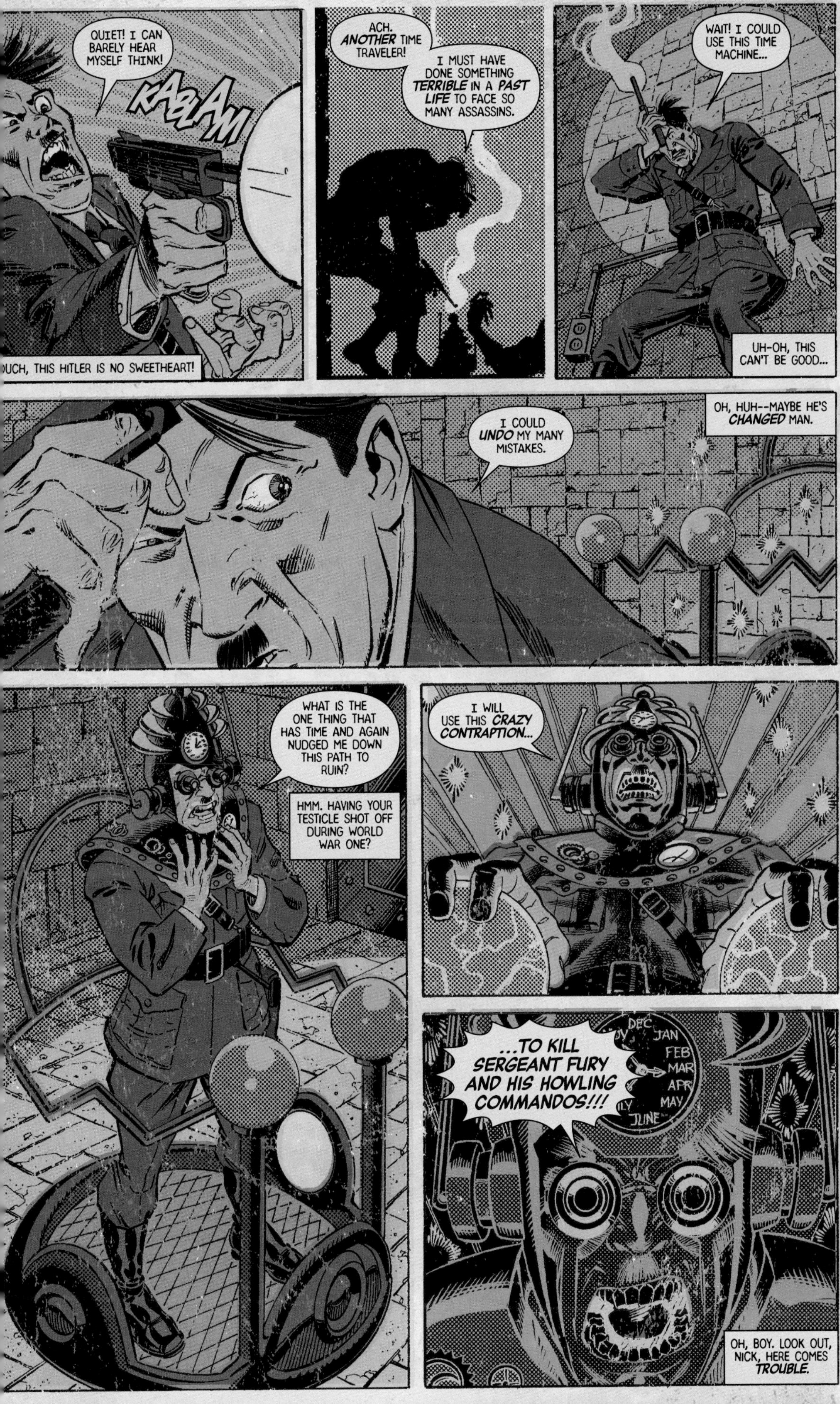
QUIET! I CAN BARELY HEAR MYSELF THINK!
KABLAM
OUCH, THIS HITLER IS NO SWEETHEART!
ACH. ANOTHER TIME TRAVELER!
I MUST HAVE DONE SOMETHING TERRIBLE IN A PAST LIFE TO FACE SO MANY ASSASSINS.
WAIT! I COULD USE THIS TIME MACHINE...
UH-OH, THIS CAN'T BE GOOD...
OH, HUH--MAYBE HE'S CHANGED MAN.
I COULD UNDO MY MANY MISTAKES.
WHAT IS THE ONE THING THAT HAS TIME AND AGAIN NUDGED ME DOWN THIS PATH TO RUIN?
HMM. HAVING YOUR TESTICLE SHOT OFF DURING WORLD WAR ONE?
I WILL USE THIS CRAZY CONTRAPTION...
...TO KILL SERGEANT FURY AND HIS HOWLING COMMANDOS!!!
DEC
JAN
FEB
MAR
APR
MAY
JUNE
OH, BOY. LOOK OUT, NICK, HERE COMES TROUBLE.

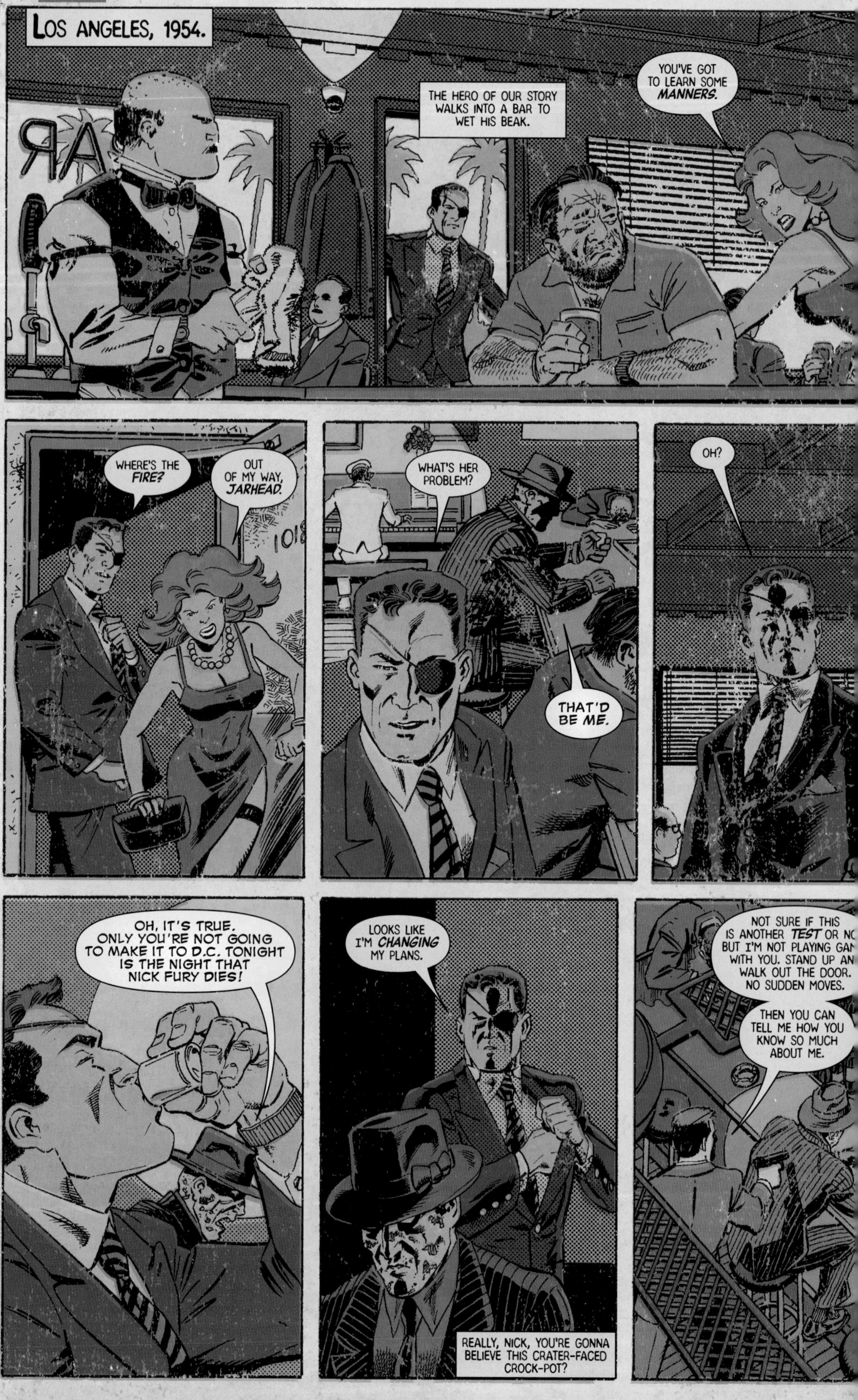
LOS ANGELES, 1954.
THE HERO OF OUR STORY WALKS INTO A BAR TO WET HIS BEAK.
YOU'VE GOT TO LEARN SOME MANNERS.
WHERE'S THE FIRE?
OUT OF MY WAY, JARHEAD.
WHAT'S HER PROBLEM?
THAT'D BE ME.
OH?
OH, IT'S TRUE. ONLY YOU'RE NOT GOING TO MAKE IT TO D.C. TONIGHT IS THE NIGHT THAT NICK FURY DIES!
LOOKS LIKE I'M CHANGING MY PLANS.
REALLY, NICK, YOU'RE GONNA BELIEVE THIS CRATER-FACED CROCK-POT?
NOT SURE IF THIS IS ANOTHER TEST OR NO BUT I'M NOT PLAYING GAM WITH YOU. STAND UP AN WALK OUT THE DOOR. NO SUDDEN MOVES.
THEN YOU CAN TELL ME HOW YOU KNOW SO MUCH ABOUT ME.

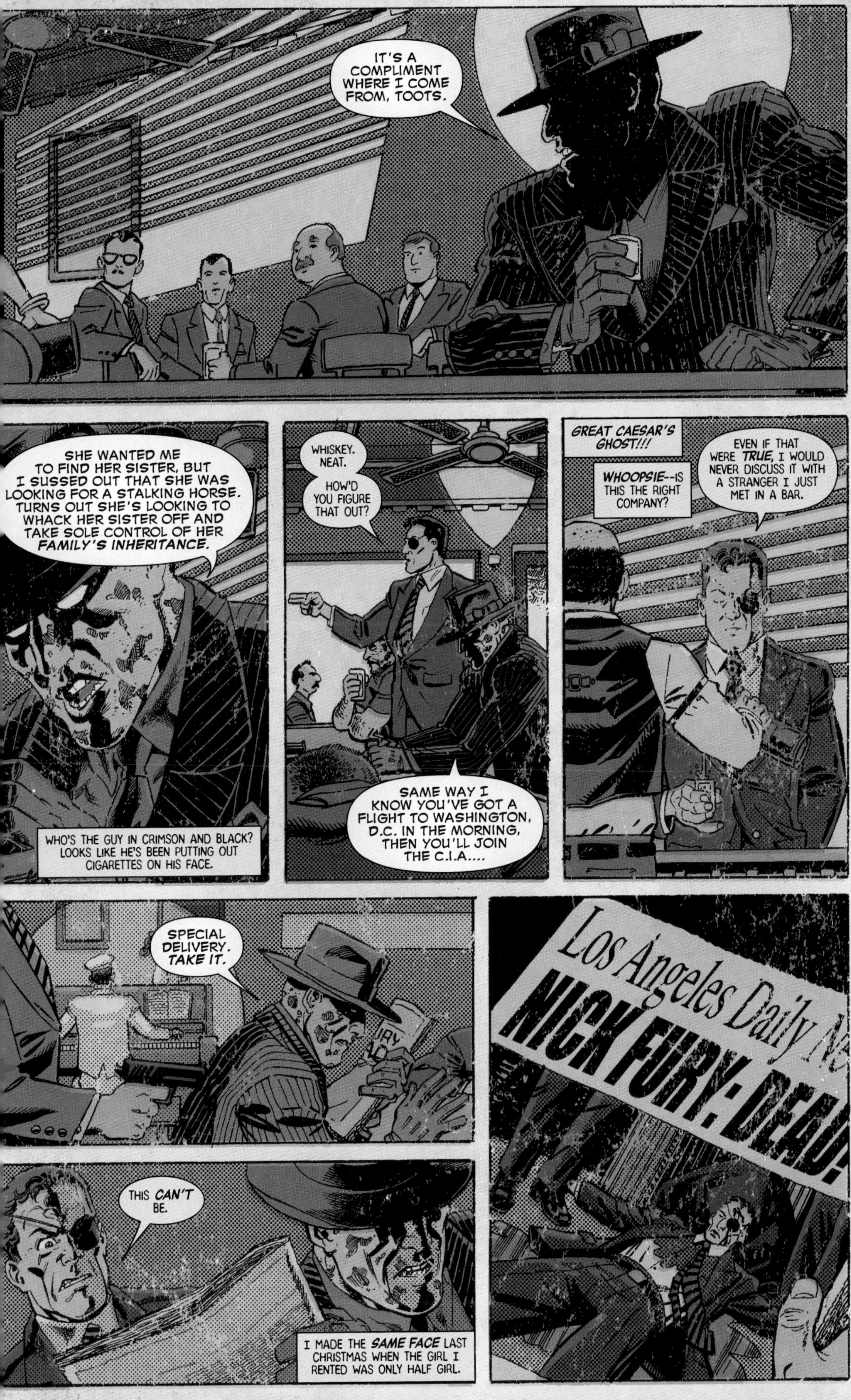
IT'S A COMPLIMENT WHERE I COME FROM, TOOTS.
SHE WANTED ME TO FIND HER SISTER, BUT I SUSSED OUT THAT SHE WAS LOOKING FOR A STALKING HORSE. TURNS OUT SHE'S LOOKING TO WHACK HER SISTER OFF AND TAKE SOLE CONTROL OF HER FAMILY'S INHERITANCE.
WHO'S THE GUY IN CRIMSON AND BLACK? LOOKS LIKE HE'S BEEN PUTTING OUT CIGARETTES ON HIS FACE.
WHISKEY. NEAT.
HOW'D YOU FIGURE THAT OUT?
SAME WAY I KNOW YOU'VE GOT A FLIGHT TO WASHINGTON, D.C. IN THE MORNING, THEN YOU'LL JOIN THE C.I.A....
GREAT CAESAR'S GHOST!!!
WHOOPSIE--IS THIS THE RIGHT COMPANY?
EVEN IF THAT WERE TRUE, I WOULD NEVER DISCUSS IT WITH A STRANGER I JUST MET IN A BAR.
SPECIAL DELIVERY. TAKE IT.
THIS CAN'T BE.
I MADE THE SAME FACE LAST CHRISTMAS WHEN THE GIRL I RENTED WAS ONLY HALF GIRL.
Los Angeles Daily N
NICK FURY: DEAD!

WHAT THE DEVIL? THIS IS GETTING SERIOUS, GUYS.

THIS COULD BE *FAKED.*

SURE. YOU SAID YOU WOULD SAY THAT...

...BUT *THIS* CAN'T.

WHAT CAN'T?!

HOLY HELL!

WHAT'S HE GOT THERE?

HUHN. TIME TRAVEL?

HEY, I WANT TO SEE, TOO.

YOU SENT ME BACK TO HELP YOU WITH A CERTAIN PROBLEM. YOU'RE NOT SUPPOSED TO DIE TONIGHT, BUT AN OLD ENEMY IS MESSING WITH THE TIME-STREAM.

WHO'S GUNNING FOR ME?

ANYONE I KNOW...*YET?*

I'M SKETCHY ON ALL THE DETAILS...

BUT HITLER'S ON THE LOOSE AND HE HAS A TIME MACHINE.

NOT ADOLF *HITLER!* HE BOUGHT THE FARM!

HOW IS HE ALIVE?!

HOW DID HE GET A TIME MACHINE?!

THIS IS REALLY GETT[...] INTERESTING...I'LL S[...] UP FOR A WHILE.

HARD TO SAY, BUT WE THINK HITLER WENT *BACK* IN TIME FIRST AND GAVE HIMSELF ONE OF HIS FAMOUS *"PEP TALKS."*

THEN HE SET HIS SIGHTS ON KILLING HIS GREATEST NEMESIS, NICK FURY.

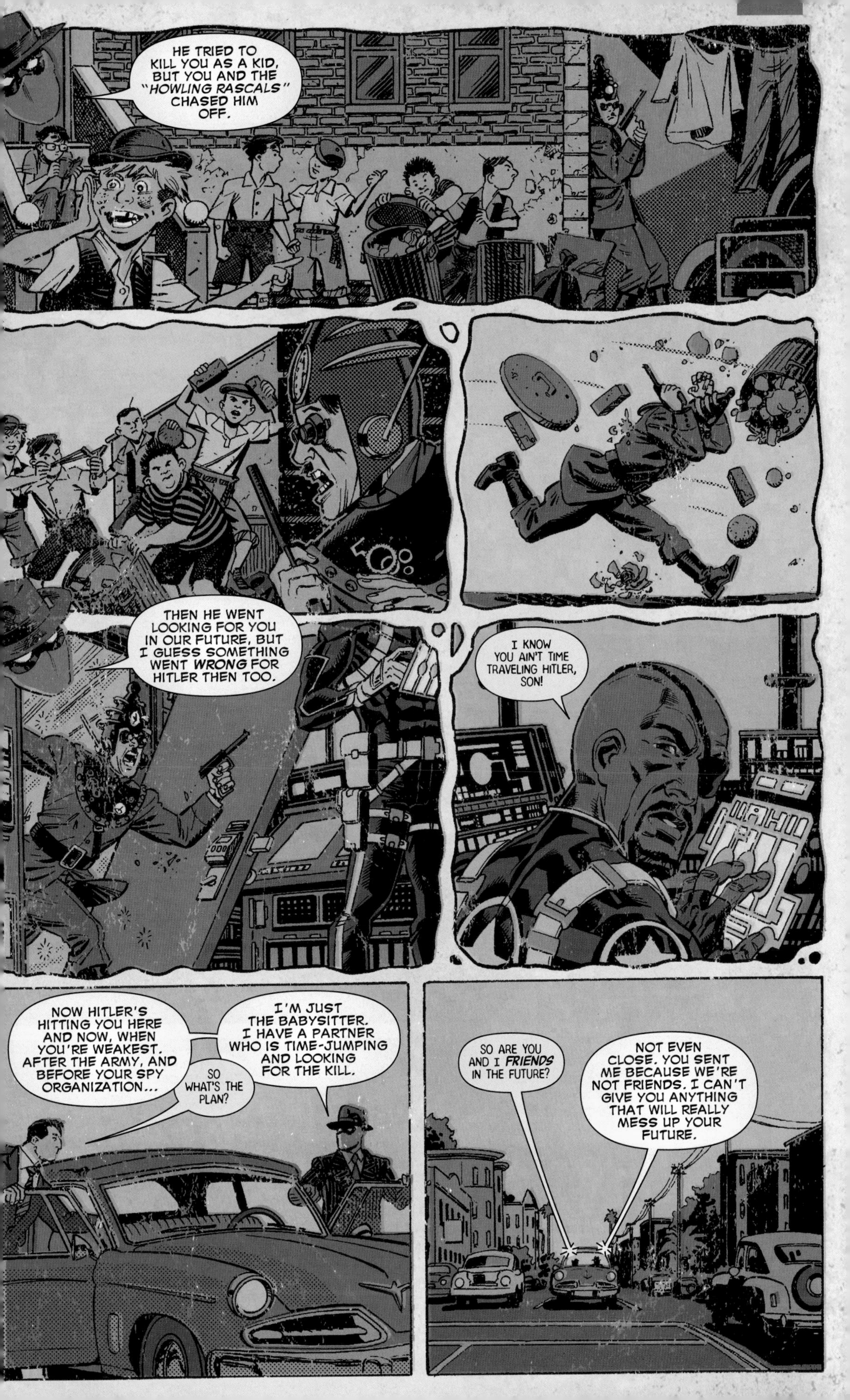
HE TRIED TO KILL YOU AS A KID, BUT YOU AND THE "HOWLING RASCALS" CHASED HIM OFF.
THEN HE WENT LOOKING FOR YOU IN OUR FUTURE, BUT I GUESS SOMETHING WENT WRONG FOR HITLER THEN TOO.
I KNOW YOU AIN'T TIME TRAVELING HITLER, SON!
NOW HITLER'S HITTING YOU HERE AND NOW, WHEN YOU'RE WEAKEST. AFTER THE ARMY, AND BEFORE YOUR SPY ORGANIZATION...
SO WHAT'S THE PLAN?
I'M JUST THE BABYSITTER. I HAVE A PARTNER WHO IS TIME-JUMPING AND LOOKING FOR THE KILL.
SO ARE YOU AND I FRIENDS IN THE FUTURE?
NOT EVEN CLOSE. YOU SENT ME BECAUSE WE'RE NOT FRIENDS. I CAN'T GIVE YOU ANYTHING THAT WILL REALLY MESS UP YOUR FUTURE.

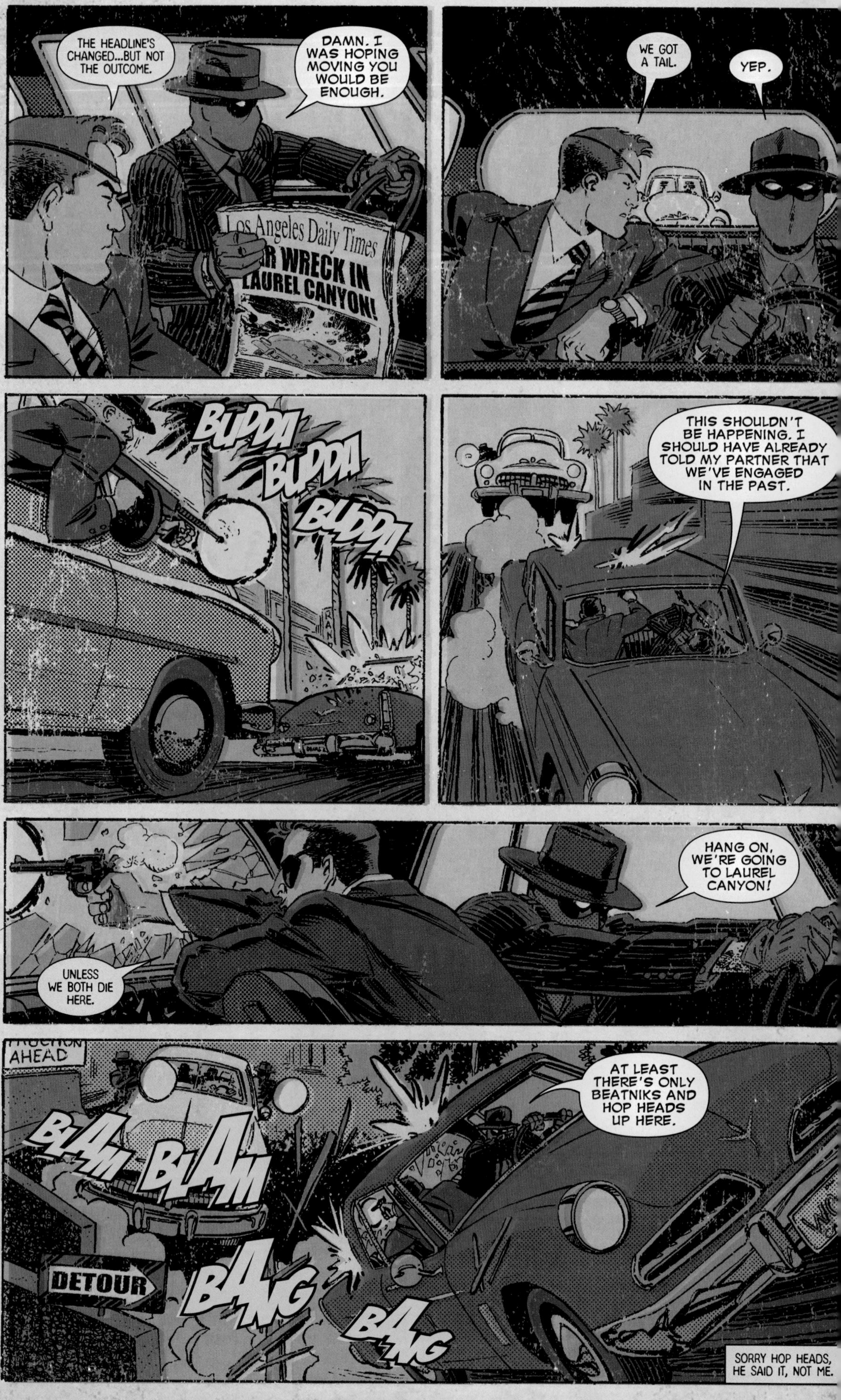
THE HEADLINE'S CHANGED...BUT NOT THE OUTCOME.
DAMN. I WAS HOPING MOVING YOU WOULD BE ENOUGH.
Los Angeles Daily Times
LAUREL CANYON!
WE GOT A TAIL.
YEP.
BUDDA
BUDDA
BUDDA
THIS SHOULDN'T BE HAPPENING. I SHOULD HAVE ALREADY TOLD MY PARTNER THAT WE'VE ENGAGED IN THE PAST.
HANG ON, WE'RE GOING TO LAUREL CANYON!
UNLESS WE BOTH DIE HERE.
AHEAD
AT LEAST THERE'S ONLY BEATNIKS AND HOP HEADS UP HERE.
BLAM
BLAM
DETOUR
BANG
BANG
SORRY HOP HEADS, HE SAID IT, NOT ME.

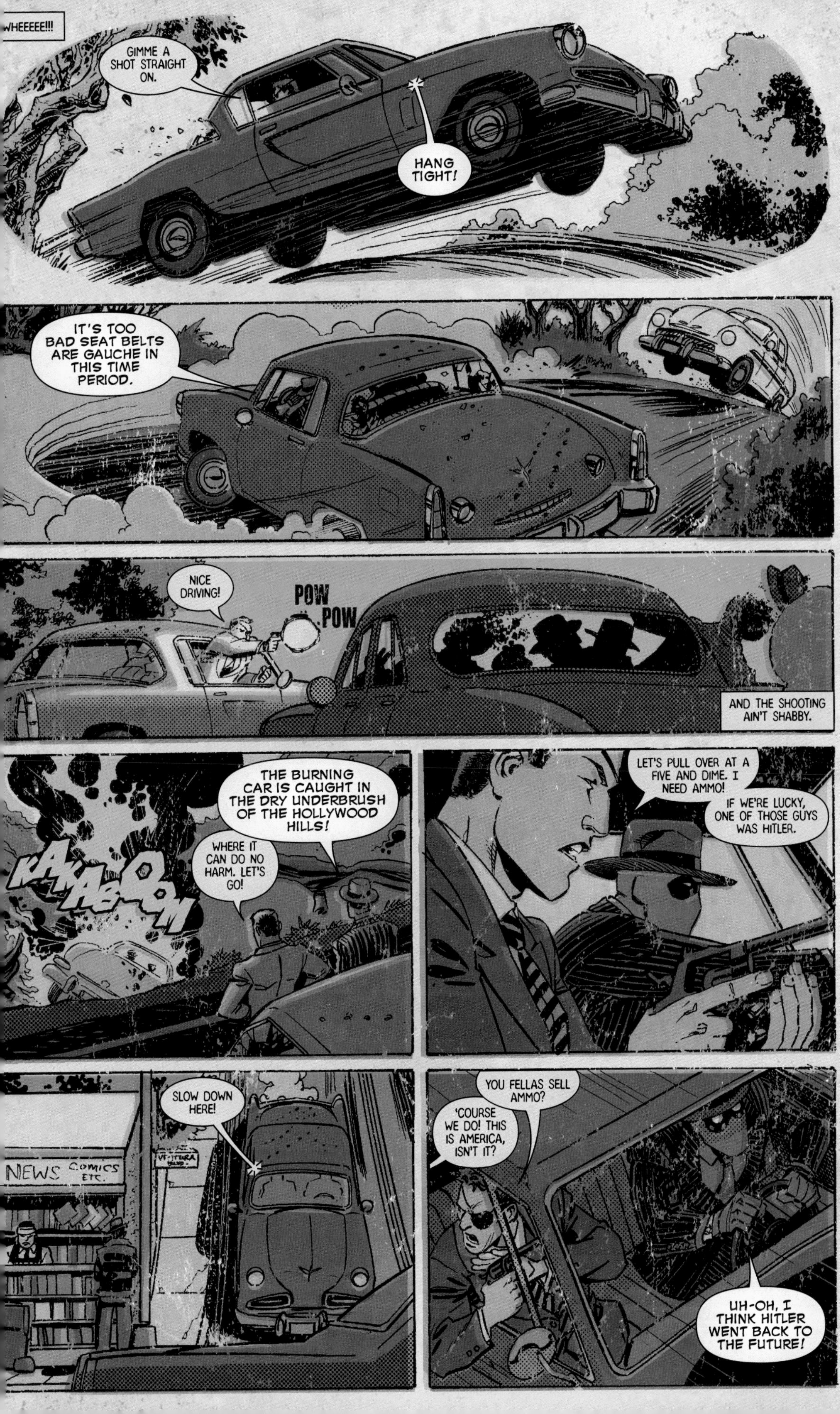
WHEEEEE!!!
GIMME A SHOT STRAIGHT ON.
HANG TIGHT!
IT'S TOO BAD SEAT BELTS ARE GAUCHE IN THIS TIME PERIOD.
NICE DRIVING!
POW
POW
AND THE SHOOTING AIN'T SHABBY.
KA-BOOM
THE BURNING CAR IS CAUGHT IN THE DRY UNDERBRUSH OF THE HOLLYWOOD HILLS!
WHERE IT CAN DO NO HARM. LET'S GO!
LET'S PULL OVER AT A FIVE AND DIME. I NEED AMMO!
IF WE'RE LUCKY, ONE OF THOSE GUYS WAS HITLER.
NEWS COMICS ETC.
SLOW DOWN HERE!
YOU FELLAS SELL AMMO?
'COURSE WE DO! THIS IS AMERICA, ISN'T IT?
UH-OH, I THINK HITLER WENT BACK TO THE FUTURE!

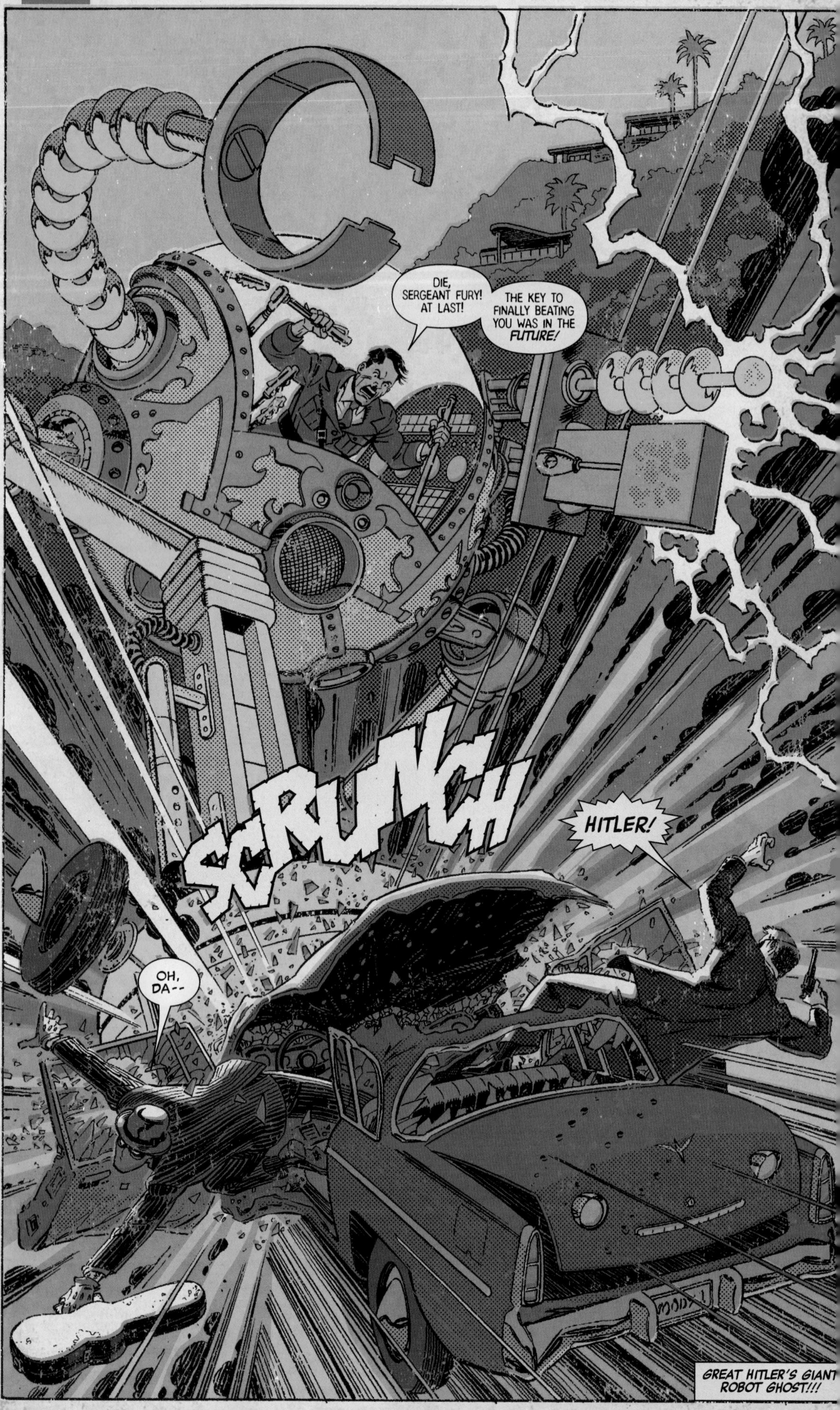
DIE, SERGEANT FURY! AT LAST!
THE KEY TO FINALLY BEATING YOU WAS IN THE FUTURE!
SCRUNCH
HITLER!
OH, DA--
GREAT HITLER'S GIANT ROBOT GHOST!!!

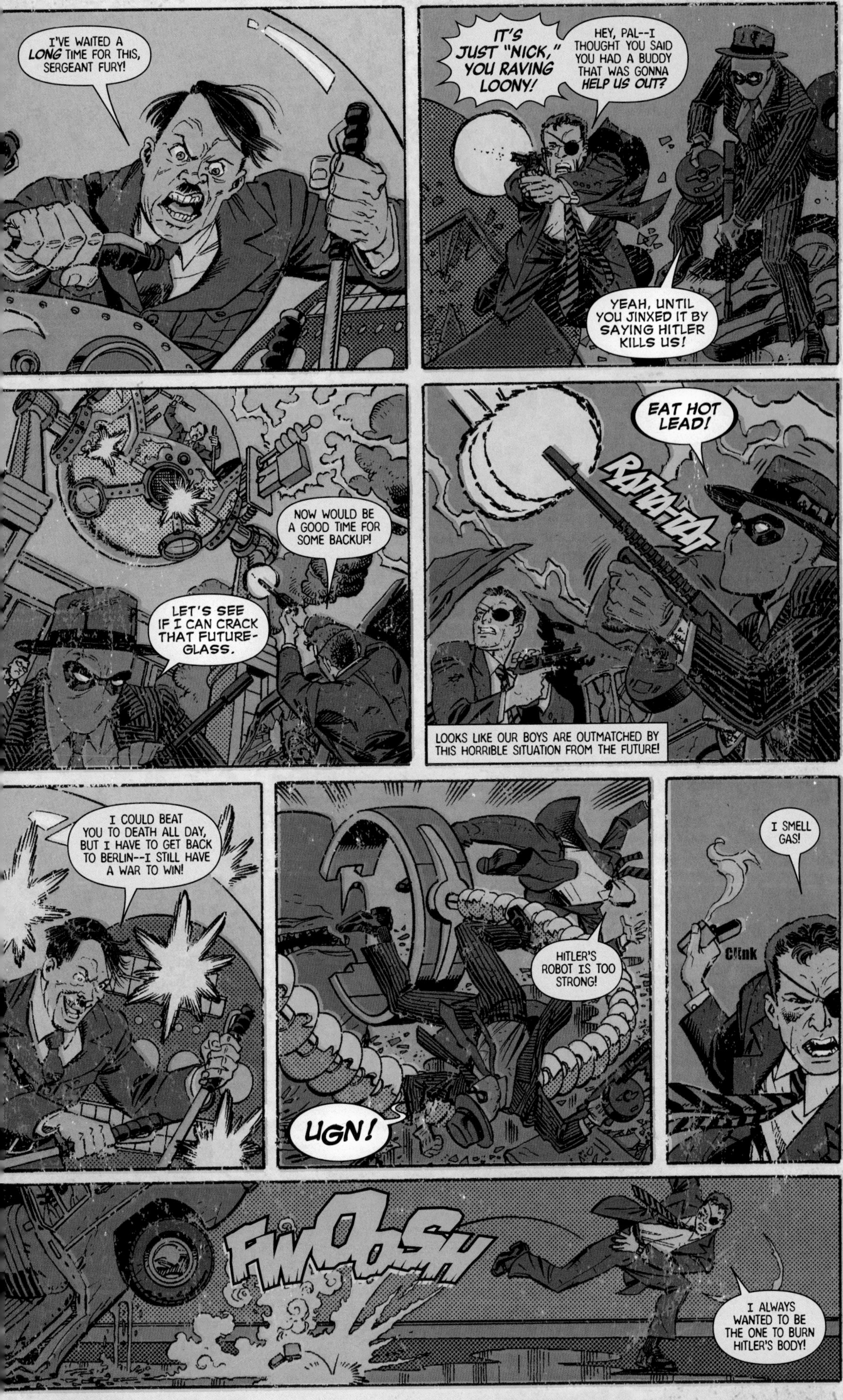
I'VE WAITED A LONG TIME FOR THIS, SERGEANT FURY!
IT'S JUST "NICK," YOU RAVING LOONY!
HEY, PAL--I THOUGHT YOU SAID YOU HAD A BUDDY THAT WAS GONNA HELP US OUT?
YEAH, UNTIL YOU JINXED IT BY SAYING HITLER KILLS US!
NOW WOULD BE A GOOD TIME FOR SOME BACKUP!
LET'S SEE IF I CAN CRACK THAT FUTURE-GLASS.
EAT HOT LEAD!
RATATAT
LOOKS LIKE OUR BOYS ARE OUTMATCHED BY THIS HORRIBLE SITUATION FROM THE FUTURE!
I COULD BEAT YOU TO DEATH ALL DAY, BUT I HAVE TO GET BACK TO BERLIN--I STILL HAVE A WAR TO WIN!
HITLER'S ROBOT IS TOO STRONG!
UGN!
I SMELL GAS!
Clink
FWOOSH
I ALWAYS WANTED TO BE THE ONE TO BURN HITLER'S BODY!

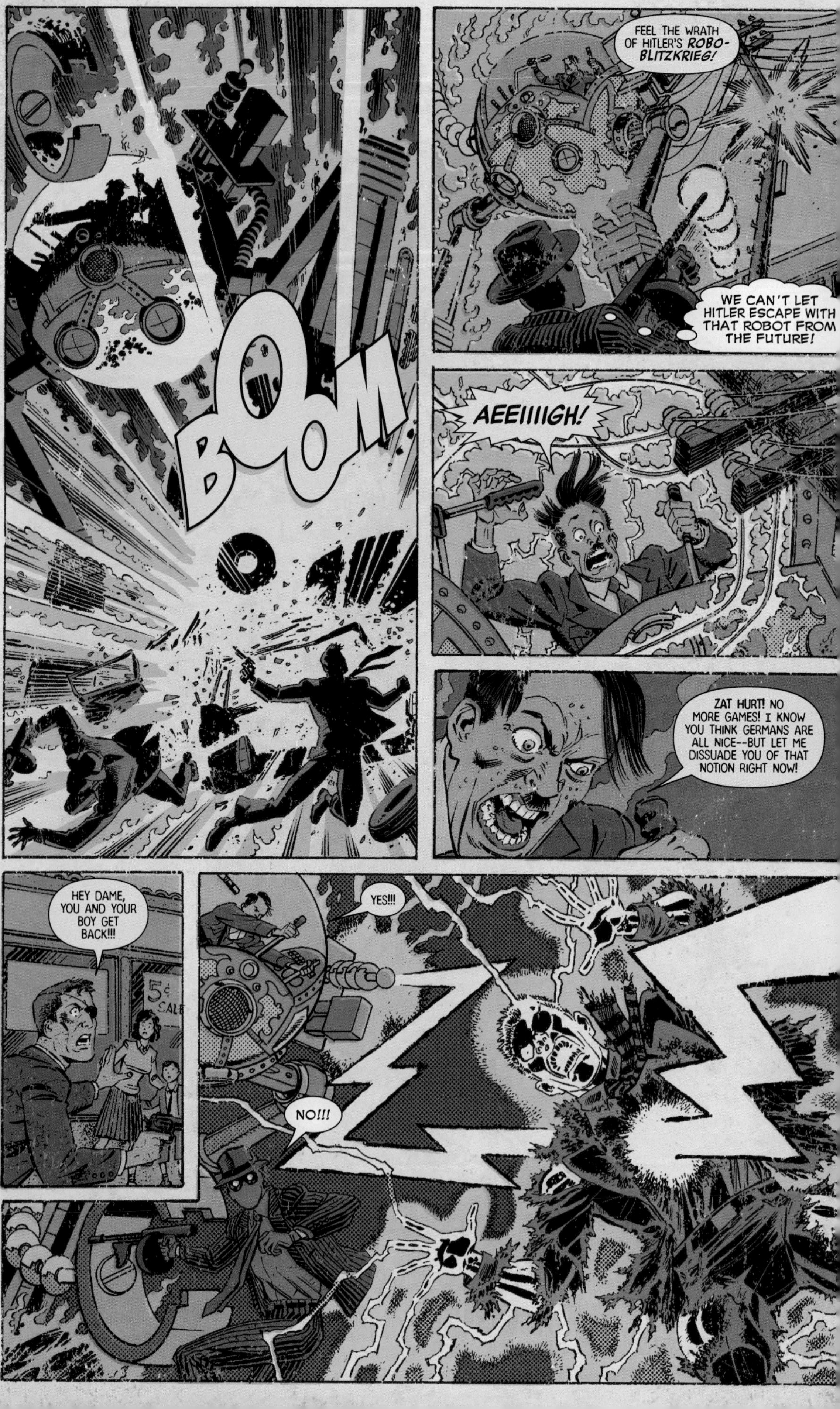
BOOM
FEEL THE WRATH OF HITLER'S ROBO-BLITZKRIEG!
WE CAN'T LET HITLER ESCAPE WITH THAT ROBOT FROM THE FUTURE!
AEEIIIIGH!
ZAT HURT! NO MORE GAMES! I KNOW YOU THINK GERMANS ARE ALL NICE--BUT LET ME DISSUADE YOU OF THAT NOTION RIGHT NOW!
HEY DAME, YOU AND YOUR BOY GET BACK!!!
5¢ SALE
YES!!!
NO!!!

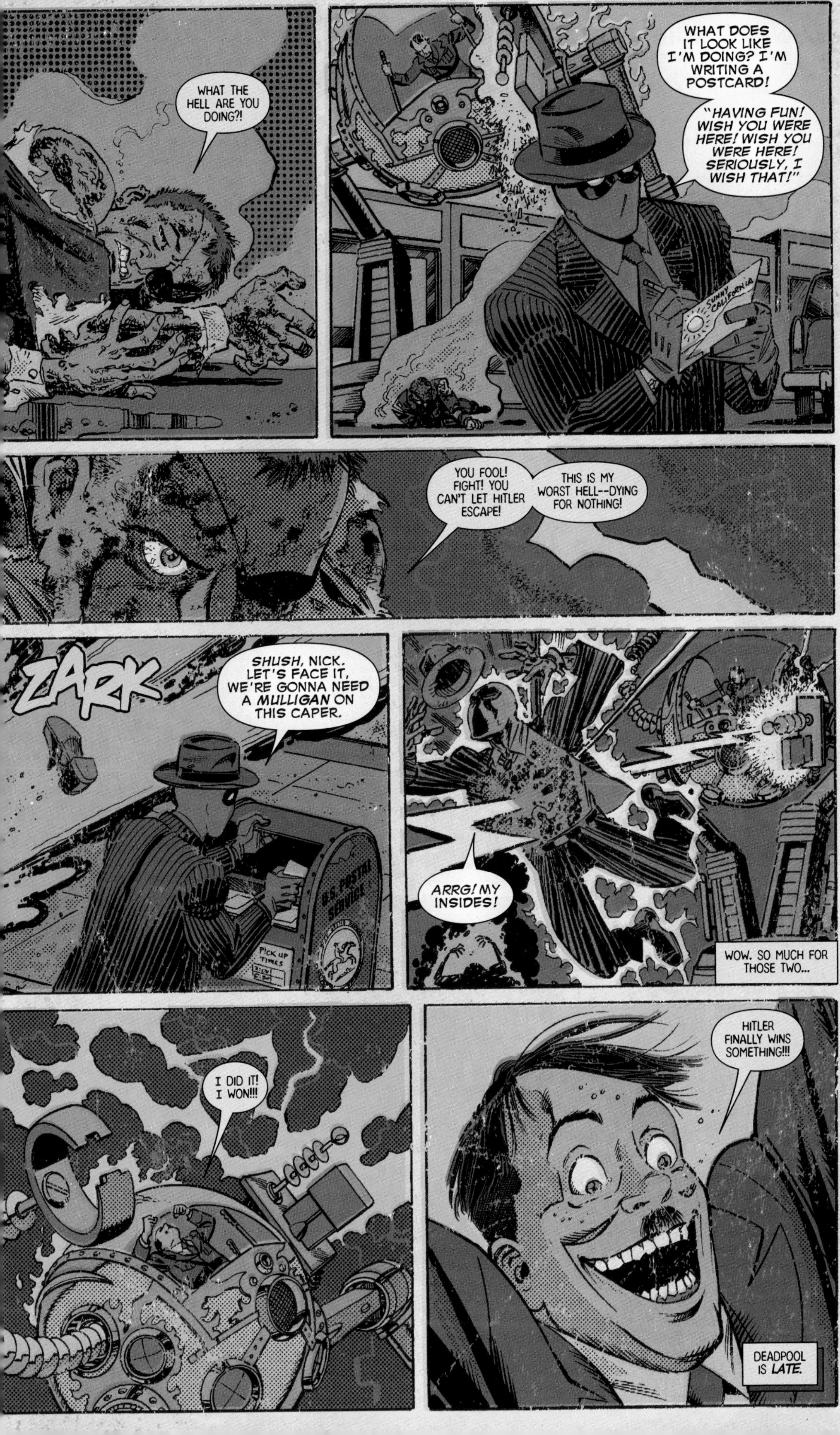
WHAT THE HELL ARE YOU DOING?!
WHAT DOES IT LOOK LIKE I'M DOING? I'M WRITING A POSTCARD!
"HAVING FUN! WISH YOU WERE HERE! WISH YOU WERE HERE! SERIOUSLY, I WISH THAT!"
SUNNY CALIFORNIA
YOU FOOL! FIGHT! YOU CAN'T LET HITLER ESCAPE!
THIS IS MY WORST HELL--DYING FOR NOTHING!
ZARK
SHUSH, NICK. LET'S FACE IT, WE'RE GONNA NEED A MULLIGAN ON THIS CAPER.
U.S. POSTAL SERVICE
PICK UP TIMES
ARRG! MY INSIDES!
WOW. SO MUCH FOR THOSE TWO...
I DID IT! I WON!!!
HITLER FINALLY WINS SOMETHING!!!
DEADPOOL IS LATE.

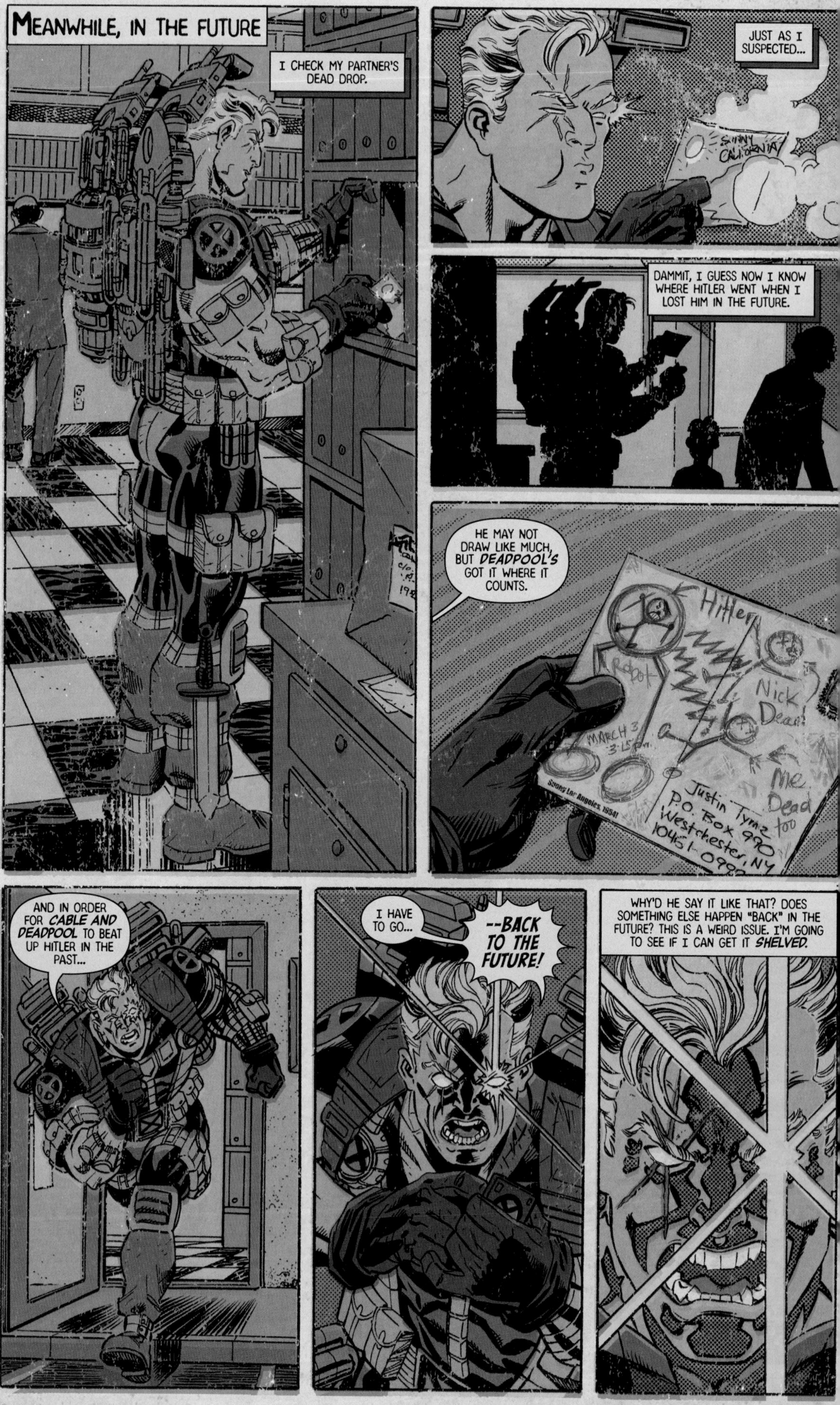
MEANWHILE, IN THE FUTURE
I CHECK MY PARTNER'S DEAD DROP.
JUST AS I SUSPECTED...
SUNNY CALIFORNIA!
DAMMIT, I GUESS NOW I KNOW WHERE HITLER WENT WHEN I LOST HIM IN THE FUTURE.
HE MAY NOT DRAW LIKE MUCH, BUT DEADPOOL'S GOT IT WHERE IT COUNTS.
Hitler
Robot
Nick Dead
MARCH 3 3:15 pm
Me Dead too
Justin Tyme
P.O. Box 990
Westchester, NY
AND IN ORDER FOR CABLE AND DEADPOOL TO BEAT UP HITLER IN THE PAST...
I HAVE TO GO...
--BACK TO THE FUTURE!
WHY'D HE SAY IT LIKE THAT? DOES SOMETHING ELSE HAPPEN "BACK" IN THE FUTURE? THIS IS A WEIRD ISSUE. I'M GOING TO SEE IF I CAN GET IT SHELVED.

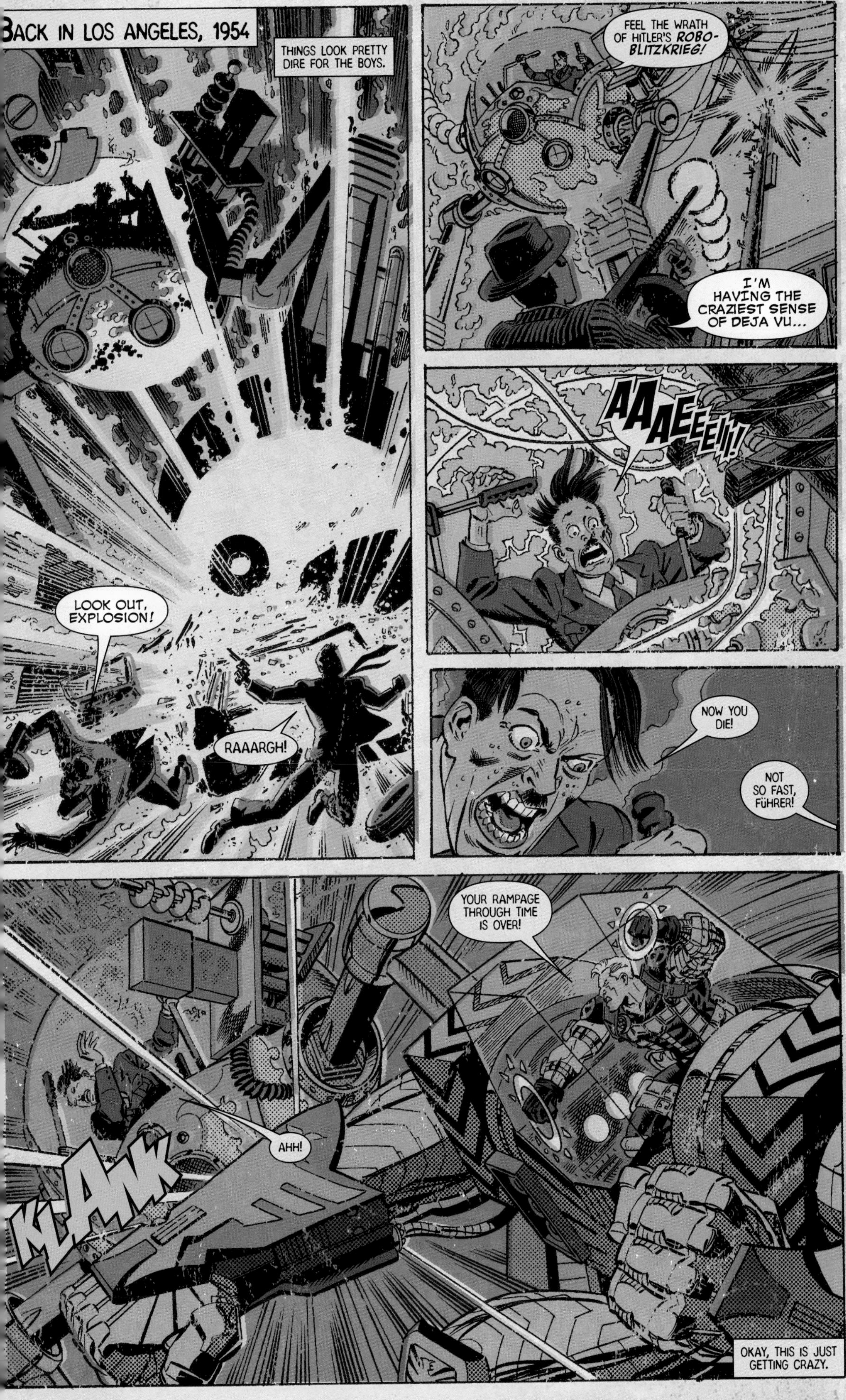
BACK IN LOS ANGELES, 1954
THINGS LOOK PRETTY DIRE FOR THE BOYS.
LOOK OUT, EXPLOSION!
RAAARGH!
FEEL THE WRATH OF HITLER'S ROBO-BLITZKRIEG!
I'M HAVING THE CRAZIEST SENSE OF DEJA VU...
AAAEEEIII!
NOW YOU DIE!
NOT SO FAST, FÜHRER!
YOUR RAMPAGE THROUGH TIME IS OVER!
AHH!
KLANK
OKAY, THIS IS JUST GETTING CRAZY.

GOOD TO SEE YOU, SERGEANT!

I GOT YOUR POSTCARD, WADE!

NICE TO SEE YOU, CABLE.

AMAZING! THESE CONTRAPTIONS MUST REPLACE CARS IN THE FUTURE.

I DON'T KNOW WHO YOU ARE, BUT I DON'T CARE, I WON'T LET YOU STOP ME FROM KILLING SERGEANT FURY!

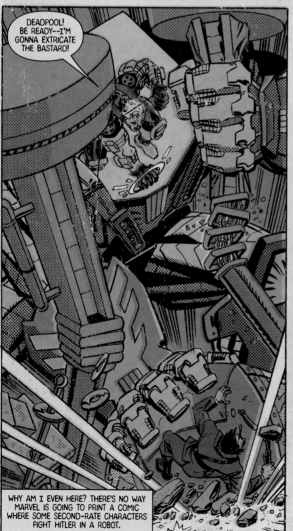

DEADPOOL! BE READY--I'M GONNA EXTRICATE THE BASTARD!

WHY AM I EVEN HERE? THERE'S NO WAY MARVEL IS GOING TO PRINT A COMIC WHERE SOME SECOND-RATE CHARACTERS FIGHT HITLER IN A ROBOT.

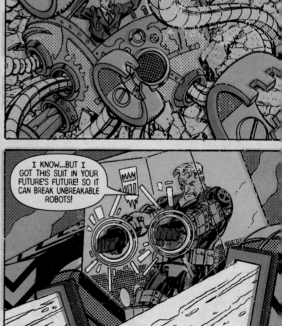

MY ROBOTIC MACHINE IS UNBREAKABLE! I GOT IT IN THE FUTURE!

I KNOW...BUT I GOT THIS SUIT IN YOUR FUTURE'S FUTURE! SO IT CAN BREAK UNBREAKABLE ROBOTS!

ACTUALLY, THAT'S NOT A BAD 1950S' SCI-FI TWIST RIGHT THERE...LET'S SEE IF OUR BOYS STRIKE PAY DIRT!

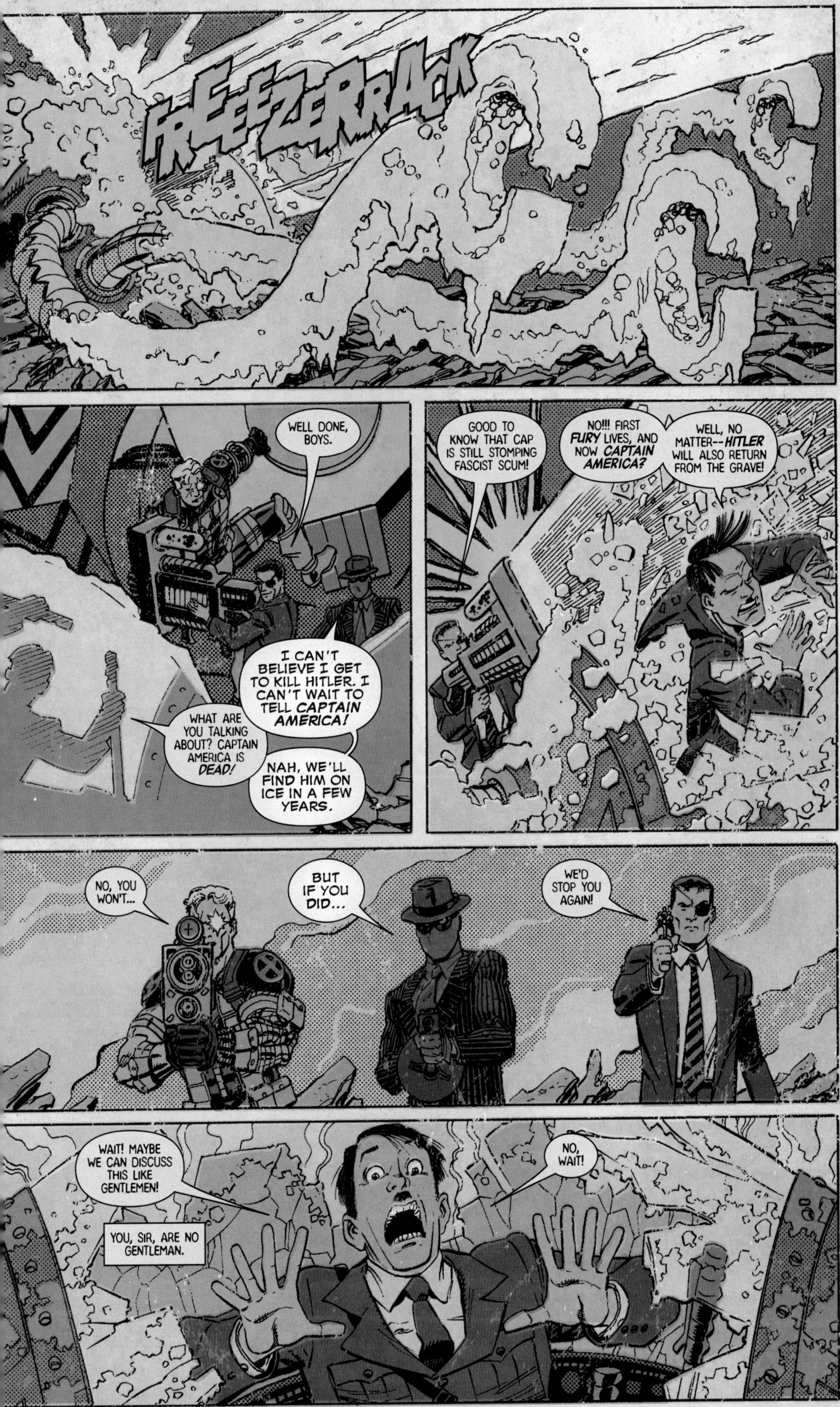
FREEEZERRACK
WELL DONE, BOYS.
I CAN'T BELIEVE I GET TO KILL HITLER. I CAN'T WAIT TO TELL CAPTAIN AMERICA!
WHAT ARE YOU TALKING ABOUT? CAPTAIN AMERICA IS DEAD!
NAH, WE'LL FIND HIM ON ICE IN A FEW YEARS.
GOOD TO KNOW THAT CAP IS STILL STOMPING FASCIST SCUM!
NO!!! FIRST FURY LIVES, AND NOW CAPTAIN AMERICA?
WELL, NO MATTER--HITLER WILL ALSO RETURN FROM THE GRAVE!
NO, YOU WON'T...
BUT IF YOU DID...
WE'D STOP YOU AGAIN!
WAIT! MAYBE WE CAN DISCUSS THIS LIKE GENTLEMEN!
YOU, SIR, ARE NO GENTLEMAN.
NO, WAIT!

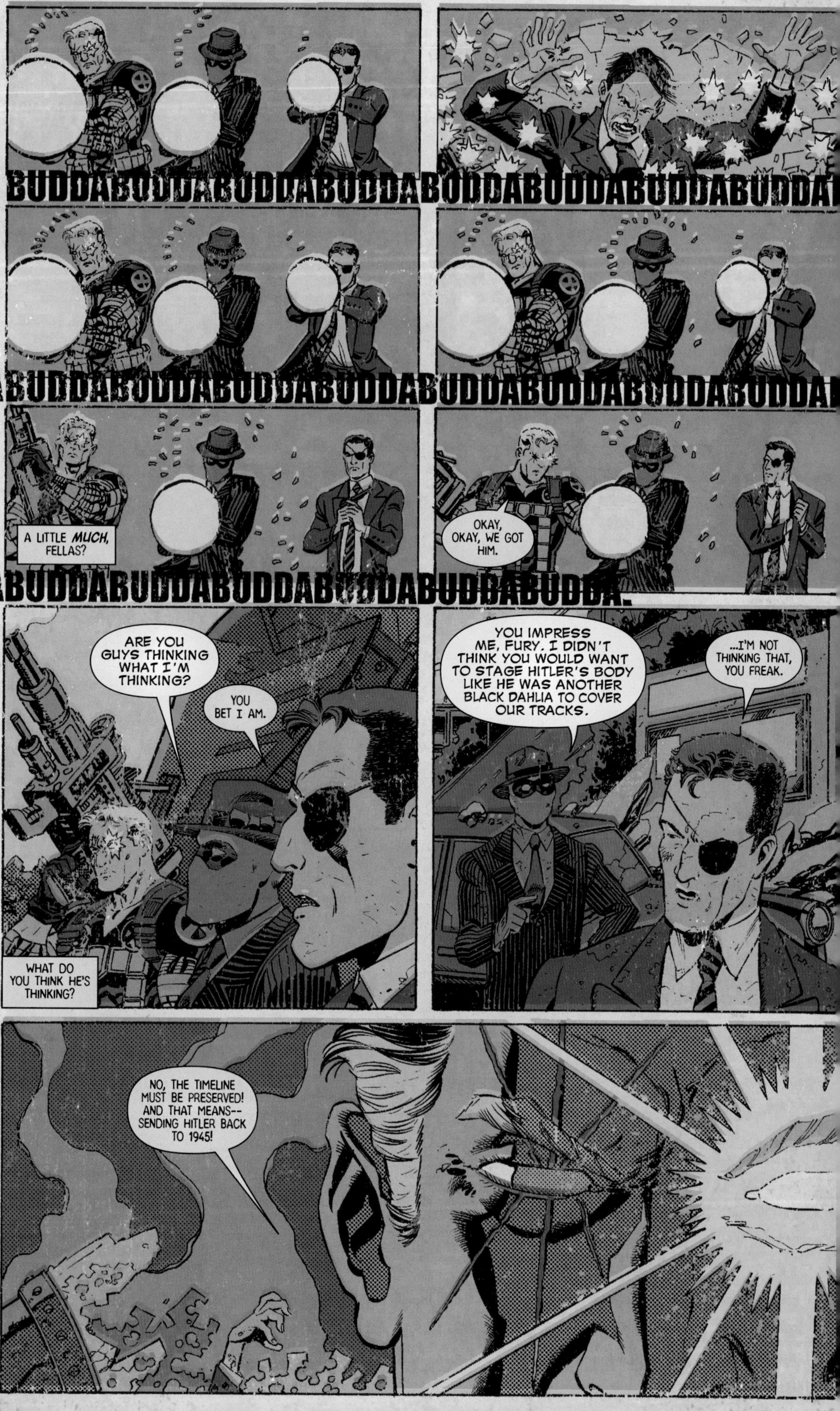
BUDDABUDDABUDDABUDDABUDDABUDDABUDDA
DABUDDABUDDABUDDABUDDABUDDABUDDABUDDA
A LITTLE *MUCH*, FELLAS?
OKAY, OKAY, WE GOT HIM.
ABUDDABUDDABUDDABUDDABUDDA.
ARE YOU GUYS THINKING WHAT I'M THINKING?
YOU BET I AM.
WHAT DO YOU THINK HE'S THINKING?
YOU IMPRESS ME, FURY. I DIDN'T THINK YOU WOULD WANT TO STAGE HITLER'S BODY LIKE HE WAS ANOTHER BLACK DAHLIA TO COVER OUR TRACKS.
...I'M NOT THINKING THAT, YOU FREAK.
NO, THE TIMELINE MUST BE PRESERVED! AND THAT MEANS--SENDING HITLER BACK TO 1945!

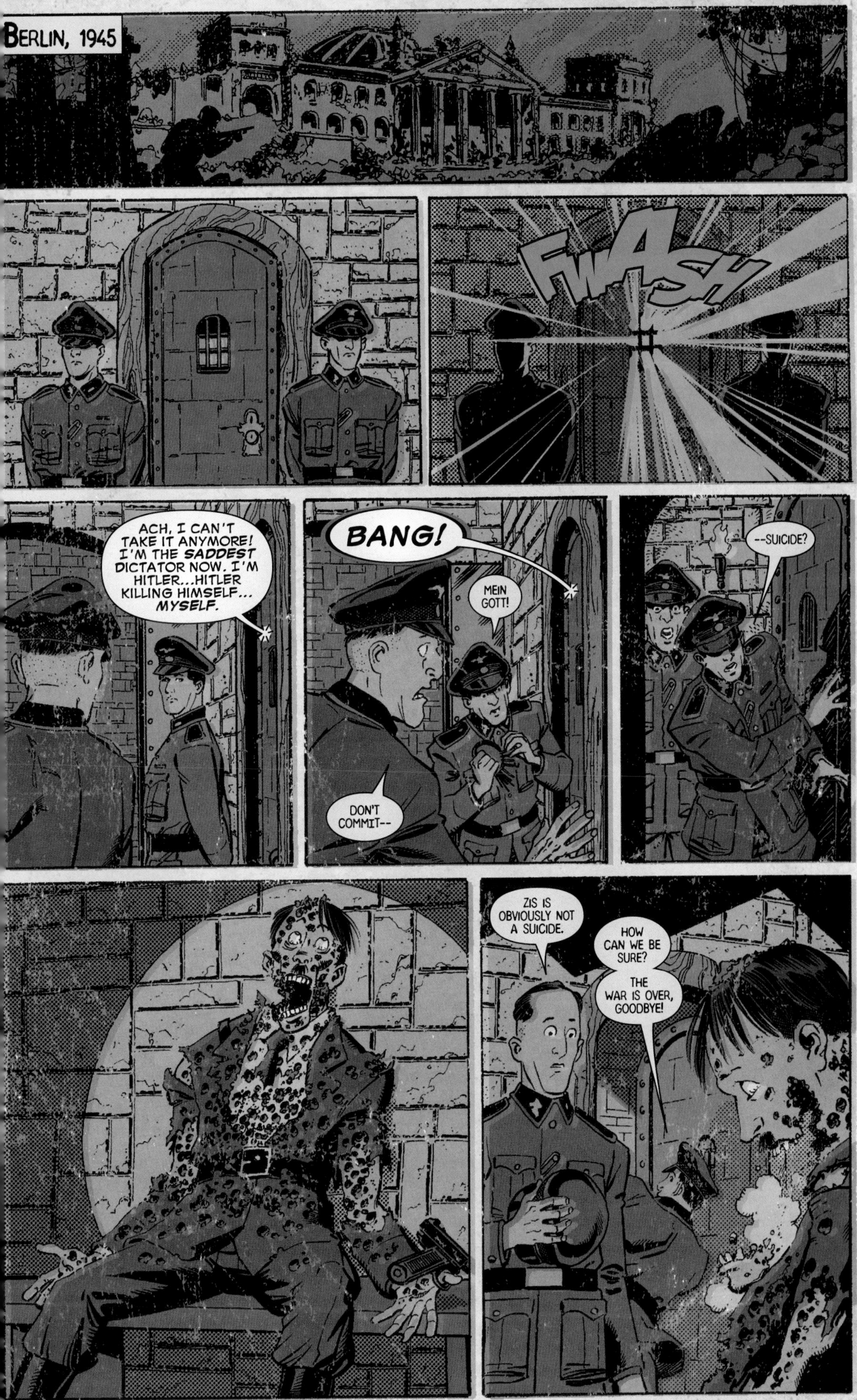
BERLIN, 1945
FWASH
ACH, I CAN'T TAKE IT ANYMORE! I'M THE SADDEST DICTATOR NOW. I'M HITLER...HITLER KILLING HIMSELF... MYSELF.
BANG!
MEIN GOTT!
DON'T COMMIT--
--SUICIDE?
ZIS IS OBVIOUSLY NOT A SUICIDE.
HOW CAN WE BE SURE?
THE WAR IS OVER, GOODBYE!

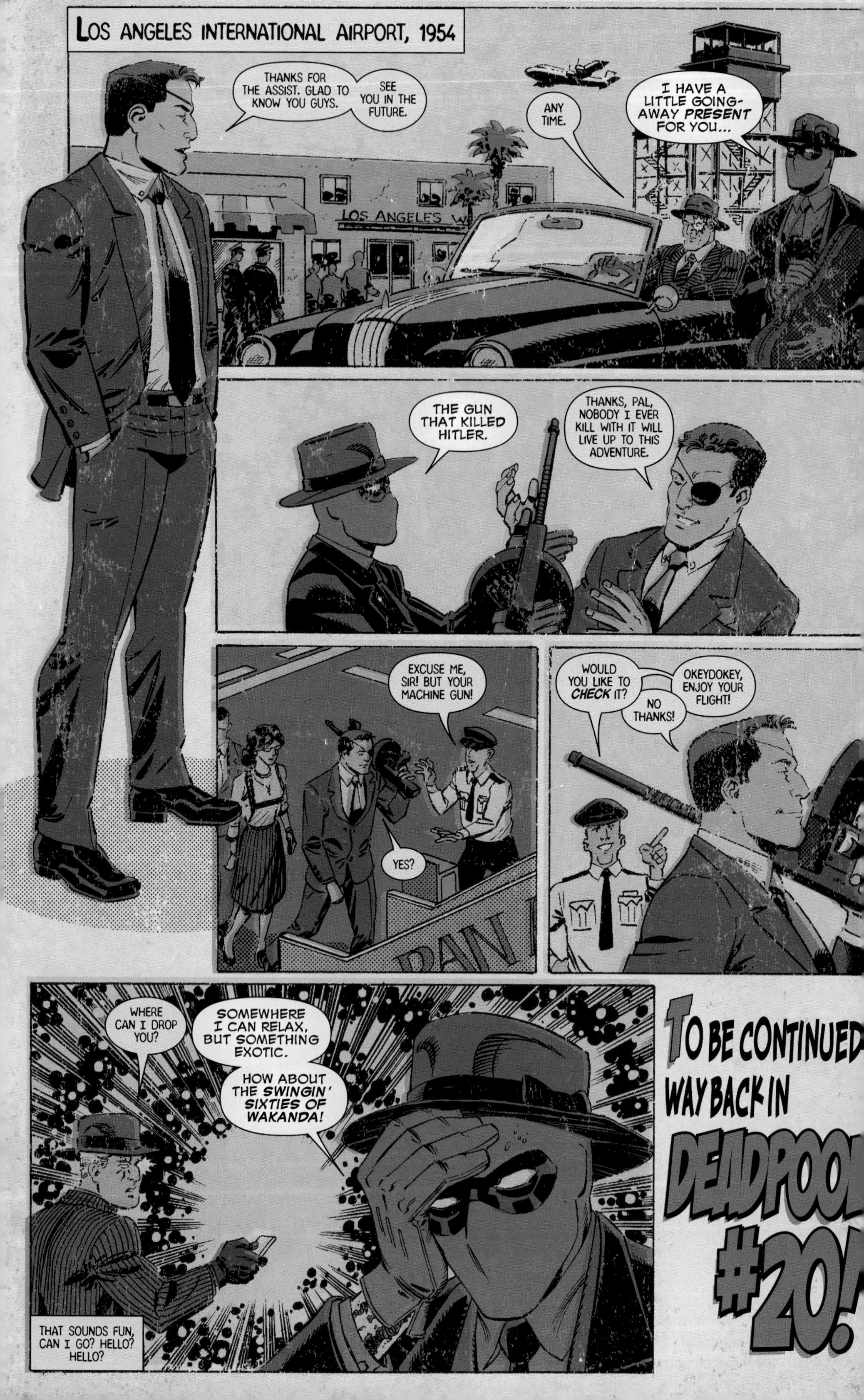

LOS ANGELES INTERNATIONAL AIRPORT, 1954
THANKS FOR THE ASSIST. GLAD TO KNOW YOU GUYS.
SEE YOU IN THE FUTURE.
ANY TIME.
I HAVE A LITTLE GOING-AWAY PRESENT FOR YOU...
LOS ANGELES
THE GUN THAT KILLED HITLER.
THANKS, PAL, NOBODY I EVER KILL WITH IT WILL LIVE UP TO THIS ADVENTURE.
EXCUSE ME, SIR! BUT YOUR MACHINE GUN!
YES?
WOULD YOU LIKE TO CHECK IT?
NO THANKS!
OKEYDOKEY, ENJOY YOUR FLIGHT!
WHERE CAN I DROP YOU?
SOMEWHERE I CAN RELAX, BUT SOMETHING EXOTIC.
HOW ABOUT THE SWINGIN' SIXTIES OF WAKANDA!
THAT SOUNDS FUN, CAN I GO? HELLO? HELLO?
TO BE CONTINUED WAY BACK IN DEADPOOL #20!

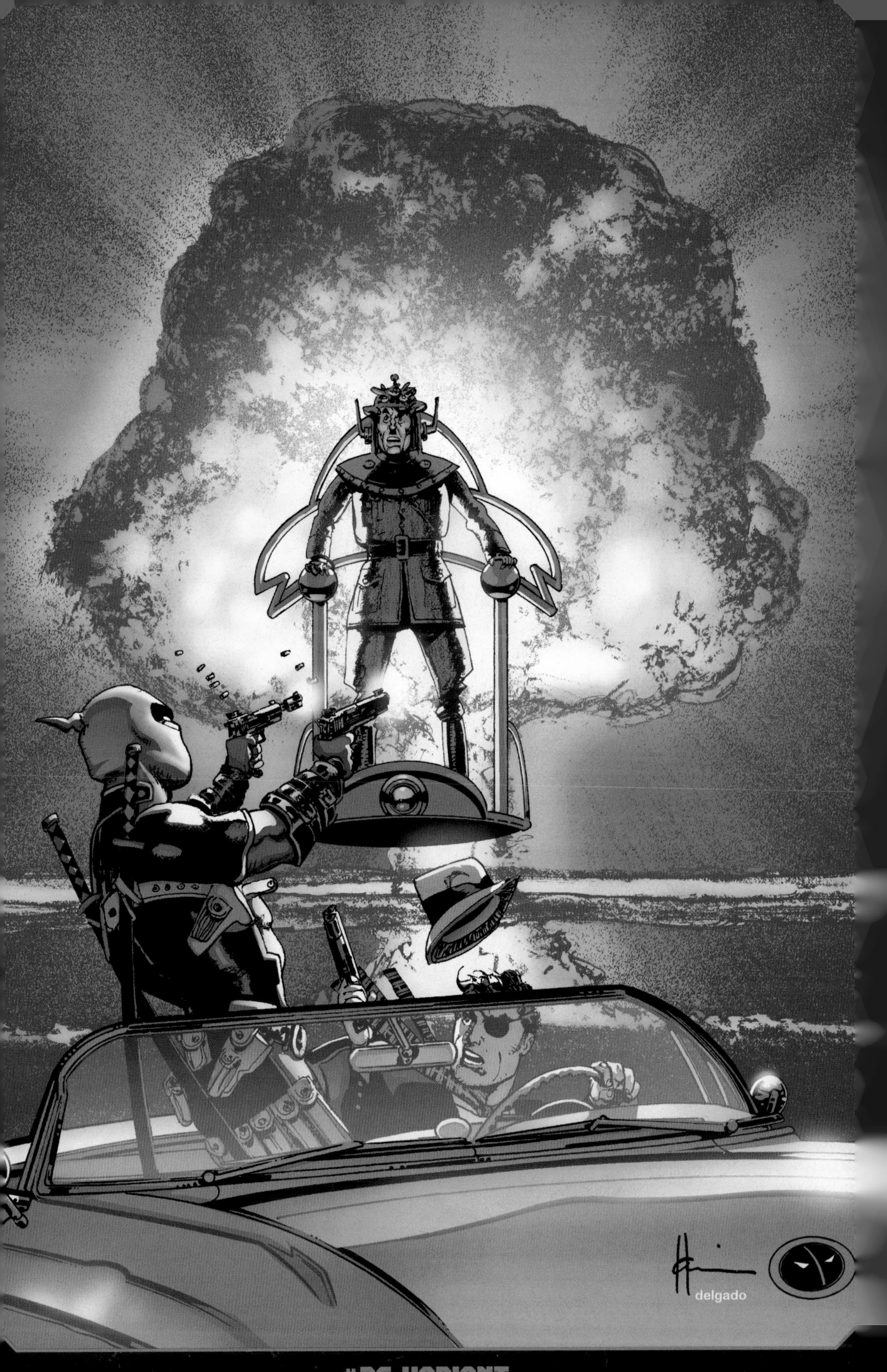
delgado

#26 VARIANT

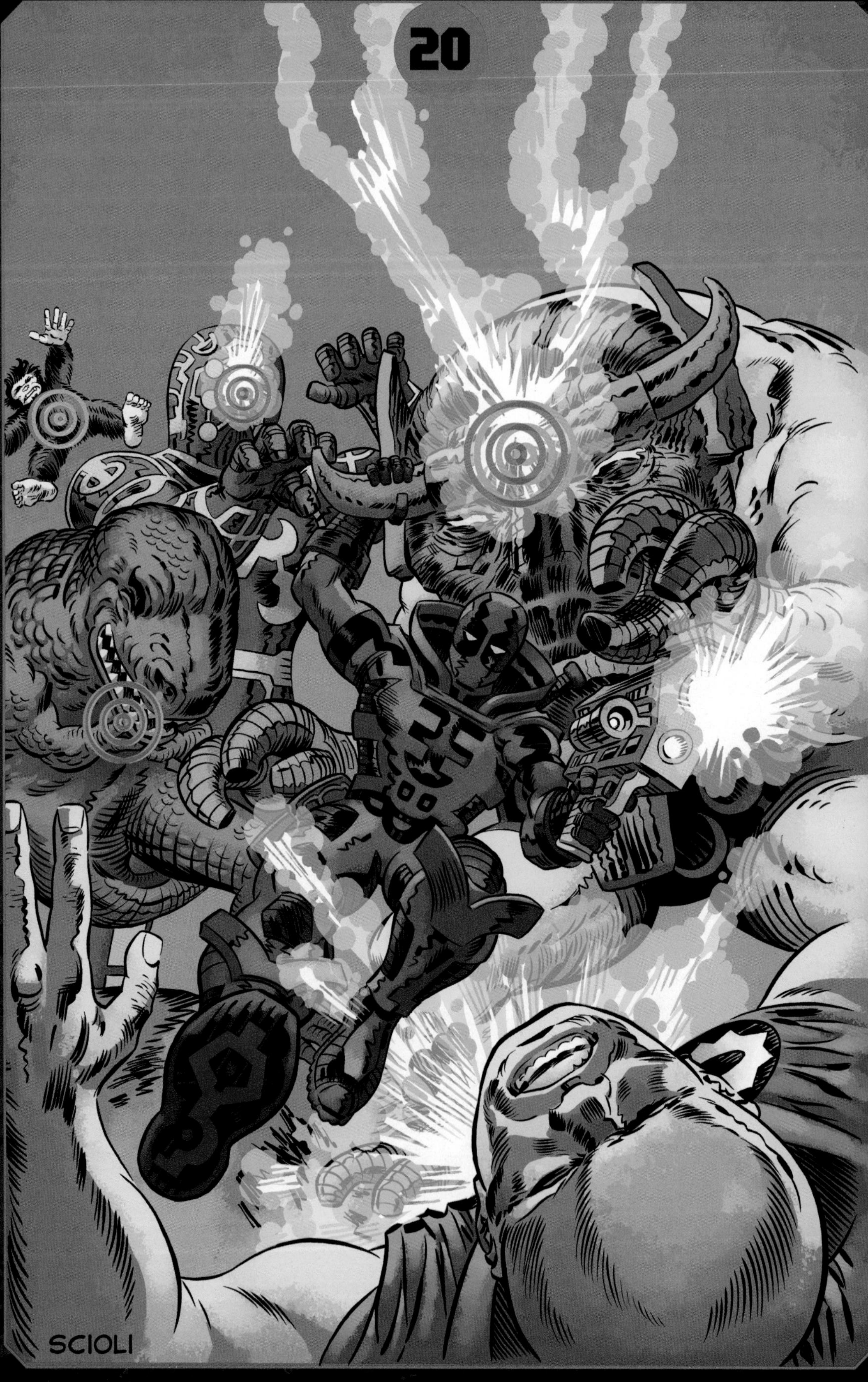
20
SCIOLI

WAKANDAN VACATION!

POSSIBLY THE WORLD'S MOST SKILLED MERCENARY, DEFINITELY THE WORLD'S MOST ANNOYING, WADE WILSON WAS CHOSEN FOR A TOP-SECRET GOVERNMENT PROGRAM THAT GAVE HIM A HEALING FACTOR ALLOWING HIM TO HEAL FROM ANY WOUND. NOW, WADE MAKES HIS WAY AS A GUN FOR HIRE, SHOOTING HIS PREY'S FACES OFF WHILE TALKING HIS FRIENDS' EARS OFF. CALL HIM THE MERC WITH THE MOUTH...CALL HIM THE REGENERATIN' DEGENERATE...CALL HIM...

DEADPOOL!

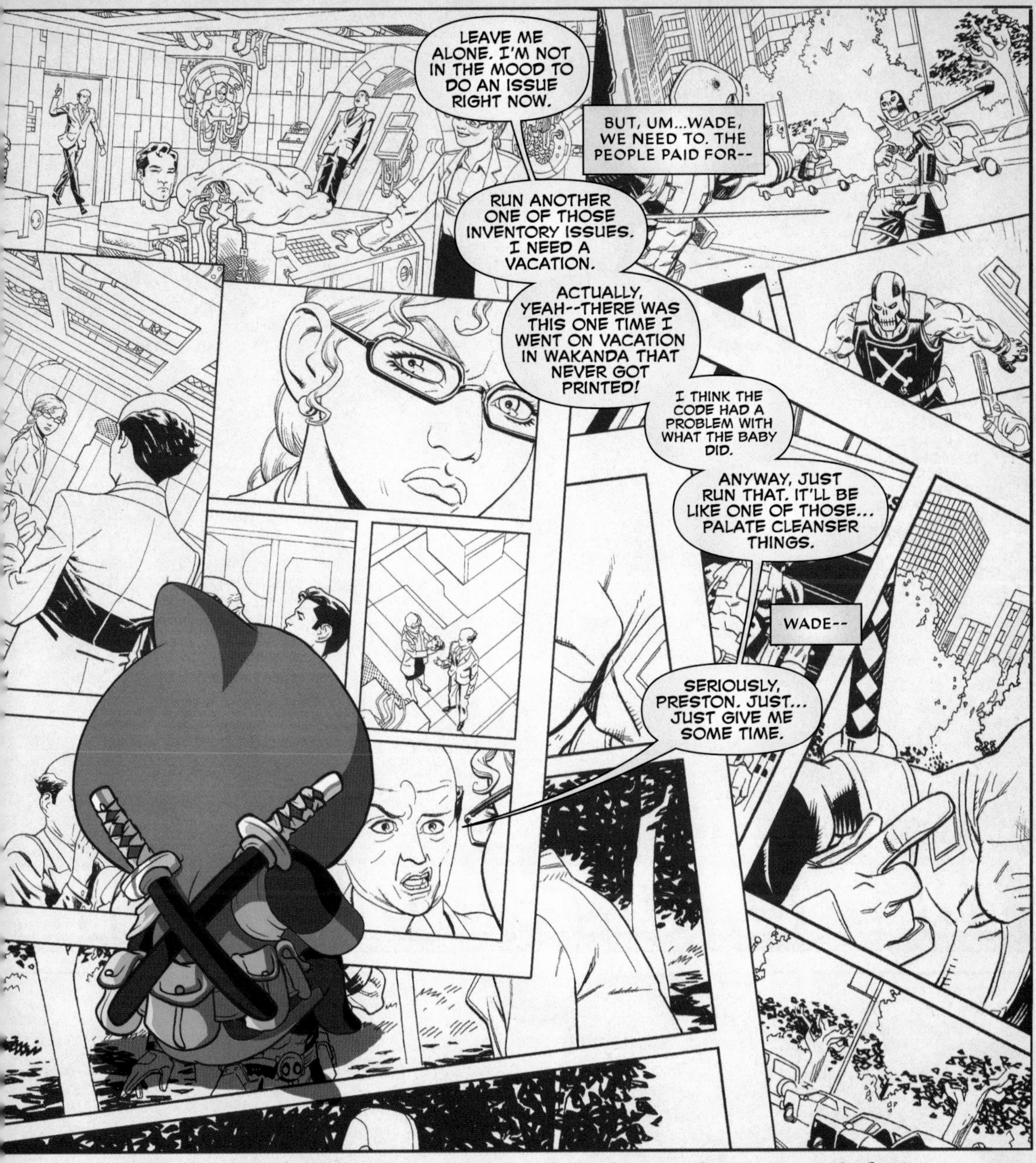
LEAVE ME ALONE. I'M NOT IN THE MOOD TO DO AN ISSUE RIGHT NOW.
BUT, UM...WADE, WE NEED TO. THE PEOPLE PAID FOR--
RUN ANOTHER ONE OF THOSE INVENTORY ISSUES. I NEED A VACATION.
ACTUALLY, YEAH--THERE WAS THIS ONE TIME I WENT ON VACATION IN WAKANDA THAT NEVER GOT PRINTED!
I THINK THE CODE HAD A PROBLEM WITH WHAT THE BABY DID.
ANYWAY, JUST RUN THAT. IT'LL BE LIKE ONE OF THOSE... PALATE CLEANSER THINGS.
WADE--
SERIOUSLY, PRESTON. JUST... JUST GIVE ME SOME TIME.

WAKANDAN VACATION!

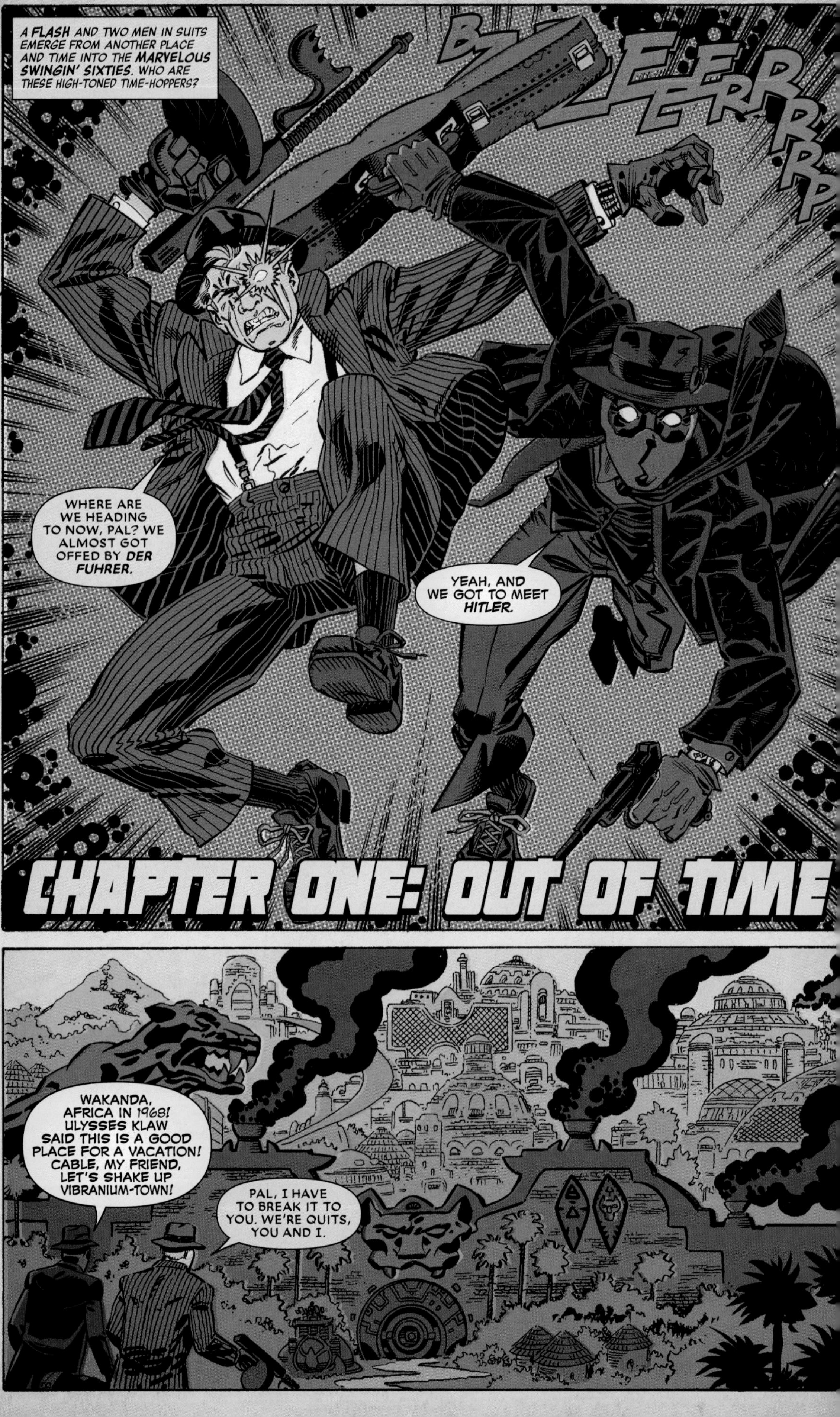

A FLASH AND TWO MEN IN SUITS EMERGE FROM ANOTHER PLACE AND TIME INTO THE MARVELOUS SWINGIN' SIXTIES. WHO ARE THESE HIGH-TONED TIME-HOPPERS?
WHERE ARE WE HEADING TO NOW, PAL? WE ALMOST GOT OFFED BY DER FUHRER.
YEAH, AND WE GOT TO MEET HITLER.
CHAPTER ONE: OUT OF TIME
WAKANDA, AFRICA IN 1968! ULYSSES KLAW SAID THIS IS A GOOD PLACE FOR A VACATION! CABLE, MY FRIEND, LET'S SHAKE UP VIBRANIUM-TOWN!
PAL, I HAVE TO BREAK IT TO YOU. WE'RE QUITS, YOU AND I.

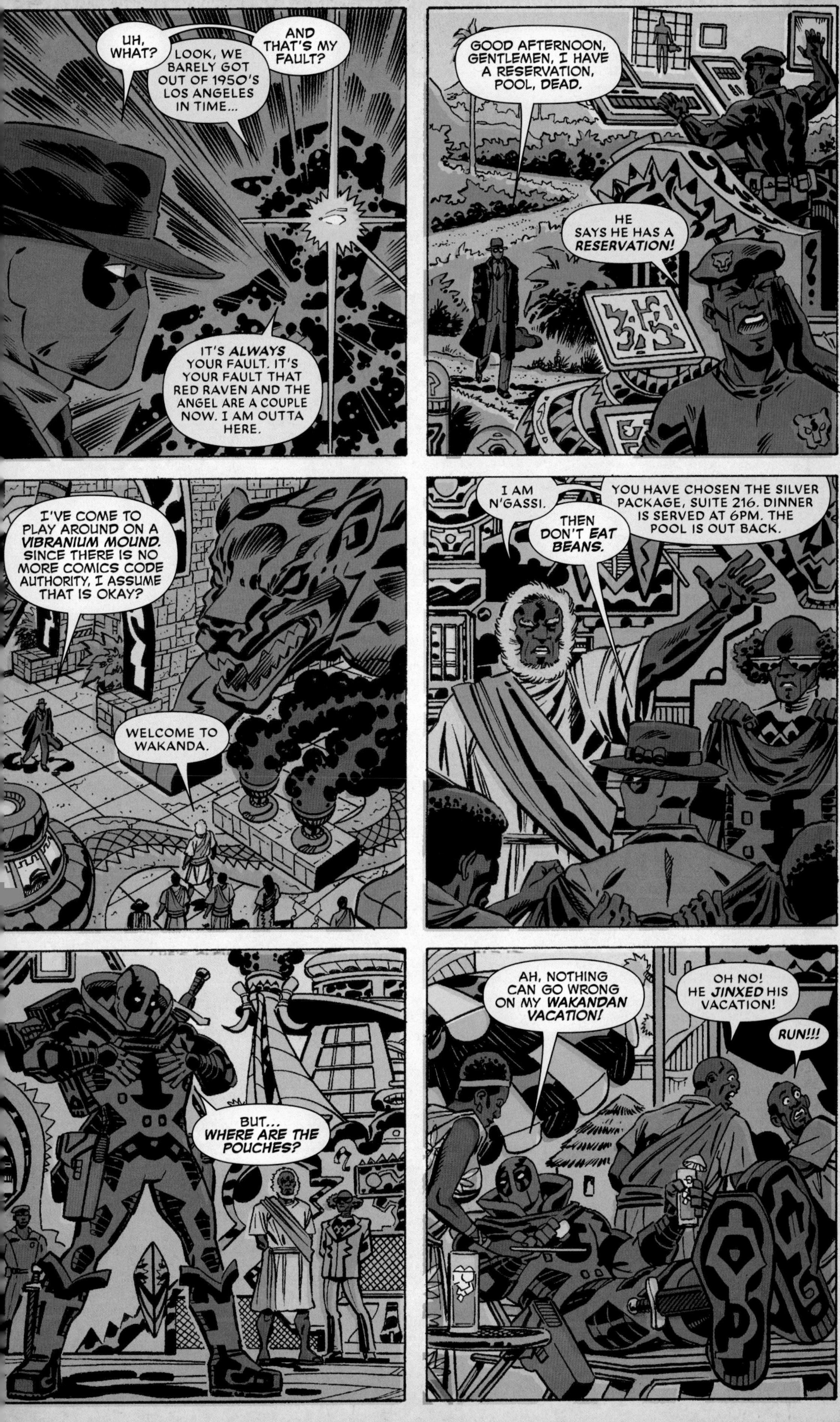
UH, WHAT?
AND THAT'S MY FAULT?
LOOK, WE BARELY GOT OUT OF 1950'S LOS ANGELES IN TIME...
IT'S ALWAYS YOUR FAULT. IT'S YOUR FAULT THAT RED RAVEN AND THE ANGEL ARE A COUPLE NOW. I AM OUTTA HERE.
GOOD AFTERNOON, GENTLEMEN, I HAVE A RESERVATION. POOL, DEAD.
HE SAYS HE HAS A RESERVATION!
I'VE COME TO PLAY AROUND ON A VIBRANIUM MOUND. SINCE THERE IS NO MORE COMICS CODE AUTHORITY, I ASSUME THAT IS OKAY?
WELCOME TO WAKANDA.
I AM N'GASSI.
YOU HAVE CHOSEN THE SILVER PACKAGE, SUITE 216. DINNER IS SERVED AT 6PM. THE POOL IS OUT BACK.
THEN DON'T EAT BEANS.
BUT... WHERE ARE THE POUCHES?
AH, NOTHING CAN GO WRONG ON MY WAKANDAN VACATION!
OH NO! HE JINXED HIS VACATION!
RUN!!!

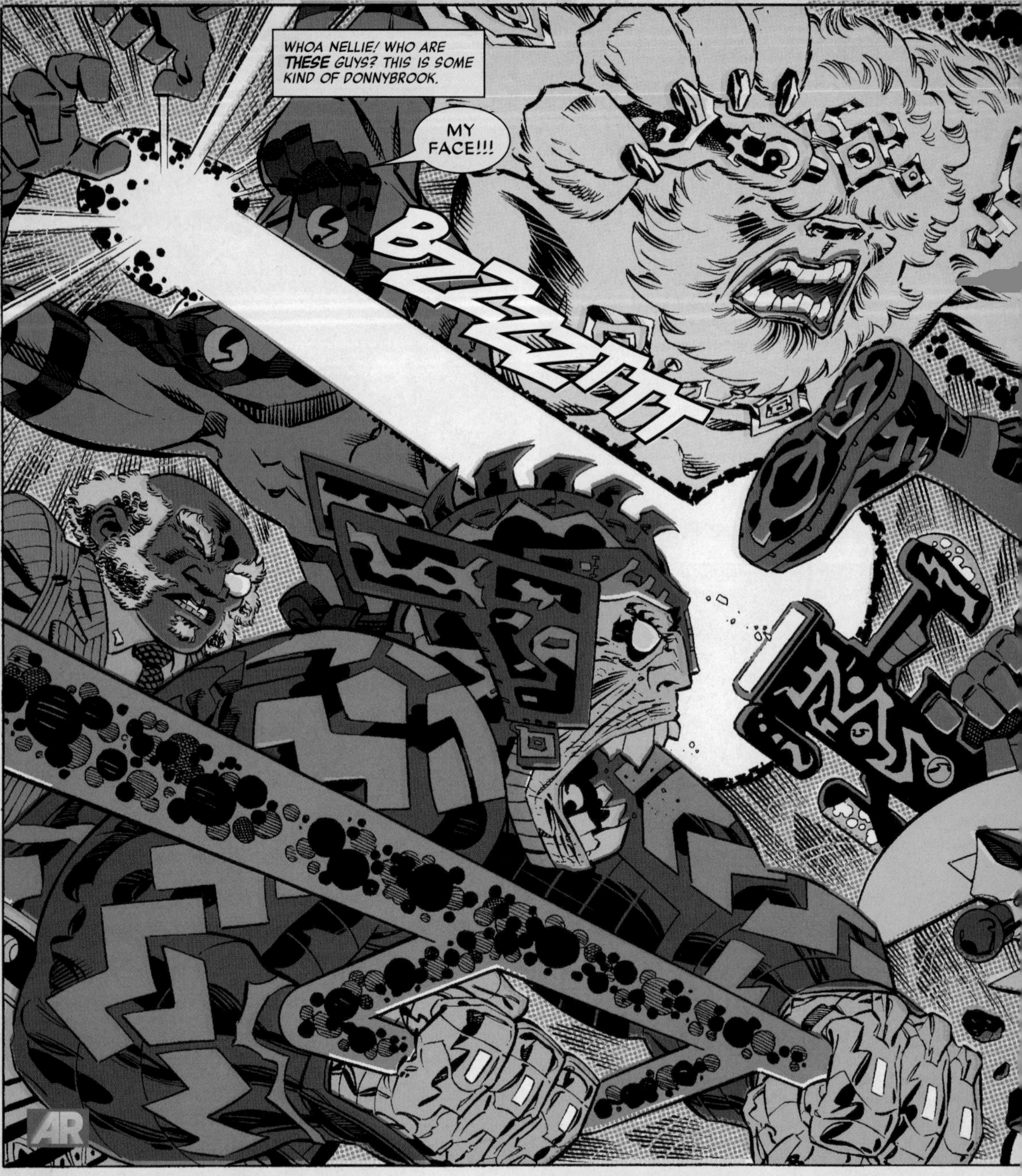
WHOA NELLIE! WHO ARE THESE GUYS? THIS IS SOME KIND OF DONNYBROOK.
MY FACE!!!
BZZZZTTTT

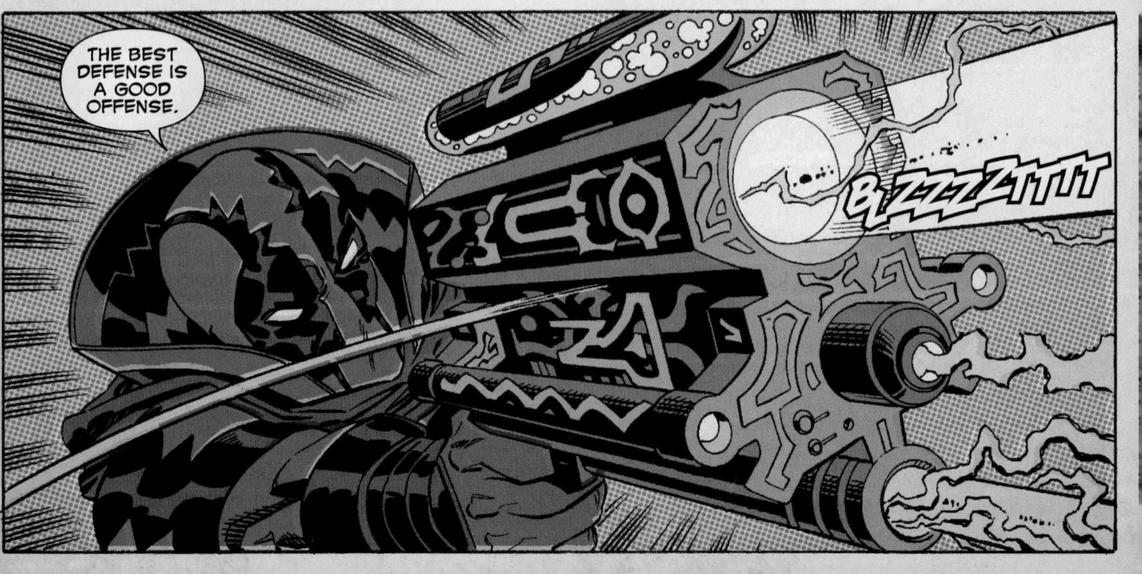
THE BEST DEFENSE IS A GOOD OFFENSE.
BZZZZZTTTT

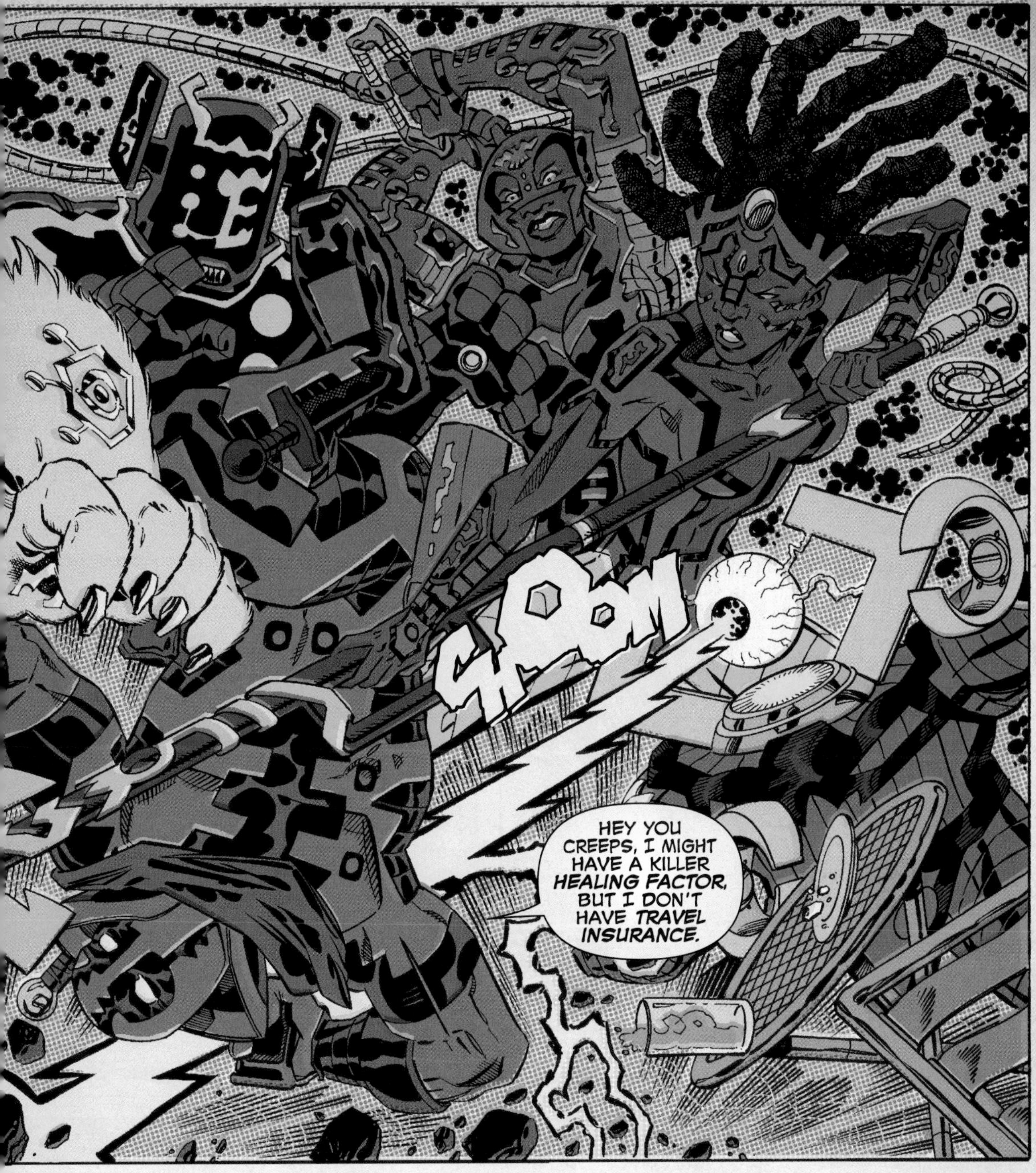
SPROM
HEY YOU CREEPS, I MIGHT HAVE A KILLER HEALING FACTOR, BUT I DON'T HAVE TRAVEL INSURANCE.

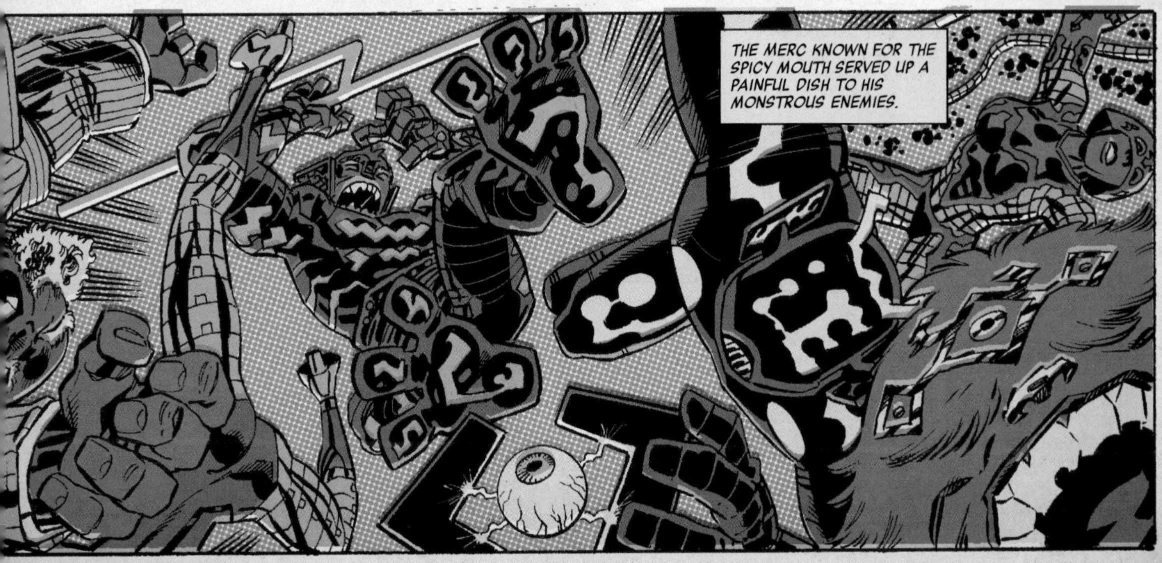
THE MERC KNOWN FOR THE SPICY MOUTH SERVED UP A PAINFUL DISH TO HIS MONSTROUS ENEMIES.

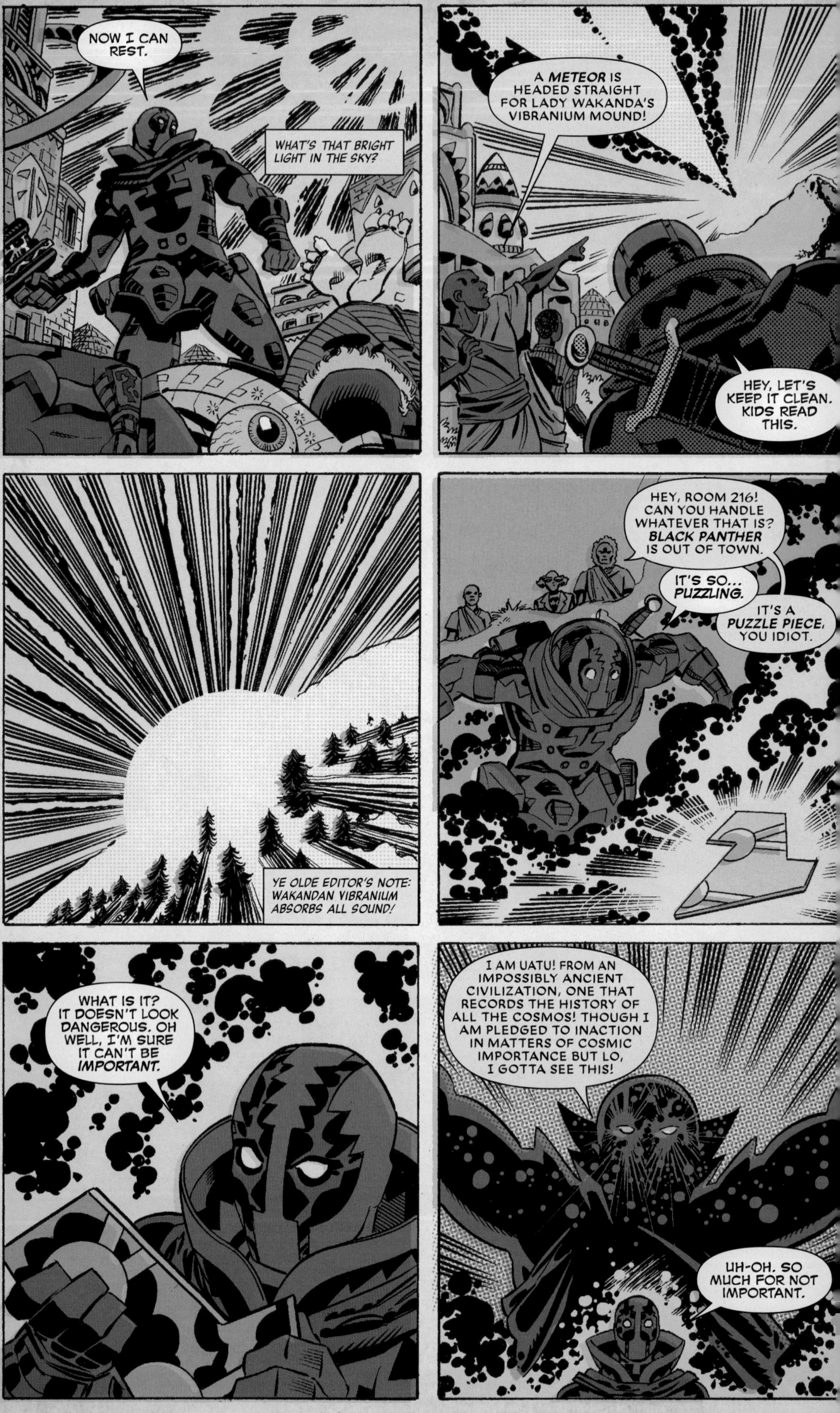
NOW I CAN REST.
WHAT'S THAT BRIGHT LIGHT IN THE SKY?
A METEOR IS HEADED STRAIGHT FOR LADY WAKANDA'S VIBRANIUM MOUND!
HEY, LET'S KEEP IT CLEAN. KIDS READ THIS.
YE OLDE EDITOR'S NOTE: WAKANDAN VIBRANIUM ABSORBS ALL SOUND!
HEY, ROOM 216! CAN YOU HANDLE WHATEVER THAT IS? BLACK PANTHER IS OUT OF TOWN.
IT'S SO... PUZZLING.
IT'S A PUZZLE PIECE, YOU IDIOT.
WHAT IS IT? IT DOESN'T LOOK DANGEROUS. OH WELL, I'M SURE IT CAN'T BE IMPORTANT.
I AM UATU! FROM AN IMPOSSIBLY ANCIENT CIVILIZATION, ONE THAT RECORDS THE HISTORY OF ALL THE COSMOS! THOUGH I AM PLEDGED TO INACTION IN MATTERS OF COSMIC IMPORTANCE BUT LO, I GOTTA SEE THIS!
UH-OH. SO MUCH FOR NOT IMPORTANT.

AND IN MY TRUSTED POSITION AS COSMIC MC, I HAVE ARRIVED AT THIS MOMENT SO THAT I MAY PRESENT TO YOU--

THE RULER OF THE EARTH!

DEADPOOL, TROUBLE IS *AFOOT*. YOU ALONE MUST FIND THREE OTHER COSMIC PUZZLE PIECES, AND THERE WILL BE OTHERS WHO WILL TRY AND TAKE THEM FIRST! I AM HERE TO TAKE YOUR *MEASURE. INCH BY INCH*, YOU WILL APPROACH THE FINISH LINE! AN *OUNCE* OF PREVENTION IS WORTH A *POUND* OF CURE...

I GET IT, YOU'RE "*THE RULER*" AND YOU MAKE MEASUREMENT JOKES. SAVE IT FOR THE BRICK WALL, HACK!

I DON'T KNOW WHAT YOU'RE TALKING ABOUT.

THIS COSMIC *DEVICE* WILL HELP YOU FIND THE PIECES YOU NEED.

I *LOVE* PUZZLES. I USED TO EAT THEM WHEN I WAS LITTLE.

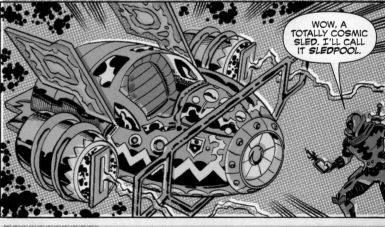

WOW, A TOTALLY COSMIC SLED. I'LL CALL IT *SLEDPOOL*.

GOOD LUCK! DON'T DIE!

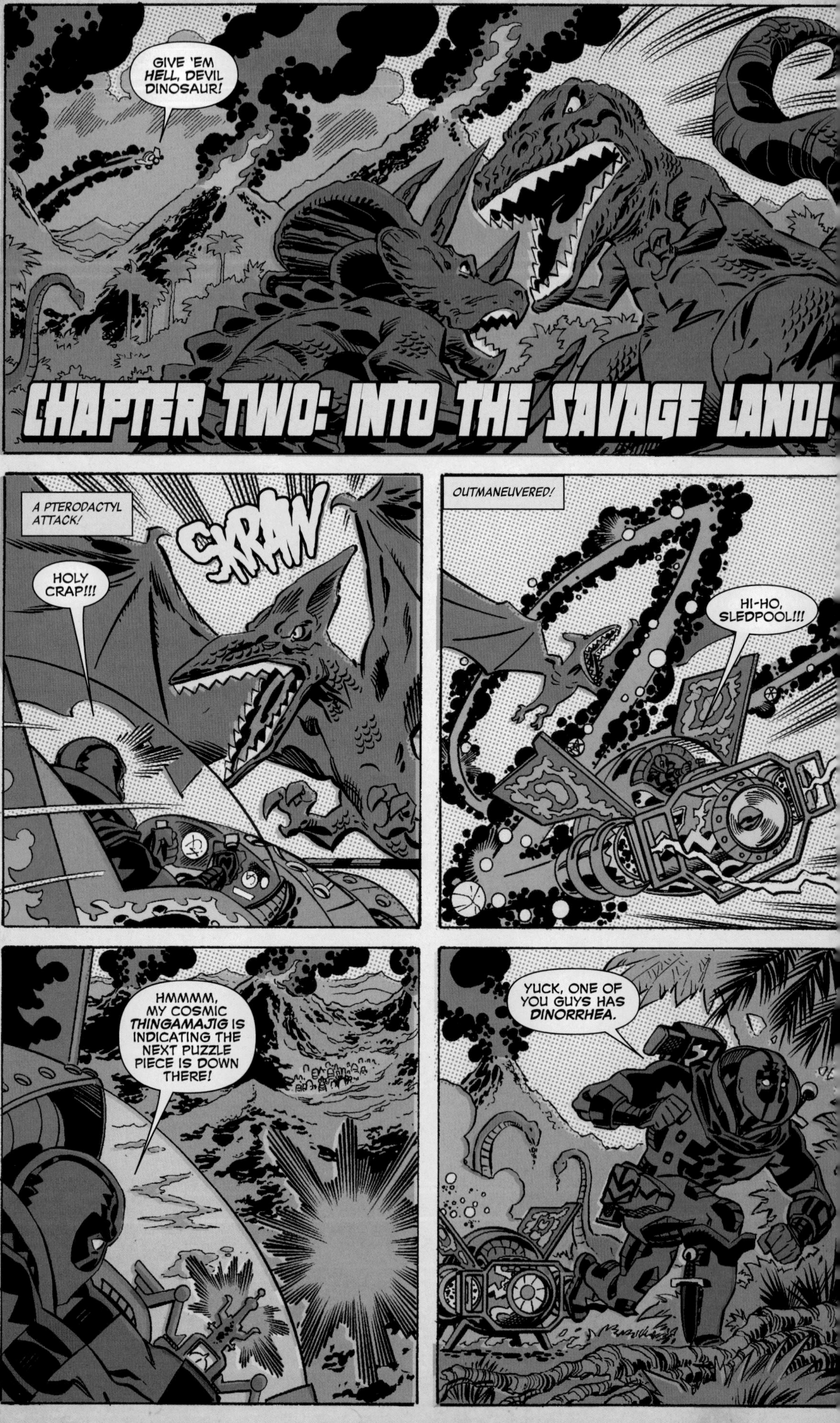

GIVE 'EM HELL, DEVIL DINOSAUR!
CHAPTER TWO: INTO THE SAVAGE LAND!
A PTERODACTYL ATTACK!
SKRAW
HOLY CRAP!!!
OUTMANEUVERED!
HI-HO, SLEDPOOL!!!
HMMMM, MY COSMIC THINGAMAJIG IS INDICATING THE NEXT PUZZLE PIECE IS DOWN THERE!
YUCK, ONE OF YOU GUYS HAS DINORRHEA.

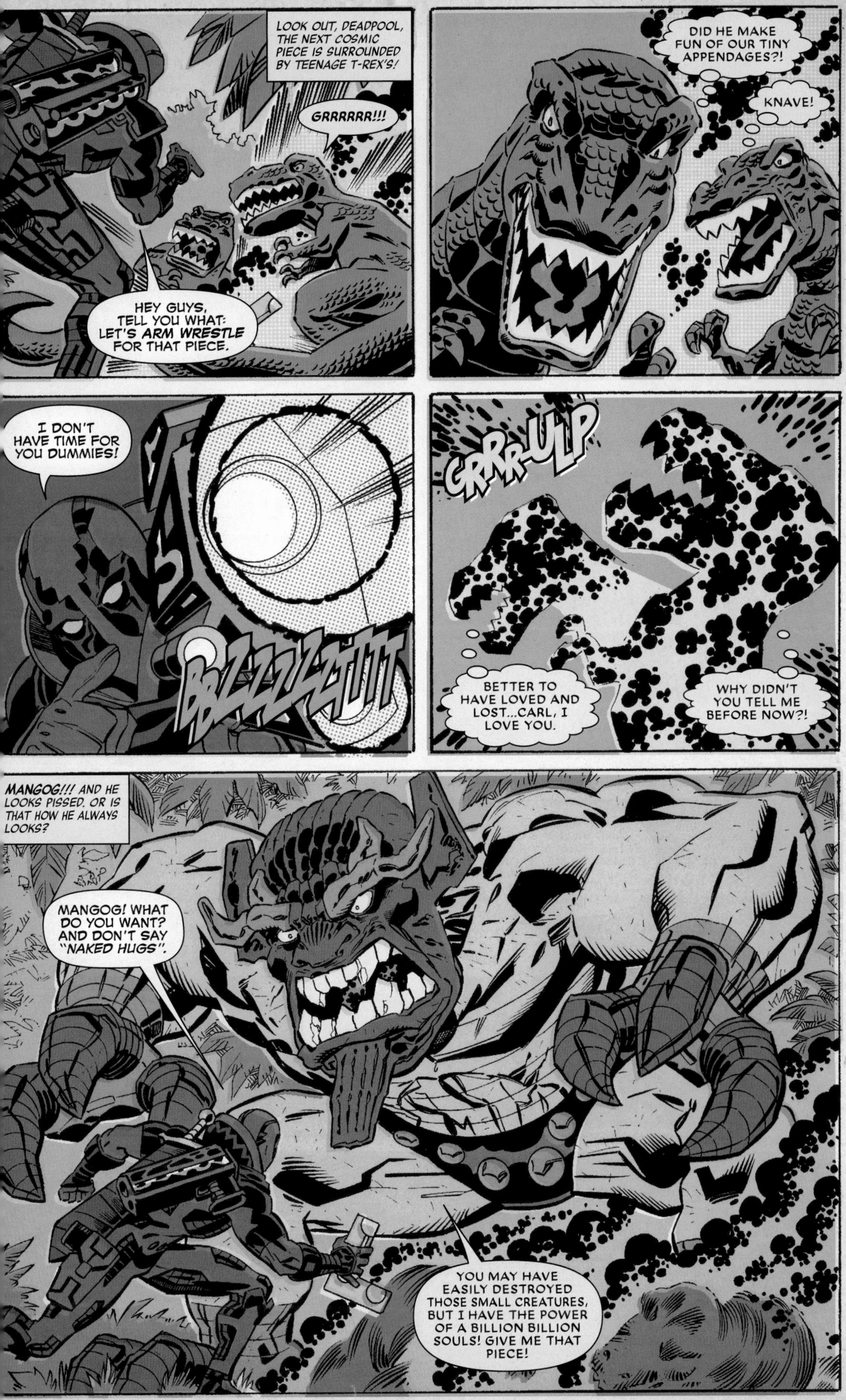

LOOK OUT, DEADPOOL, THE NEXT COSMIC PIECE IS SURROUNDED BY TEENAGE T-REX'S!
GRRRRRR!!!
HEY GUYS, TELL YOU WHAT: LET'S ARM WRESTLE FOR THAT PIECE.
DID HE MAKE FUN OF OUR TINY APPENDAGES?!
KNAVE!
I DON'T HAVE TIME FOR YOU DUMMIES!
BRZZZZZZTTTT
GRRR-ULP
BETTER TO HAVE LOVED AND LOST...CARL, I LOVE YOU.
WHY DIDN'T YOU TELL ME BEFORE NOW?!
MANGOG!!! AND HE LOOKS PISSED. OR IS THAT HOW HE ALWAYS LOOKS?
MANGOG! WHAT DO YOU WANT? AND DON'T SAY "NAKED HUGS".
YOU MAY HAVE EASILY DESTROYED THOSE SMALL CREATURES, BUT I HAVE THE POWER OF A BILLION BILLION SOULS! GIVE ME THAT PIECE!

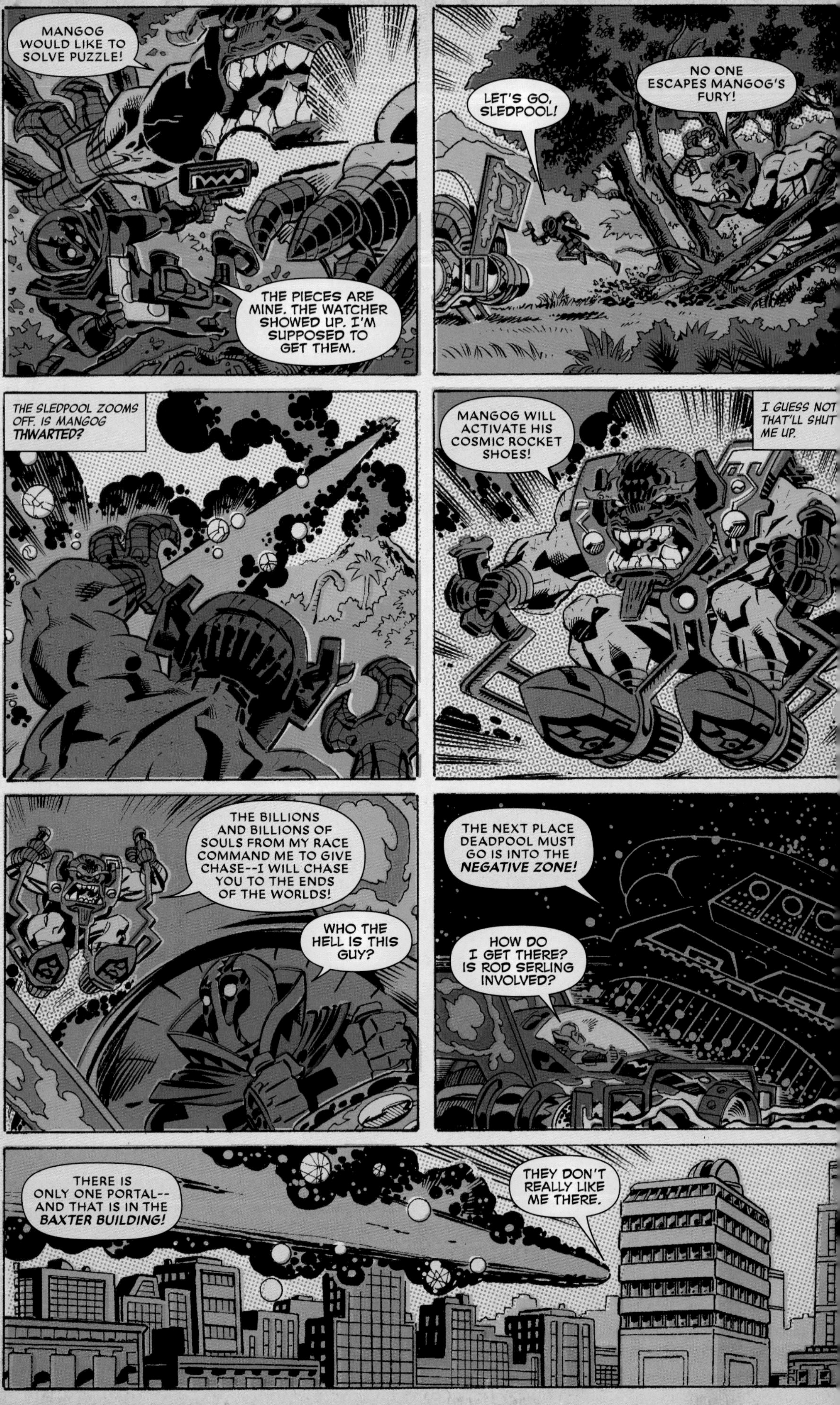
MANGOG WOULD LIKE TO SOLVE PUZZLE!
THE PIECES ARE MINE. THE WATCHER SHOWED UP. I'M SUPPOSED TO GET THEM.
LET'S GO, SLEDPOOL!
NO ONE ESCAPES MANGOG'S FURY!
THE SLEDPOOL ZOOMS OFF. IS MANGOG THWARTED?
MANGOG WILL ACTIVATE HIS COSMIC ROCKET SHOES!
I GUESS NOT THAT'LL SHUT ME UP.
THE BILLIONS AND BILLIONS OF SOULS FROM MY RACE COMMAND ME TO GIVE CHASE--I WILL CHASE YOU TO THE ENDS OF THE WORLDS!
WHO THE HELL IS THIS GUY?
THE NEXT PLACE DEADPOOL MUST GO IS INTO THE NEGATIVE ZONE!
HOW DO I GET THERE? IS ROD SERLING INVOLVED?
THERE IS ONLY ONE PORTAL--AND THAT IS IN THE BAXTER BUILDING!
THEY DON'T REALLY LIKE ME THERE.

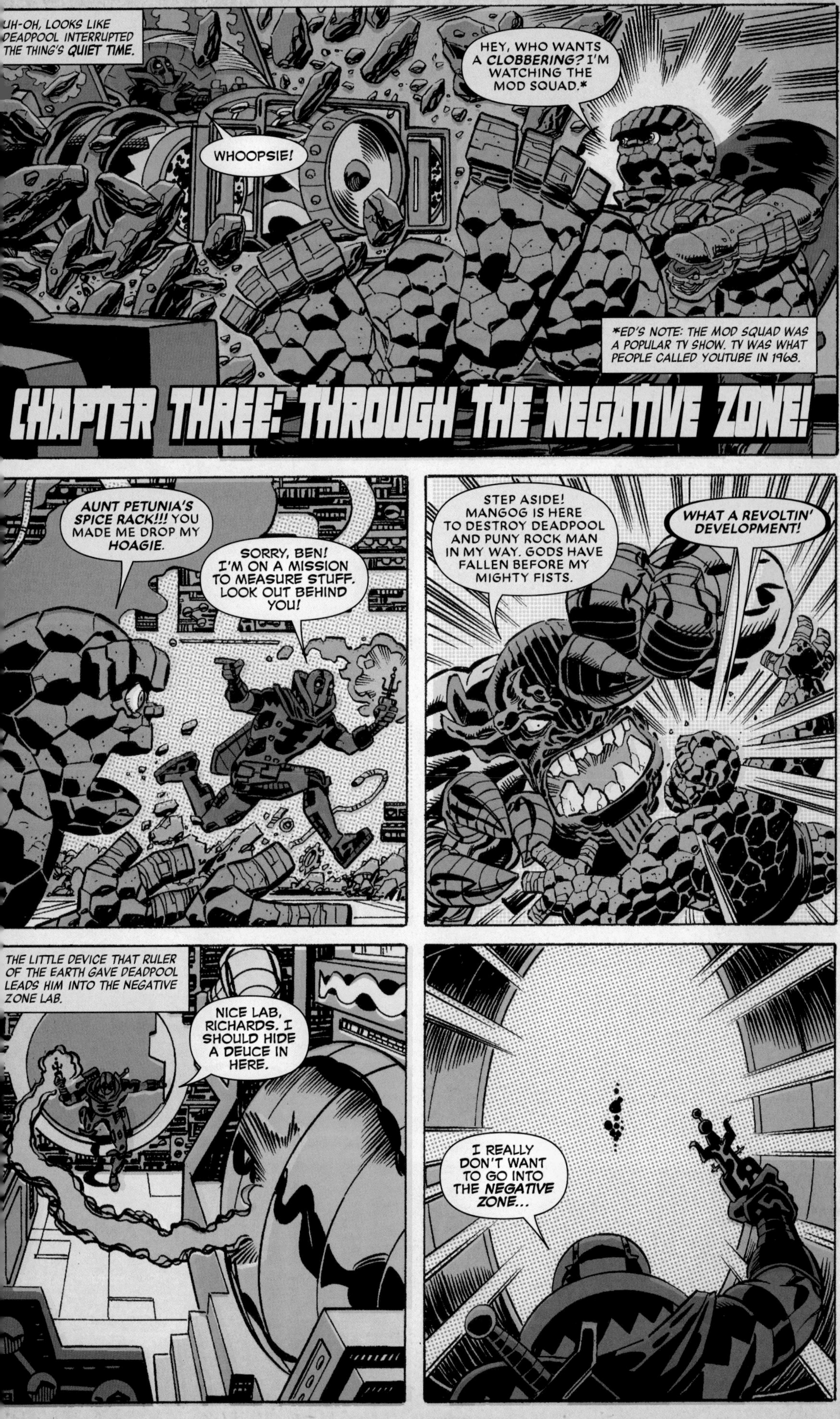
UH-OH, LOOKS LIKE DEADPOOL INTERRUPTED THE THING'S QUIET TIME.
HEY, WHO WANTS A CLOBBERING? I'M WATCHING THE MOD SQUAD.*
WHOOPSIE!
*ED'S NOTE: THE MOD SQUAD WAS A POPULAR TV SHOW. TV WAS WHAT PEOPLE CALLED YOUTUBE IN 1968.
CHAPTER THREE: THROUGH THE NEGATIVE ZONE!
AUNT PETUNIA'S SPICE RACK!!! YOU MADE ME DROP MY HOAGIE.
SORRY, BEN! I'M ON A MISSION TO MEASURE STUFF. LOOK OUT BEHIND YOU!
STEP ASIDE! MANGOG IS HERE TO DESTROY DEADPOOL AND PUNY ROCK MAN IN MY WAY. GODS HAVE FALLEN BEFORE MY MIGHTY FISTS.
WHAT A REVOLTIN' DEVELOPMENT!
THE LITTLE DEVICE THAT RULER OF THE EARTH GAVE DEADPOOL LEADS HIM INTO THE NEGATIVE ZONE LAB.
NICE LAB, RICHARDS. I SHOULD HIDE A DEUCE IN HERE.
I REALLY DON'T WANT TO GO INTO THE NEGATIVE ZONE...

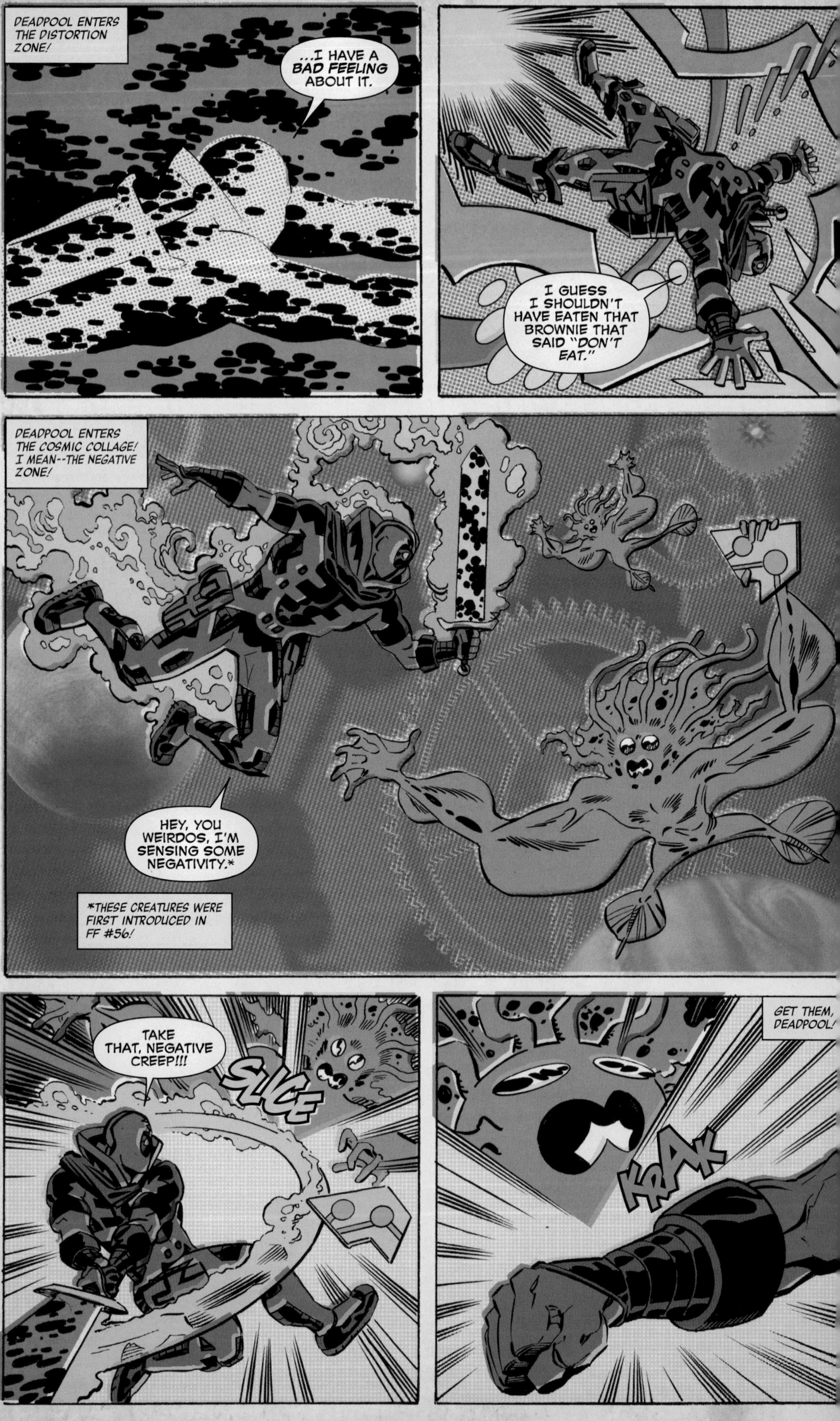
DEADPOOL ENTERS THE DISTORTION ZONE!
...I HAVE A BAD FEELING ABOUT IT.
I GUESS I SHOULDN'T HAVE EATEN THAT BROWNIE THAT SAID "DON'T EAT."
DEADPOOL ENTERS THE COSMIC COLLAGE! I MEAN--THE NEGATIVE ZONE!
HEY, YOU WEIRDOS, I'M SENSING SOME NEGATIVITY.*
*THESE CREATURES WERE FIRST INTRODUCED IN FF #56!
TAKE THAT, NEGATIVE CREEP!!!
SLICE
GET THEM, DEADPOOL!
KRAK

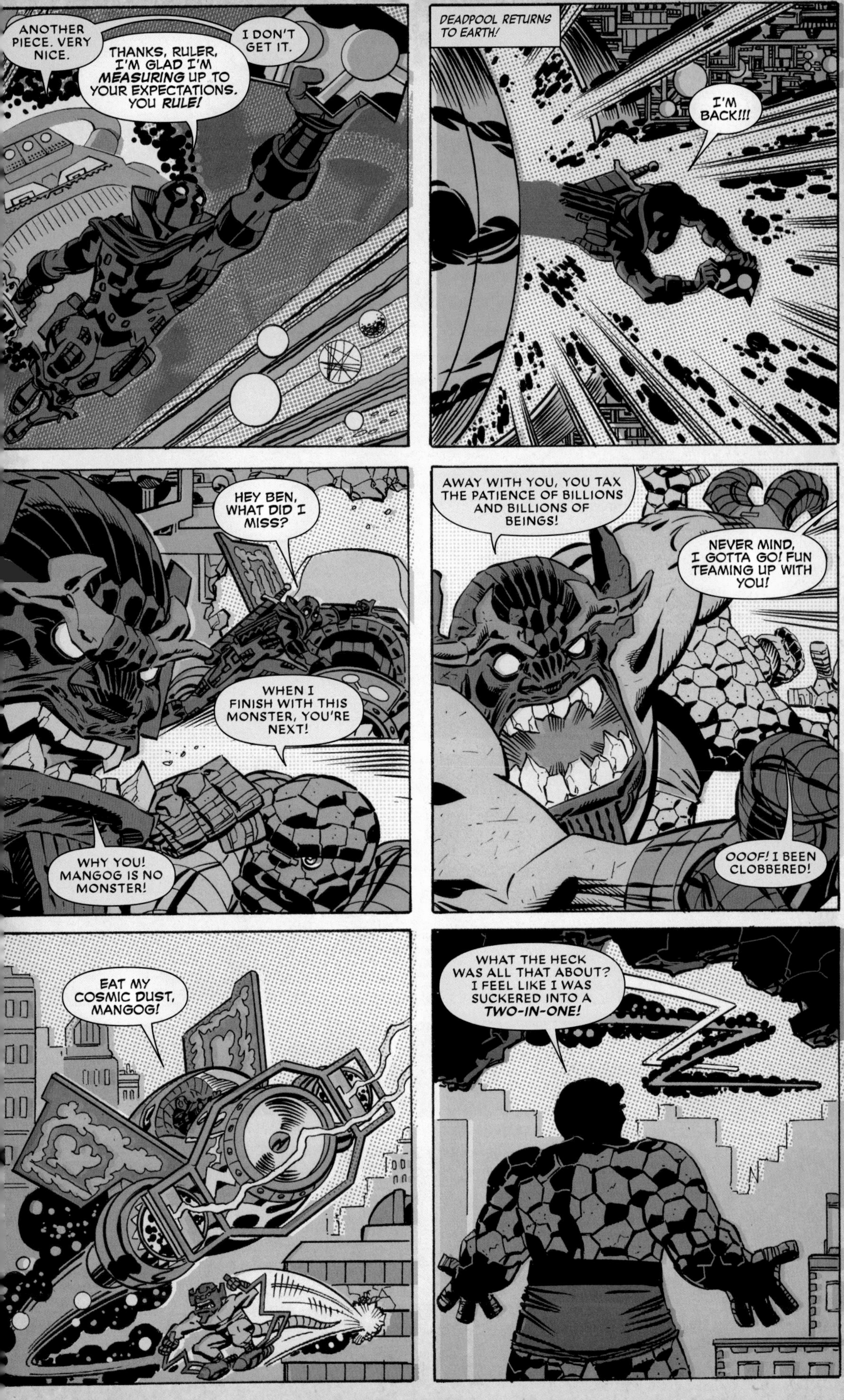
ANOTHER PIECE. VERY NICE.
THANKS, RULER, I'M GLAD I'M *MEASURING* UP TO YOUR EXPECTATIONS. YOU *RULE!*
I DON'T GET IT.
DEADPOOL RETURNS TO EARTH!
I'M BACK!!!
HEY BEN, WHAT DID I MISS?
WHEN I FINISH WITH THIS MONSTER, YOU'RE NEXT!
WHY YOU! MANGOG IS NO MONSTER!
AWAY WITH YOU, YOU TAX THE PATIENCE OF BILLIONS AND BILLIONS OF BEINGS!
NEVER MIND, I GOTTA GO! FUN TEAMING UP WITH YOU!
OOOF! I BEEN CLOBBERED!
EAT MY COSMIC DUST, MANGOG!
WHAT THE HECK WAS ALL THAT ABOUT? I FEEL LIKE I WAS SUCKERED INTO A *TWO-IN-ONE!*

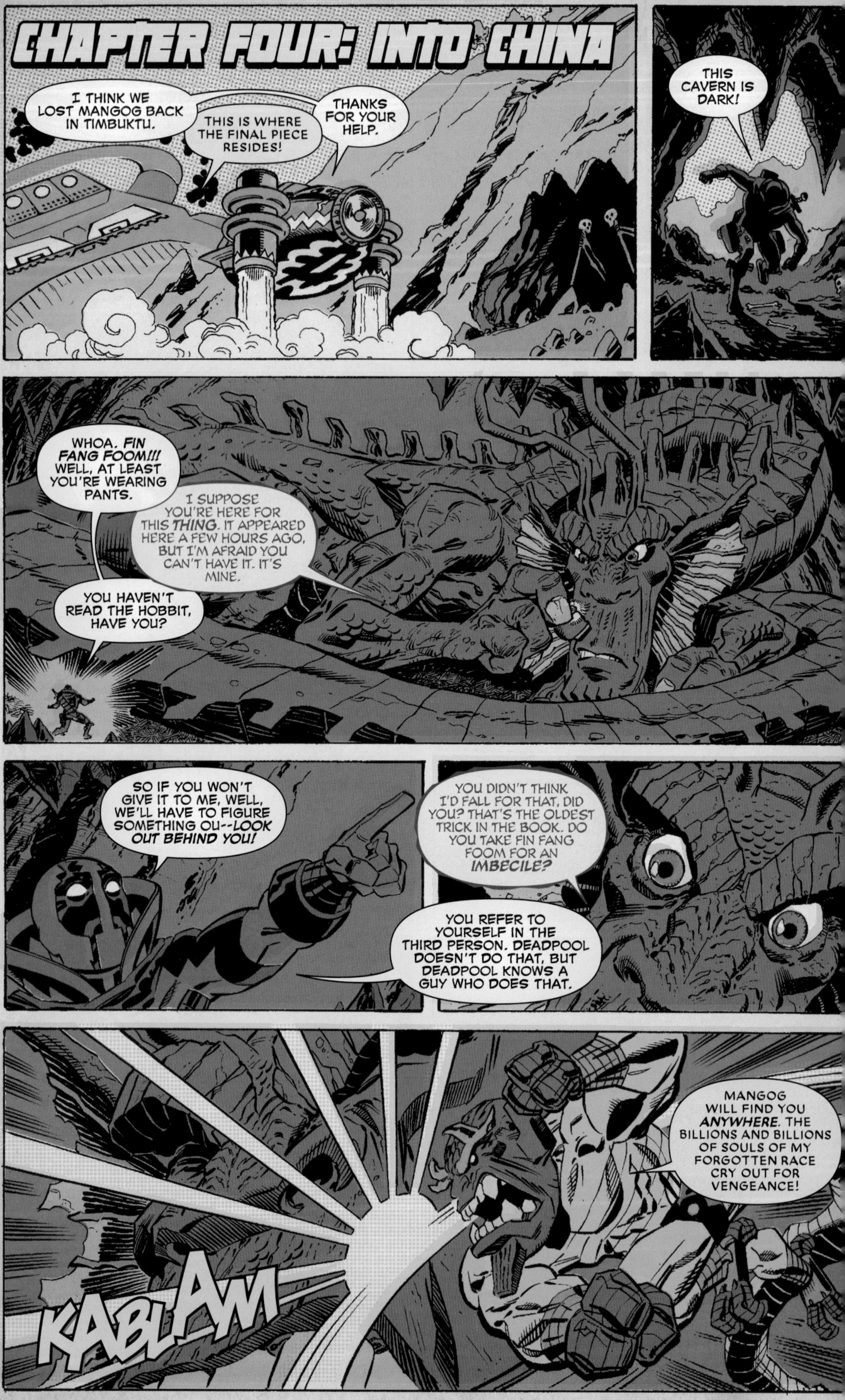
CHAPTER FOUR: INTO CHINA
I THINK WE LOST MANGOG BACK IN TIMBUKTU.
THIS IS WHERE THE FINAL PIECE RESIDES!
THANKS FOR YOUR HELP.
THIS CAVERN IS DARK!
WHOA. FIN FANG FOOM!!! WELL, AT LEAST YOU'RE WEARING PANTS.
I SUPPOSE YOU'RE HERE FOR THIS THING. IT APPEARED HERE A FEW HOURS AGO, BUT I'M AFRAID YOU CAN'T HAVE IT. IT'S MINE.
YOU HAVEN'T READ THE HOBBIT, HAVE YOU?
SO IF YOU WON'T GIVE IT TO ME, WELL, WE'LL HAVE TO FIGURE SOMETHING OU--LOOK OUT BEHIND YOU!
YOU DIDN'T THINK I'D FALL FOR THAT, DID YOU? THAT'S THE OLDEST TRICK IN THE BOOK. DO YOU TAKE FIN FANG FOOM FOR AN IMBECILE?
YOU REFER TO YOURSELF IN THE THIRD PERSON. DEADPOOL DOESN'T DO THAT, BUT DEADPOOL KNOWS A GUY WHO DOES THAT.
KABLAM
MANGOG WILL FIND YOU ANYWHERE. THE BILLIONS AND BILLIONS OF SOULS OF MY FORGOTTEN RACE CRY OUT FOR VENGEANCE!

OOOOOFFF!!!

KFERRUNCHH

WELL, THAT OUGHT TO KEEP THEM ENTERTAINED. I DON'T HEAR THE RULER OF THE EARTH GLOATING IN MY EAR. IT'S NICE TO NOT HAVE TO WORRY ABOUT ANYBODY IN MY HEAD.

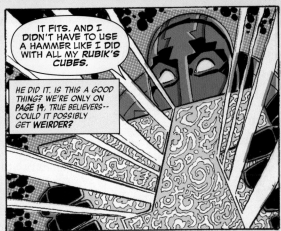

IT FITS. AND I DIDN'T HAVE TO USE A HAMMER LIKE I DID WITH ALL MY RUBIK'S CUBES.

HE DID IT. IS THIS A GOOD THING? WE'RE ONLY ON PAGE 14, TRUE BELIEVERS-- COULD IT POSSIBLY GET WEIRDER?

IT GETS WEIRDER.

CONGRATULATIONS DEADPOOL, YOU HAVE COMPLETED THE COSMIC PUZZLE.

THANKS, COSMIC BABY...WAIT, YOUR LIPS DIDN'T MOVE WHEN YOU TALKED, YOU'RE LIKE JEFF DUNHAM, BUT FUNNY.

IT'S TIME FOR MY OLD-SCHOOL CLOSE-UP ON MY EYES AS I SAY SOMETHING OF IMPORTANCE, HEIGHTENING THE DRAMA, AS I ASK YOU--WHAT'S NEXT, COSMIC BABY? WHERE DO WE GO FROM HERE?

WHERE ALL BLOCKHEADS GO...!

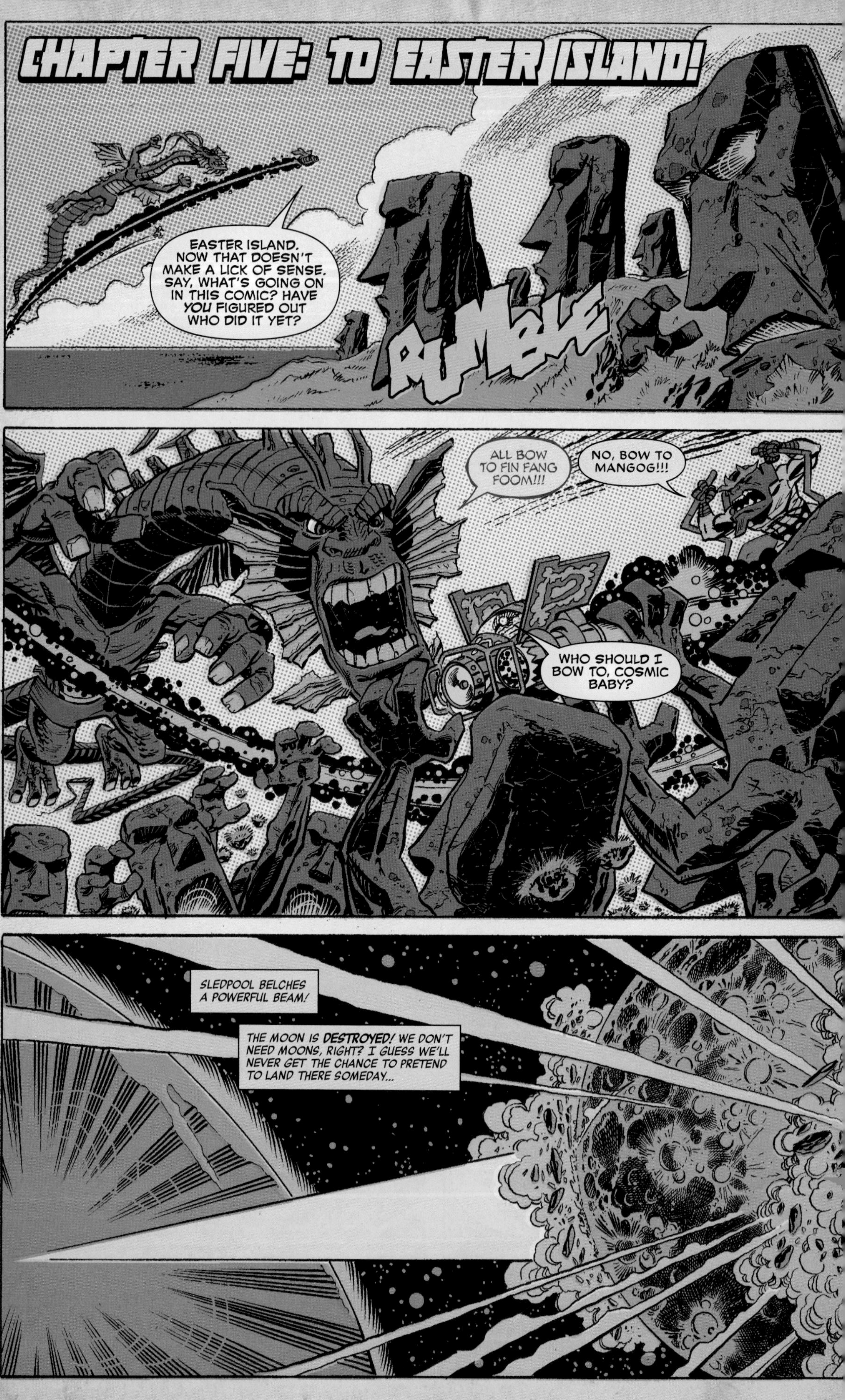
CHAPTER FIVE: TO EASTER ISLAND!
EASTER ISLAND. NOW THAT DOESN'T MAKE A LICK OF SENSE. SAY, WHAT'S GOING ON IN THIS COMIC? HAVE YOU FIGURED OUT WHO DID IT YET?
RUMBLE
ALL BOW TO FIN FANG FOOM!!!
NO, BOW TO MANGOG!!!
WHO SHOULD I BOW TO, COSMIC BABY?
SLEDPOOL BELCHES A POWERFUL BEAM!
THE MOON IS DESTROYED! WE DON'T NEED MOONS, RIGHT? I GUESS WE'LL NEVER GET THE CHANCE TO PRETEND TO LAND THERE SOMEDAY...

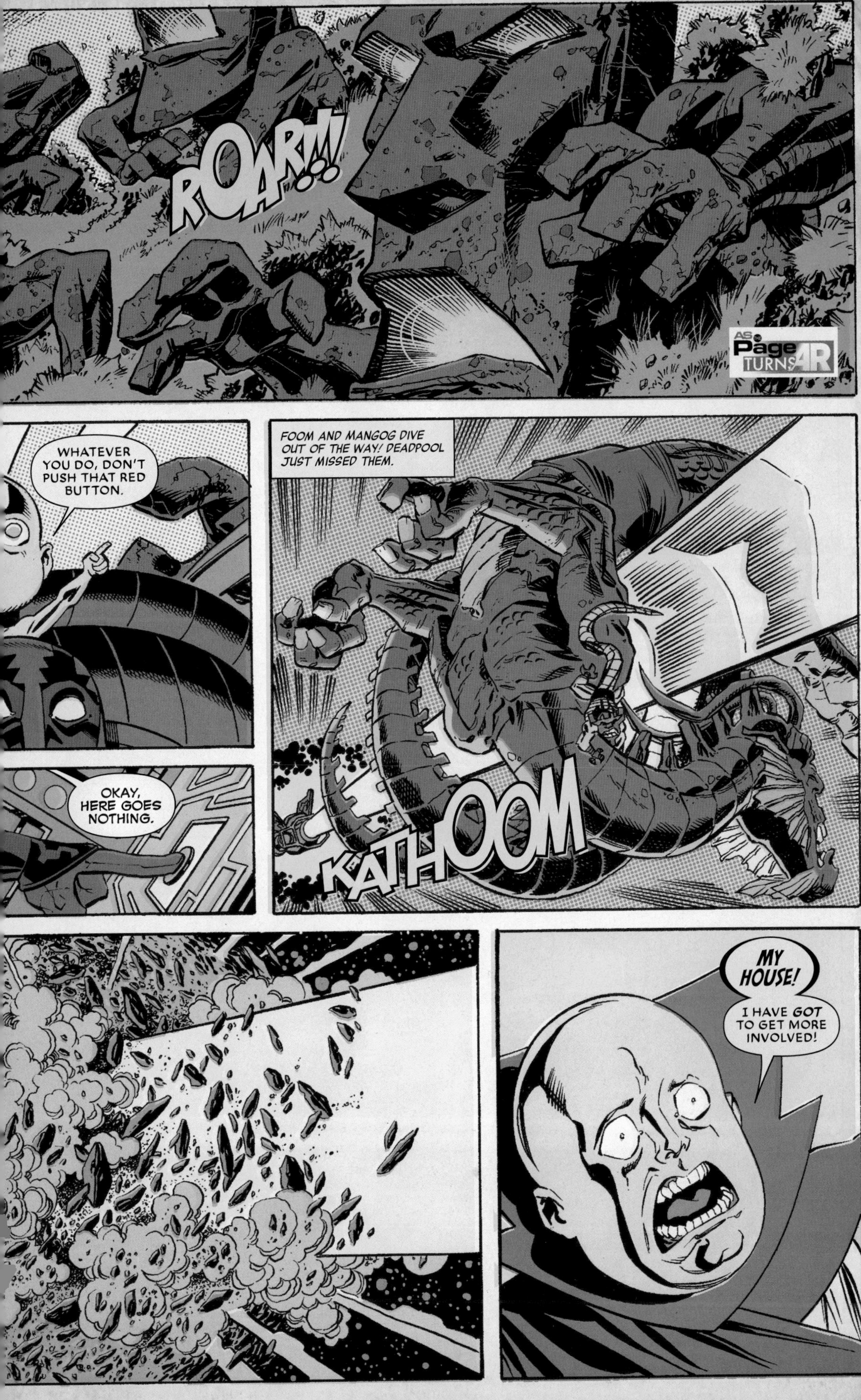
ROAR!!!
WHATEVER YOU DO, DON'T PUSH THAT RED BUTTON.
FOOM AND MANGOG DIVE OUT OF THE WAY! DEADPOOL JUST MISSED THEM.
OKAY, HERE GOES NOTHING.
KATHOOM
MY HOUSE!
I HAVE GOT TO GET MORE INVOLVED!

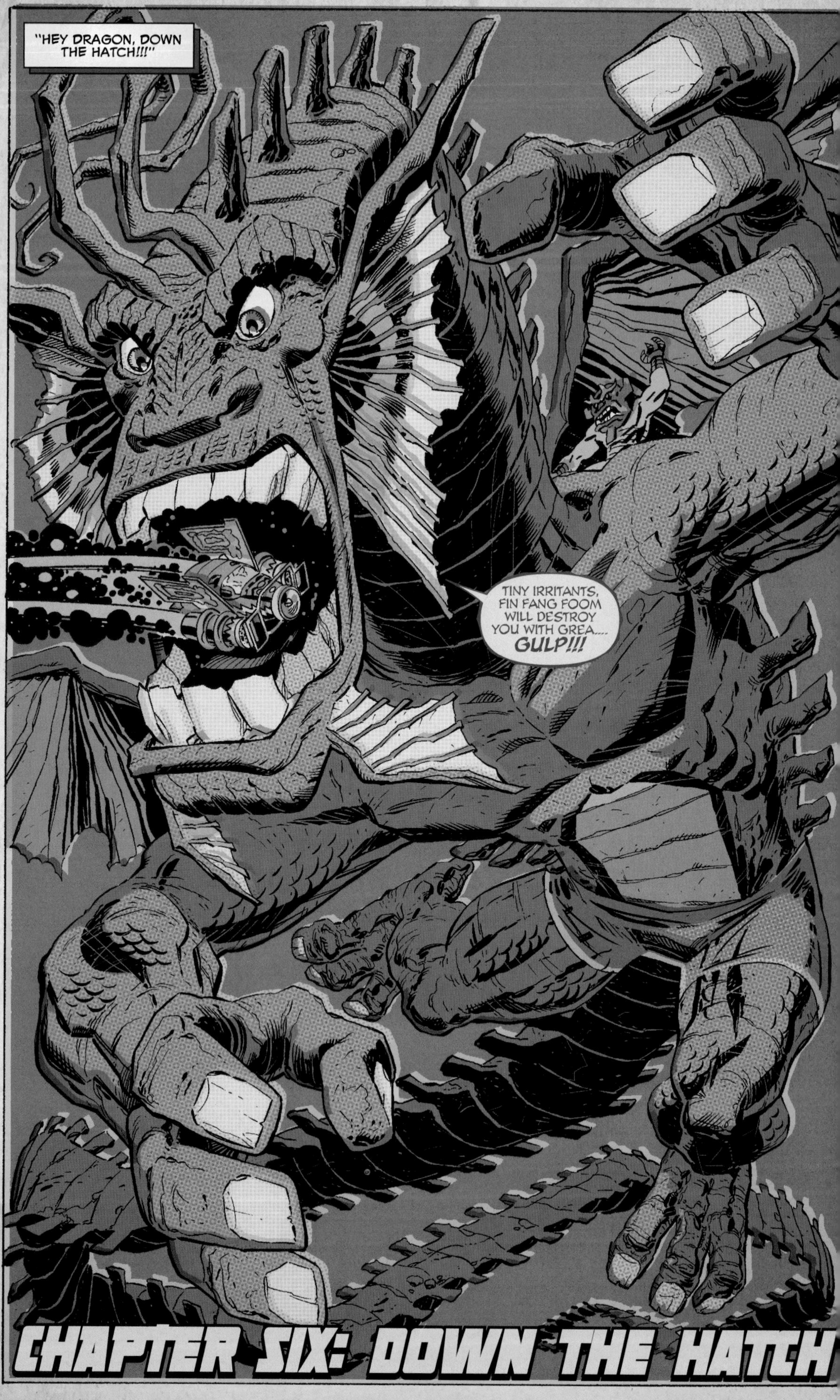
"HEY DRAGON, DOWN THE HATCH!!!"
TINY IRRITANTS, FIN FANG FOOM WILL DESTROY YOU WITH GREA.... GULP!!!
CHAPTER SIX: DOWN THE HATCH

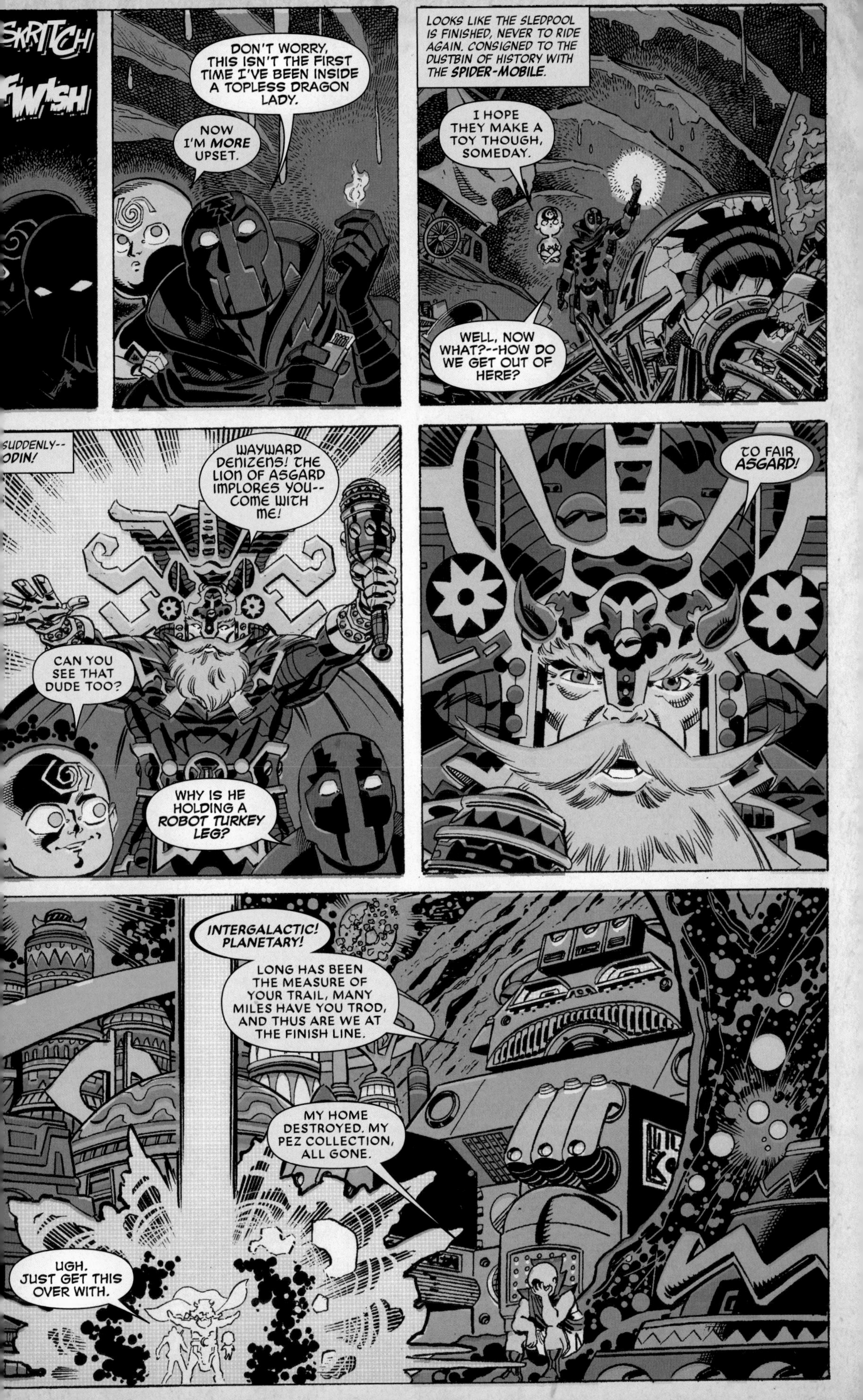
SKRITCH
FWISH
DON'T WORRY, THIS ISN'T THE FIRST TIME I'VE BEEN INSIDE A TOPLESS DRAGON LADY.
NOW I'M MORE UPSET.
LOOKS LIKE THE SLEDPOOL IS FINISHED, NEVER TO RIDE AGAIN. CONSIGNED TO THE DUSTBIN OF HISTORY WITH THE SPIDER-MOBILE.
I HOPE THEY MAKE A TOY THOUGH, SOMEDAY.
WELL, NOW WHAT?--HOW DO WE GET OUT OF HERE?
SUDDENLY-- ODIN!
WAYWARD DENIZENS! THE LION OF ASGARD IMPLORES YOU-- COME WITH ME!
CAN YOU SEE THAT DUDE TOO?
WHY IS HE HOLDING A ROBOT TURKEY LEG?
TO FAIR ASGARD!
INTERGALACTIC! PLANETARY!
LONG HAS BEEN THE MEASURE OF YOUR TRAIL, MANY MILES HAVE YOU TROD, AND THUS ARE WE AT THE FINISH LINE.
MY HOME DESTROYED. MY PEZ COLLECTION, ALL GONE.
UGH. JUST GET THIS OVER WITH.

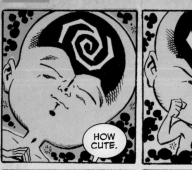

HOW CUTE.

WAIT...

THAT'S A HAPPY BABY. SOMEBODY'S GOTTA DO THE DIRTY WORK, ODIN WILL HANDLE IT.

IS...

HE...???

YUCK.

EVERYONE POOPS.

I KNOW. IT'S MY FAVORITE BOOK. I JUST NEVER SAW A COSMIC BABY DO IT BEFORE. AND LOOK AT IT, IT'S HULK-SIZED.

UNCOUTH AS IT MAY BE TO YOU, BUT THIS WILL POWER ASGARD FOR THE NEXT 1,000 YEARS.

I MET A HIPPIE ONCE, HE HAD A VW BUS THAT RAN ON FERTILIZER.

SO IT IS DONE!

DO YOU CLEAN THE COSMIC TOILET OR DO YOU HAVE A HOUSEKEEPER?

WHISPER WHISPER UNIVERSES WHISPER UNKNOWN WHISPER WHISPER SAVIOR WHISPER WHISPER.

WHISPER WHISPER JIM BELUSHI WHISPER WHISPER.

WHISPER OOOPS WHISPER MINOR PROBLEM WHISPER EXPLAIN LATER WHISPER...

BYE EVERYONE.

SAFE TRAVELS, MY FRIENDS AND I WISH YOU THE SPEED OF THE GODS.

WHAT WERE THOR'S DEUCES LIKE? BIG, RIGHT? COULD ONLY THOR LIFT THEM?

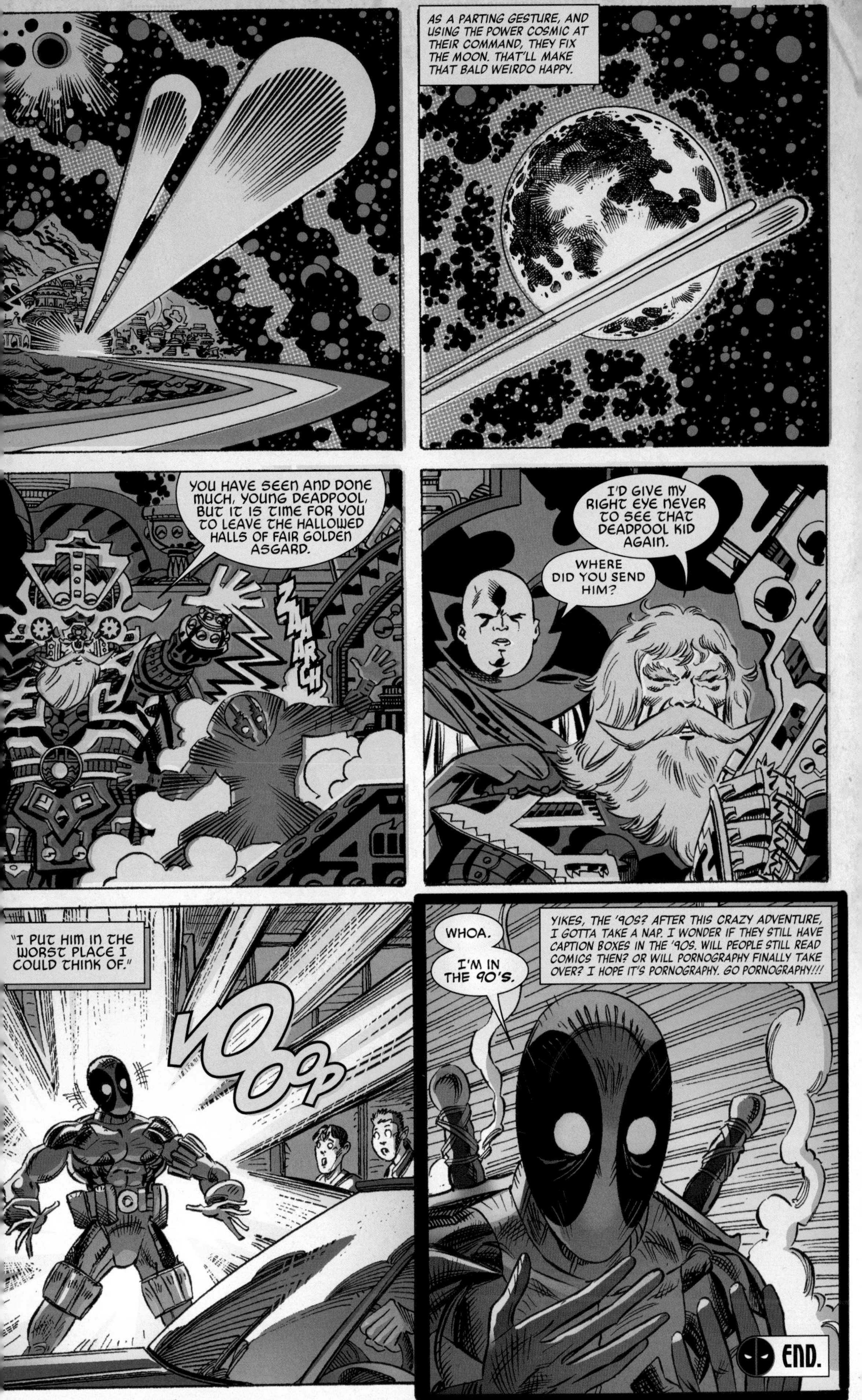
AS A PARTING GESTURE, AND USING THE POWER COSMIC AT THEIR COMMAND, THEY FIX THE MOON. THAT'LL MAKE THAT BALD WEIRDO HAPPY.
YOU HAVE SEEN AND DONE MUCH, YOUNG DEADPOOL, BUT IT IS TIME FOR YOU TO LEAVE THE HALLOWED HALLS OF FAIR GOLDEN ASGARD.
ZAARCH
I'D GIVE MY RIGHT EYE NEVER TO SEE THAT DEADPOOL KID AGAIN.
WHERE DID YOU SEND HIM?
"I PUT HIM IN THE WORST PLACE I COULD THINK OF."
VOOOP
WHOA.
I'M IN THE 90'S.
YIKES, THE '90S? AFTER THIS CRAZY ADVENTURE, I GOTTA TAKE A NAP. I WONDER IF THEY STILL HAVE CAPTION BOXES IN THE '90S. WILL PEOPLE STILL READ COMICS THEN? OR WILL PORNOGRAPHY FINALLY TAKE OVER? I HOPE IT'S PORNOGRAPHY. GO PORNOGRAPHY!!!
END.

DEADPOOL

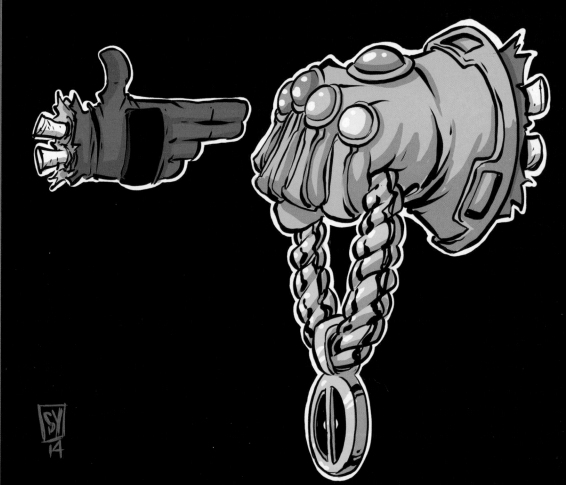

#45 VARIANT
BY SKOTTIE YOUNG

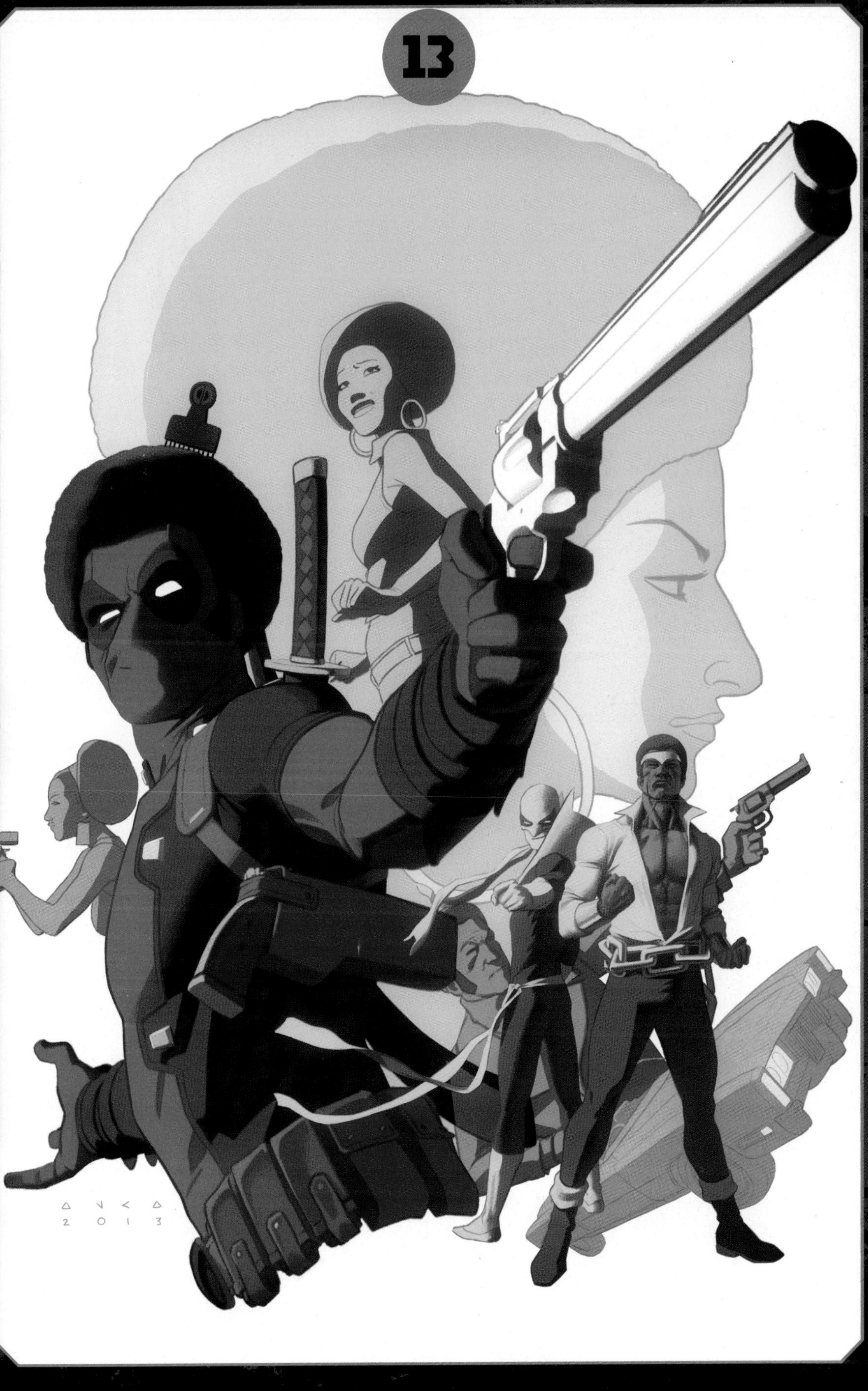
13

DEADPOOL, POWER MAN AND IRON FIST

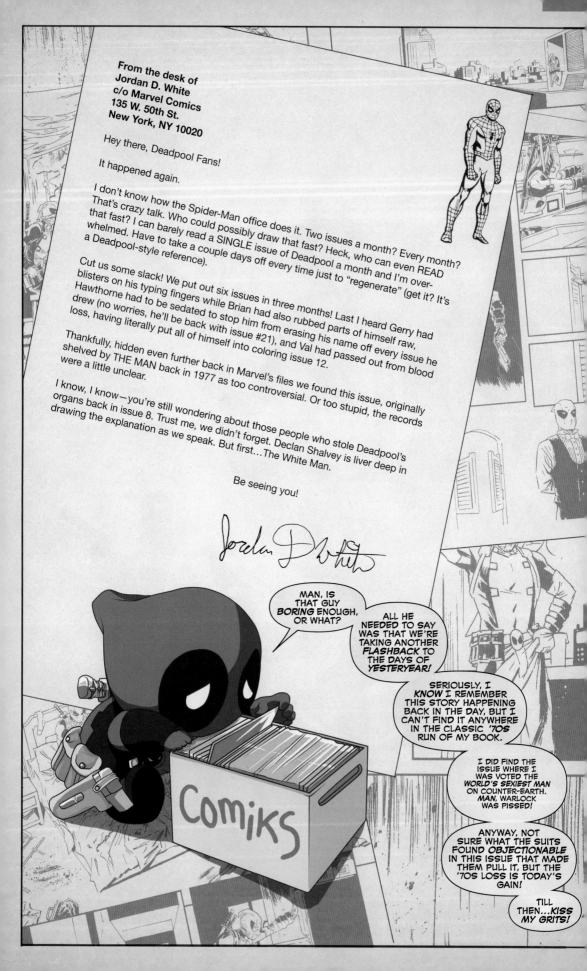

From the desk of
Jordan D. White
c/o Marvel Comics
135 W. 50th St.
New York, NY 10020

Hey there, Deadpool Fans!

It happened again.

I don't know how the Spider-Man office does it. Two issues a month? Every month? That's crazy talk. Who could possibly draw that fast? Heck, who can even READ that fast? I can barely read a SINGLE issue of Deadpool a month and I'm over-whelmed. Have to take a couple days off every time just to "regenerate" (get it? It's a Deadpool-style reference).

Cut us some slack! We put out six issues in three months! Last I heard Gerry had blisters on his typing fingers while Brian had also rubbed parts of himself raw, Hawthorne had to be sedated to stop him from erasing his name off every issue he drew (no worries, he'll be back with issue #21), and Val had passed out from blood loss, having literally put all of himself into coloring issue 12.

Thankfully, hidden even further back in Marvel's files we found this issue, originally shelved by THE MAN back in 1977 as too controversial. Or too stupid, the records were a little unclear.

I know, I know—you're still wondering about those people who stole Deadpool's organs back in issue 8. Trust me, we didn't forget. Declan Shalvey is liver deep in drawing the explanation as we speak. But first…The White Man.

Be seeing you!

Jordan D. White

MAN, IS THAT GUY *BORING* ENOUGH, OR WHAT?

ALL HE NEEDED TO SAY WAS THAT WE'RE TAKING ANOTHER *FLASHBACK* TO THE DAYS OF *YESTERYEAR!*

SERIOUSLY, I *KNOW* I REMEMBER THIS STORY HAPPENING BACK IN THE DAY, BUT I CAN'T FIND IT ANYWHERE IN THE CLASSIC *'70S* RUN OF MY BOOK.

I DID FIND THE ISSUE WHERE I WAS VOTED THE *WORLD'S SEXIEST MAN* ON COUNTER-EARTH. MAN, WARLOCK WAS PISSED!

ANYWAY, NOT SURE WHAT THE SUITS FOUND *OBJECTIONABLE* IN THIS ISSUE THAT MADE THEM PULL IT, BUT THE '70S LOSS IS TODAY'S GAIN!

TILL THEN…*KISS MY GRITS!*

COMIKS

UKE CAGE: a child of the streets…DANIEL RAND: a son of the mystic city of K'un-Lun…WADE WILSON: government experiment gone wrong… Three men from different worlds—all reborn with **strength** and **power beyond belief!** And together, no one can stop them!

DEADPOOL, POWER MAN AND IRON FIST

GERRY DUGGAN
BRIAN POSEHN
WRITERS

SCOTT KOBLISH
ARTIST

VAL STAPLES
COLORIST

VC'S JOE SABINO
LETTERER

JORDAN D. WHITE
EDITOR

AXEL ALONSO
EDITOR IN CHIEF

JOE QUESADA
CHIEF CREATIVE OFFICER

DAN BUCKLEY
PUBLISHER

ALAN FINE
EXEC. PRODUCER

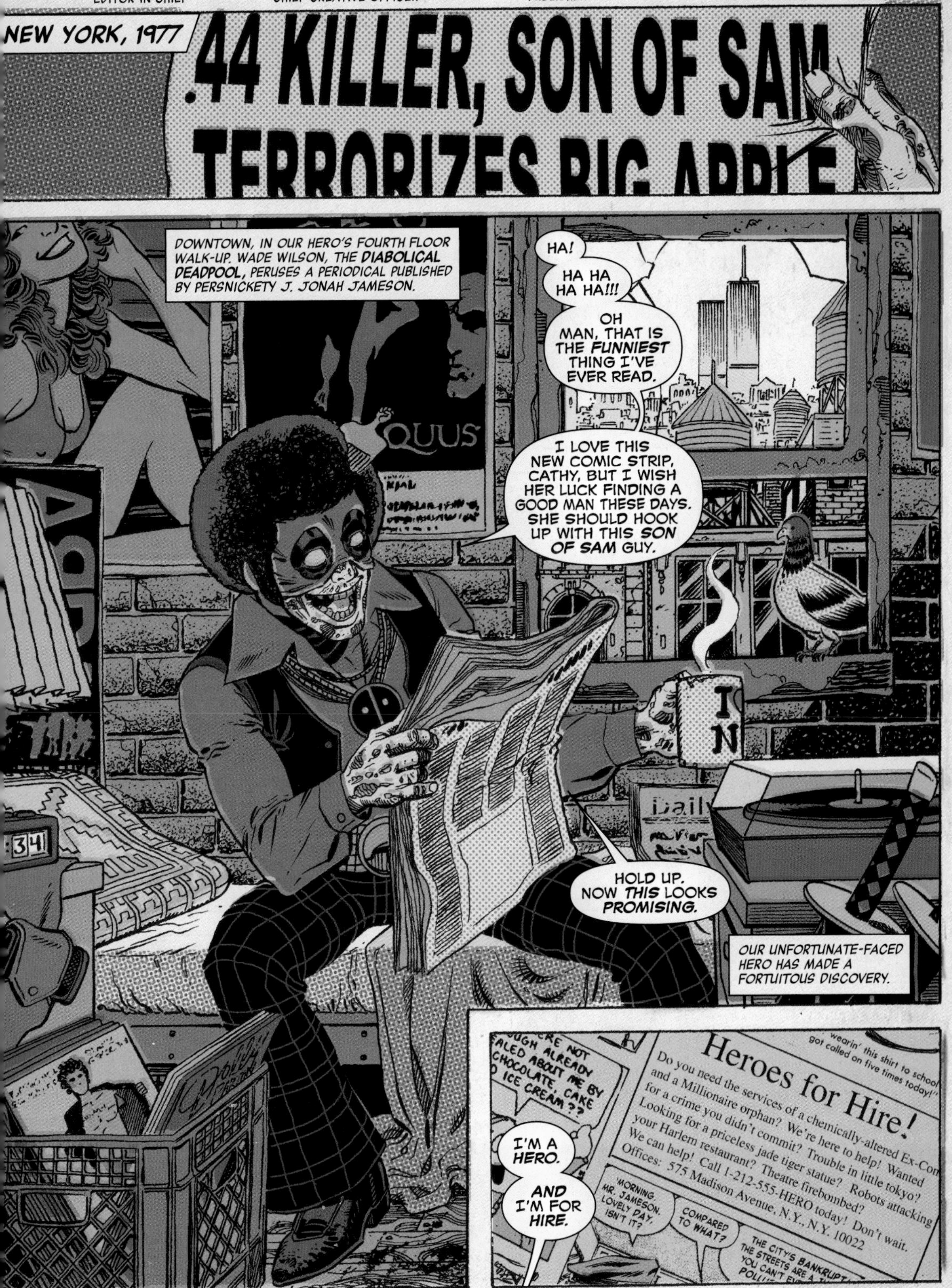

NEW YORK, 1977
.44 KILLER, SON OF SAM
TERRORIZES BIG APPLE
DOWNTOWN, IN OUR HERO'S FOURTH FLOOR WALK-UP. WADE WILSON, THE DIABOLICAL DEADPOOL, PERUSES A PERIODICAL PUBLISHED BY PERSNICKETY J. JONAH JAMESON.
HA!
HA HA HA HA!!!
OH MAN, THAT IS THE FUNNIEST THING I'VE EVER READ.
I LOVE THIS NEW COMIC STRIP, CATHY, BUT I WISH HER LUCK FINDING A GOOD MAN THESE DAYS. SHE SHOULD HOOK UP WITH THIS SON OF SAM GUY.
QUUS
HOLD UP. NOW THIS LOOKS PROMISING.
OUR UNFORTUNATE-FACED HERO HAS MADE A FORTUITOUS DISCOVERY.
Heroes for Hire!
Do you need the services of a chemically-altered Ex-Con and a Millionaire orphan? We're here to help! Wanted for a crime you didn't commit? Trouble in little tokyo? Looking for a priceless jade tiger statue? Robots attacking your Harlem restaurant? Theatre firebombed? We can help! Call 1-212-555-HERO today! Don't wait. Offices: 575 Madison Avenue, N.Y., N.Y. 10022
wearin' this shirt to school got called on five times today!"
I'M A HERO.
AND I'M FOR HIRE.
'MORNING, MR. JAMESON. LOVELY DAY, ISN'T IT?
COMPARED TO WHAT?

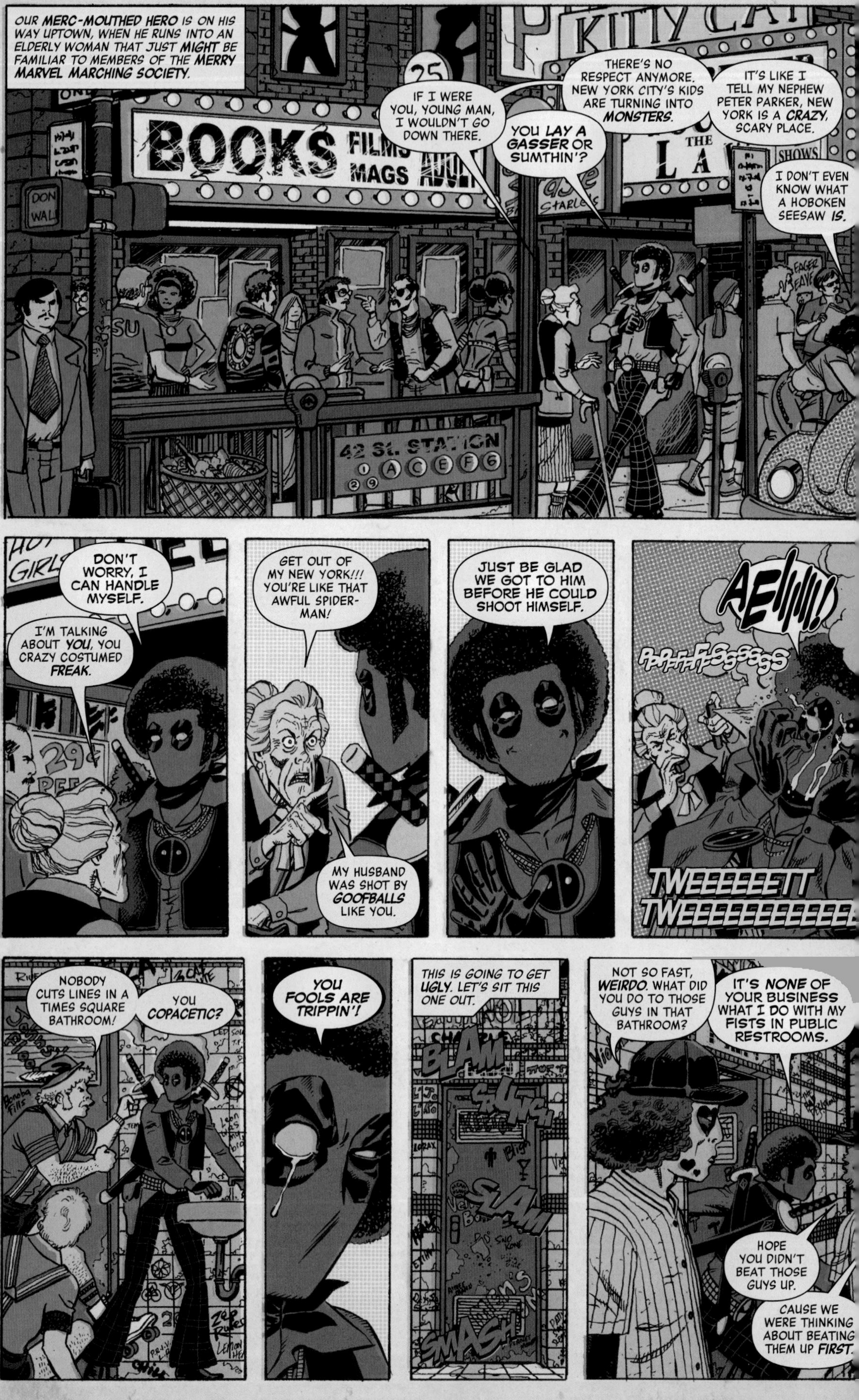
OUR MERC-MOUTHED HERO IS ON HIS WAY UPTOWN, WHEN HE RUNS INTO AN ELDERLY WOMAN THAT JUST MIGHT BE FAMILIAR TO MEMBERS OF THE MERRY MARVEL MARCHING SOCIETY.
KITTY CAT
BOOKS FILMS MAGS ADULT
IF I WERE YOU, YOUNG MAN, I WOULDN'T GO DOWN THERE.
YOU LAY A GASSER OR SUMTHIN'?
THERE'S NO RESPECT ANYMORE. NEW YORK CITY'S KIDS ARE TURNING INTO MONSTERS.
IT'S LIKE I TELL MY NEPHEW PETER PARKER, NEW YORK IS A CRAZY, SCARY PLACE.
I DON'T EVEN KNOW WHAT A HOBOKEN SEESAW IS.
42 St. STATION
DON'T WORRY, I CAN HANDLE MYSELF.
I'M TALKING ABOUT YOU, YOU CRAZY COSTUMED FREAK.
GET OUT OF MY NEW YORK!!! YOU'RE LIKE THAT AWFUL SPIDER-MAN!
MY HUSBAND WAS SHOT BY GOOFBALLS LIKE YOU.
JUST BE GLAD WE GOT TO HIM BEFORE HE COULD SHOOT HIMSELF.
AEIIIII!
PPPFFFTSSSSSS
TWEEEEEEETT TWEEEEEEEEEEEE
NOBODY CUTS LINES IN A TIMES SQUARE BATHROOM!
YOU COPACETIC?
YOU FOOLS ARE TRIPPIN'!
THIS IS GOING TO GET UGLY. LET'S SIT THIS ONE OUT.
BLAM
SLUNCH
SLAM
SMASH
NOT SO FAST, WEIRDO. WHAT DID YOU DO TO THOSE GUYS IN THAT BATHROOM?
IT'S NONE OF YOUR BUSINESS WHAT I DO WITH MY FISTS IN PUBLIC RESTROOMS.
HOPE YOU DIDN'T BEAT THOSE GUYS UP.
CAUSE WE WERE THINKING ABOUT BEATING THEM UP FIRST.

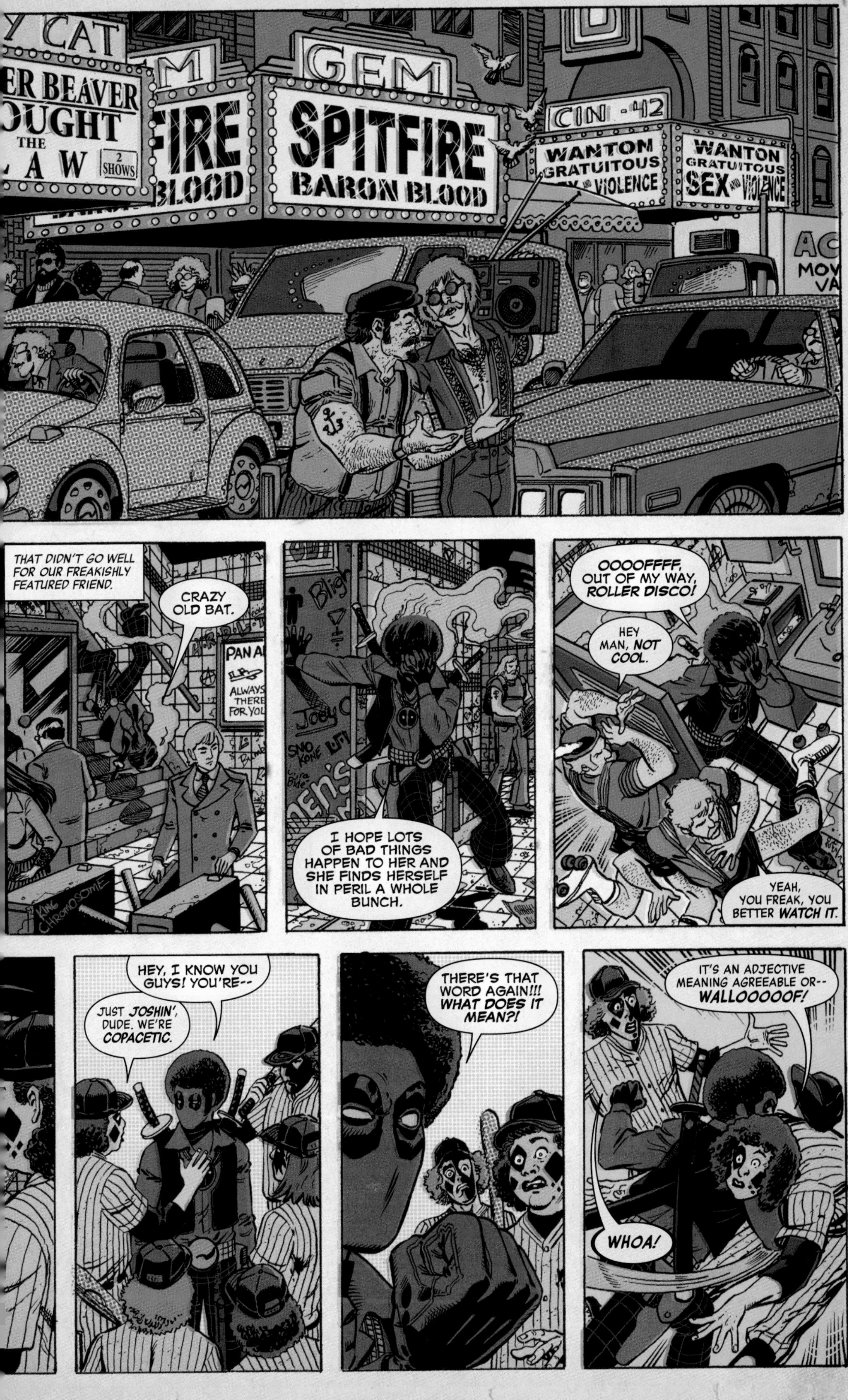
GEM
SPITFIRE
BARON BLOOD
CIN -42
WANTON GRATUITOUS
WANTON GRATUITOUS SEX AND VIOLENCE
PAN AM
ALWAYS THERE FOR YOU
THAT DIDN'T GO WELL FOR OUR FREAKISHLY FEATURED FRIEND.
CRAZY OLD BAT.
I HOPE LOTS OF BAD THINGS HAPPEN TO HER AND SHE FINDS HERSELF IN PERIL A WHOLE BUNCH.
OOOOFFFF, OUT OF MY WAY, ROLLER DISCO!
HEY MAN, NOT COOL.
YEAH, YOU FREAK, YOU BETTER WATCH IT.
HEY, I KNOW YOU GUYS! YOU'RE--
JUST JOSHIN', DUDE. WE'RE COPACETIC.
THERE'S THAT WORD AGAIN!!! WHAT DOES IT MEAN?!
IT'S AN ADJECTIVE MEANING AGREEABLE OR--
WALLOOOOF!
WHOA!

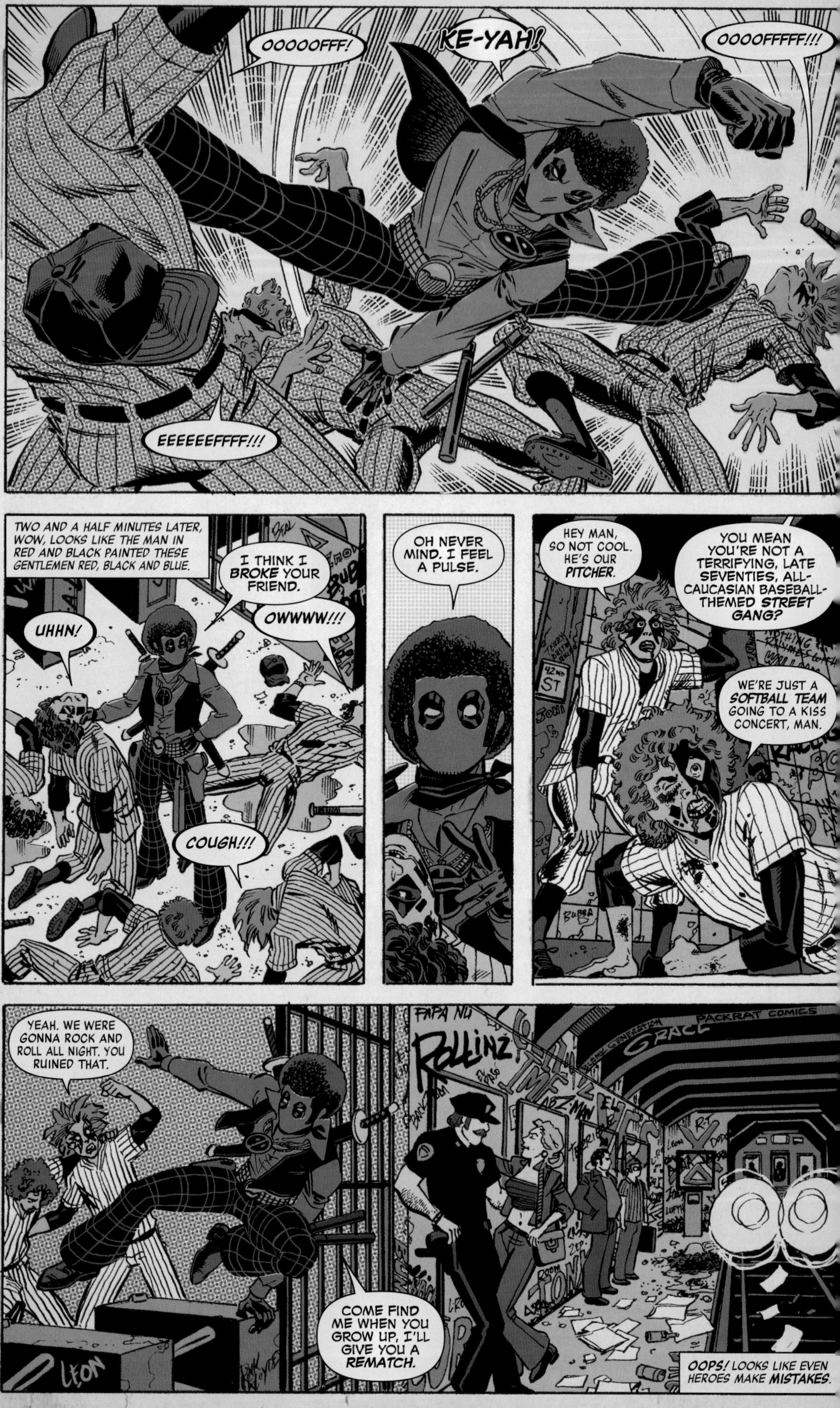
OOOOOFFF!
KE-YAH!
OOOOFFFFF!!!
EEEEEEFFFF!!!
TWO AND A HALF MINUTES LATER, WOW, LOOKS LIKE THE MAN IN RED AND BLACK PAINTED THESE GENTLEMEN RED, BLACK AND BLUE.
I THINK I BROKE YOUR FRIEND.
OWWWW!!!
UHHN!
COUGH!!!
OH NEVER MIND. I FEEL A PULSE.
HEY MAN, SO NOT COOL. HE'S OUR PITCHER.
YOU MEAN YOU'RE NOT A TERRIFYING, LATE SEVENTIES, ALL-CAUCASIAN BASEBALL-THEMED STREET GANG?
WE'RE JUST A SOFTBALL TEAM GOING TO A KISS CONCERT, MAN.
42ND ST
YEAH. WE WERE GONNA ROCK AND ROLL ALL NIGHT. YOU RUINED THAT.
PACKRAT COMICS
ROLLINZ
COME FIND ME WHEN YOU GROW UP, I'LL GIVE YOU A REMATCH.
OOPS! LOOKS LIKE EVEN HEROES MAKE MISTAKES.
LEON

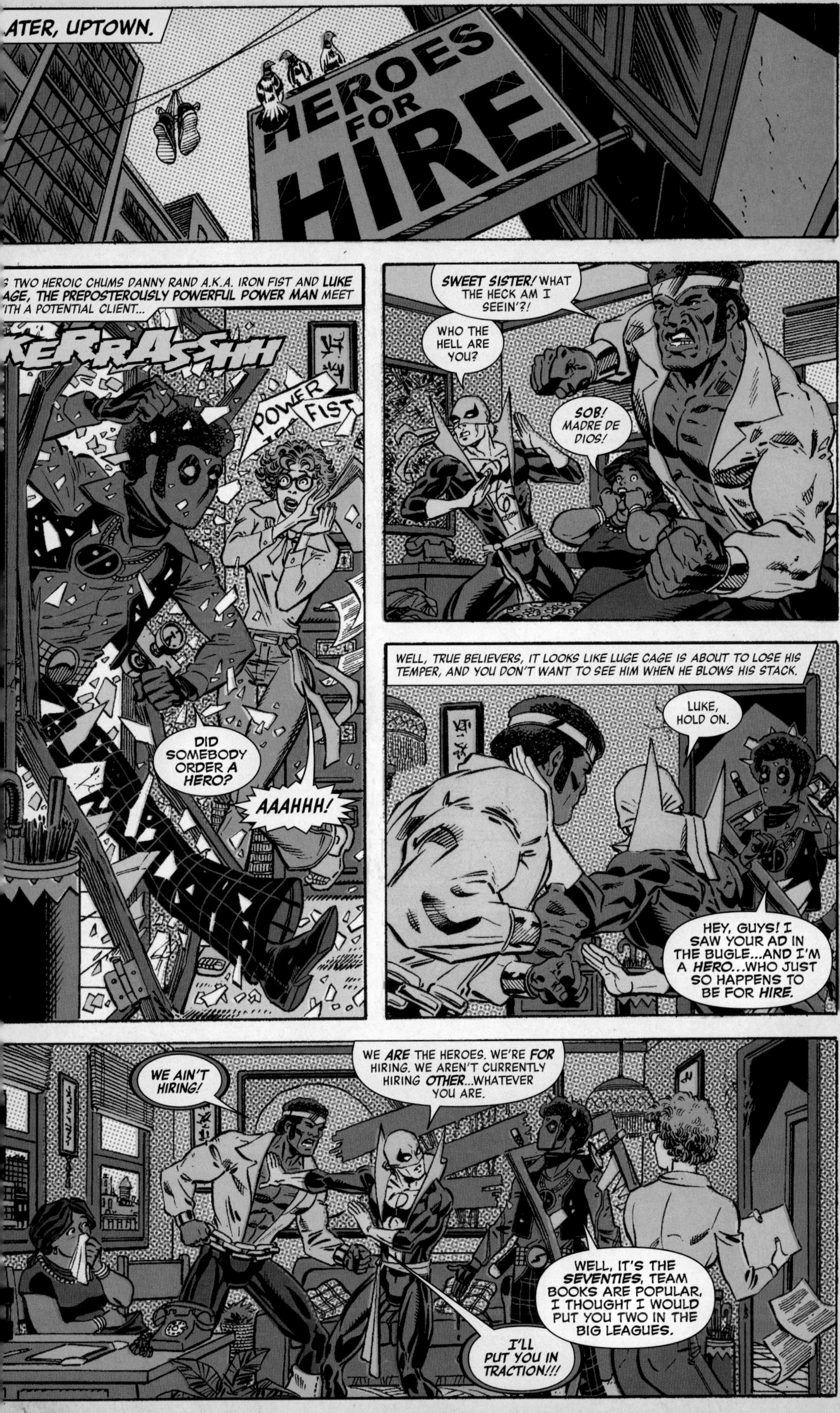

ATER, UPTOWN.
HEROES FOR HIRE
S TWO HEROIC CHUMS DANNY RAND A.K.A. IRON FIST AND LUKE AGE, THE PREPOSTEROUSLY POWERFUL POWER MAN MEET ITH A POTENTIAL CLIENT...
KERRASSHH
POWER FIST
DID SOMEBODY ORDER A HERO?
AAAHHH!
SWEET SISTER! WHAT THE HECK AM I SEEIN'?!
WHO THE HELL ARE YOU?
SOB! MADRE DE DIOS!
WELL, TRUE BELIEVERS, IT LOOKS LIKE LUGE CAGE IS ABOUT TO LOSE HIS TEMPER, AND YOU DON'T WANT TO SEE HIM WHEN HE BLOWS HIS STACK.
LUKE, HOLD ON.
HEY, GUYS! I SAW YOUR AD IN THE BUGLE...AND I'M A HERO...WHO JUST SO HAPPENS TO BE FOR HIRE.
WE AIN'T HIRING!
WE ARE THE HEROES. WE'RE FOR HIRING. WE AREN'T CURRENTLY HIRING OTHER...WHATEVER YOU ARE.
WELL, IT'S THE SEVENTIES, TEAM BOOKS ARE POPULAR, I THOUGHT I WOULD PUT YOU TWO IN THE BIG LEAGUES.
I'LL PUT YOU IN TRACTION!!!

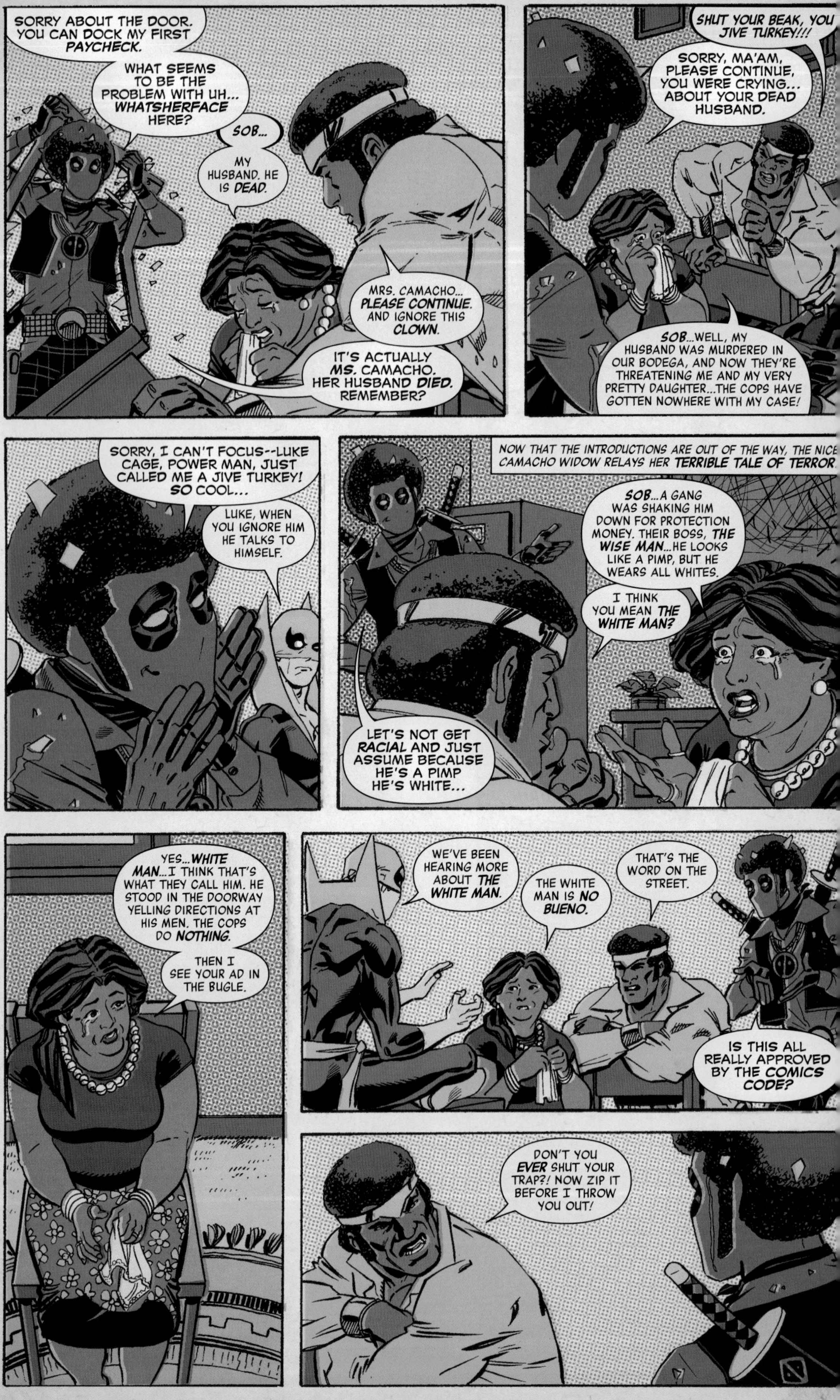

SORRY ABOUT THE DOOR. YOU CAN DOCK MY FIRST PAYCHECK.
WHAT SEEMS TO BE THE PROBLEM WITH UH... WHATSHERFACE HERE?
SOB...
MY HUSBAND. HE IS DEAD.
MRS. CAMACHO... PLEASE CONTINUE. AND IGNORE THIS CLOWN.
IT'S ACTUALLY MS. CAMACHO. HER HUSBAND DIED. REMEMBER?
SHUT YOUR BEAK, YOU JIVE TURKEY!!!
SORRY, MA'AM, PLEASE CONTINUE, YOU WERE CRYING... ABOUT YOUR DEAD HUSBAND.
SOB...WELL, MY HUSBAND WAS MURDERED IN OUR BODEGA, AND NOW THEY'RE THREATENING ME AND MY VERY PRETTY DAUGHTER...THE COPS HAVE GOTTEN NOWHERE WITH MY CASE!
SORRY, I CAN'T FOCUS--LUKE CAGE, POWER MAN, JUST CALLED ME A JIVE TURKEY! SO COOL...
LUKE, WHEN YOU IGNORE HIM HE TALKS TO HIMSELF.
NOW THAT THE INTRODUCTIONS ARE OUT OF THE WAY, THE NICE CAMACHO WIDOW RELAYS HER TERRIBLE TALE OF TERROR.
SOB...A GANG WAS SHAKING HIM DOWN FOR PROTECTION MONEY. THEIR BOSS, THE WISE MAN...HE LOOKS LIKE A PIMP, BUT HE WEARS ALL WHITES.
I THINK YOU MEAN THE WHITE MAN?
LET'S NOT GET RACIAL AND JUST ASSUME BECAUSE HE'S A PIMP HE'S WHITE...
YES...WHITE MAN...I THINK THAT'S WHAT THEY CALL HIM. HE STOOD IN THE DOORWAY YELLING DIRECTIONS AT HIS MEN. THE COPS DO NOTHING.
THEN I SEE YOUR AD IN THE BUGLE.
WE'VE BEEN HEARING MORE ABOUT THE WHITE MAN.
THE WHITE MAN IS NO BUENO.
THAT'S THE WORD ON THE STREET.
IS THIS ALL REALLY APPROVED BY THE COMICS CODE?
DON'T YOU EVER SHUT YOUR TRAP?! NOW ZIP IT BEFORE I THROW YOU OUT!

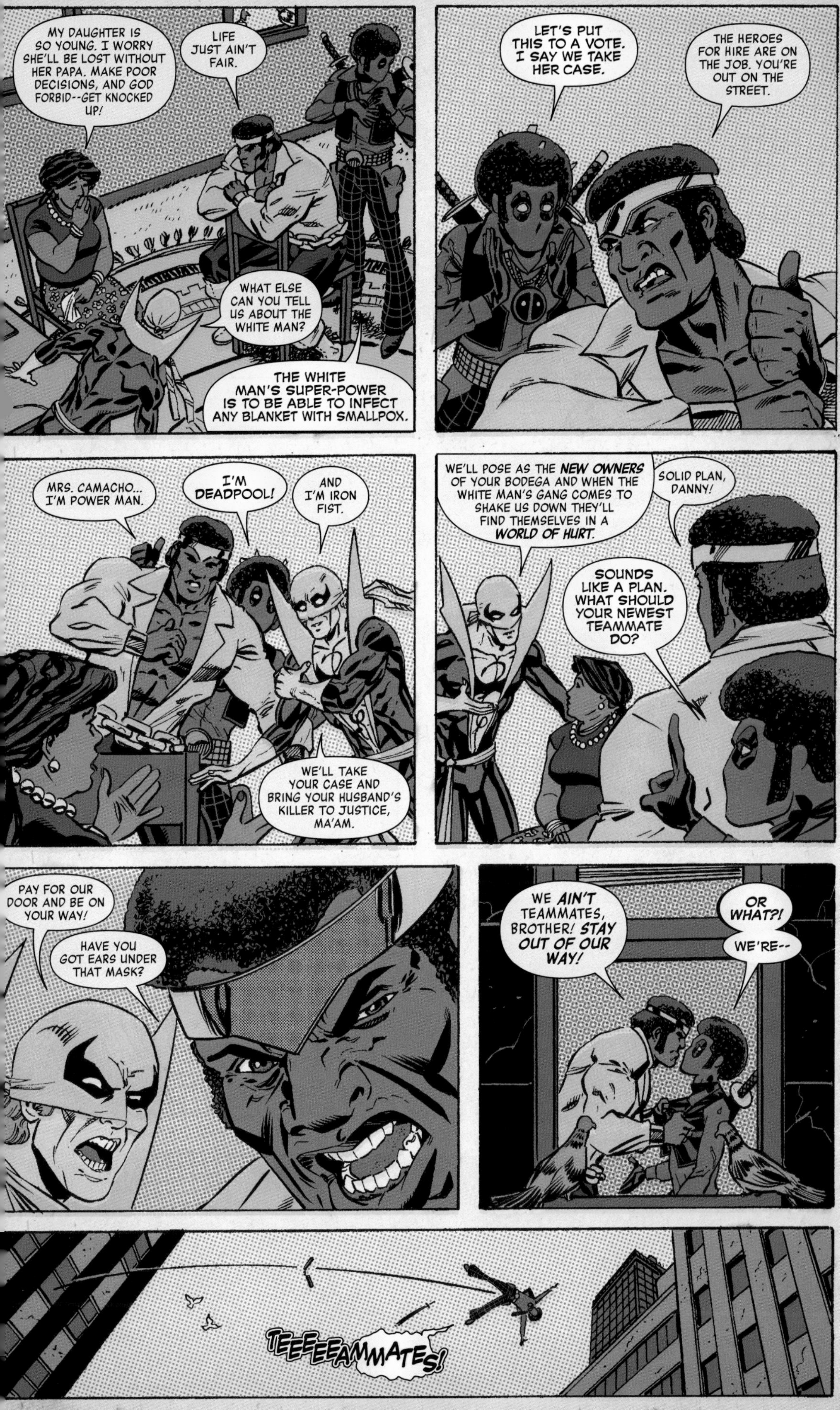
MY DAUGHTER IS SO YOUNG. I WORRY SHE'LL BE LOST WITHOUT HER PAPA. MAKE POOR DECISIONS, AND GOD FORBID--GET KNOCKED UP!
LIFE JUST AIN'T FAIR.
WHAT ELSE CAN YOU TELL US ABOUT THE WHITE MAN?
THE WHITE MAN'S SUPER-POWER IS TO BE ABLE TO INFECT ANY BLANKET WITH SMALLPOX.
LET'S PUT THIS TO A VOTE. I SAY WE TAKE HER CASE.
THE HEROES FOR HIRE ARE ON THE JOB. YOU'RE OUT ON THE STREET.
MRS. CAMACHO... I'M POWER MAN.
I'M DEADPOOL!
AND I'M IRON FIST.
WE'LL TAKE YOUR CASE AND BRING YOUR HUSBAND'S KILLER TO JUSTICE, MA'AM.
WE'LL POSE AS THE NEW OWNERS OF YOUR BODEGA AND WHEN THE WHITE MAN'S GANG COMES TO SHAKE US DOWN THEY'LL FIND THEMSELVES IN A WORLD OF HURT.
SOLID PLAN, DANNY!
SOUNDS LIKE A PLAN. WHAT SHOULD YOUR NEWEST TEAMMATE DO?
PAY FOR OUR DOOR AND BE ON YOUR WAY!
HAVE YOU GOT EARS UNDER THAT MASK?
WE AIN'T TEAMMATES, BROTHER! STAY OUT OF OUR WAY!
OR WHAT?!
WE'RE--
TEEEEEAMMATES!

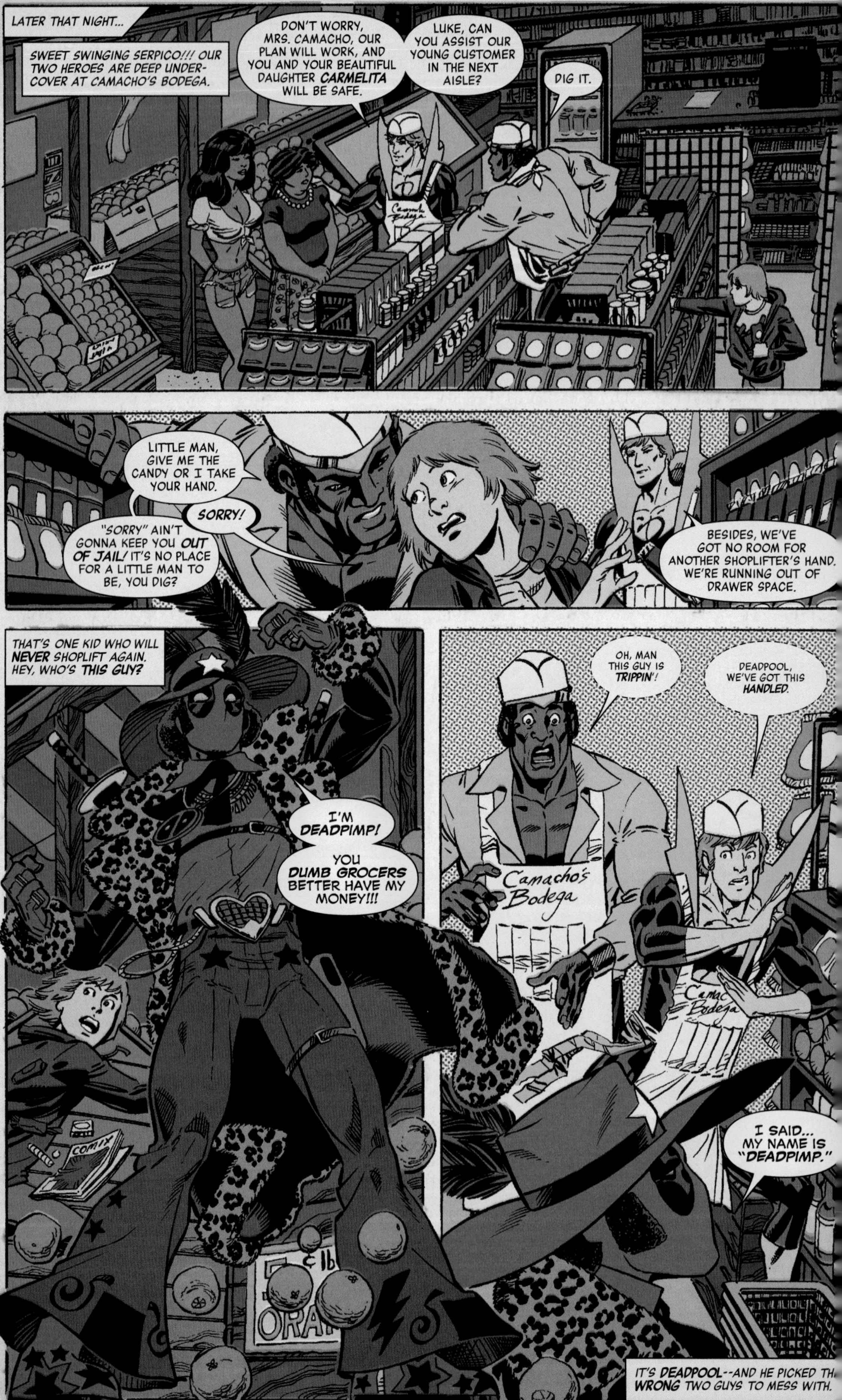
LATER THAT NIGHT...
SWEET SWINGING SERPICO!!! OUR TWO HEROES ARE DEEP UNDER-COVER AT CAMACHO'S BODEGA.
DON'T WORRY, MRS. CAMACHO, OUR PLAN WILL WORK, AND YOU AND YOUR BEAUTIFUL DAUGHTER CARMELITA WILL BE SAFE.
LUKE, CAN YOU ASSIST OUR YOUNG CUSTOMER IN THE NEXT AISLE?
DIG IT.
LITTLE MAN, GIVE ME THE CANDY OR I TAKE YOUR HAND.
SORRY!
"SORRY" AIN'T GONNA KEEP YOU OUT OF JAIL! IT'S NO PLACE FOR A LITTLE MAN TO BE, YOU DIG?
BESIDES, WE'VE GOT NO ROOM FOR ANOTHER SHOPLIFTER'S HAND. WE'RE RUNNING OUT OF DRAWER SPACE.
THAT'S ONE KID WHO WILL NEVER SHOPLIFT AGAIN. HEY, WHO'S THIS GUY?
I'M DEADPIMP!
YOU DUMB GROCERS BETTER HAVE MY MONEY!!!
OH, MAN THIS GUY IS TRIPPIN'!
DEADPOOL, WE'VE GOT THIS HANDLED.
Camacho's Bodega
COMIX
I SAID... MY NAME IS "DEADPIMP."
IT'S DEADPOOL--AND HE PICKED TH WRONG TWO GUYS TO MESS WITH.

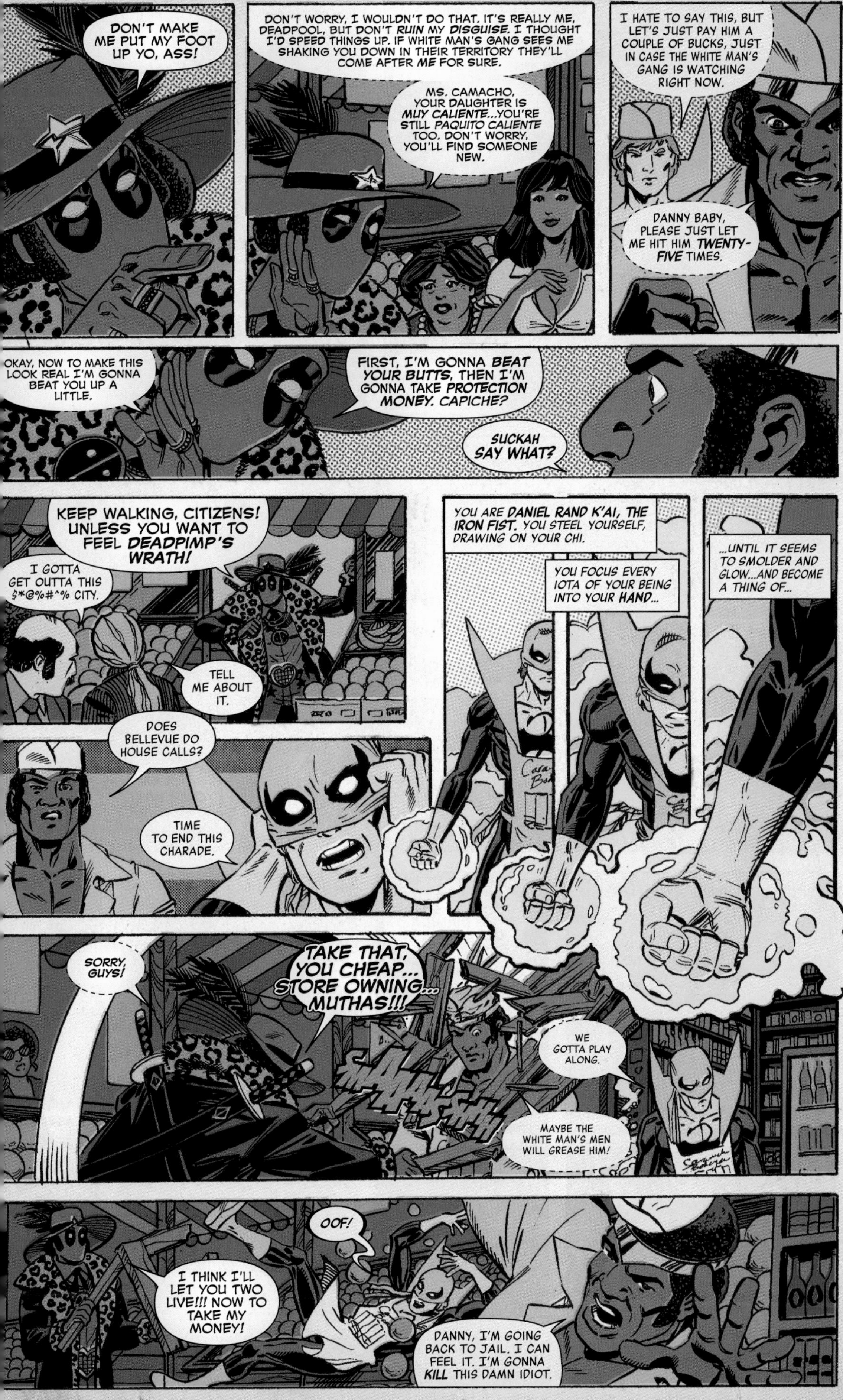
DON'T MAKE ME PUT MY FOOT UP YO, ASS!
DON'T WORRY, I WOULDN'T DO THAT. IT'S REALLY ME, DEADPOOL, BUT DON'T RUIN MY DISGUISE. I THOUGHT I'D SPEED THINGS UP. IF WHITE MAN'S GANG SEES ME SHAKING YOU DOWN IN THEIR TERRITORY THEY'LL COME AFTER ME FOR SURE.
MS. CAMACHO, YOUR DAUGHTER IS MUY CALIENTE...YOU'RE STILL PAQUITO CALIENTE TOO. DON'T WORRY, YOU'LL FIND SOMEONE NEW.
I HATE TO SAY THIS, BUT LET'S JUST PAY HIM A COUPLE OF BUCKS, JUST IN CASE THE WHITE MAN'S GANG IS WATCHING RIGHT NOW.
DANNY BABY, PLEASE JUST LET ME HIT HIM TWENTY-FIVE TIMES.
OKAY, NOW TO MAKE THIS LOOK REAL I'M GONNA BEAT YOU UP A LITTLE.
FIRST, I'M GONNA BEAT YOUR BUTTS, THEN I'M GONNA TAKE PROTECTION MONEY. CAPICHE?
SUCKAH SAY WHAT?
KEEP WALKING, CITIZENS! UNLESS YOU WANT TO FEEL DEADPIMP'S WRATH!
I GOTTA GET OUTTA THIS $*@%#^% CITY.
TELL ME ABOUT IT.
YOU ARE DANIEL RAND K'AI, THE IRON FIST. YOU STEEL YOURSELF, DRAWING ON YOUR CHI.
YOU FOCUS EVERY IOTA OF YOUR BEING INTO YOUR HAND...
...UNTIL IT SEEMS TO SMOLDER AND GLOW...AND BECOME A THING OF...
DOES BELLEVUE DO HOUSE CALLS?
TIME TO END THIS CHARADE.
SORRY, GUYS!
TAKE THAT, YOU CHEAP... STORE OWNING... MUTHAS!!!
WE GOTTA PLAY ALONG.
MAYBE THE WHITE MAN'S MEN WILL GREASE HIM!
OOF!
I THINK I'LL LET YOU TWO LIVE!!! NOW TO TAKE MY MONEY!
DANNY, I'M GOING BACK TO JAIL. I CAN FEEL IT. I'M GONNA KILL THIS DAMN IDIOT.

I HAD AN IDEA: CAN WE JUST SAY THIS SCRATCH IS MY FIRST HEROES FOR HIRE PAYCHECK?

POOL, I'M SO DEADPOOL. AND I'D SAY YOU ARE SO RAVEN, BUT I DOUBT YOU'D GET IT.

SUCKAH, YOU ARE SO DEAD.

YOU BETTER RUN, DEADPOOL.

RUN, DEADPOOL, RUN!

OOPS, NOT FOR LONG.

HEY GUYS, DON'T MIND ME. I'M JUST EXTORTING PROTECTION MONEY FROM THE NEW OWNERS OF THE CAMACHO BODEGA.

OUR BOSS AIN'T GONNA LIKE YOU GETTING PROTECTION MONEY FROM PEOPLE HE WAS GONNA GET PROTECTION MONEY FROM.

LET'S GET HIM. FOR THE WHITE MAN!

EWWW...THAT SOUNDS RACIST. WHY DON'T YOU GET ME FOR YOURSELVES?

LET'S TEACH THIS FOOL A LESSON...

A LESSON IN VIOLENCE!

THUMP BONK CRUNCH

OOOF!!! OWWWW!!! UGGHHH!!!

HEY, WHO ARE YOU GUYS? IS IT MY BIRTHDAY? DID I MAKE IN MY PANTS?

HIT THAT MUTHA AGAIN.

NIGHTY-NIGHT!

WOMP

LOOKS LIKE IT'S LIGHTS OUT FOR DEADPOOL.

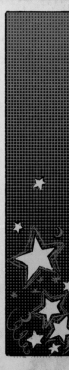

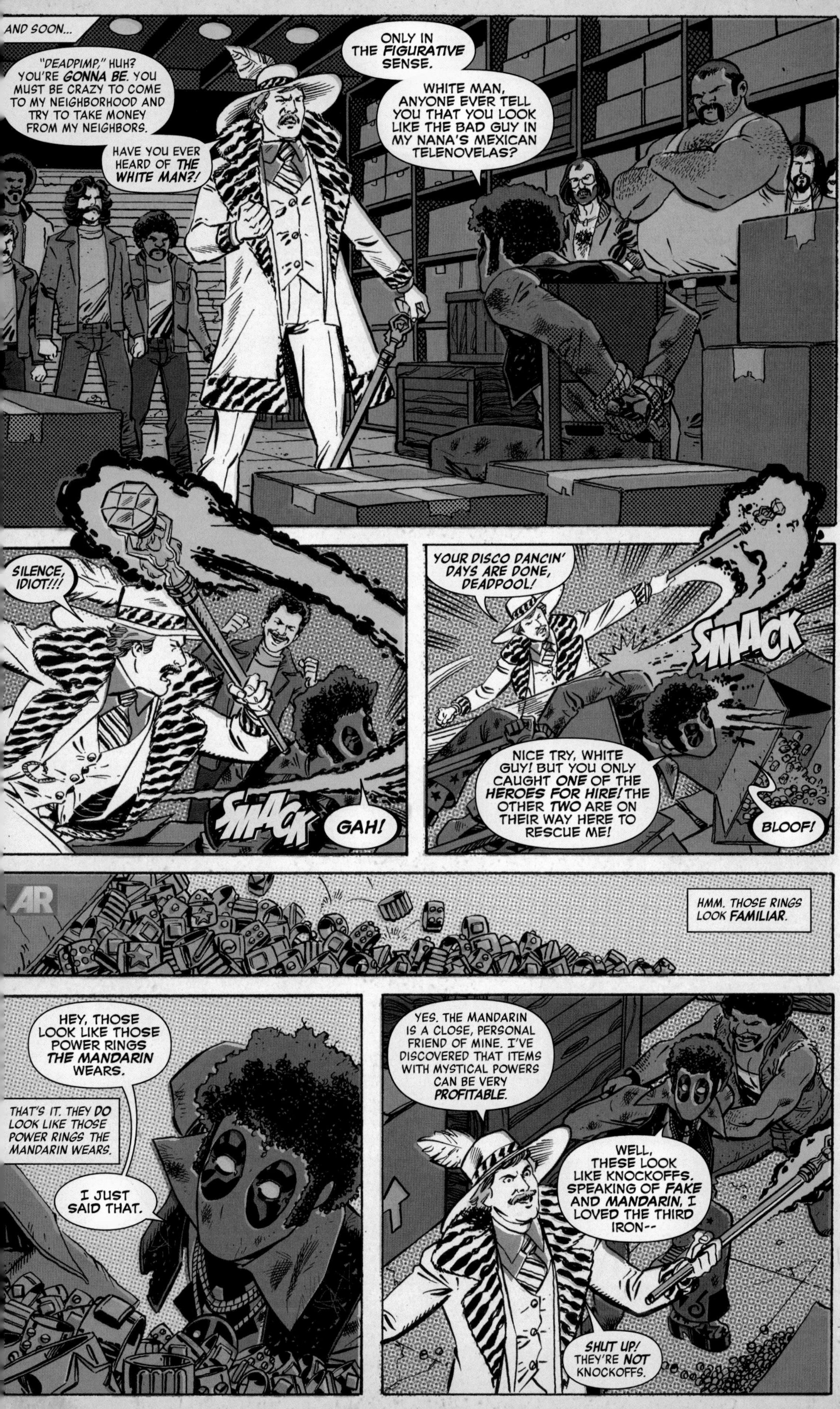
AND SOON...
"DEADPIMP," HUH? YOU'RE GONNA BE. YOU MUST BE CRAZY TO COME TO MY NEIGHBORHOOD AND TRY TO TAKE MONEY FROM MY NEIGHBORS.
HAVE YOU EVER HEARD OF THE WHITE MAN?!
ONLY IN THE FIGURATIVE SENSE.
WHITE MAN, ANYONE EVER TELL YOU THAT YOU LOOK LIKE THE BAD GUY IN MY NANA'S MEXICAN TELENOVELAS?
SILENCE, IDIOT!!!
SMACK
GAH!
YOUR DISCO DANCIN' DAYS ARE DONE, DEADPOOL!
SMACK
NICE TRY, WHITE GUY! BUT YOU ONLY CAUGHT ONE OF THE HEROES FOR HIRE! THE OTHER TWO ARE ON THEIR WAY HERE TO RESCUE ME!
BLOOF!
HMM. THOSE RINGS LOOK FAMILIAR.
HEY, THOSE LOOK LIKE THOSE POWER RINGS THE MANDARIN WEARS.
THAT'S IT. THEY DO LOOK LIKE THOSE POWER RINGS THE MANDARIN WEARS.
I JUST SAID THAT.
YES. THE MANDARIN IS A CLOSE, PERSONAL FRIEND OF MINE. I'VE DISCOVERED THAT ITEMS WITH MYSTICAL POWERS CAN BE VERY PROFITABLE.
WELL, THESE LOOK LIKE KNOCKOFFS. SPEAKING OF FAKE AND MANDARIN, I LOVED THE THIRD IRON--
SHUT UP! THEY'RE NOT KNOCKOFFS.

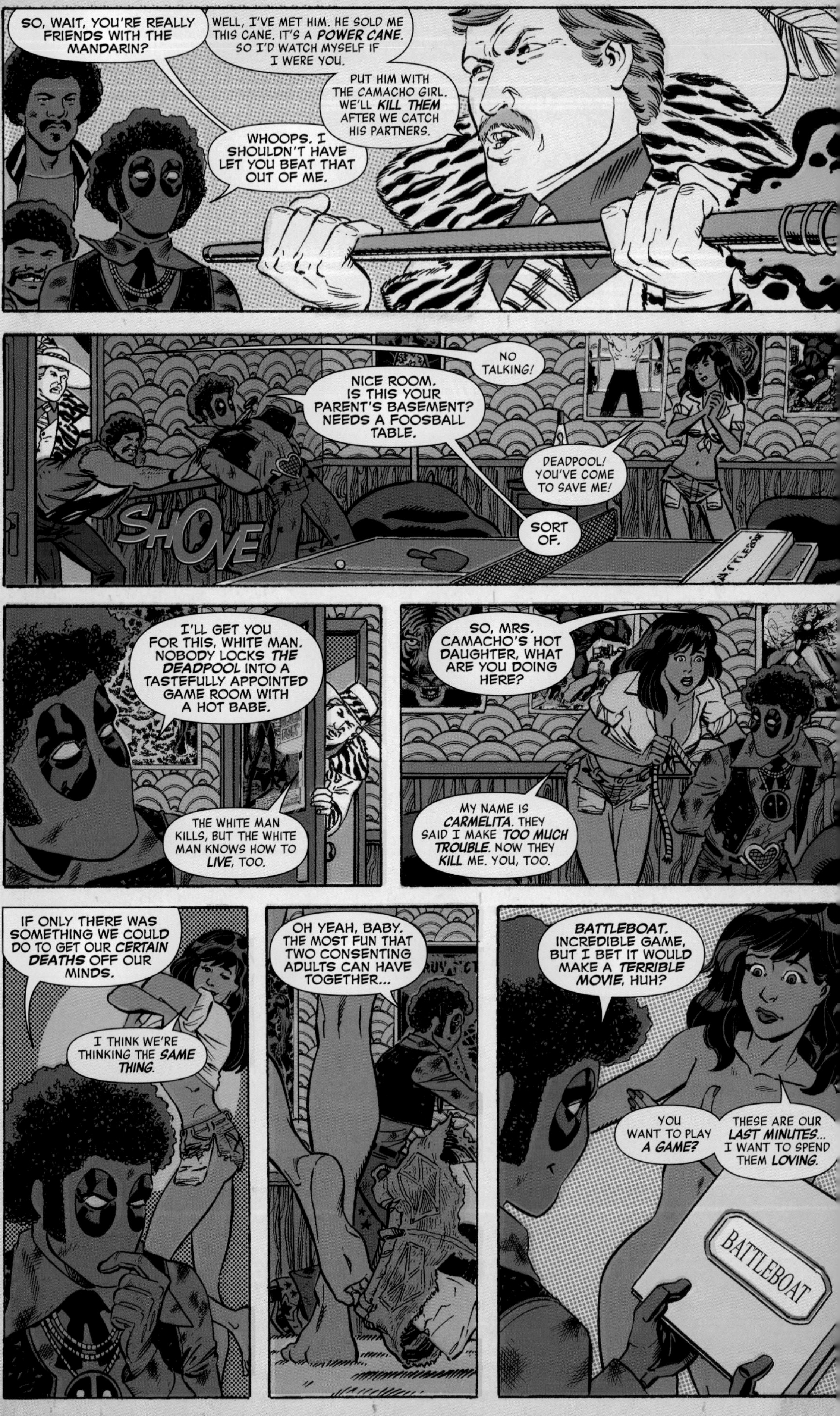
SO, WAIT, YOU'RE REALLY FRIENDS WITH THE MANDARIN?
WELL, I'VE MET HIM. HE SOLD ME THIS CANE. IT'S A POWER CANE. SO I'D WATCH MYSELF IF I WERE YOU.
PUT HIM WITH THE CAMACHO GIRL. WE'LL KILL THEM AFTER WE CATCH HIS PARTNERS.
WHOOPS. I SHOULDN'T HAVE LET YOU BEAT THAT OUT OF ME.
NO TALKING!
NICE ROOM. IS THIS YOUR PARENT'S BASEMENT? NEEDS A FOOSBALL TABLE.
DEADPOOL! YOU'VE COME TO SAVE ME!
SORT OF.
SHOVE
I'LL GET YOU FOR THIS, WHITE MAN. NOBODY LOCKS THE DEADPOOL INTO A TASTEFULLY APPOINTED GAME ROOM WITH A HOT BABE.
THE WHITE MAN KILLS, BUT THE WHITE MAN KNOWS HOW TO LIVE, TOO.
SO, MRS. CAMACHO'S HOT DAUGHTER, WHAT ARE YOU DOING HERE?
MY NAME IS CARMELITA. THEY SAID I MAKE TOO MUCH TROUBLE. NOW THEY KILL ME. YOU, TOO.
IF ONLY THERE WAS SOMETHING WE COULD DO TO GET OUR CERTAIN DEATHS OFF OUR MINDS.
I THINK WE'RE THINKING THE SAME THING.
OH YEAH, BABY. THE MOST FUN THAT TWO CONSENTING ADULTS CAN HAVE TOGETHER...
BATTLEBOAT. INCREDIBLE GAME, BUT I BET IT WOULD MAKE A TERRIBLE MOVIE, HUH?
YOU WANT TO PLAY A GAME?
THESE ARE OUR LAST MINUTES... I WANT TO SPEND THEM LOVING.
BATTLEBOAT

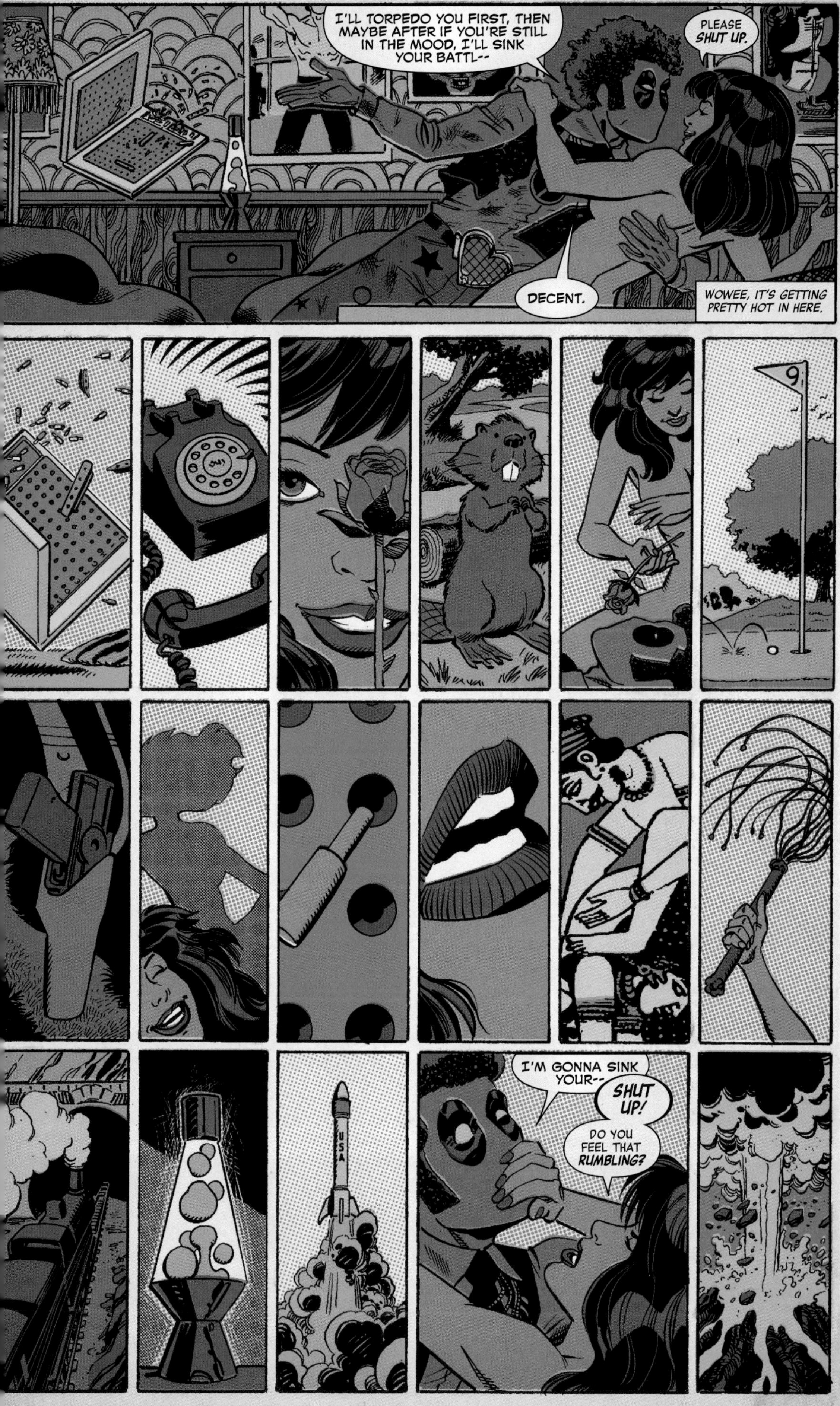
I'LL TORPEDO YOU FIRST, THEN MAYBE AFTER IF YOU'RE STILL IN THE MOOD, I'LL SINK YOUR BATTL--
PLEASE SHUT UP.
DECENT.
WOWEE, IT'S GETTING PRETTY HOT IN HERE.
I'M GONNA SINK YOUR--
SHUT UP!
DO YOU FEEL THAT RUMBLING?

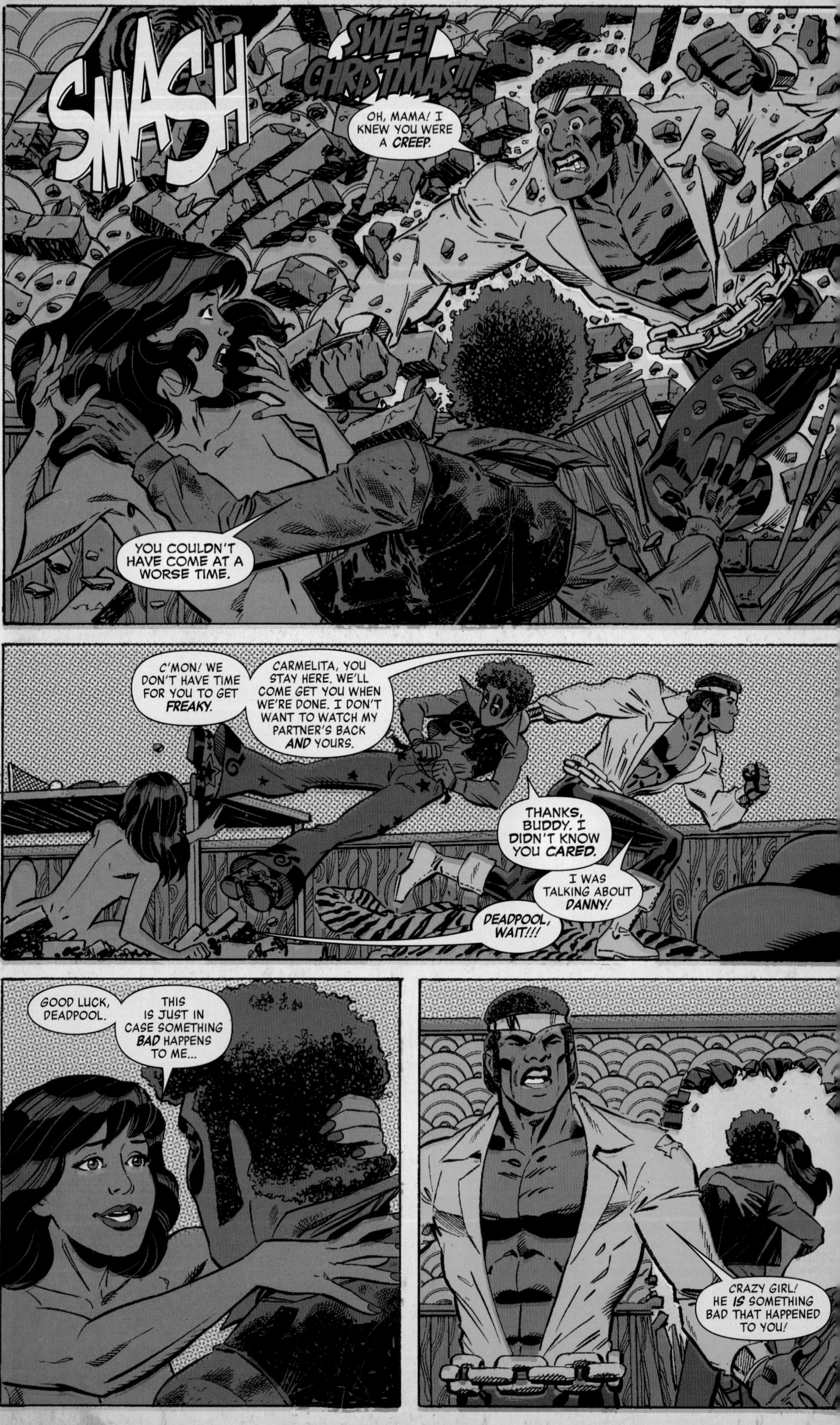
SWASH
SWEET CHRISTMAS!!!
OH, MAMA! I KNEW YOU WERE A CREEP.
YOU COULDN'T HAVE COME AT A WORSE TIME.
C'MON! WE DON'T HAVE TIME FOR YOU TO GET FREAKY.
CARMELITA, YOU STAY HERE. WE'LL COME GET YOU WHEN WE'RE DONE. I DON'T WANT TO WATCH MY PARTNER'S BACK AND YOURS.
THANKS, BUDDY. I DIDN'T KNOW YOU CARED.
I WAS TALKING ABOUT DANNY!
DEADPOOL, WAIT!!!
GOOD LUCK, DEADPOOL.
THIS IS JUST IN CASE SOMETHING BAD HAPPENS TO ME...
CRAZY GIRL! HE IS SOMETHING BAD THAT HAPPENED TO YOU!

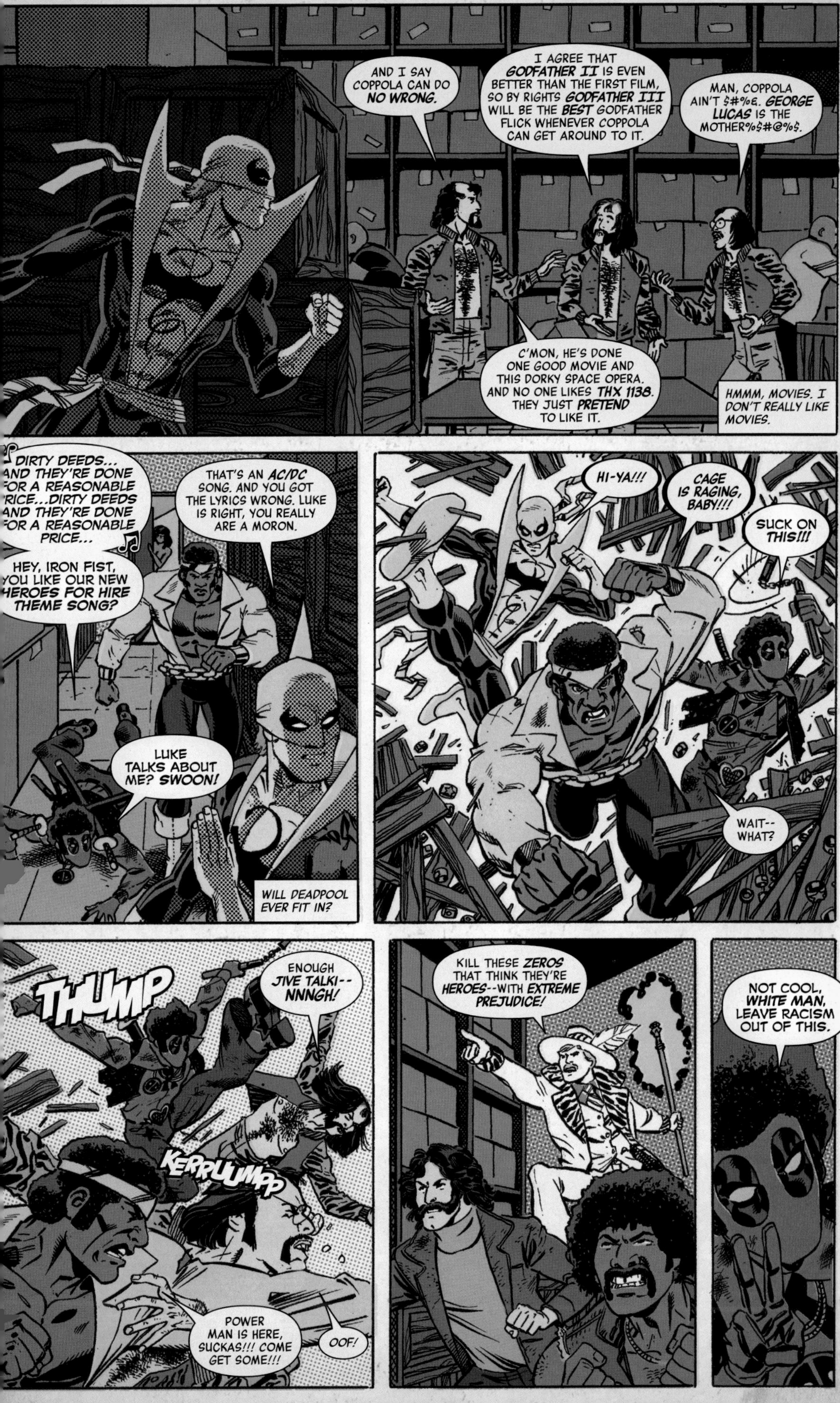
AND I SAY COPPOLA CAN DO NO WRONG.
I AGREE THAT GODFATHER II IS EVEN BETTER THAN THE FIRST FILM, SO BY RIGHTS GODFATHER III WILL BE THE BEST GODFATHER FLICK WHENEVER COPPOLA CAN GET AROUND TO IT.
MAN, COPPOLA AIN'T $#%£. GEORGE LUCAS IS THE MOTHER%$#@%$.
C'MON, HE'S DONE ONE GOOD MOVIE AND THIS DORKY SPACE OPERA. AND NO ONE LIKES THX 1138. THEY JUST PRETEND TO LIKE IT.
HMMM, MOVIES. I DON'T REALLY LIKE MOVIES.
DIRTY DEEDS... AND THEY'RE DONE FOR A REASONABLE PRICE...DIRTY DEEDS AND THEY'RE DONE FOR A REASONABLE PRICE...
THAT'S AN AC/DC SONG. AND YOU GOT THE LYRICS WRONG. LUKE IS RIGHT, YOU REALLY ARE A MORON.
HEY, IRON FIST, YOU LIKE OUR NEW HEROES FOR HIRE THEME SONG?
LUKE TALKS ABOUT ME? SWOON!
WILL DEADPOOL EVER FIT IN?
HI-YA!!!
CAGE IS RAGING, BABY!!!
SUCK ON THIS!!!
WAIT-- WHAT?
THUMP
ENOUGH JIVE TALKI-- NNNGH!
KERRUUMPP
POWER MAN IS HERE, SUCKAS!!! COME GET SOME!!!
OOF!
KILL THESE ZEROS THAT THINK THEY'RE HEROES--WITH EXTREME PREJUDICE!
NOT COOL, WHITE MAN. LEAVE RACISM OUT OF THIS.

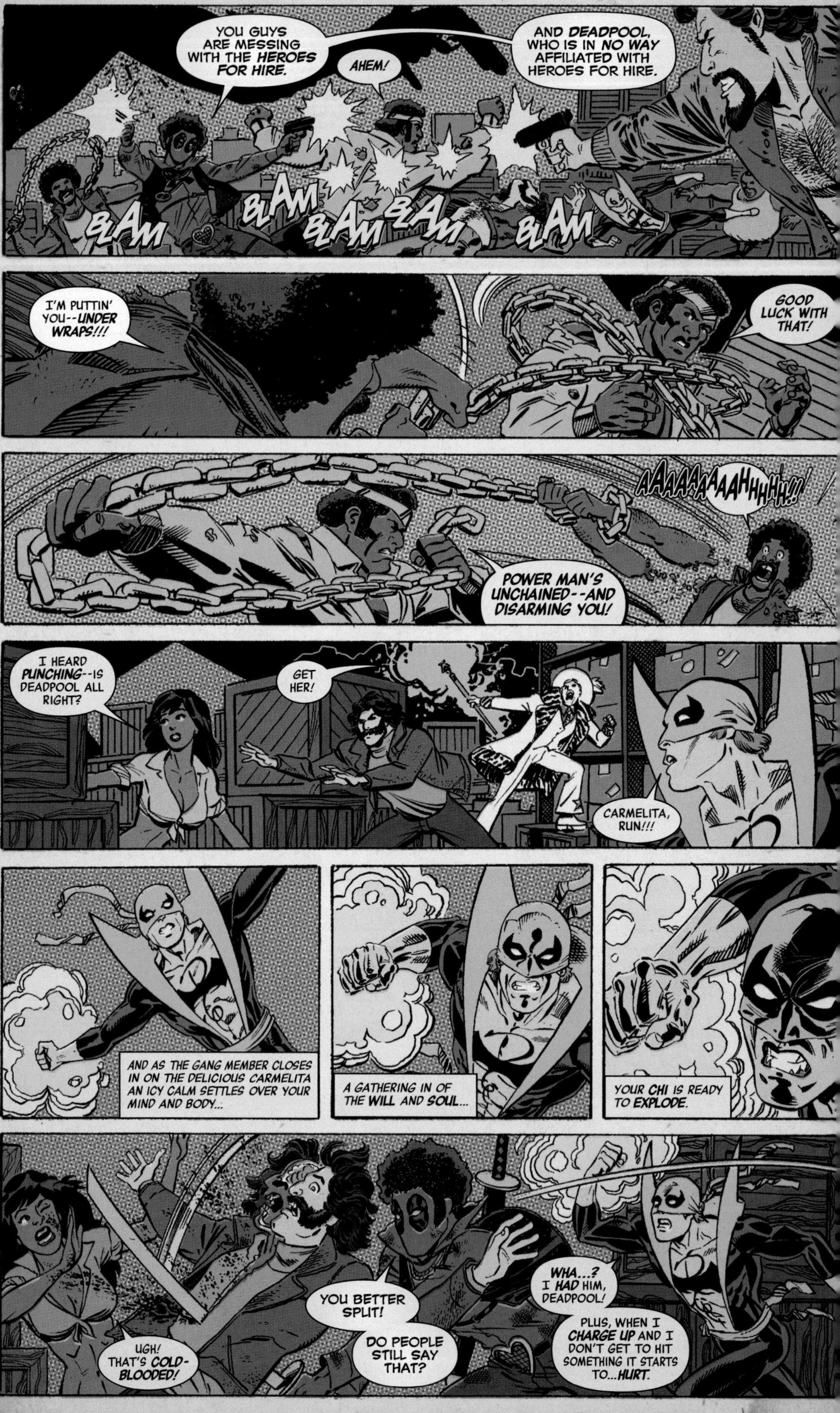
YOU GUYS ARE MESSING WITH THE HEROES FOR HIRE.
AHEM!
AND DEADPOOL, WHO IS IN NO WAY AFFILIATED WITH HEROES FOR HIRE.
BLAM
BLAM
BLAM
BLAM
BLAM
I'M PUTTIN' YOU--UNDER WRAPS!!!
GOOD LUCK WITH THAT!
AAAAAAAAHHHHH!!!
POWER MAN'S UNCHAINED--AND DISARMING YOU!
I HEARD PUNCHING--IS DEADPOOL ALL RIGHT?
GET HER!
CARMELITA, RUN!!!
AND AS THE GANG MEMBER CLOSES IN ON THE DELICIOUS CARMELITA AN ICY CALM SETTLES OVER YOUR MIND AND BODY...
A GATHERING IN OF THE WILL AND SOUL...
YOUR CHI IS READY TO EXPLODE.
UGH! THAT'S COLD-BLOODED!
YOU BETTER SPLIT!
DO PEOPLE STILL SAY THAT?
WHA...? I HAD HIM, DEADPOOL!
PLUS, WHEN I CHARGE UP AND I DON'T GET TO HIT SOMETHING IT STARTS TO...HURT.

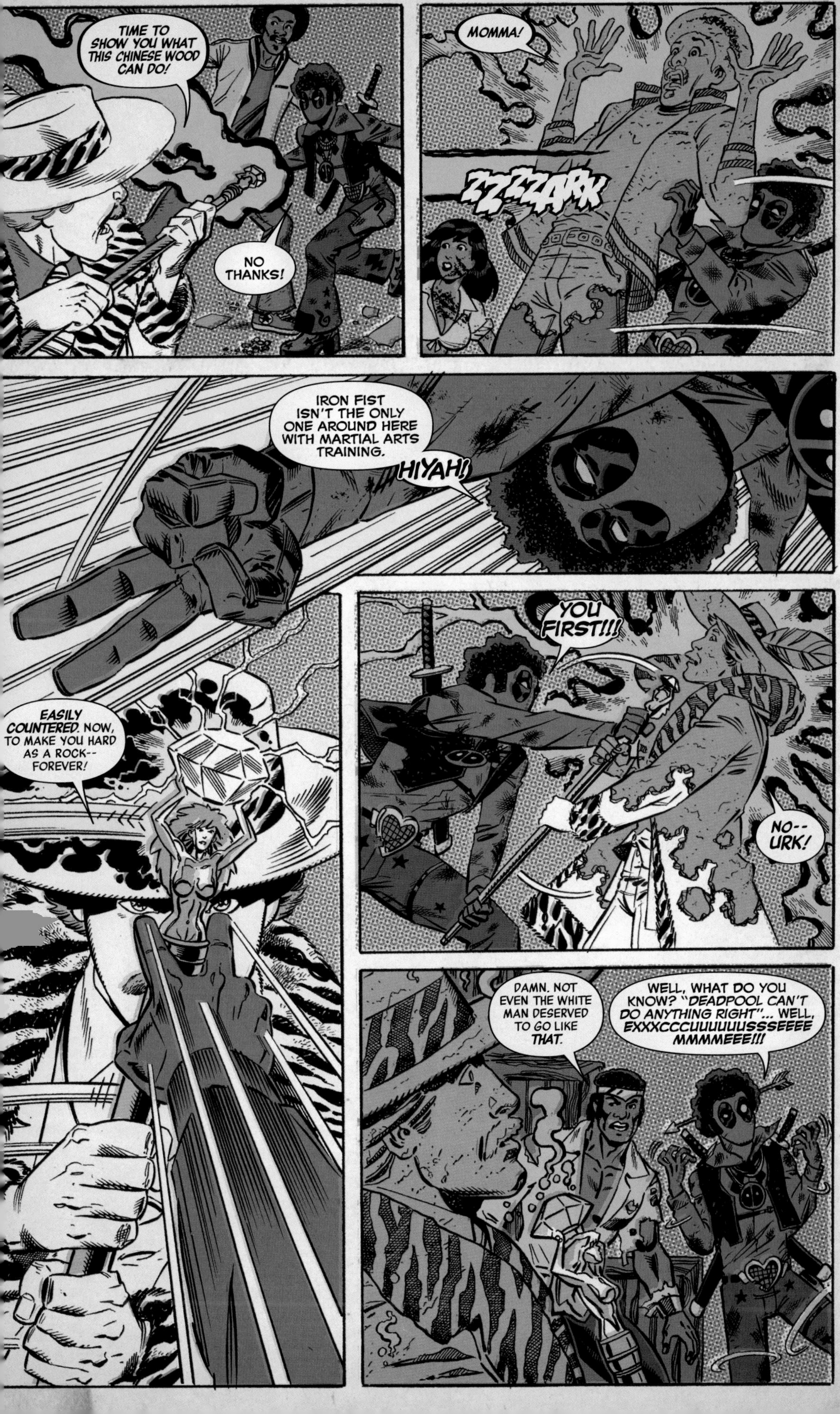
TIME TO SHOW YOU WHAT THIS CHINESE WOOD CAN DO!
NO THANKS!
MOMMA!
ZZZZZARK
IRON FIST ISN'T THE ONLY ONE AROUND HERE WITH MARTIAL ARTS TRAINING.
HIYAH!
EASILY COUNTERED. NOW, TO MAKE YOU HARD AS A ROCK-- FOREVER!
YOU FIRST!!!
NO-- URK!
DAMN. NOT EVEN THE WHITE MAN DESERVED TO GO LIKE THAT.
WELL, WHAT DO YOU KNOW? "DEADPOOL CAN'T DO ANYTHING RIGHT"... WELL, EXXXCCCUUUUUUSSSEEEE MMMMEEE!!!

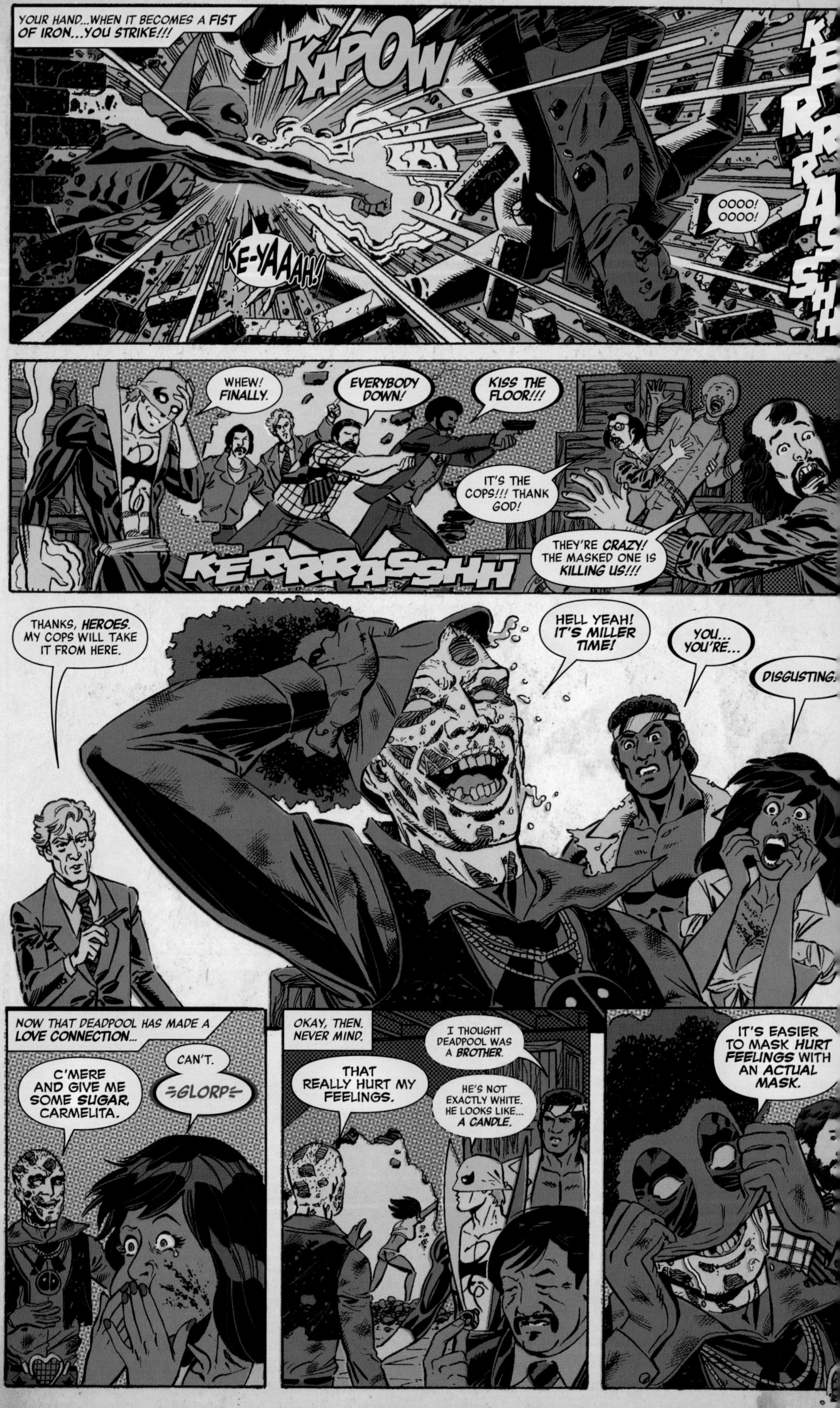
YOUR HAND...WHEN IT BECOMES A FIST OF IRON...YOU STRIKE!!!
KAPOW
KE-YAAAH!
OOOO! OOOO!
KERRRASHH
WHEW! FINALLY.
EVERYBODY DOWN!
KISS THE FLOOR!!!
IT'S THE COPS!!! THANK GOD!
THEY'RE CRAZY! THE MASKED ONE IS KILLING US!!!
KERRRRASSHH
THANKS, HEROES. MY COPS WILL TAKE IT FROM HERE.
HELL YEAH! IT'S MILLER TIME!
YOU... YOU'RE...
DISGUSTING!
NOW THAT DEADPOOL HAS MADE A LOVE CONNECTION...
C'MERE AND GIVE ME SOME SUGAR, CARMELITA.
CAN'T.
GLORP
OKAY, THEN. NEVER MIND.
THAT REALLY HURT MY FEELINGS.
I THOUGHT DEADPOOL WAS A BROTHER.
HE'S NOT EXACTLY WHITE. HE LOOKS LIKE... A CANDLE.
IT'S EASIER TO MASK HURT FEELINGS WITH AN ACTUAL MASK.

DON'T WORRY, THERE ARE OTHER BIRDS OUT THERE FOR YOU, DEADPOOL.

SETTLE DOWN, FISH. NOBODY'S LAUGHING ABOUT HOW YOU LOOK.

YEAH, SORRY, BROTHER WHO AIN'T A BROTHER.

I BET YOU'VE HAD IT UP TO THE GILLS WITH THAT.

I'M REPORTING YOU FOR HARASSMENT. I DIDN'T EVEN HAVE ANYTHING TO DO WITH THIS.

HANKS, GUYS. GOOD THINGS ARE GONNA START HAPPENING FOR ME RIGHT NOW.

I CAN HEAR YOU CRYING.

THERE HE IS. THE UGLY GUY WITH THE AFRO. HE DID IT.

DAMN. LOOKS LIKE YOU GOT SOME COMPANY.

GET THAT DUDE. TEACH HIM NOT TO MESS WITH US.

I SHOULD WARN YOU, I'VE ALREADY BEATEN UP ONE SOFTBALL TEAM TONIGHT. TWO DON'T MAKE NO DIFFERENCE.

THAT WAS US!!! WE JUST WASHED OFF OUR MAKE-UP!

C'MON, KISS FANS! GET USED TO A LIFE OF DISAPPOINTMENT.

THUMP

SLAM

CRACK

THUMP THUMP

ALRIGHT, THAT'S ENOUGH. GO BACK TO YOUR LITTLE PIECE OF NEW YORK AND HIT EACH OTHER WITH BATS. I DON'T CARE. JUST GET OUT OF HERE.

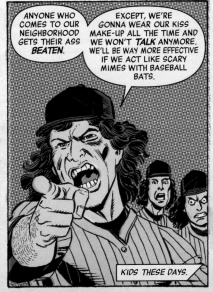

ANYONE WHO COMES TO OUR NEIGHBORHOOD GETS THEIR ASS BEATEN.

EXCEPT, WE'RE GONNA WEAR OUR KISS MAKE-UP ALL THE TIME AND WE WON'T TALK ANYMORE. WE'LL BE WAY MORE EFFECTIVE IF WE ACT LIKE SCARY MIMES WITH BASEBALL BATS.

KIDS THESE DAYS.

THANKS. YOU HAVE A GOOD ONE, CAPTAIN STACY.

I ALWAYS HAVE A GOOD ONE.

LET'S PRETEND WE DIDN'T READ THAT.

HOW COULD I NOT HAVE A GOOD ONE? I'VE GOT MY HEALTH AND THE GREATEST DAUGHTER IN THE WORLD. MY LIFE IS PERFECT.

YEEEESHH. YEAH, LISTEN, I DON'T WRITE THIS STUFF. I'M GONNA STAY OUT OF THIS.

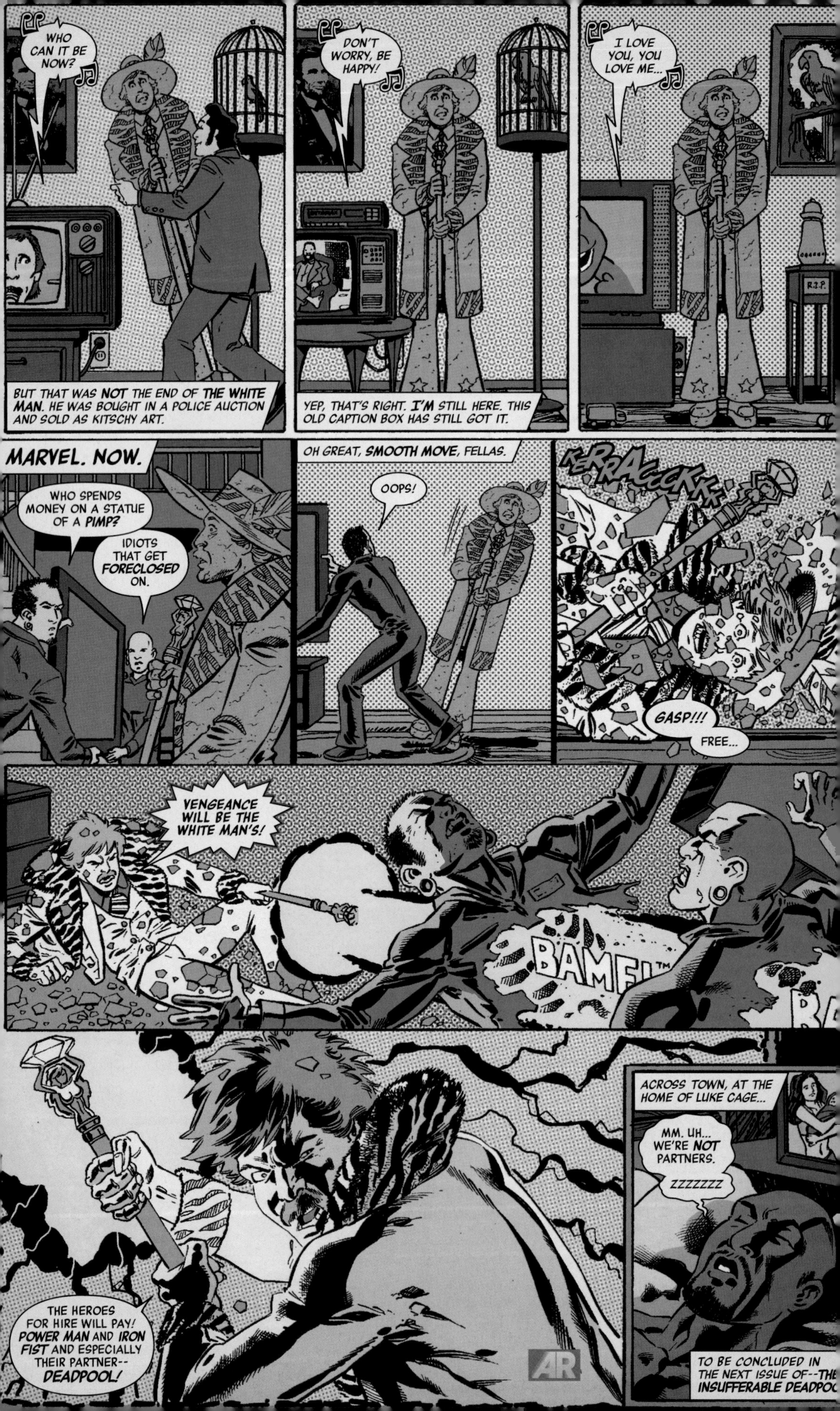
WHO CAN IT BE NOW?
BUT THAT WAS NOT THE END OF THE WHITE MAN. HE WAS BOUGHT IN A POLICE AUCTION AND SOLD AS KITSCHY ART.
DON'T WORRY, BE HAPPY!
YEP, THAT'S RIGHT. I'M STILL HERE. THIS OLD CAPTION BOX HAS STILL GOT IT.
I LOVE YOU, YOU LOVE ME...
MARVEL. NOW.
WHO SPENDS MONEY ON A STATUE OF A PIMP?
IDIOTS THAT GET FORECLOSED ON.
OH GREAT, SMOOTH MOVE, FELLAS.
OOPS!
KERRACCCKKK
GASP!!!
FREE...
VENGEANCE WILL BE THE WHITE MAN'S!
BAMF!
THE HEROES FOR HIRE WILL PAY! POWER MAN AND IRON FIST AND ESPECIALLY THEIR PARTNER-- DEADPOOL!
ACROSS TOWN, AT THE HOME OF LUKE CAGE...
MM. UH... WE'RE NOT PARTNERS.
ZZZZZZZ
TO BE CONCLUDED IN THE NEXT ISSUE OF--THE INSUFFERABLE DEADPOOL

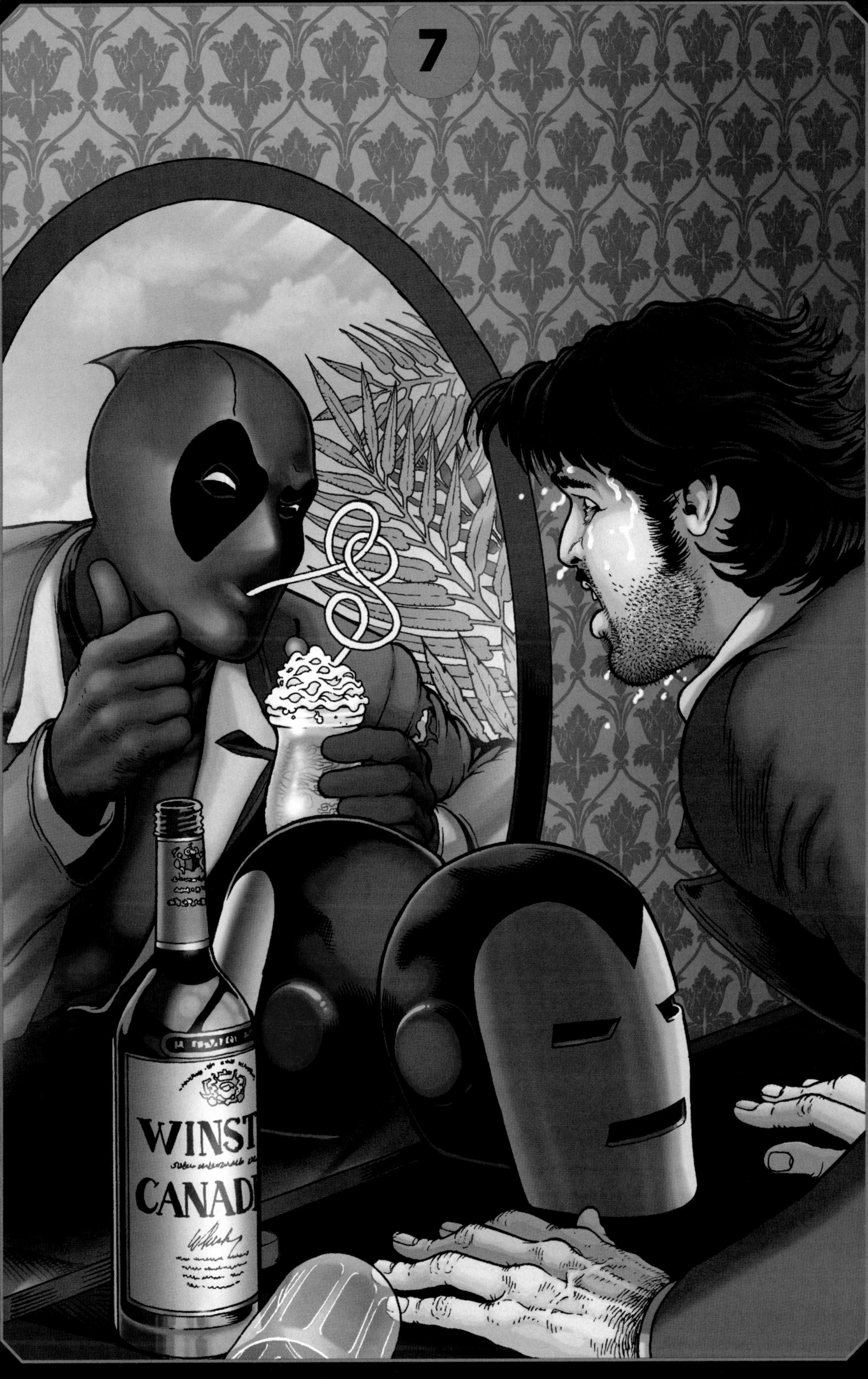
7
WINST
CANAD

DRINKING GAME

Possibly the world's most skilled mercenary, definitely the world's most annoying, Wade Wilson was chosen for a top-secret government program that gave him a healing factor allowing him to heal from any wound. Now, Wade makes his way as a gun for hire, shooting his prey's faces off while talking his friends' ears off. Call him the Merc with the Mouth…call him the Regeneratin' Degenerate…call him…DEADPOOL.

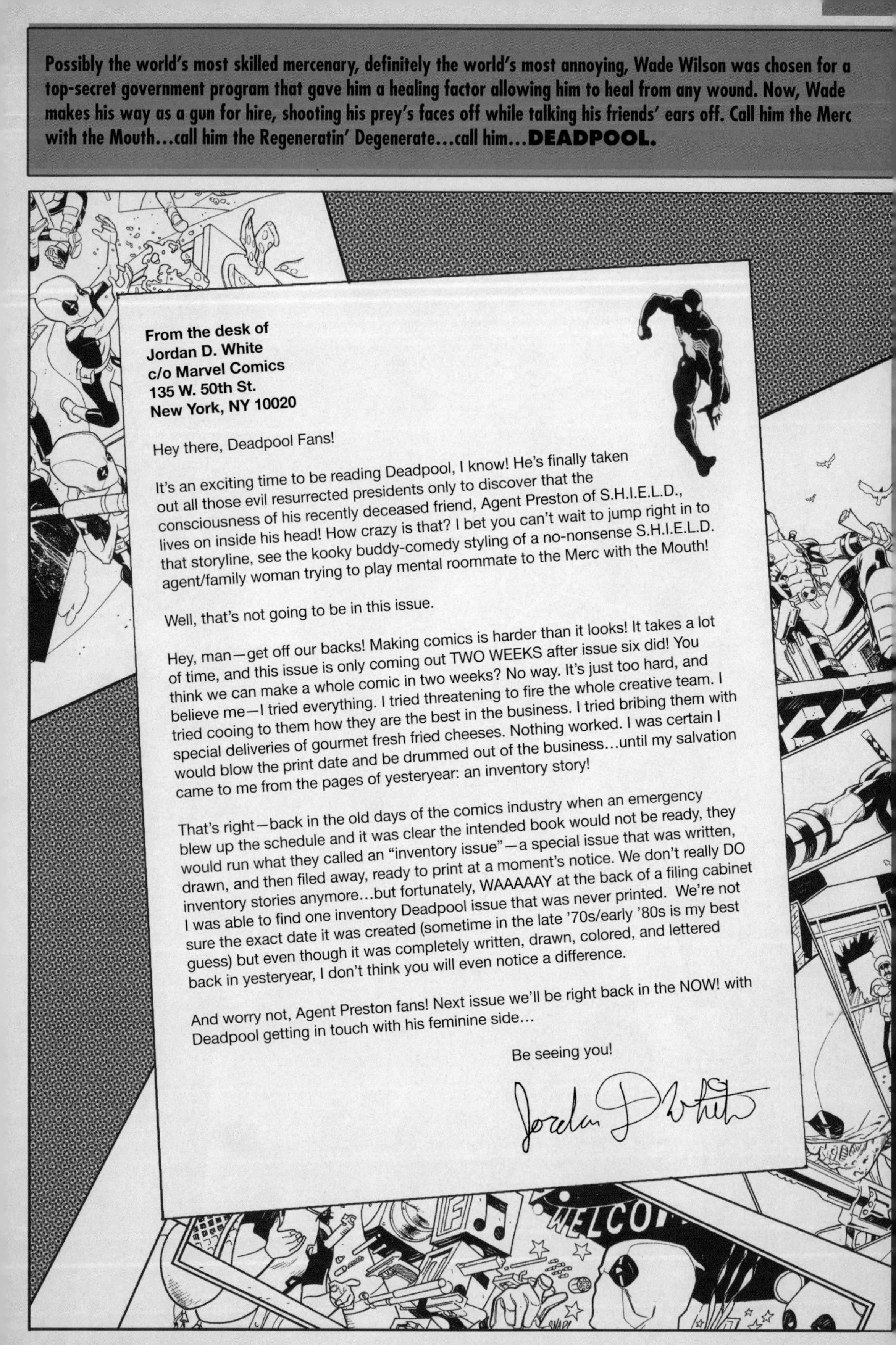

WELCO

From the desk of
Jordan D. White
c/o Marvel Comics
135 W. 50th St.
New York, NY 10020

Hey there, Deadpool Fans!

It's an exciting time to be reading Deadpool, I know! He's finally taken out all those evil resurrected presidents only to discover that the consciousness of his recently deceased friend, Agent Preston of S.H.I.E.L.D., lives on inside his head! How crazy is that? I bet you can't wait to jump right in to that storyline, see the kooky buddy-comedy styling of a no-nonsense S.H.I.E.L.D. agent/family woman trying to play mental roommate to the Merc with the Mouth!

Well, that's not going to be in this issue.

Hey, man—get off our backs! Making comics is harder than it looks! It takes a lot of time, and this issue is only coming out TWO WEEKS after issue six did! You think we can make a whole comic in two weeks? No way. It's just too hard, and believe me—I tried everything. I tried threatening to fire the whole creative team. I tried cooing to them how they are the best in the business. I tried bribing them with special deliveries of gourmet fresh fried cheeses. Nothing worked. I was certain I would blow the print date and be drummed out of the business…until my salvation came to me from the pages of yesteryear: an inventory story!

That's right—back in the old days of the comics industry when an emergency blew up the schedule and it was clear the intended book would not be ready, they would run what they called an "inventory issue"—a special issue that was written, drawn, and then filed away, ready to print at a moment's notice. We don't really DO inventory stories anymore…but fortunately, WAAAAAY at the back of a filing cabinet I was able to find one inventory Deadpool issue that was never printed. We're not sure the exact date it was created (sometime in the late '70s/early '80s is my best guess) but even though it was completely written, drawn, colored, and lettered back in yesteryear, I don't think you will even notice a difference.

And worry not, Agent Preston fans! Next issue we'll be right back in the NOW! with Deadpool getting in touch with his feminine side…

Be seeing you!

Jordan D White

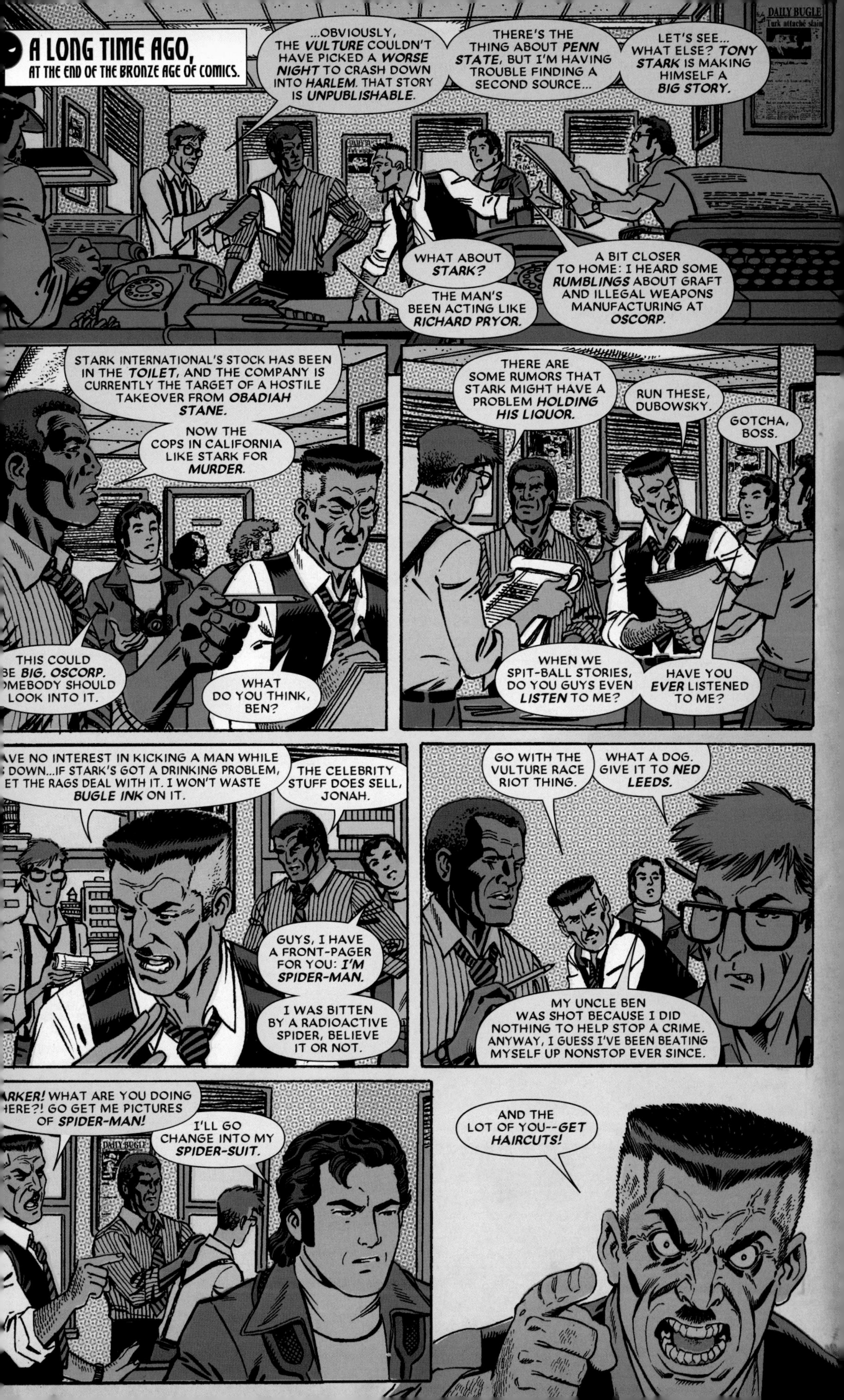
A LONG TIME AGO, AT THE END OF THE BRONZE AGE OF COMICS.
...OBVIOUSLY, THE VULTURE COULDN'T HAVE PICKED A WORSE NIGHT TO CRASH DOWN INTO HARLEM. THAT STORY IS UNPUBLISHABLE.
THERE'S THE THING ABOUT PENN STATE, BUT I'M HAVING TROUBLE FINDING A SECOND SOURCE...
LET'S SEE... WHAT ELSE? TONY STARK IS MAKING HIMSELF A BIG STORY.
DAILY BUGLE
Turk attaché slain
WHAT ABOUT STARK?
THE MAN'S BEEN ACTING LIKE RICHARD PRYOR.
A BIT CLOSER TO HOME: I HEARD SOME RUMBLINGS ABOUT GRAFT AND ILLEGAL WEAPONS MANUFACTURING AT OSCORP.
STARK INTERNATIONAL'S STOCK HAS BEEN IN THE TOILET, AND THE COMPANY IS CURRENTLY THE TARGET OF A HOSTILE TAKEOVER FROM OBADIAH STANE.
NOW THE COPS IN CALIFORNIA LIKE STARK FOR MURDER.
THIS COULD BE BIG. OSCORP. OMEBODY SHOULD LOOK INTO IT.
WHAT DO YOU THINK, BEN?
THERE ARE SOME RUMORS THAT STARK MIGHT HAVE A PROBLEM HOLDING HIS LIQUOR.
RUN THESE, DUBOWSKY.
GOTCHA, BOSS.
WHEN WE SPIT-BALL STORIES, DO YOU GUYS EVEN LISTEN TO ME?
HAVE YOU EVER LISTENED TO ME?
AVE NO INTEREST IN KICKING A MAN WHILE S DOWN...IF STARK'S GOT A DRINKING PROBLEM, ET THE RAGS DEAL WITH IT. I WON'T WASTE BUGLE INK ON IT.
THE CELEBRITY STUFF DOES SELL, JONAH.
GUYS, I HAVE A FRONT-PAGER FOR YOU: I'M SPIDER-MAN.
I WAS BITTEN BY A RADIOACTIVE SPIDER, BELIEVE IT OR NOT.
GO WITH THE VULTURE RACE RIOT THING.
WHAT A DOG. GIVE IT TO NED LEEDS.
MY UNCLE BEN WAS SHOT BECAUSE I DID NOTHING TO HELP STOP A CRIME. ANYWAY, I GUESS I'VE BEEN BEATING MYSELF UP NONSTOP EVER SINCE.
ARKER! WHAT ARE YOU DOING HERE?! GO GET ME PICTURES OF SPIDER-MAN!
I'LL GO CHANGE INTO MY SPIDER-SUIT.
DAILY BUGLE
AND THE LOT OF YOU--GET HAIRCUTS!

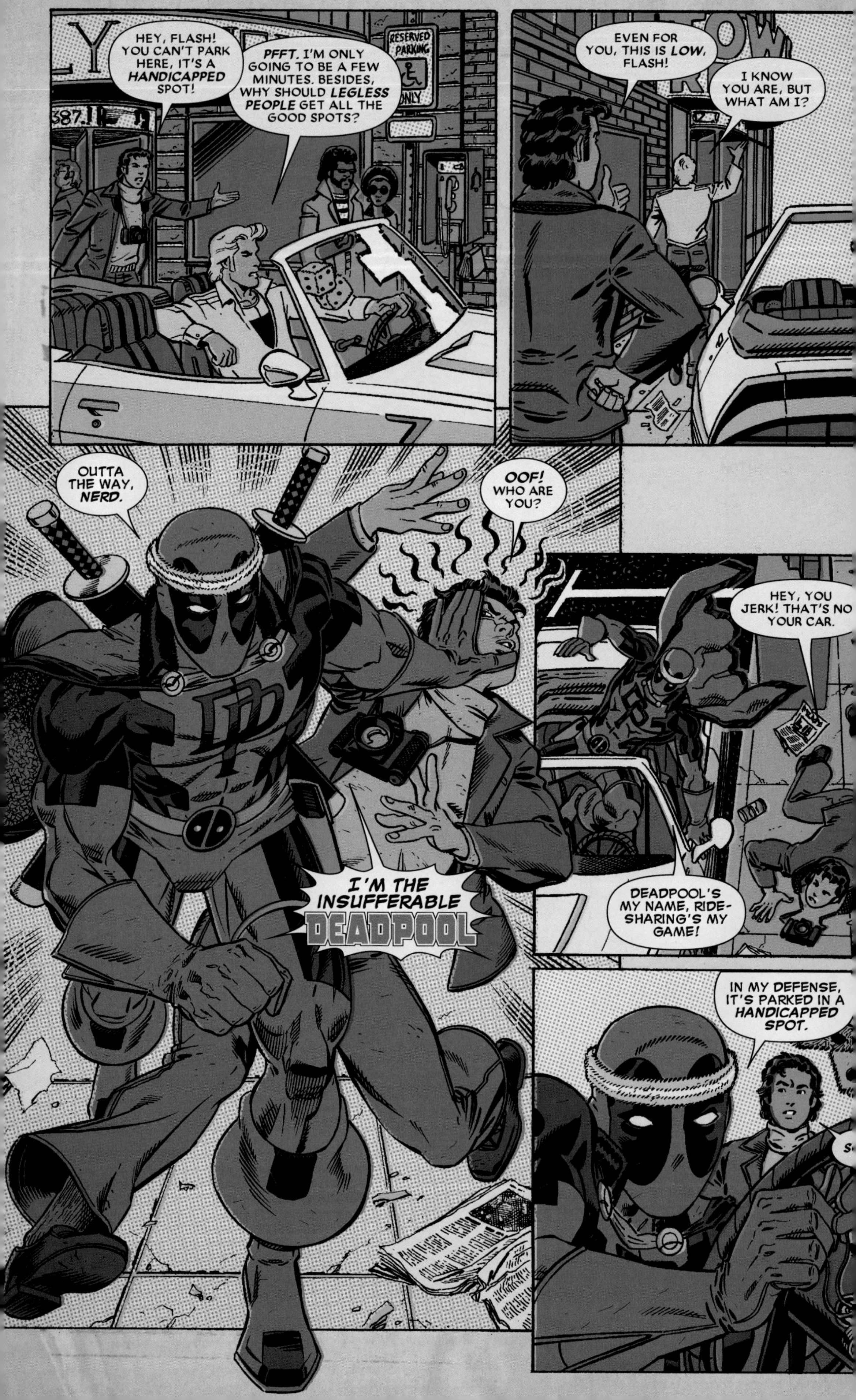

HEY, FLASH! YOU CAN'T PARK HERE, IT'S A *HANDICAPPED* SPOT!
PFFT. I'M ONLY GOING TO BE A FEW MINUTES. BESIDES, WHY SHOULD *LEGLESS PEOPLE* GET ALL THE GOOD SPOTS?
RESERVED PARKING ONLY
EVEN FOR YOU, THIS IS *LOW*, FLASH!
I KNOW YOU ARE, BUT WHAT AM I?
OUTTA THE WAY, *NERD.*
OOF! WHO ARE YOU?
I'M THE INSUFFERABLE DEADPOOL
HEY, YOU JERK! THAT'S NO YOUR CAR.
DEADPOOL'S MY NAME, RIDE-SHARING'S MY GAME!
IN MY DEFENSE, IT'S PARKED IN A *HANDICAPPED SPOT.*

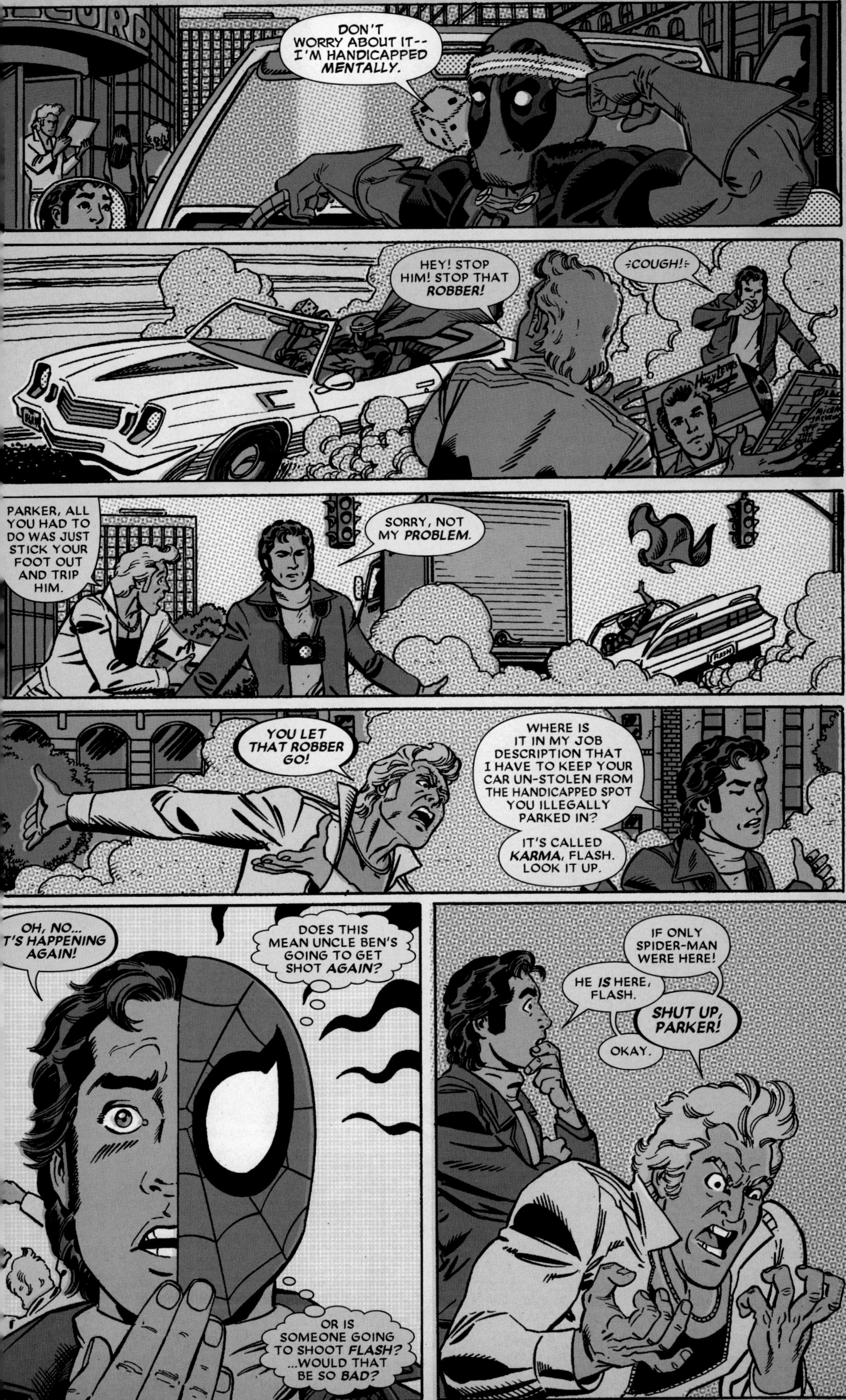

DON'T WORRY ABOUT IT-- I'M HANDICAPPED *MENTALLY.*
HEY! STOP HIM! STOP THAT *ROBBER!*
COUGH!
PARKER, ALL YOU HAD TO DO WAS JUST STICK YOUR FOOT OUT AND TRIP HIM.
SORRY, NOT MY *PROBLEM.*
YOU LET THAT ROBBER GO!
WHERE IS IT IN MY JOB DESCRIPTION THAT I HAVE TO KEEP YOUR CAR UN-STOLEN FROM THE HANDICAPPED SPOT YOU ILLEGALLY PARKED IN?
IT'S CALLED *KARMA,* FLASH. LOOK IT UP.
OH, NO... IT'S HAPPENING AGAIN!
DOES THIS MEAN UNCLE BEN'S GOING TO GET SHOT *AGAIN?*
OR IS SOMEONE GOING TO SHOOT *FLASH?* ...WOULD THAT BE SO *BAD?*
IF ONLY SPIDER-MAN WERE HERE!
HE *IS* HERE, FLASH.
SHUT UP, PARKER!
OKAY.

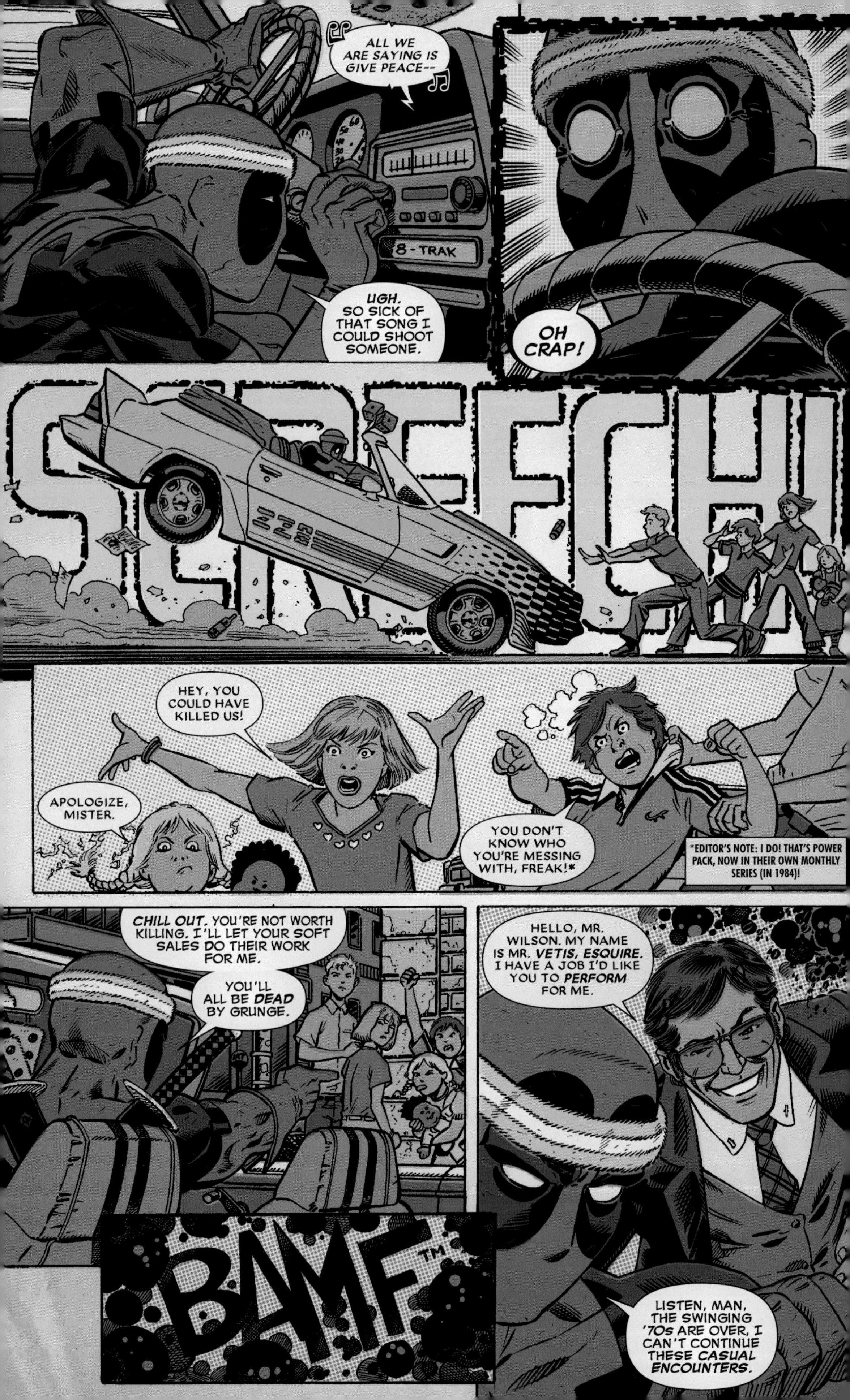

ALL WE ARE SAYING IS GIVE PEACE--
8-TRAK
UGH. SO SICK OF THAT SONG I COULD SHOOT SOMEONE.
OH CRAP!
HEY, YOU COULD HAVE KILLED US!
APOLOGIZE, MISTER.
YOU DON'T KNOW WHO YOU'RE MESSING WITH, FREAK!*
*EDITOR'S NOTE: I DO! THAT'S POWER PACK, NOW IN THEIR OWN MONTHLY SERIES (IN 1984)!
CHILL OUT. YOU'RE NOT WORTH KILLING. I'LL LET YOUR SOFT SALES DO THEIR WORK FOR ME.
YOU'LL ALL BE DEAD BY GRUNGE.
BAMF™
HELLO, MR. WILSON. MY NAME IS MR. VETIS, ESQUIRE. I HAVE A JOB I'D LIKE YOU TO PERFORM FOR ME.
LISTEN, MAN, THE SWINGING '70s ARE OVER, I CAN'T CONTINUE THESE CASUAL ENCOUNTERS.

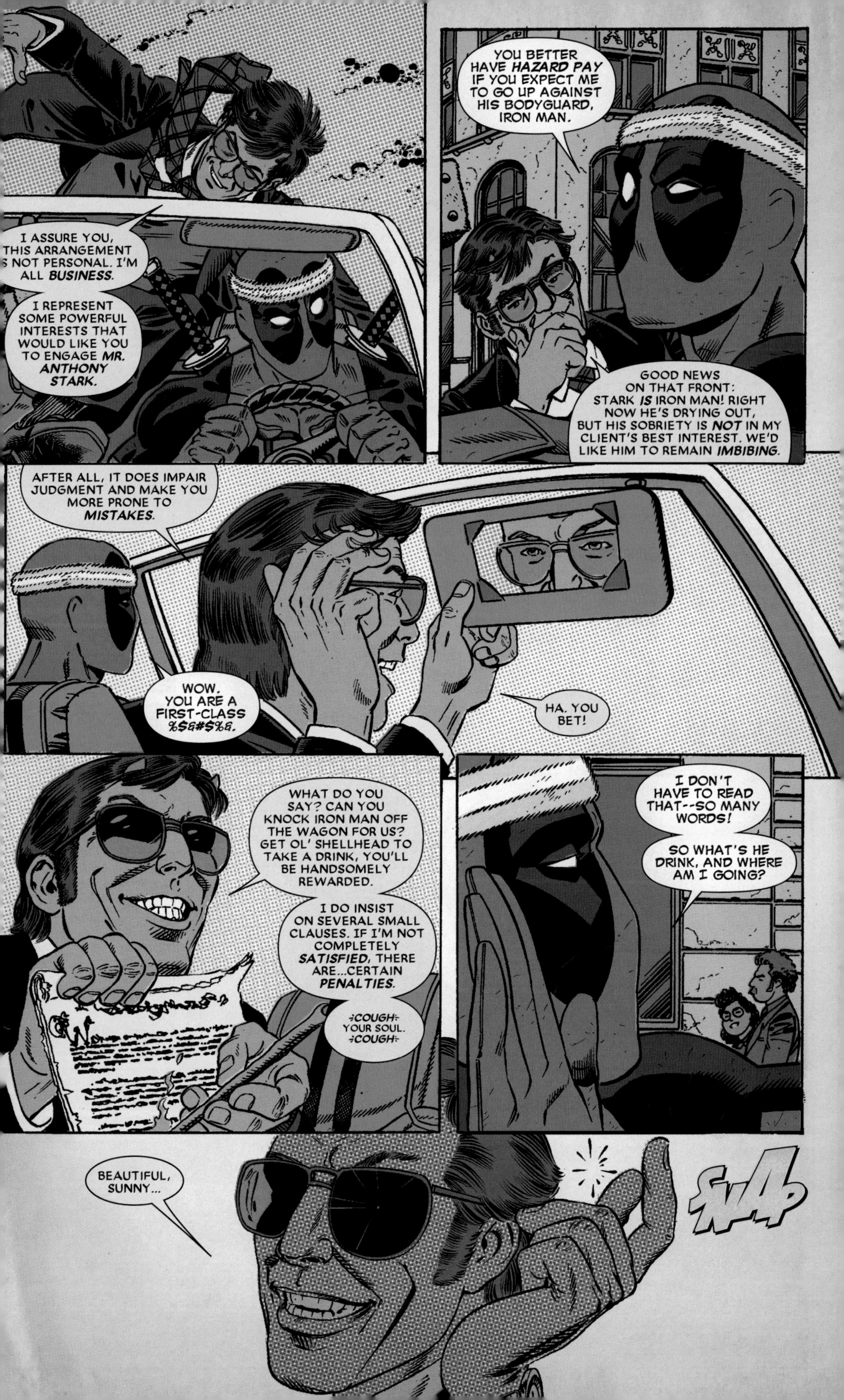
I ASSURE YOU, THIS ARRANGEMENT IS NOT PERSONAL. I'M ALL BUSINESS.
I REPRESENT SOME POWERFUL INTERESTS THAT WOULD LIKE YOU TO ENGAGE MR. ANTHONY STARK.
YOU BETTER HAVE HAZARD PAY IF YOU EXPECT ME TO GO UP AGAINST HIS BODYGUARD, IRON MAN.
GOOD NEWS ON THAT FRONT: STARK IS IRON MAN! RIGHT NOW HE'S DRYING OUT, BUT HIS SOBRIETY IS NOT IN MY CLIENT'S BEST INTEREST. WE'D LIKE HIM TO REMAIN IMBIBING.
AFTER ALL, IT DOES IMPAIR JUDGMENT AND MAKE YOU MORE PRONE TO MISTAKES.
WOW. YOU ARE A FIRST-CLASS %$&#$%&.
HA. YOU BET!
WHAT DO YOU SAY? CAN YOU KNOCK IRON MAN OFF THE WAGON FOR US? GET OL' SHELLHEAD TO TAKE A DRINK, YOU'LL BE HANDSOMELY REWARDED.
I DO INSIST ON SEVERAL SMALL CLAUSES. IF I'M NOT COMPLETELY SATISFIED, THERE ARE...CERTAIN PENALTIES.
COUGH YOUR SOUL. COUGH
I DON'T HAVE TO READ THAT--SO MANY WORDS!
SO WHAT'S HE DRINK, AND WHERE AM I GOING?
BEAUTIFUL, SUNNY...
SNAP

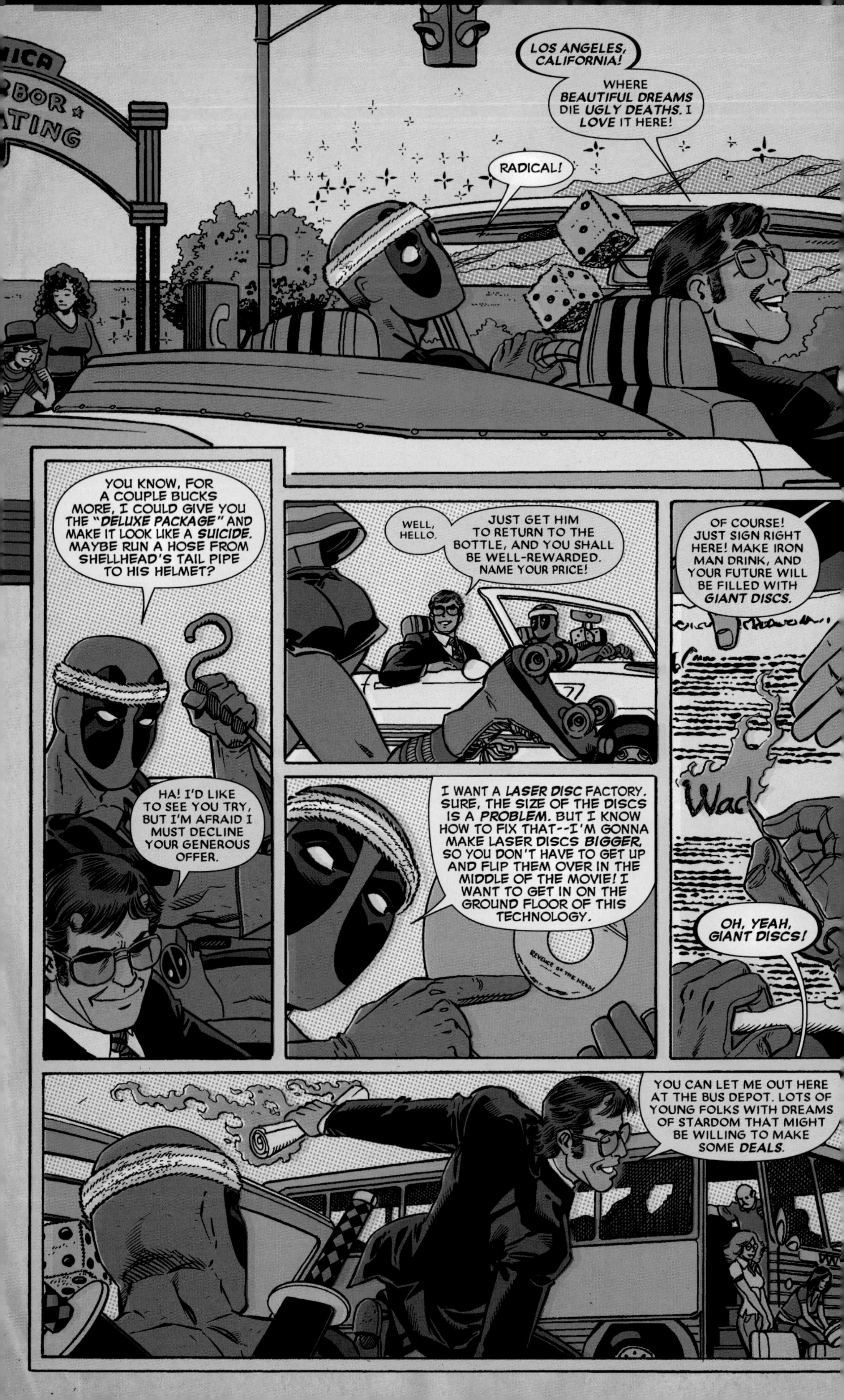

LOS ANGELES, CALIFORNIA!
WHERE BEAUTIFUL DREAMS DIE UGLY DEATHS. I LOVE IT HERE!
RADICAL!
YOU KNOW, FOR A COUPLE BUCKS MORE, I COULD GIVE YOU THE "DELUXE PACKAGE" AND MAKE IT LOOK LIKE A SUICIDE. MAYBE RUN A HOSE FROM SHELLHEAD'S TAIL PIPE TO HIS HELMET?
HA! I'D LIKE TO SEE YOU TRY, BUT I'M AFRAID I MUST DECLINE YOUR GENEROUS OFFER.
WELL, HELLO.
JUST GET HIM TO RETURN TO THE BOTTLE, AND YOU SHALL BE WELL-REWARDED. NAME YOUR PRICE!
I WANT A LASER DISC FACTORY. SURE, THE SIZE OF THE DISCS IS A PROBLEM. BUT I KNOW HOW TO FIX THAT--I'M GONNA MAKE LASER DISCS BIGGER, SO YOU DON'T HAVE TO GET UP AND FLIP THEM OVER IN THE MIDDLE OF THE MOVIE! I WANT TO GET IN ON THE GROUND FLOOR OF THIS TECHNOLOGY.
REVENGE OF THE NERDS
OF COURSE! JUST SIGN RIGHT HERE! MAKE IRON MAN DRINK, AND YOUR FUTURE WILL BE FILLED WITH GIANT DISCS.
OH, YEAH, GIANT DISCS!
YOU CAN LET ME OUT HERE AT THE BUS DEPOT. LOTS OF YOUNG FOLKS WITH DREAMS OF STARDOM THAT MIGHT BE WILLING TO MAKE SOME DEALS.

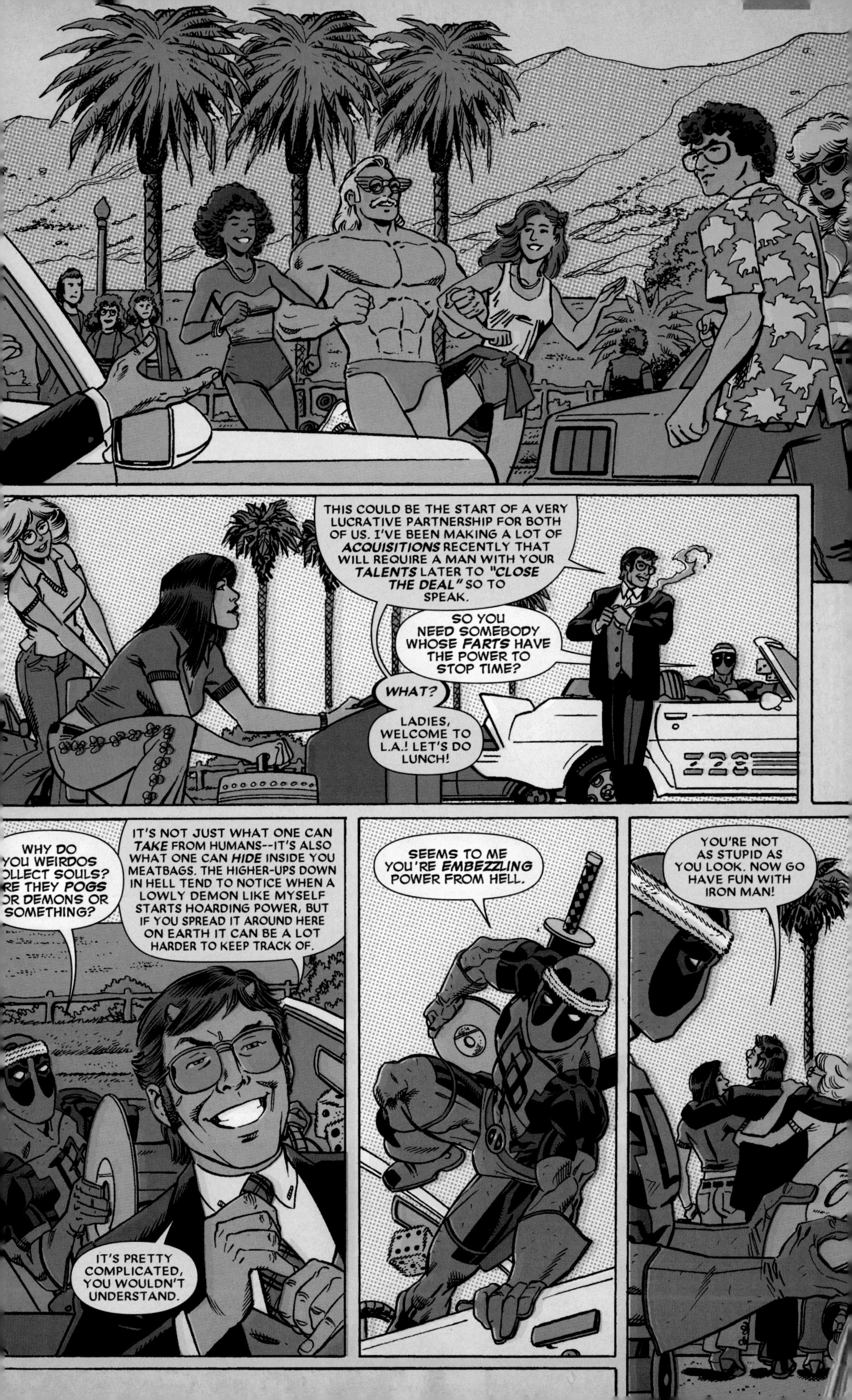

THIS COULD BE THE START OF A VERY LUCRATIVE PARTNERSHIP FOR BOTH OF US. I'VE BEEN MAKING A LOT OF ACQUISITIONS RECENTLY THAT WILL REQUIRE A MAN WITH YOUR TALENTS LATER TO "CLOSE THE DEAL" SO TO SPEAK.
SO YOU NEED SOMEBODY WHOSE FARTS HAVE THE POWER TO STOP TIME?
WHAT?
LADIES, WELCOME TO L.A.! LET'S DO LUNCH!
WHY DO YOU WEIRDOS OLLECT SOULS? RE THEY POGS OR DEMONS OR SOMETHING?
IT'S NOT JUST WHAT ONE CAN TAKE FROM HUMANS--IT'S ALSO WHAT ONE CAN HIDE INSIDE YOU MEATBAGS. THE HIGHER-UPS DOWN IN HELL TEND TO NOTICE WHEN A LOWLY DEMON LIKE MYSELF STARTS HOARDING POWER, BUT IF YOU SPREAD IT AROUND HERE ON EARTH IT CAN BE A LOT HARDER TO KEEP TRACK OF.
IT'S PRETTY COMPLICATED, YOU WOULDN'T UNDERSTAND.
SEEMS TO ME YOU'RE EMBEZZLING POWER FROM HELL.
YOU'RE NOT AS STUPID AS YOU LOOK. NOW GO HAVE FUN WITH IRON MAN!

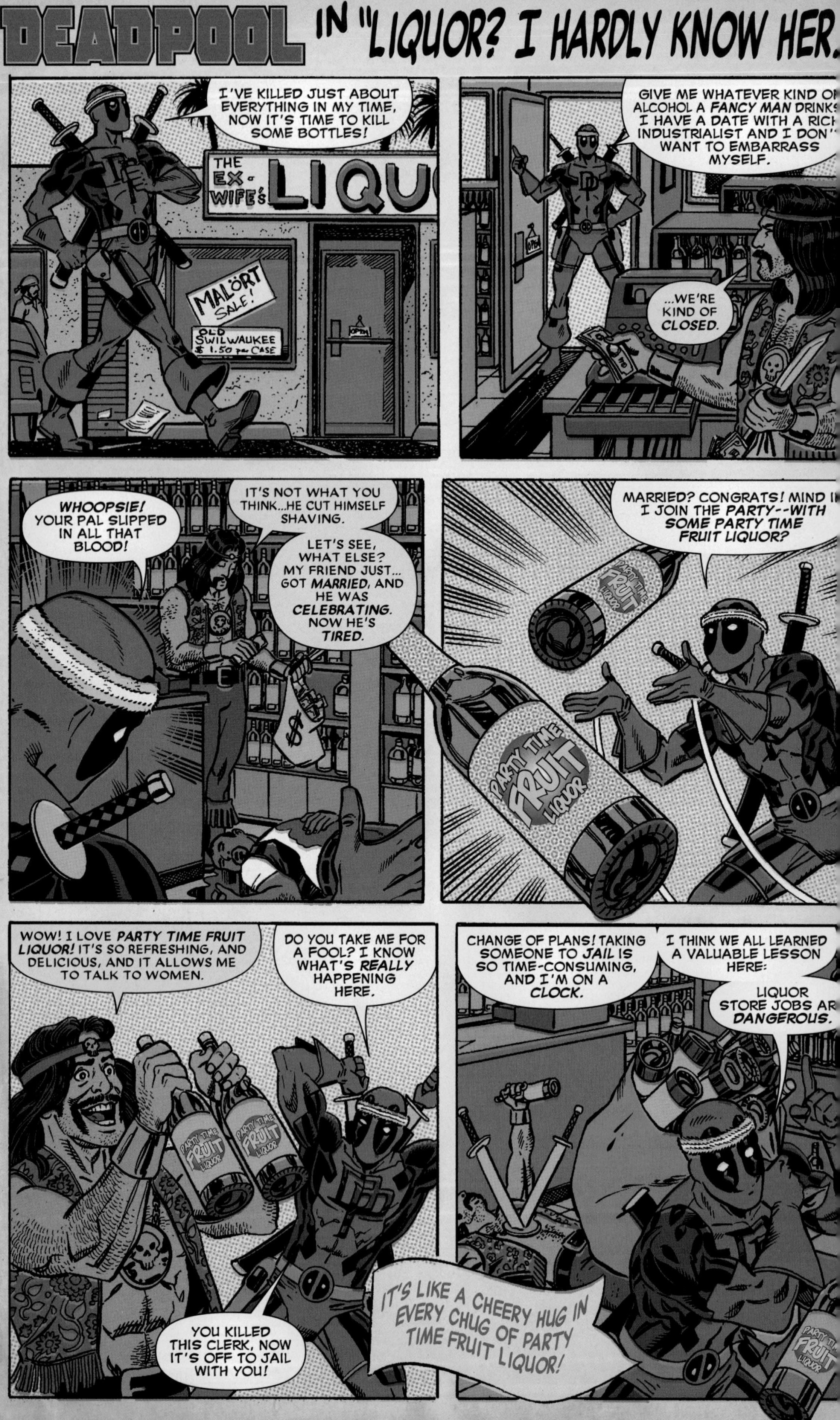
DEADPOOL IN "LIQUOR? I HARDLY KNOW HER.
I'VE KILLED JUST ABOUT EVERYTHING IN MY TIME, NOW IT'S TIME TO KILL SOME BOTTLES!
THE EX-WIFE'S LIQU
MALÖRT SALE!
OLD SWILWAUKEE $1.50 per CASE
OPEN
GIVE ME WHATEVER KIND OF ALCOHOL A FANCY MAN DRINKS. I HAVE A DATE WITH A RICH INDUSTRIALIST AND I DON'T WANT TO EMBARRASS MYSELF.
...WE'RE KIND OF CLOSED.
WHOOPSIE! YOUR PAL SLIPPED IN ALL THAT BLOOD!
IT'S NOT WHAT YOU THINK...HE CUT HIMSELF SHAVING.
LET'S SEE, WHAT ELSE? MY FRIEND JUST... GOT MARRIED, AND HE WAS CELEBRATING. NOW HE'S TIRED.
MARRIED? CONGRATS! MIND IF I JOIN THE PARTY--WITH SOME PARTY TIME FRUIT LIQUOR?
PARTY TIME FRUIT LIQUOR
WOW! I LOVE PARTY TIME FRUIT LIQUOR! IT'S SO REFRESHING, AND DELICIOUS, AND IT ALLOWS ME TO TALK TO WOMEN.
DO YOU TAKE ME FOR A FOOL? I KNOW WHAT'S REALLY HAPPENING HERE.
YOU KILLED THIS CLERK, NOW IT'S OFF TO JAIL WITH YOU!
CHANGE OF PLANS! TAKING SOMEONE TO JAIL IS SO TIME-CONSUMING, AND I'M ON A CLOCK.
I THINK WE ALL LEARNED A VALUABLE LESSON HERE:
LIQUOR STORE JOBS AR DANGEROUS.
IT'S LIKE A CHEERY HUG IN EVERY CHUG OF PARTY TIME FRUIT LIQUOR!

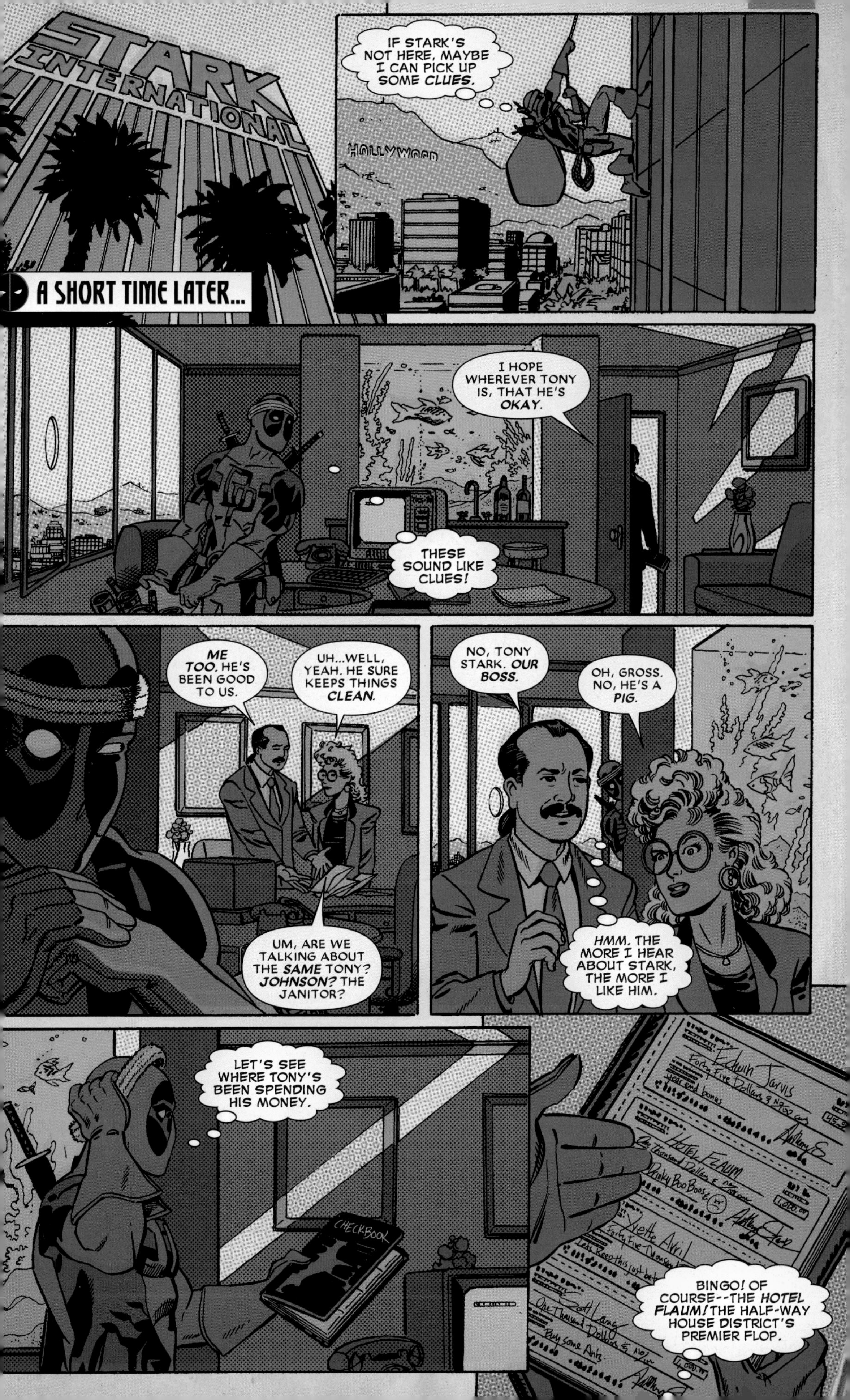
STARK INTERNATIONAL
A SHORT TIME LATER...
IF STARK'S NOT HERE, MAYBE I CAN PICK UP SOME *CLUES*.
HOLLYWOOD
I HOPE WHEREVER TONY IS, THAT HE'S *OKAY*.
THESE SOUND LIKE CLUES!
ME TOO. HE'S BEEN GOOD TO US.
UH...WELL, YEAH. HE SURE KEEPS THINGS *CLEAN*.
UM, ARE WE TALKING ABOUT THE *SAME* TONY? *JOHNSON?* THE JANITOR?
NO, TONY STARK. *OUR BOSS.*
OH, GROSS. NO, HE'S A *PIG*.
HMM. THE MORE I HEAR ABOUT STARK, THE MORE I LIKE HIM.
LET'S SEE WHERE TONY'S BEEN SPENDING HIS MONEY.
CHECKBOOK
Edwin Jarvis
year end bonus
HOTEL FLAUM
One Thousand Dollars
Yvette Avril
Scott Lang
One Thousand Dollars
Buy some Ants
BINGO! OF COURSE--THE *HOTEL FLAUM!* THE HALF-WAY HOUSE DISTRICT'S PREMIER FLOP.

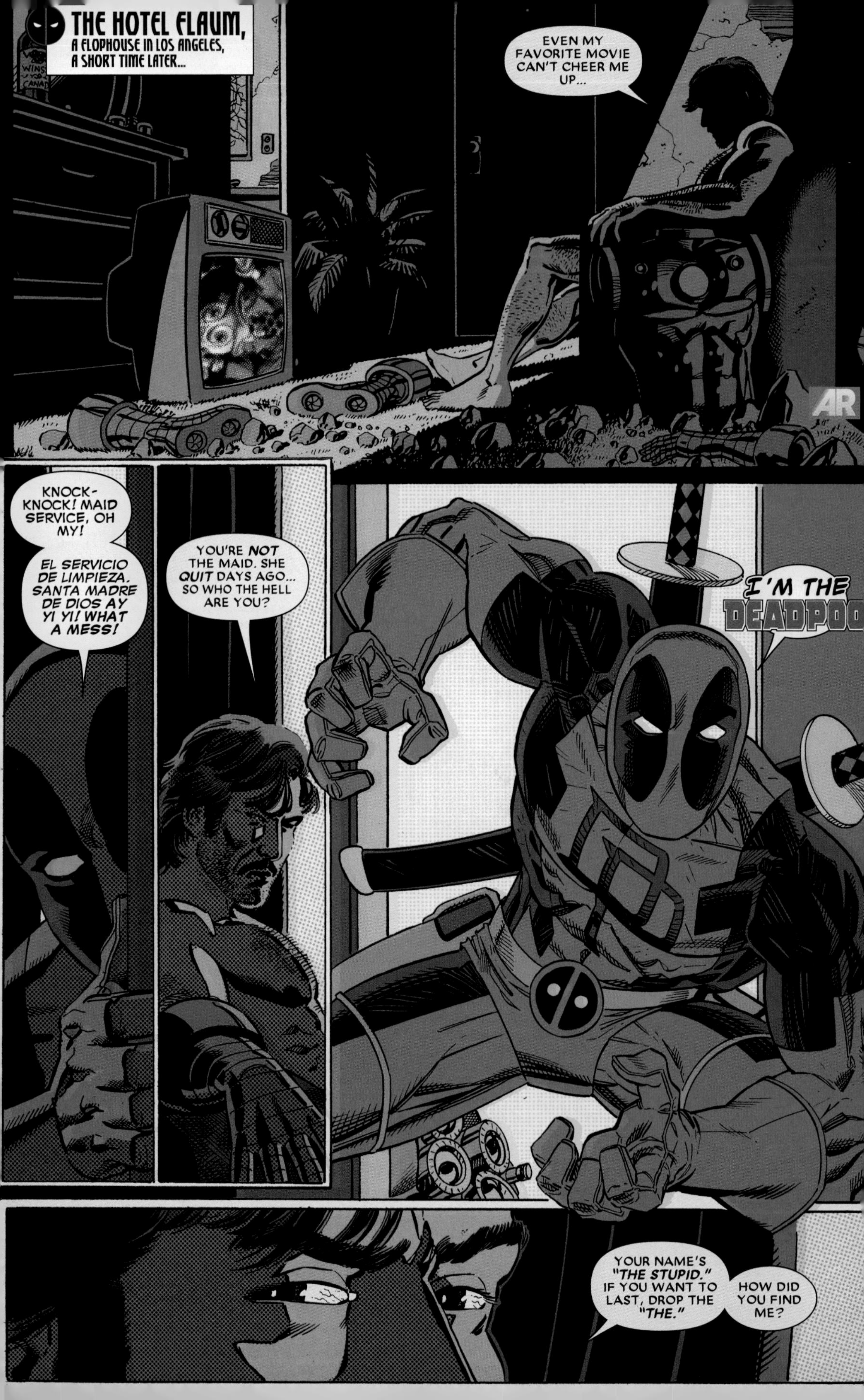
THE HOTEL FLAUM, A FLOPHOUSE IN LOS ANGELES, A SHORT TIME LATER...
EVEN MY FAVORITE MOVIE CAN'T CHEER ME UP...
KNOCK-KNOCK! MAID SERVICE, OH MY!
EL SERVICIO DE LIMPIEZA. SANTA MADRE DE DIOS AY YI YI! WHAT A MESS!
YOU'RE NOT THE MAID. SHE QUIT DAYS AGO... SO WHO THE HELL ARE YOU?
I'M THE DEADPOOL
YOUR NAME'S "THE STUPID." IF YOU WANT TO LAST, DROP THE "THE."
HOW DID YOU FIND ME?

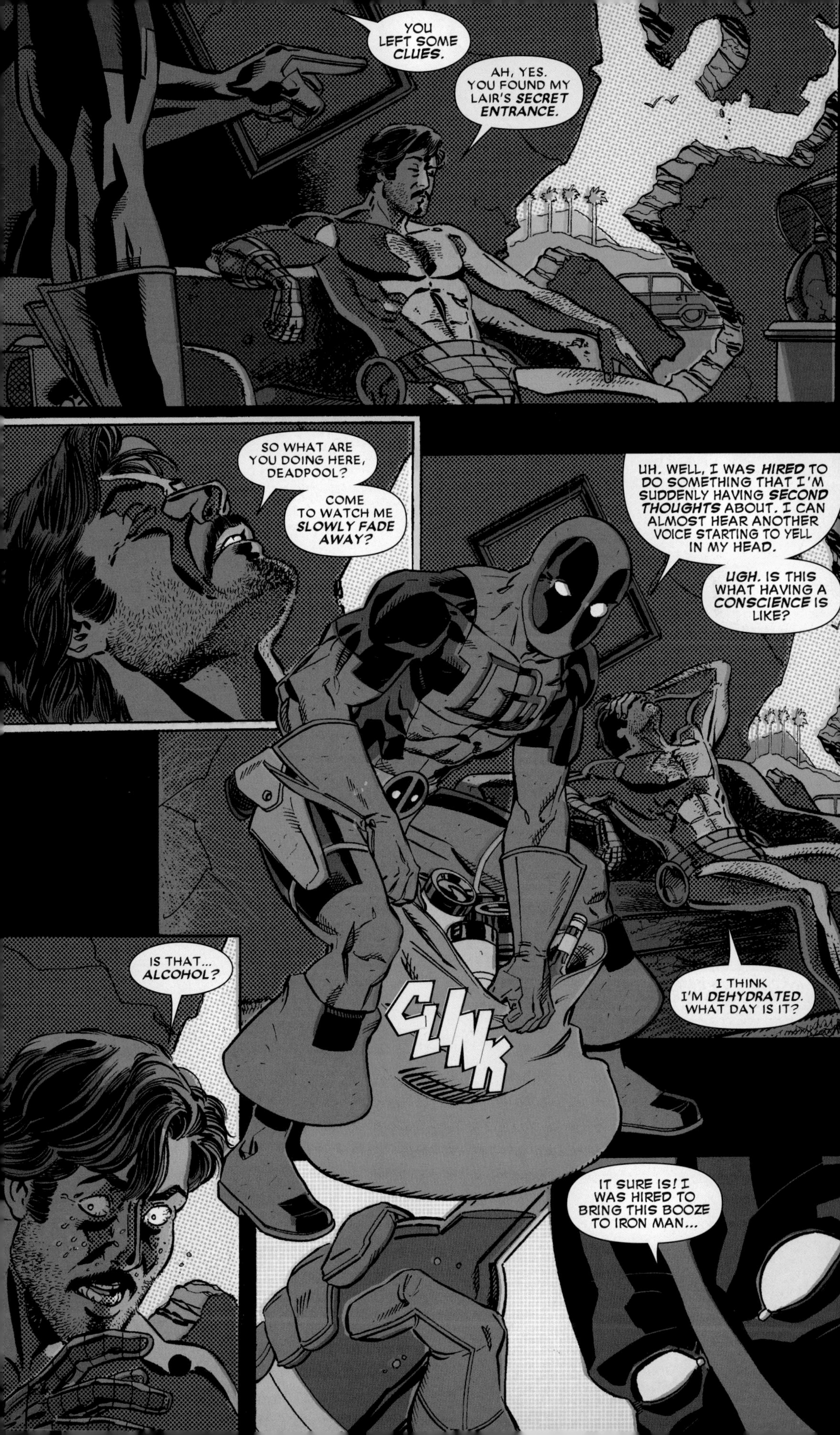
YOU LEFT SOME CLUES.
AH, YES. YOU FOUND MY LAIR'S SECRET ENTRANCE.
SO WHAT ARE YOU DOING HERE, DEADPOOL?
COME TO WATCH ME SLOWLY FADE AWAY?
UH. WELL, I WAS HIRED TO DO SOMETHING THAT I'M SUDDENLY HAVING SECOND THOUGHTS ABOUT. I CAN ALMOST HEAR ANOTHER VOICE STARTING TO YELL IN MY HEAD.
UGH. IS THIS WHAT HAVING A CONSCIENCE IS LIKE?
I THINK I'M DEHYDRATED. WHAT DAY IS IT?
IS THAT... ALCOHOL?
CLINK
IT SURE IS! I WAS HIRED TO BRING THIS BOOZE TO IRON MAN...

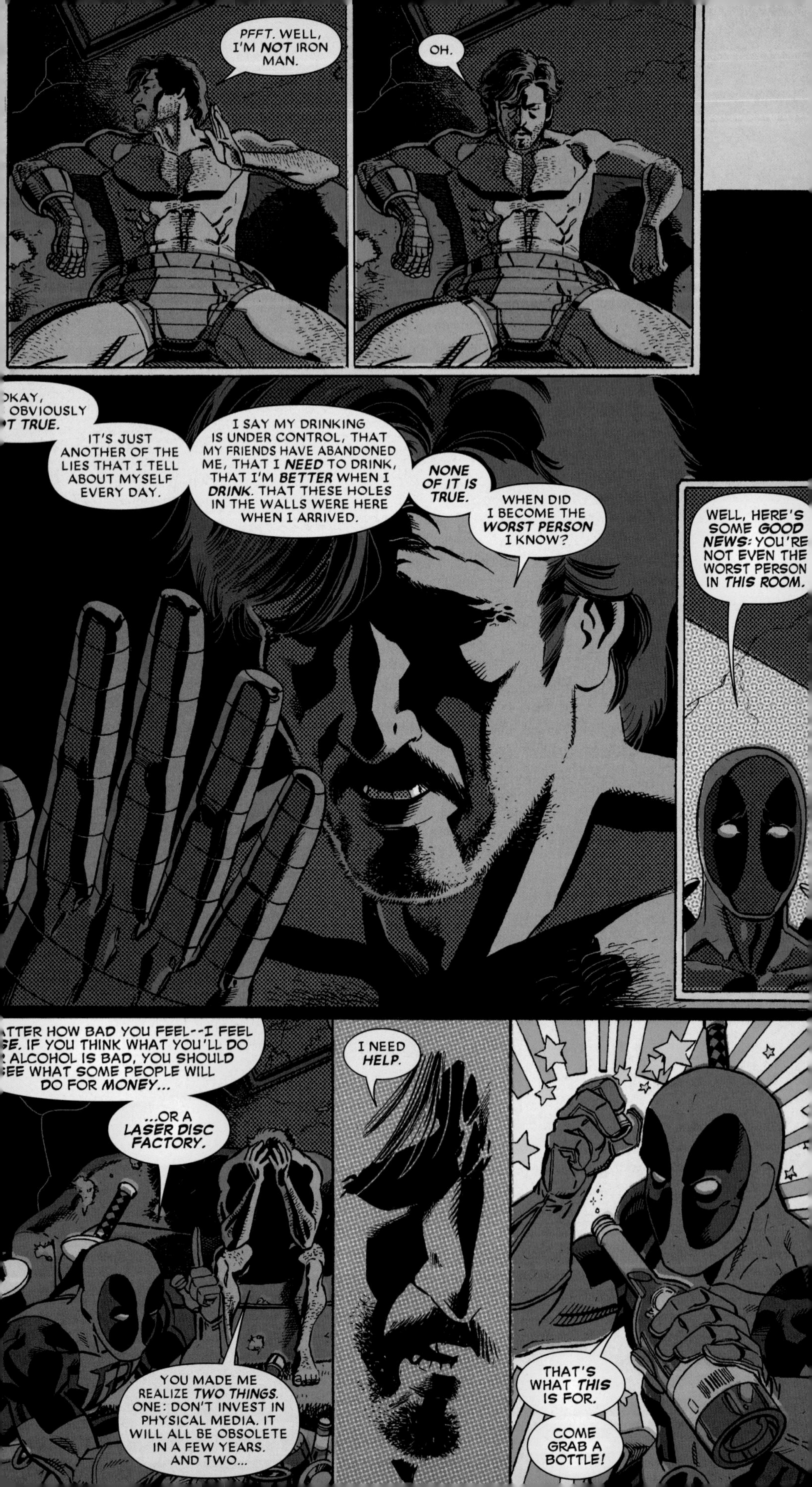
PFFT. WELL, I'M NOT IRON MAN.
OH.
OKAY, OBVIOUSLY NOT TRUE.
IT'S JUST ANOTHER OF THE LIES THAT I TELL ABOUT MYSELF EVERY DAY.
I SAY MY DRINKING IS UNDER CONTROL, THAT MY FRIENDS HAVE ABANDONED ME, THAT I NEED TO DRINK, THAT I'M BETTER WHEN I DRINK. THAT THESE HOLES IN THE WALLS WERE HERE WHEN I ARRIVED.
NONE OF IT IS TRUE.
WHEN DID I BECOME THE WORST PERSON I KNOW?
WELL, HERE'S SOME GOOD NEWS: YOU'RE NOT EVEN THE WORST PERSON IN THIS ROOM.
ATTER HOW BAD YOU FEEL--I FEEL SE. IF YOU THINK WHAT YOU'LL DO R ALCOHOL IS BAD, YOU SHOULD SEE WHAT SOME PEOPLE WILL DO FOR MONEY...
...OR A LASER DISC FACTORY.
YOU MADE ME REALIZE TWO THINGS. ONE: DON'T INVEST IN PHYSICAL MEDIA. IT WILL ALL BE OBSOLETE IN A FEW YEARS. AND TWO...
I NEED HELP.
THAT'S WHAT THIS IS FOR.
COME GRAB A BOTTLE!

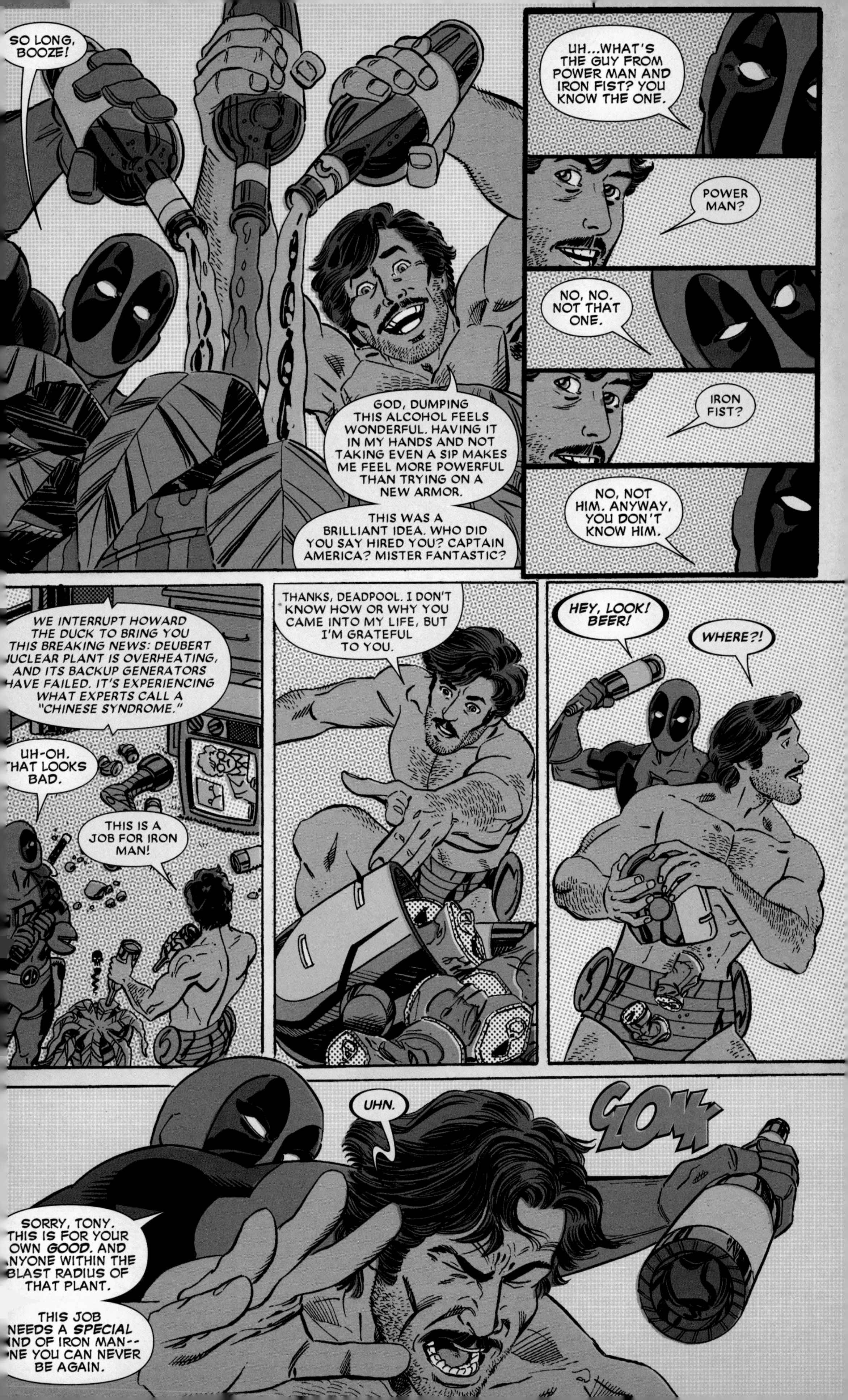
SO LONG, BOOZE!
UH...WHAT'S THE GUY FROM POWER MAN AND IRON FIST? YOU KNOW THE ONE.
POWER MAN?
NO, NO. NOT THAT ONE.
IRON FIST?
NO, NOT HIM. ANYWAY, YOU DON'T KNOW HIM.
GOD, DUMPING THIS ALCOHOL FEELS WONDERFUL. HAVING IT IN MY HANDS AND NOT TAKING EVEN A SIP MAKES ME FEEL MORE POWERFUL THAN TRYING ON A NEW ARMOR.
THIS WAS A BRILLIANT IDEA. WHO DID YOU SAY HIRED YOU? CAPTAIN AMERICA? MISTER FANTASTIC?
WE INTERRUPT HOWARD THE DUCK TO BRING YOU THIS BREAKING NEWS: DEUBERT NUCLEAR PLANT IS OVERHEATING, AND ITS BACKUP GENERATORS HAVE FAILED. IT'S EXPERIENCING WHAT EXPERTS CALL A "CHINESE SYNDROME."
UH-OH. THAT LOOKS BAD.
THIS IS A JOB FOR IRON MAN!
THANKS, DEADPOOL. I DON'T KNOW HOW OR WHY YOU CAME INTO MY LIFE, BUT I'M GRATEFUL TO YOU.
HEY, LOOK! BEER!
WHERE?!
UHN.
GONK
SORRY, TONY. THIS IS FOR YOUR OWN GOOD. AND ANYONE WITHIN THE BLAST RADIUS OF THAT PLANT.
THIS JOB NEEDS A SPECIAL KIND OF IRON MAN-- ONE YOU CAN NEVER BE AGAIN.

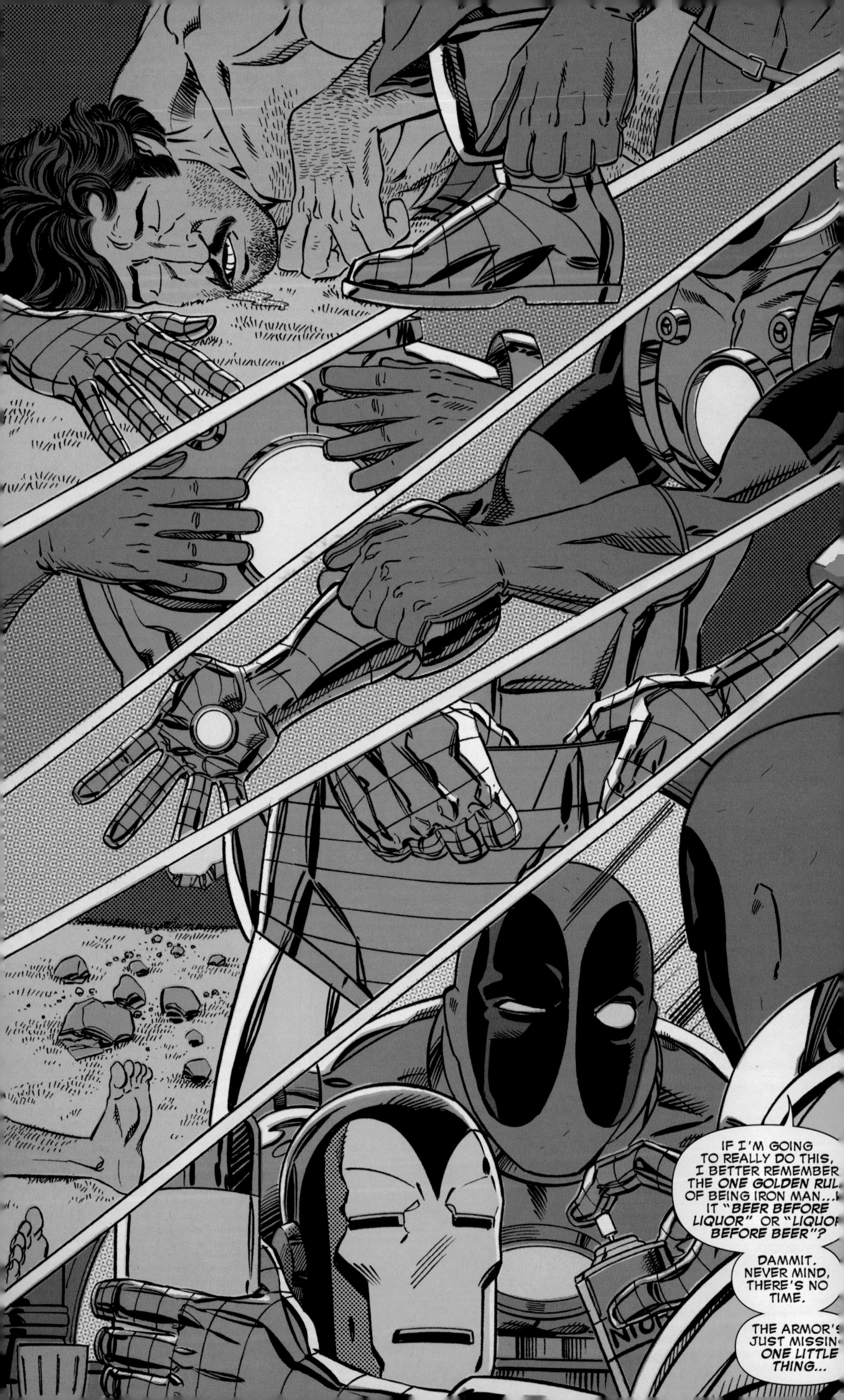
IF I'M GOING TO REALLY DO THIS, I BETTER REMEMBER THE ONE GOLDEN RUL OF BEING IRON MAN... IT "BEER BEFORE LIQUOR" OR "LIQUO BEFORE BEER"?
DAMMIT. NEVER MIND, THERE'S NO TIME.
THE ARMOR'S JUST MISSIN ONE LITTLE THING...

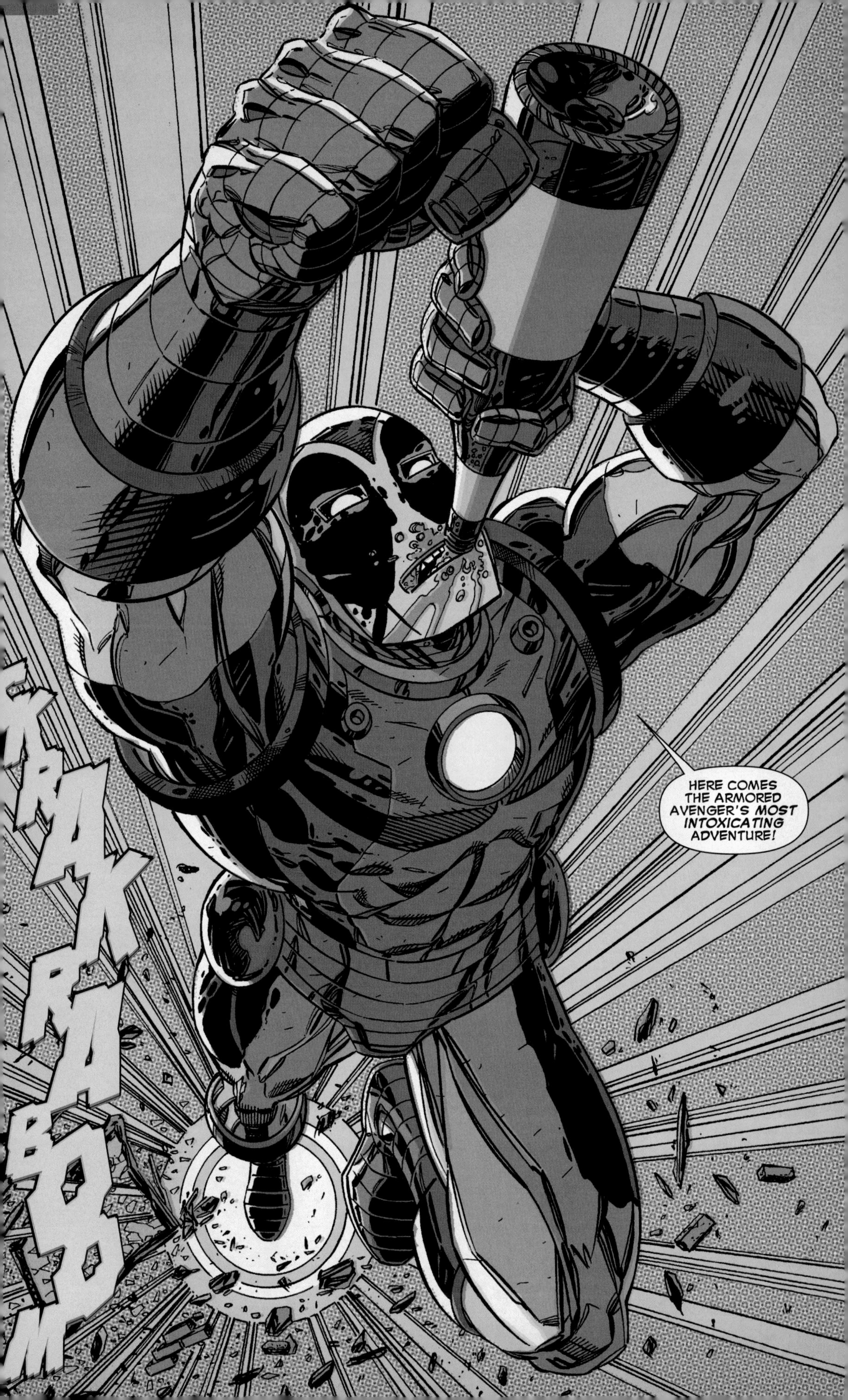
HERE COMES THE ARMORED AVENGER'S *MOST INTOXICATING* ADVENTURE!

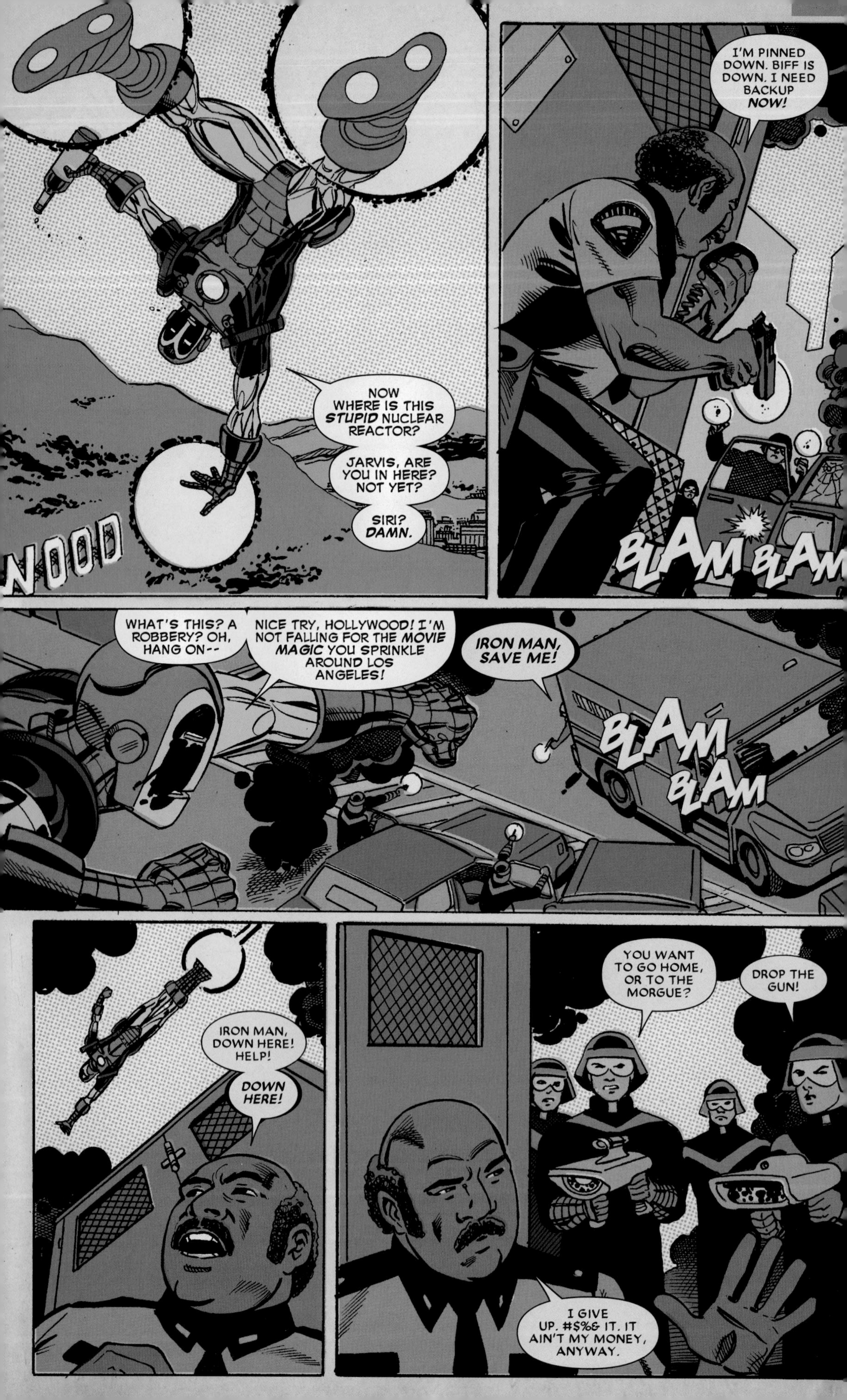

WOOD
NOW WHERE IS THIS STUPID NUCLEAR REACTOR?
JARVIS, ARE YOU IN HERE? NOT YET?
SIRI? DAMN.
I'M PINNED DOWN. BIFF IS DOWN. I NEED BACKUP NOW!
BLAM BLAM
WHAT'S THIS? A ROBBERY? OH, HANG ON--
NICE TRY, HOLLYWOOD! I'M NOT FALLING FOR THE MOVIE MAGIC YOU SPRINKLE AROUND LOS ANGELES!
IRON MAN, SAVE ME!
BLAM BLAM
IRON MAN, DOWN HERE! HELP!
DOWN HERE!
YOU WANT TO GO HOME, OR TO THE MORGUE?
DROP THE GUN!
I GIVE UP. #$%& IT. IT AIN'T MY MONEY, ANYWAY.

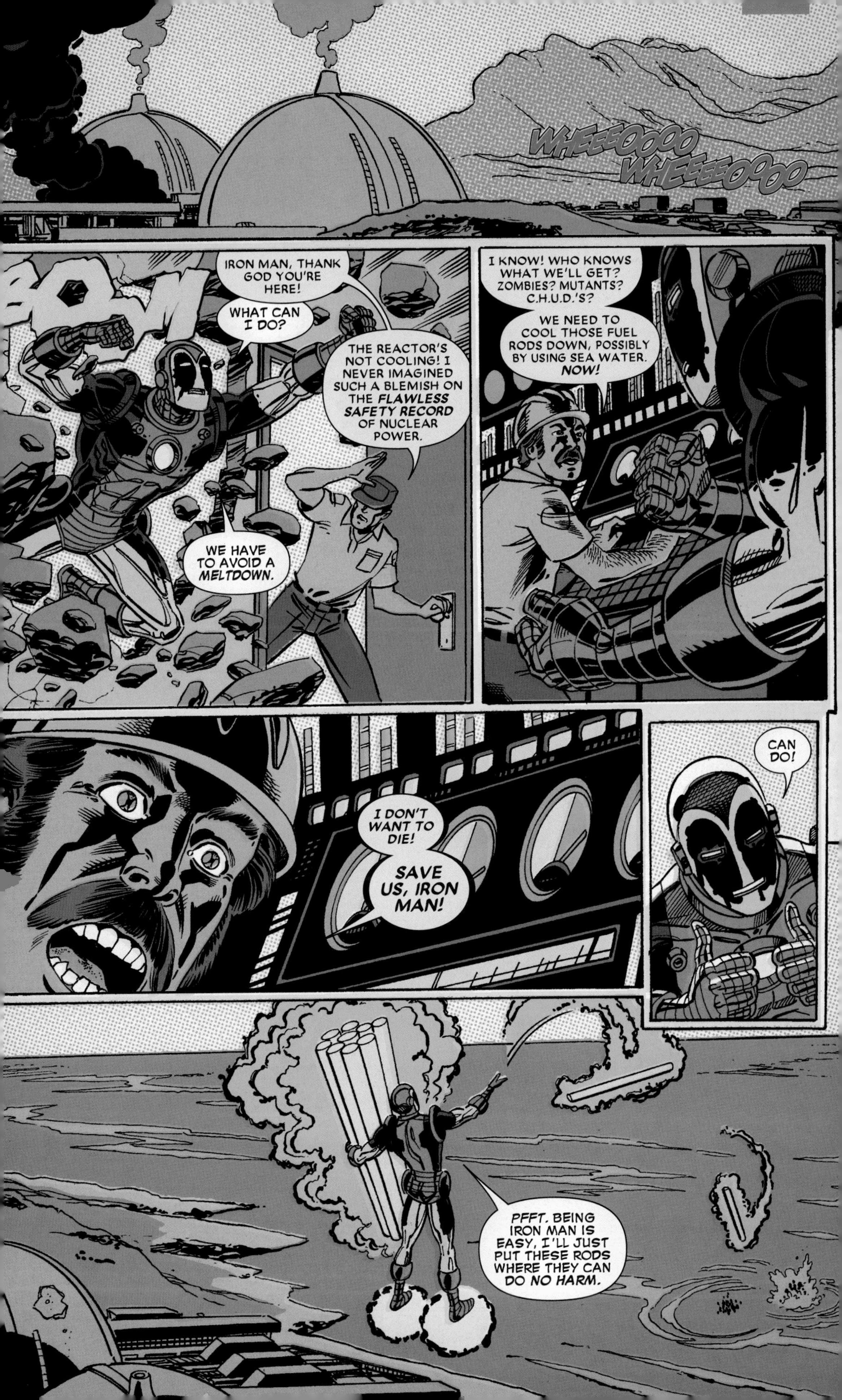
WHEEEOOOO
WHEEEEOOOO
BOOM
IRON MAN, THANK GOD YOU'RE HERE!
WHAT CAN I DO?
THE REACTOR'S NOT COOLING! I NEVER IMAGINED SUCH A BLEMISH ON THE FLAWLESS SAFETY RECORD OF NUCLEAR POWER.
WE HAVE TO AVOID A MELTDOWN.
I KNOW! WHO KNOWS WHAT WE'LL GET? ZOMBIES? MUTANTS? C.H.U.D.'S?
WE NEED TO COOL THOSE FUEL RODS DOWN, POSSIBLY BY USING SEA WATER. NOW!
I DON'T WANT TO DIE!
SAVE US, IRON MAN!
CAN DO!
PFFT. BEING IRON MAN IS EASY, I'LL JUST PUT THESE RODS WHERE THEY CAN DO NO HARM.

THE PACIFIC COAST HIGHWAY, LATER.

WE'LL BE CLEANING UP THE OCEAN FOR *YEARS* AFTER WHAT YOU DID.

OH, YOU'RE WELCOME, *MY LITTLE TONY!* AND I DIDN'T MIND SAVING THE NUKE PLANT WHILE YOU TOOK A NAP!

I GUESS I DID... *BLACK OUT* IN THAT HOTEL ROOM.

THAT'S RIGHT, YOU DID BLACK OUT! YOU SHOULD STOP DOING THAT.

AND SOON...

HOW DARE YOU, DEADPOOL! DO YOU KNOW WHAT YOU'VE DONE?!

YES, I LIVED UP TO MY END OF THE BARGAIN.

YOU HIRED ME TO MAKE SURE *IRON MAN* DRANK. AND IRON MAN *DID DRINK*-- I COULD BARELY WORK THAT CRAZY SUIT I WAS SO *BUZZED.*

IT'S TRUE WHAT THEY SAY, KIDS. ABUSING ALCOHOL IS LIKE BEING BITTEN BY A RADIOACTIVE... BAD DECISION? OKAY, THAT'S NOT THE GREATEST ANALOGY, BUT YOU GET WHAT I'M SAYING.

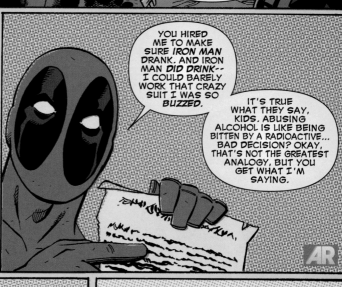

WHAT ARE YOU TALKING ABOUT? STARK IS *MORE* SOBER THAN HE *EVER* WAS.

NO, NO, WAIT! I WANTED *STARK* TO DRINK, OUR CONTRACT SHOULD SAY--

OUR CONTRACT SAID "*IRON MAN.*" *NOT* STARK. AND I DIDN'T MAKE A BAD IRON MAN--EVEN IF I WAS DRINKING ON THE JOB.

YETIS!

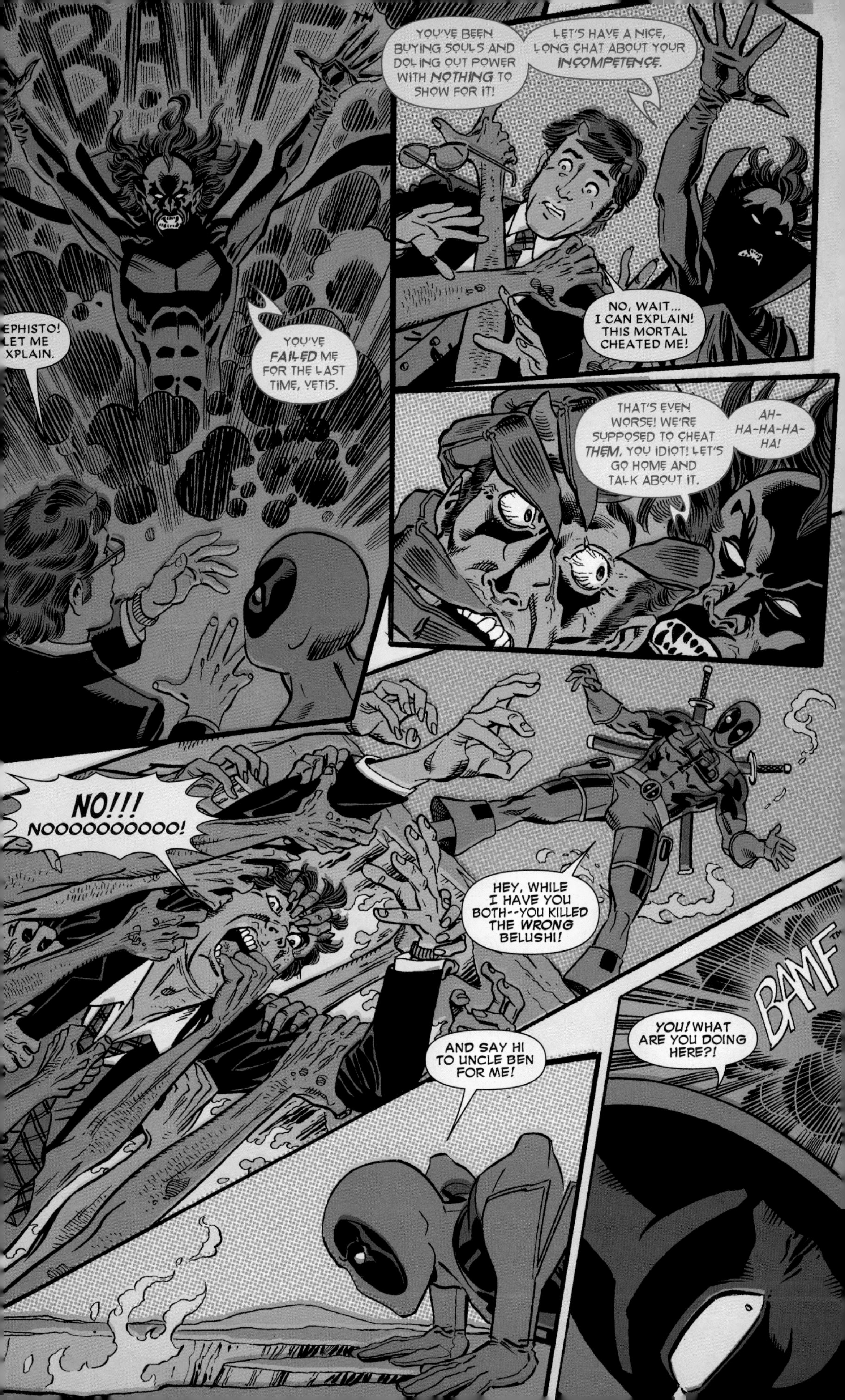
BAMF
EPHISTO! LET ME XPLAIN.
YOU'VE FAILED ME FOR THE LAST TIME, VETIS.
YOU'VE BEEN BUYING SOULS AND DOLING OUT POWER WITH NOTHING TO SHOW FOR IT!
LET'S HAVE A NICE, LONG CHAT ABOUT YOUR INCOMPETENCE.
NO, WAIT... I CAN EXPLAIN! THIS MORTAL CHEATED ME!
THAT'S EVEN WORSE! WE'RE SUPPOSED TO CHEAT THEM, YOU IDIOT! LET'S GO HOME AND TALK ABOUT IT.
AH-HA-HA-HA-HA!
NO!!! NOOOOOOOOOO!
HEY, WHILE I HAVE YOU BOTH--YOU KILLED THE WRONG BELUSHI!
AND SAY HI TO UNCLE BEN FOR ME!
BAMF
YOU! WHAT ARE YOU DOING HERE?!

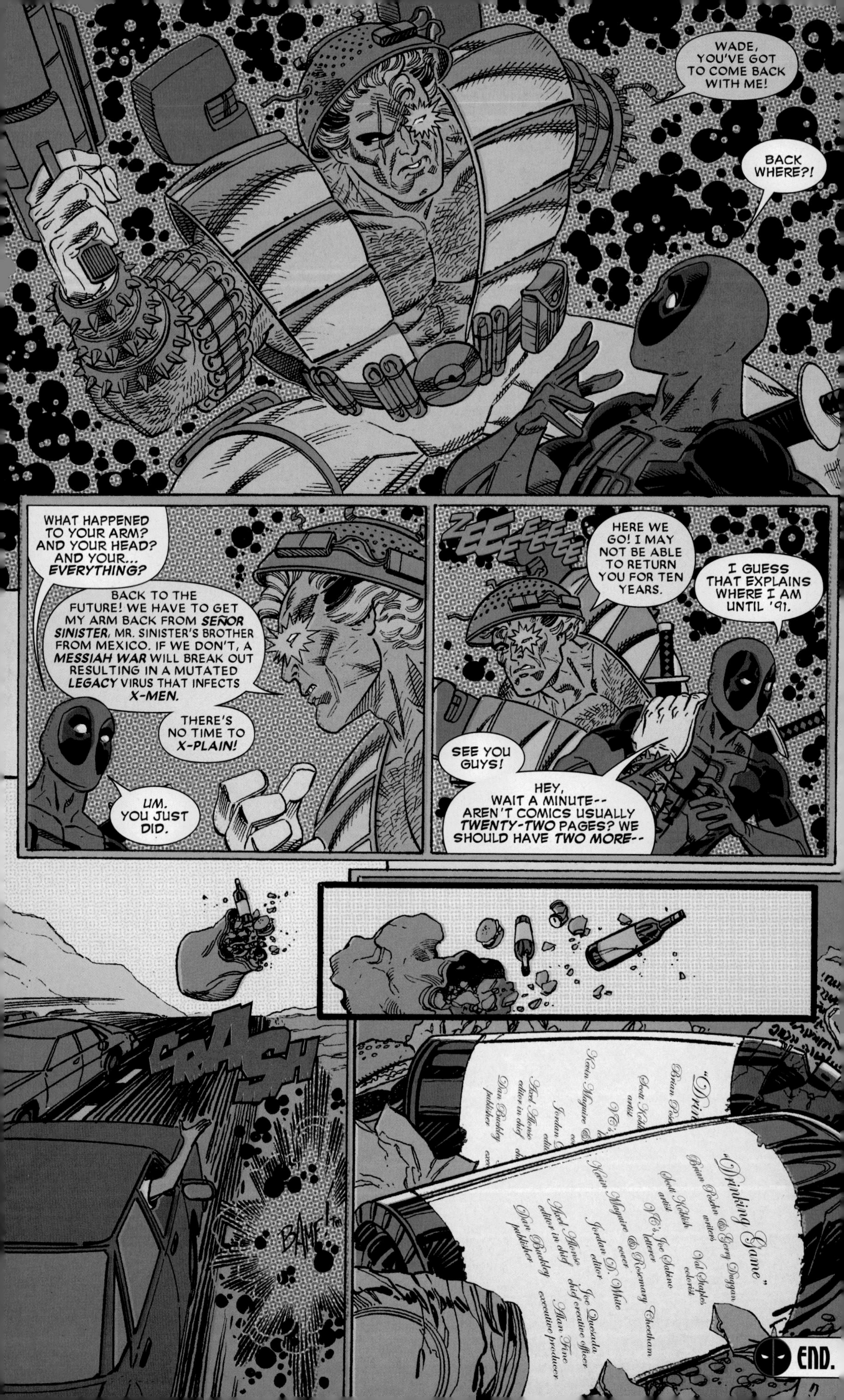
WADE, YOU'VE GOT TO COME BACK WITH ME!
BACK WHERE?!
WHAT HAPPENED TO YOUR ARM? AND YOUR HEAD? AND YOUR... EVERYTHING?
BACK TO THE FUTURE! WE HAVE TO GET MY ARM BACK FROM SEÑOR SINISTER, MR. SINISTER'S BROTHER FROM MEXICO. IF WE DON'T, A MESSIAH WAR WILL BREAK OUT RESULTING IN A MUTATED LEGACY VIRUS THAT INFECTS X-MEN.
THERE'S NO TIME TO X-PLAIN!
UM. YOU JUST DID.
ZEEEEEEEEE
HERE WE GO! I MAY NOT BE ABLE TO RETURN YOU FOR TEN YEARS.
I GUESS THAT EXPLAINS WHERE I AM UNTIL '91.
SEE YOU GUYS!
HEY, WAIT A MINUTE-- AREN'T COMICS USUALLY TWENTY-TWO PAGES? WE SHOULD HAVE TWO MORE--
CRASH
BAM!
"Drinking Game"
Brian Posehn & Gerry Duggan writers
Scott Koblish artist
Val Staples colorist
VC's Joe Sabino letterer
Kevin Maguire & Rosemary Cheetham cover
Jordan D. White editor
Axel Alonso editor in chief
Joe Quesada chief creative officer
Dan Buckley publisher
Alan Fine executive producer
END.

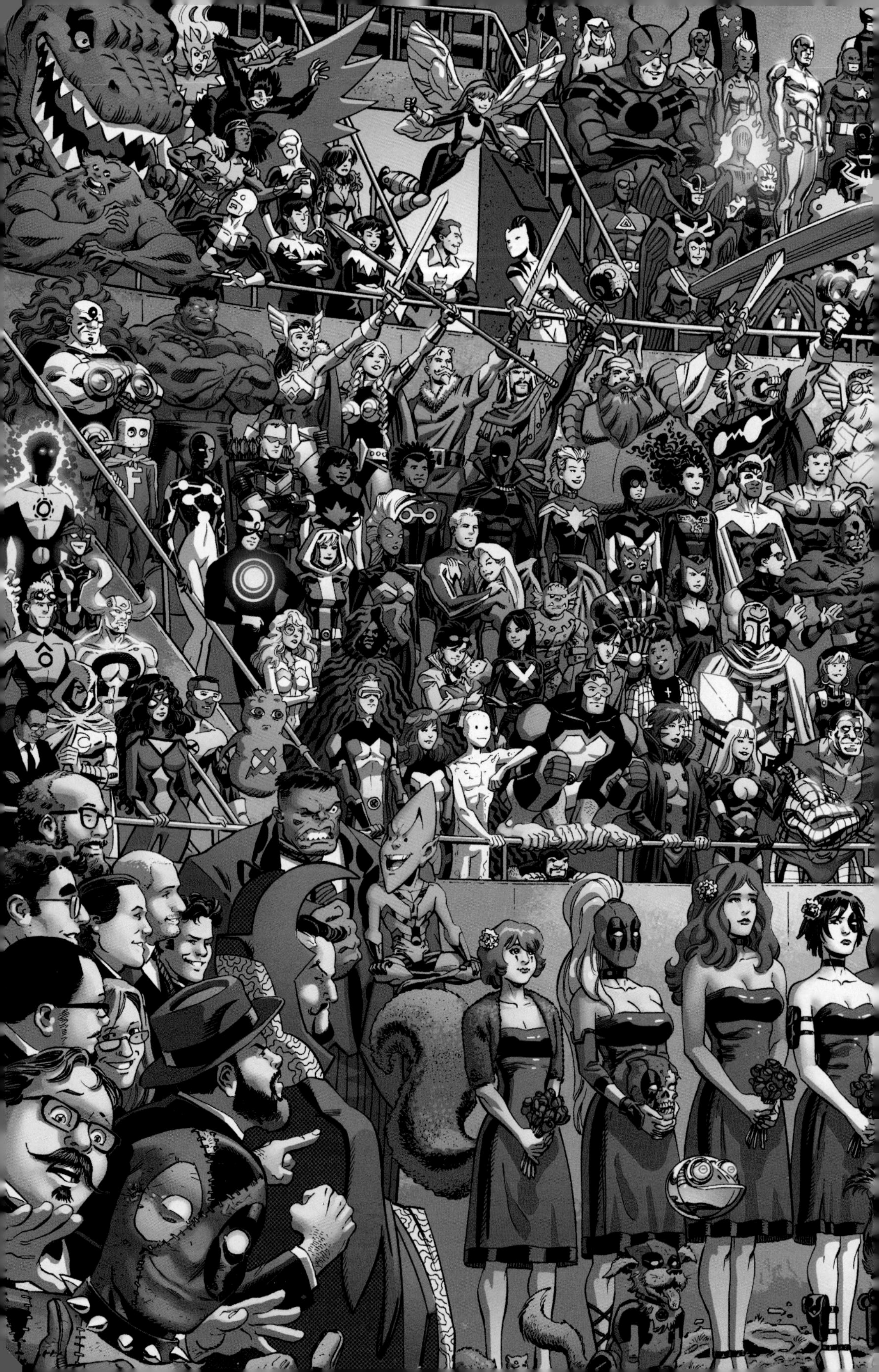

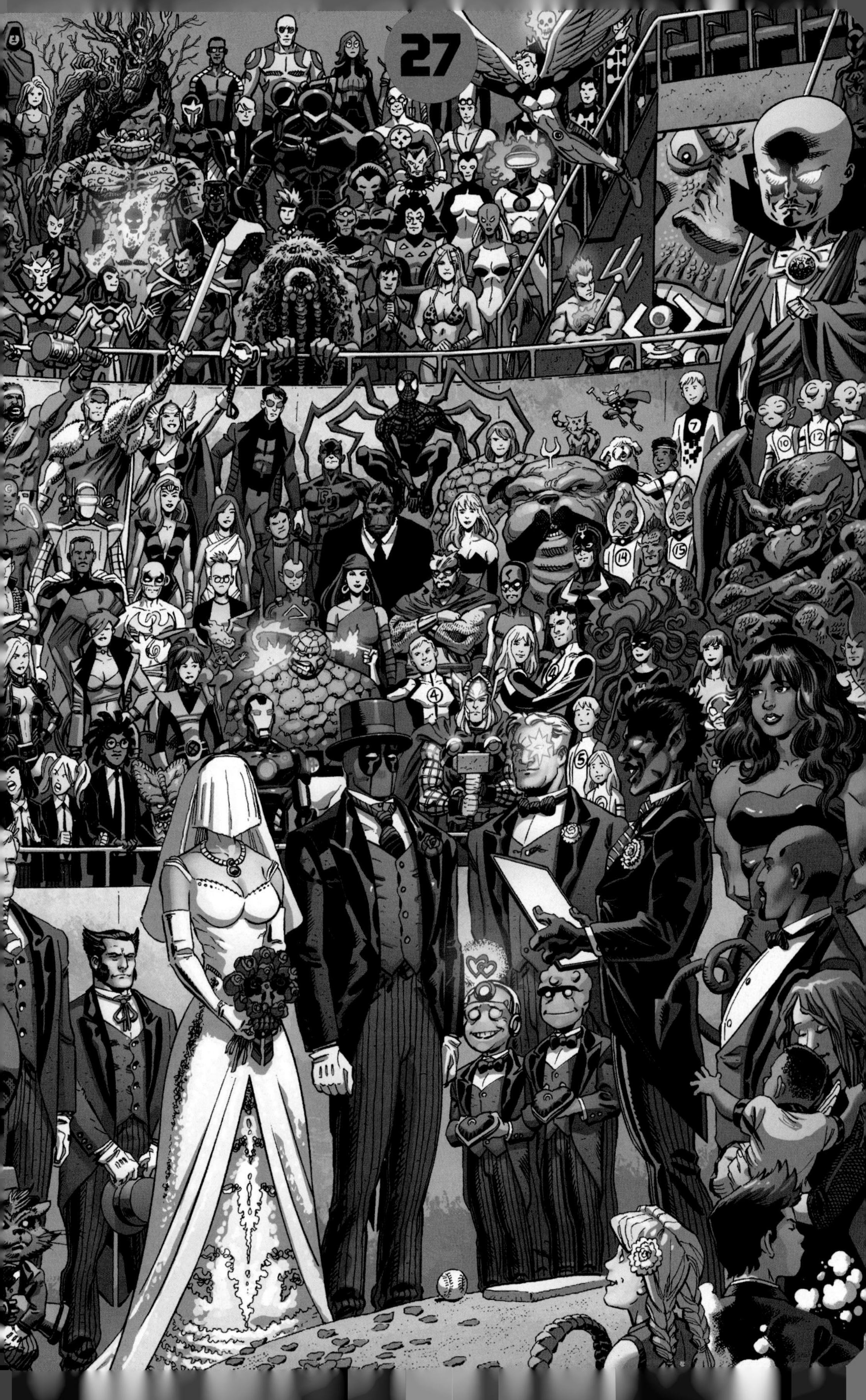
27

WELCOME TO Fabulous LAS VEGAS NEVADA

The Desert Wind

Tonight:
FRANK SINA
GALLAGH

I REMEMBER IT... LIKE IT WAS THIRTY YEARS AGO.

LAS VEGAS...THE WINDY CITY...PEARL OF THE ORIENT, THE TWIN CITIES...

EDITOR'S NOTE: THIS STORY WAS DRAWN FOR DEADPOOL ANNUAL #17 IN 1982, BUT WAS SHELVED WHEN THE EDITOR SAW THE ART, DEEMING THE ALIEN DESIGNS "INAPPROPRIATE." WE PRESENT THE STORY NOW IN CENSORED FORM. —JORDAN

YEAH, IT'S HAPPENED BEFORE...MAYBE A BUNCH OF TIMES. THIS TIME WAS DIFFERENT, BECAUSE IT WAS HER...

I KNEW HER FROM BEFORE...BUT I DON'T THINK SHE REALLY LIKED ME. MAYBE EVER.

WHOA! THAT IS ONE UGLY--

MYSELF AND VARIOUS AVENGERS TYPES WERE ASKED TO TAKE CARE OF THESE WEIRD-LOOKING THINGS THAT WERE ATTACHING TO PEOPLE'S FACES OUT IN THE DESERT.

HOPE THIS WORKS.

MMMMMFFFHHHH!!!

CENSORED

CENSORED

ACTUALLY, WHO AM I TALKING TO...I JUST HAPPENED TO BE IN THE DESERT GETTING RID OF SOMETHING...DON'T WORRY ABOUT IT. NOT THE POINT OF THE STORY.

YOU'RE CRAZY. YOU COULD'VE CUT MY FACE OFF!!!

COULDA, SHOULDA, WOULDA... YOU'RE WELCOME.

NOW, ON TO--

CENSORED

CENSORED

--UH-OH.

YOU NEED SOME HELP, HANDSOME?

WHO, ME?

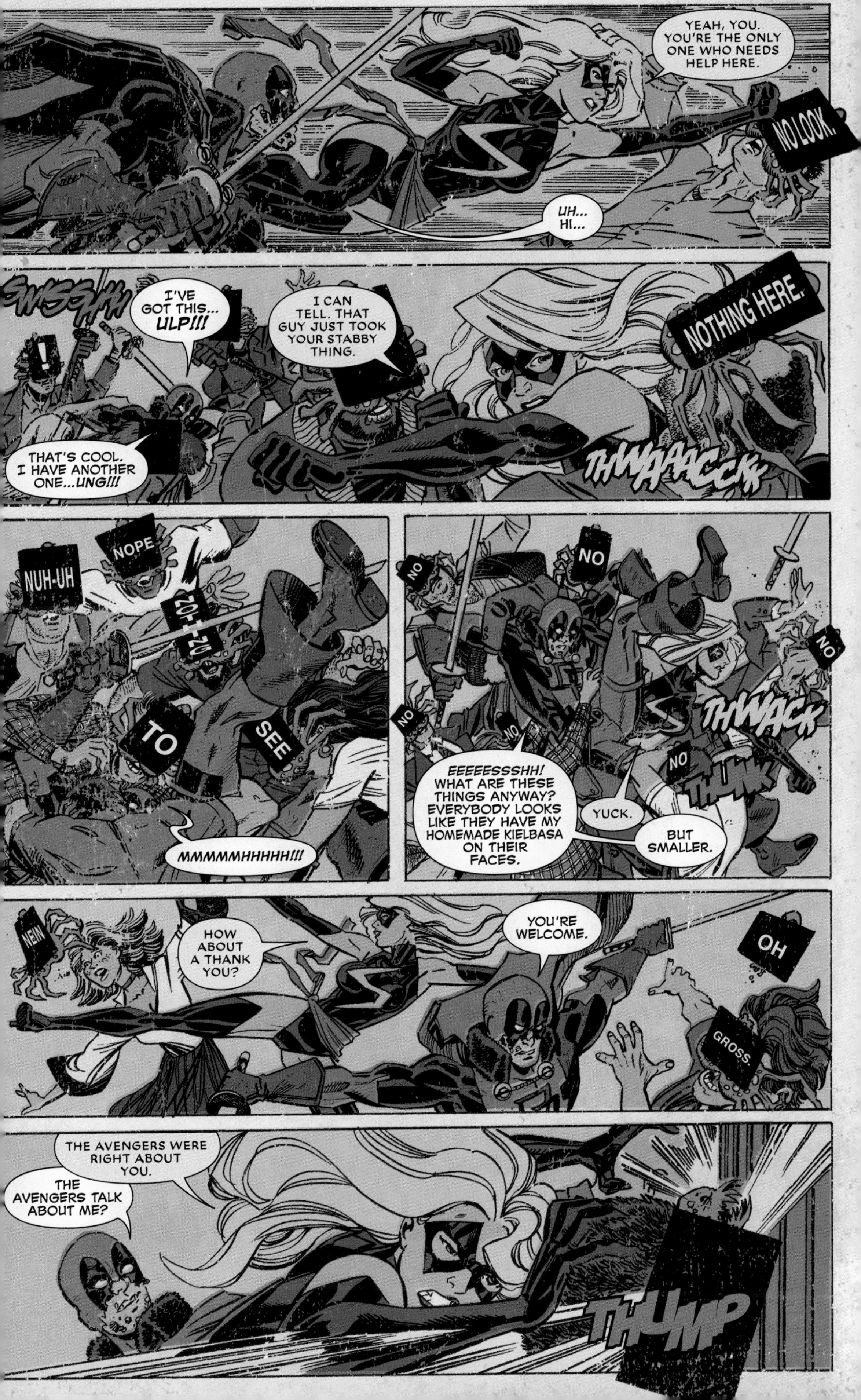

YEAH, YOU. YOU'RE THE ONLY ONE WHO NEEDS HELP HERE.
NO LOOK.
UH... HI...
SWISSHH
I'VE GOT THIS... ULP!!!
!
I CAN TELL. THAT GUY JUST TOOK YOUR STABBY THING.
NOTHING HERE.
THAT'S COOL. I HAVE ANOTHER ONE...UNG!!!
THWAAACCKK
NUH-UH
NOPE
TO
SEE
MMMMMHHHHH!!!
NO
NO
NO
NO
NO
THWACK
NO
THUNK
EEEEESSSHH! WHAT ARE THESE THINGS ANYWAY? EVERYBODY LOOKS LIKE THEY HAVE MY HOMEMADE KIELBASA ON THEIR FACES.
YUCK.
BUT SMALLER.
NEIN
HOW ABOUT A THANK YOU?
YOU'RE WELCOME.
OH
GROSS.
THE AVENGERS WERE RIGHT ABOUT YOU.
THE AVENGERS TALK ABOUT ME?
THUMP

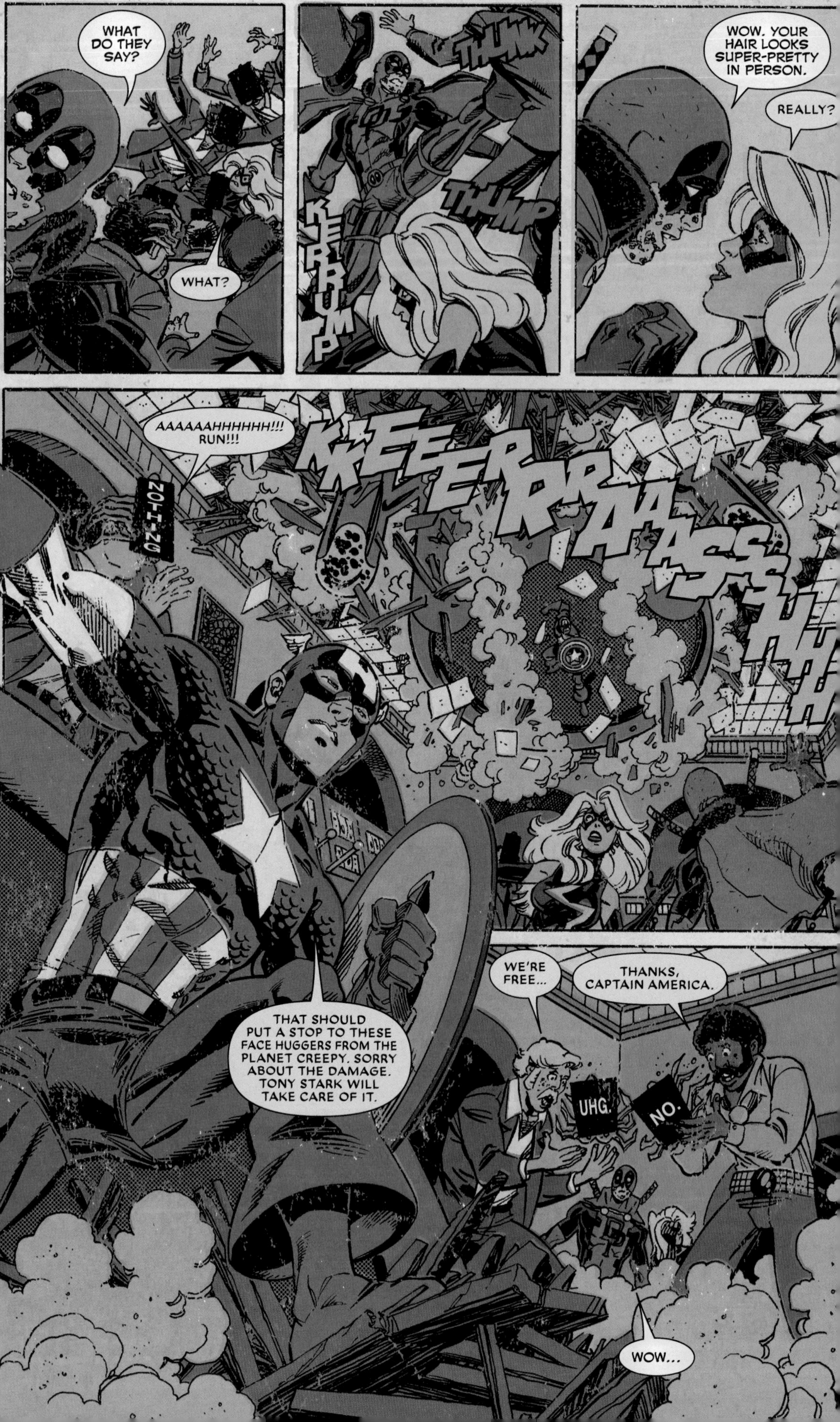
WHAT DO THEY SAY?
WHAT?
THUNK
THUMP
KERRUMP
WOW. YOUR HAIR LOOKS SUPER-PRETTY IN PERSON.
REALLY?
AAAAAAHHHHHH!!! RUN!!!
NOTHING
KKEERRAASSHH
THAT SHOULD PUT A STOP TO THESE FACE HUGGERS FROM THE PLANET CREEPY. SORRY ABOUT THE DAMAGE. TONY STARK WILL TAKE CARE OF IT.
WE'RE FREE...
THANKS, CAPTAIN AMERICA.
UHG.
NO.
WOW...

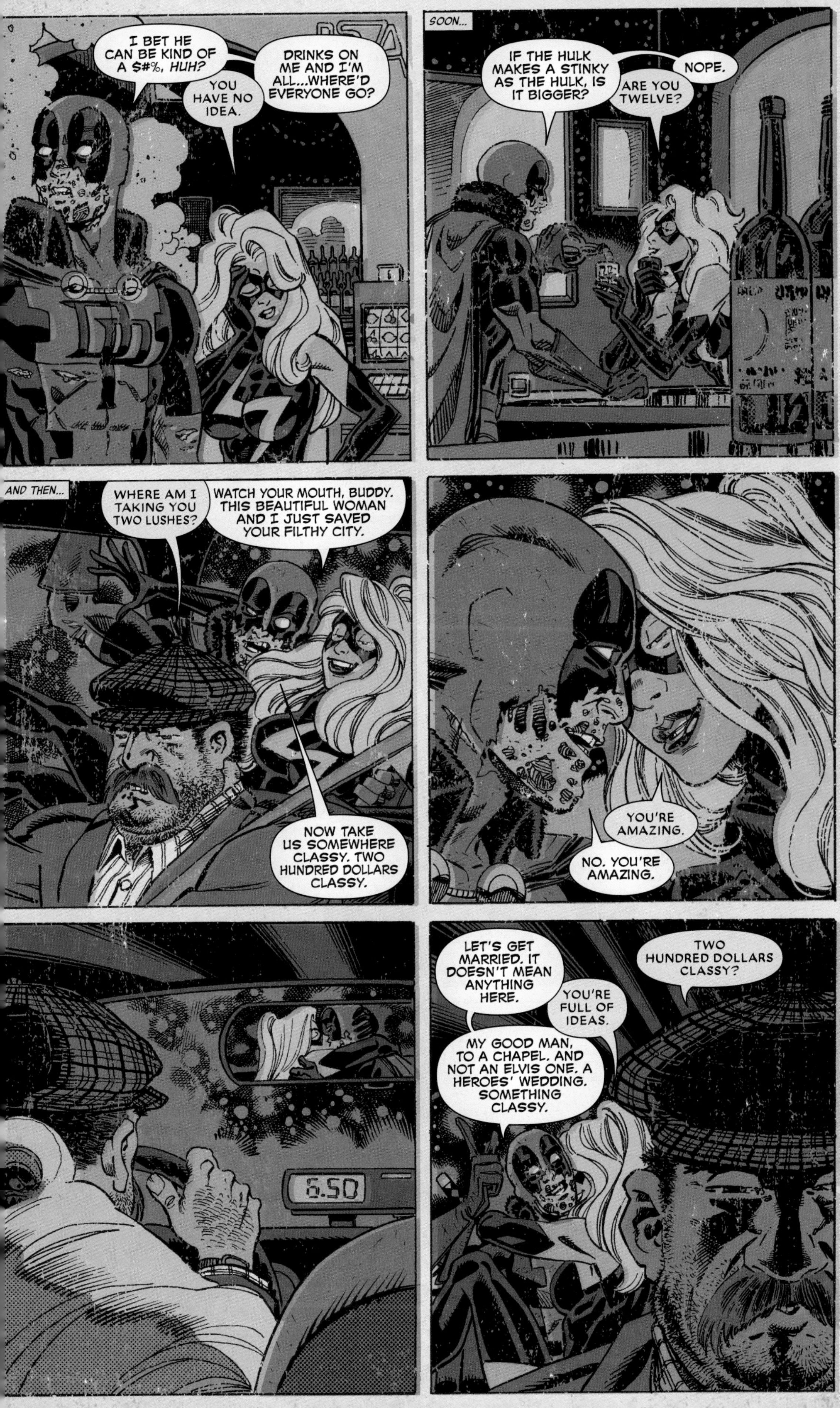
I BET HE CAN BE KIND OF A $#%, *HUH?*
YOU HAVE NO IDEA.
DRINKS ON ME AND I'M ALL...WHERE'D EVERYONE GO?
SOON...
IF THE HULK MAKES A STINKY AS THE HULK, IS IT BIGGER?
NOPE.
ARE YOU TWELVE?
AND THEN...
WHERE AM I TAKING YOU TWO LUSHES?
WATCH YOUR MOUTH, BUDDY. THIS BEAUTIFUL WOMAN AND I JUST SAVED YOUR FILTHY CITY.
NOW TAKE US SOMEWHERE CLASSY. TWO HUNDRED DOLLARS CLASSY.
YOU'RE AMAZING.
NO. YOU'RE AMAZING.
6.50
LET'S GET MARRIED. IT DOESN'T MEAN ANYTHING HERE.
YOU'RE FULL OF IDEAS.
MY GOOD MAN, TO A CHAPEL. AND NOT AN ELVIS ONE. A HEROES' WEDDING. SOMETHING CLASSY.
TWO HUNDRED DOLLARS CLASSY?

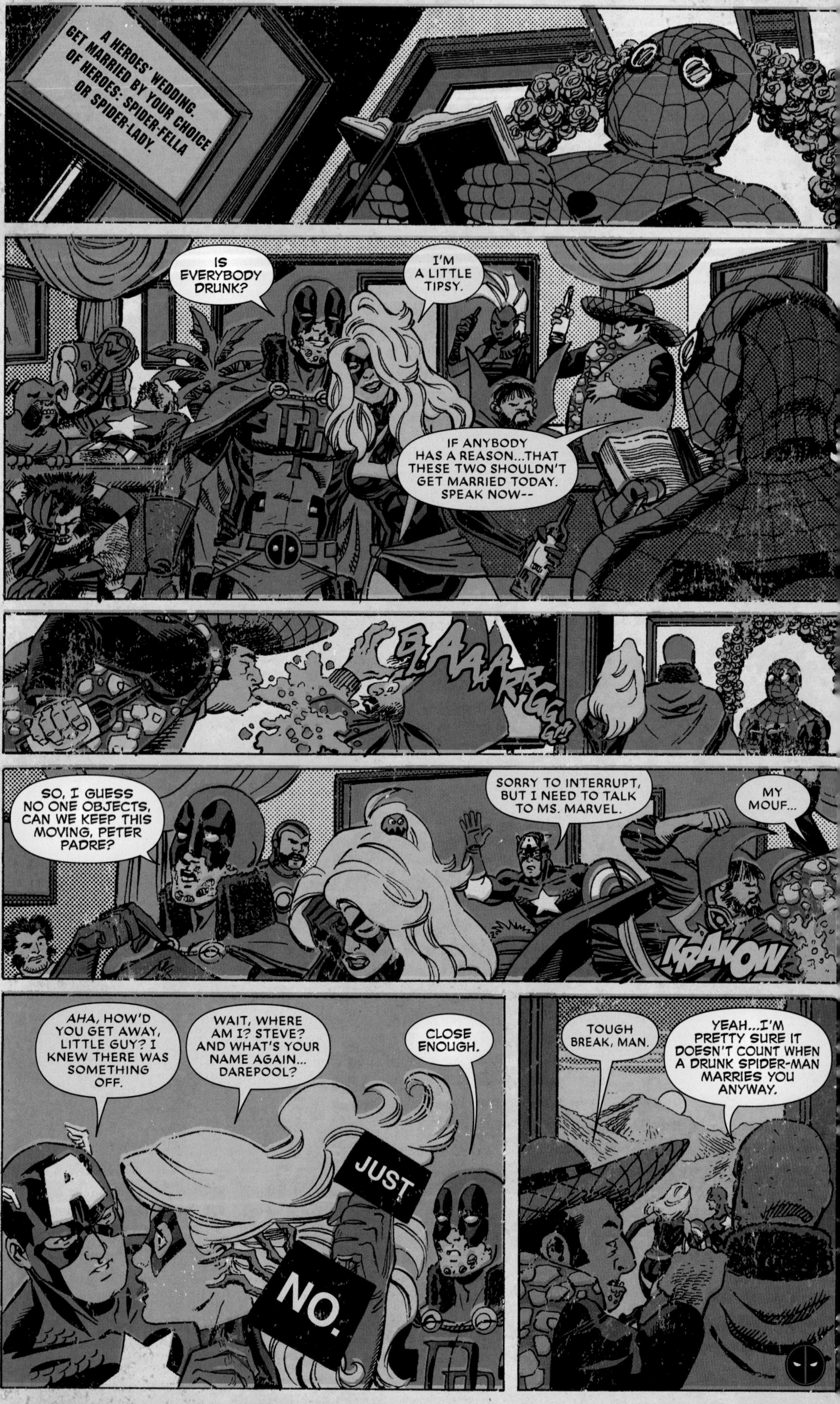
A HEROES' WEDDING. GET MARRIED BY YOUR CHOICE OF HEROES: SPIDER-FELLA OR SPIDER-LADY.
IS EVERYBODY DRUNK?
I'M A LITTLE TIPSY.
IF ANYBODY HAS A REASON...THAT THESE TWO SHOULDN'T GET MARRIED TODAY. SPEAK NOW--
BLAAARRGG!!
SO, I GUESS NO ONE OBJECTS, CAN WE KEEP THIS MOVING, PETER PADRE?
SORRY TO INTERRUPT, BUT I NEED TO TALK TO MS. MARVEL.
MY MOUF...
KRAKOW
AHA, HOW'D YOU GET AWAY, LITTLE GUY? I KNEW THERE WAS SOMETHING OFF.
WAIT, WHERE AM I? STEVE? AND WHAT'S YOUR NAME AGAIN... DAREPOOL?
CLOSE ENOUGH.
JUST
NO.
TOUGH BREAK, MAN.
YEAH...I'M PRETTY SURE IT DOESN'T COUNT WHEN A DRUNK SPIDER-MAN MARRIES YOU ANYWAY.

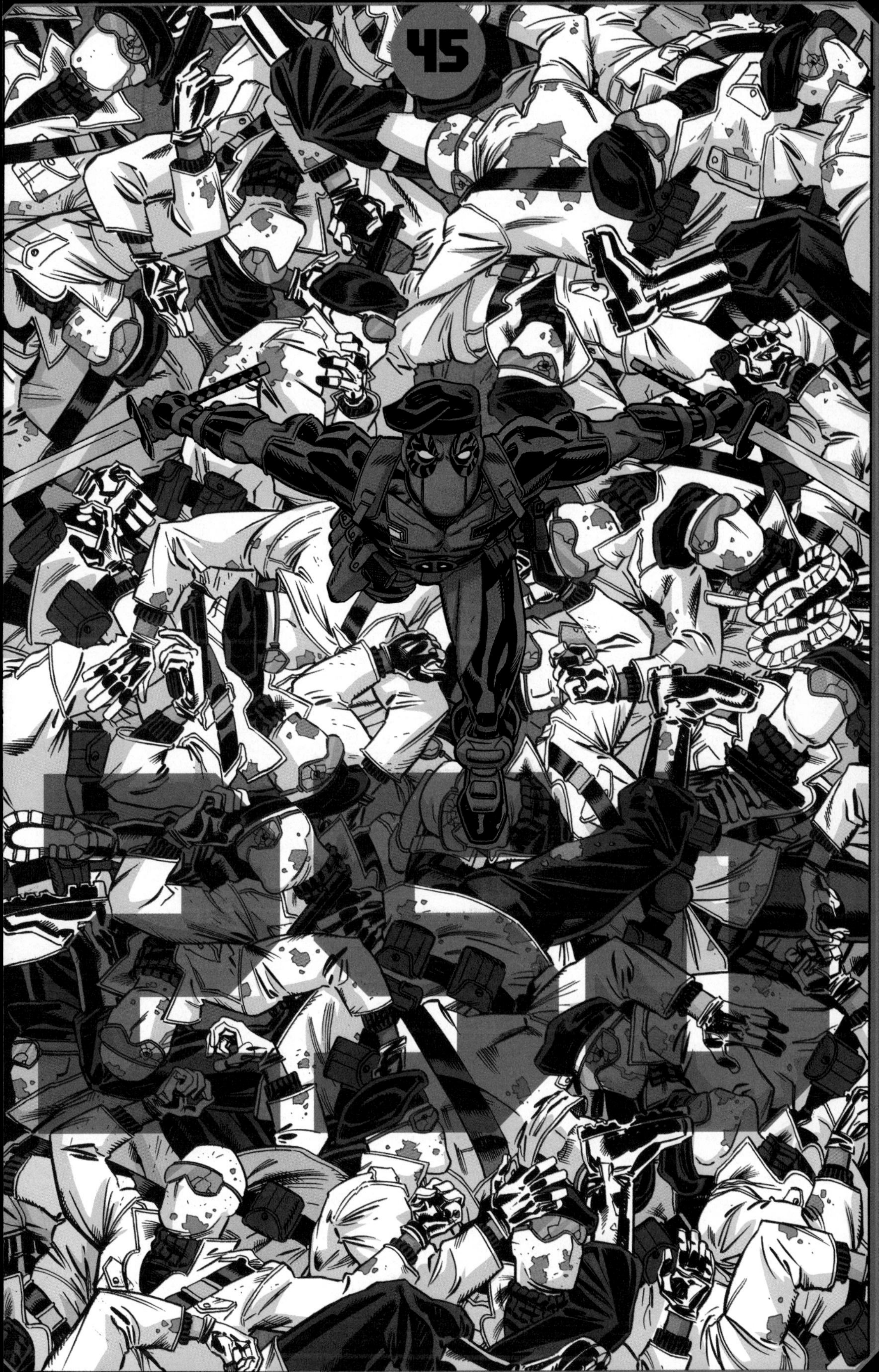
45

DEADPOOL ROASTS THE MARVEL UNIVERSE:
AN INFINITY GAUNTLET TIE-IN

Possibly the world's most skilled mercenary, definitely the world's most annoying, Wade Wilson was chosen for a top-secret government program that gave him a healing factor allowing him to heal from any wound. Now, Wade makes his way as a gun for hire, shooting his prey's faces off while talking his friends' ears off. Call him the Merc with the Mouth...call him the Regeneratin' Degenerate... call him...**DEADPOOL**.

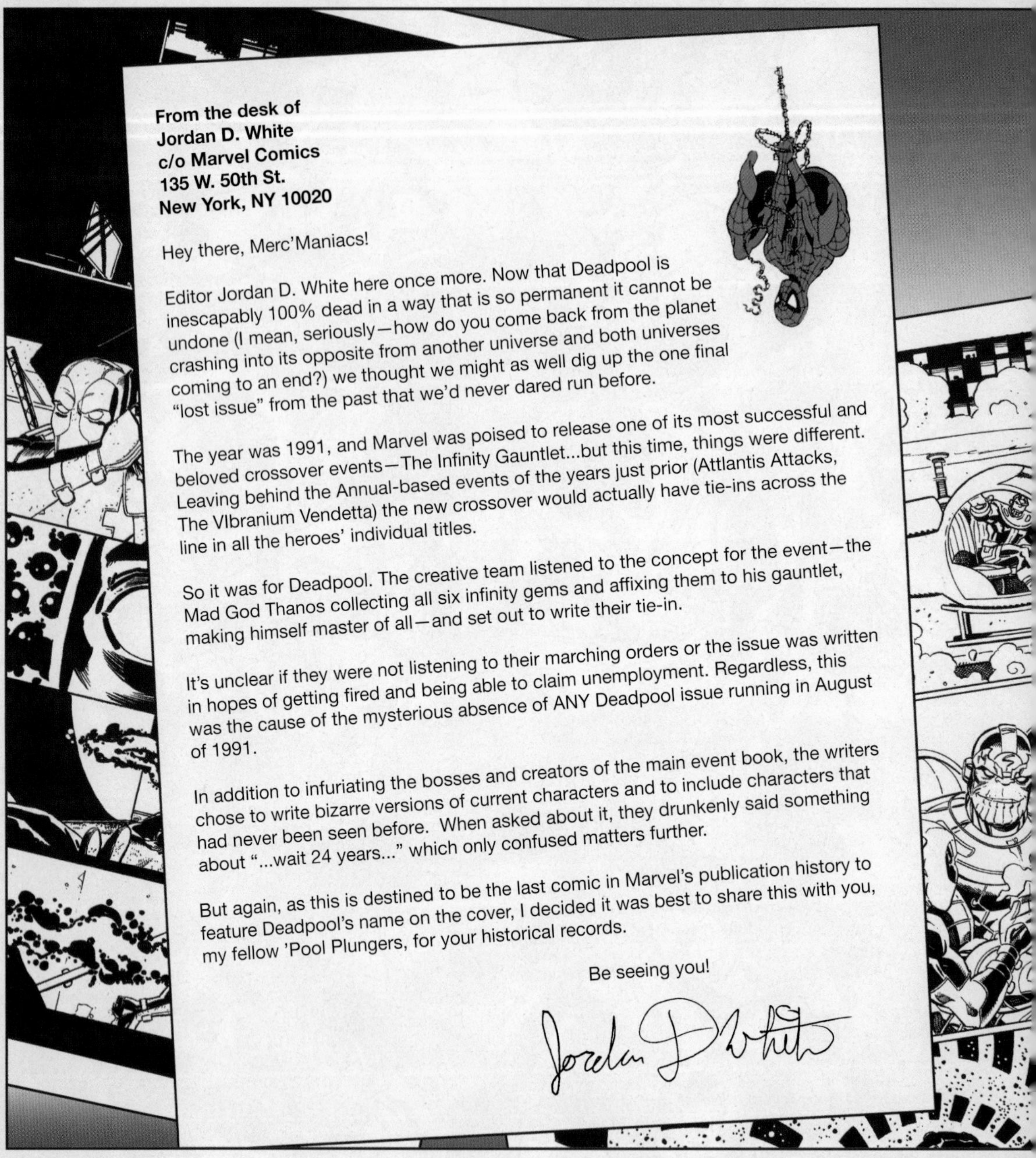

From the desk of
Jordan D. White
c/o Marvel Comics
135 W. 50th St.
New York, NY 10020

Hey there, Merc'Maniacs!

Editor Jordan D. White here once more. Now that Deadpool is inescapably 100% dead in a way that is so permanent it cannot be undone (I mean, seriously—how do you come back from the planet crashing into its opposite from another universe and both universes coming to an end?) we thought we might as well dig up the one final "lost issue" from the past that we'd never dared run before.

The year was 1991, and Marvel was poised to release one of its most successful and beloved crossover events—The Infinity Gauntlet...but this time, things were different. Leaving behind the Annual-based events of the years just prior (Atlantis Attacks, The VIbranium Vendetta) the new crossover would actually have tie-ins across the line in all the heroes' individual titles.

So it was for Deadpool. The creative team listened to the concept for the event—the Mad God Thanos collecting all six infinity gems and affixing them to his gauntlet, making himself master of all—and set out to write their tie-in.

It's unclear if they were not listening to their marching orders or the issue was written in hopes of getting fired and being able to claim unemployment. Regardless, this was the cause of the mysterious absence of ANY Deadpool issue running in August of 1991.

In addition to infuriating the bosses and creators of the main event book, the writers chose to write bizarre versions of current characters and to include characters that had never been seen before. When asked about it, they drunkenly said something about "...wait 24 years..." which only confused matters further.

But again, as this is destined to be the last comic in Marvel's publication history to feature Deadpool's name on the cover, I decided it was best to share this with you, my fellow 'Pool Plungers, for your historical records.

Be seeing you!

Jordan D White

DEADPOOL ROASTS THE MARVEL UNIVERSE

AN INFINITY GAUNTLET TIE-IN

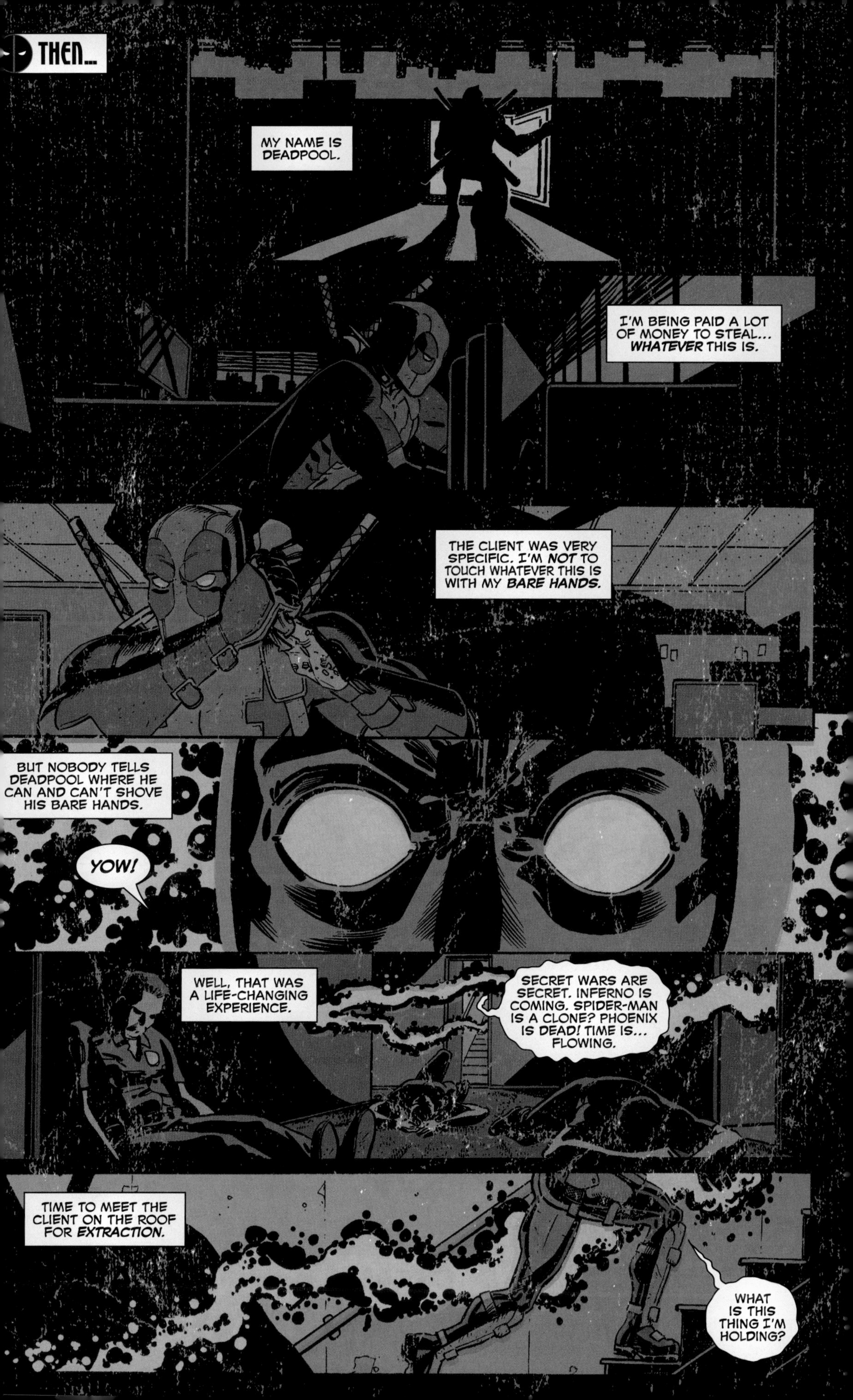
THEN...
MY NAME IS DEADPOOL.
I'M BEING PAID A LOT OF MONEY TO STEAL... WHATEVER THIS IS.
THE CLIENT WAS VERY SPECIFIC. I'M NOT TO TOUCH WHATEVER THIS IS WITH MY BARE HANDS.
BUT NOBODY TELLS DEADPOOL WHERE HE CAN AND CAN'T SHOVE HIS BARE HANDS.
YOW!
WELL, THAT WAS A LIFE-CHANGING EXPERIENCE.
SECRET WARS ARE SECRET. INFERNO IS COMING. SPIDER-MAN IS A CLONE? PHOENIX IS DEAD! TIME IS... FLOWING.
TIME TO MEET THE CLIENT ON THE ROOF FOR EXTRACTION.
WHAT IS THIS THING I'M HOLDING?

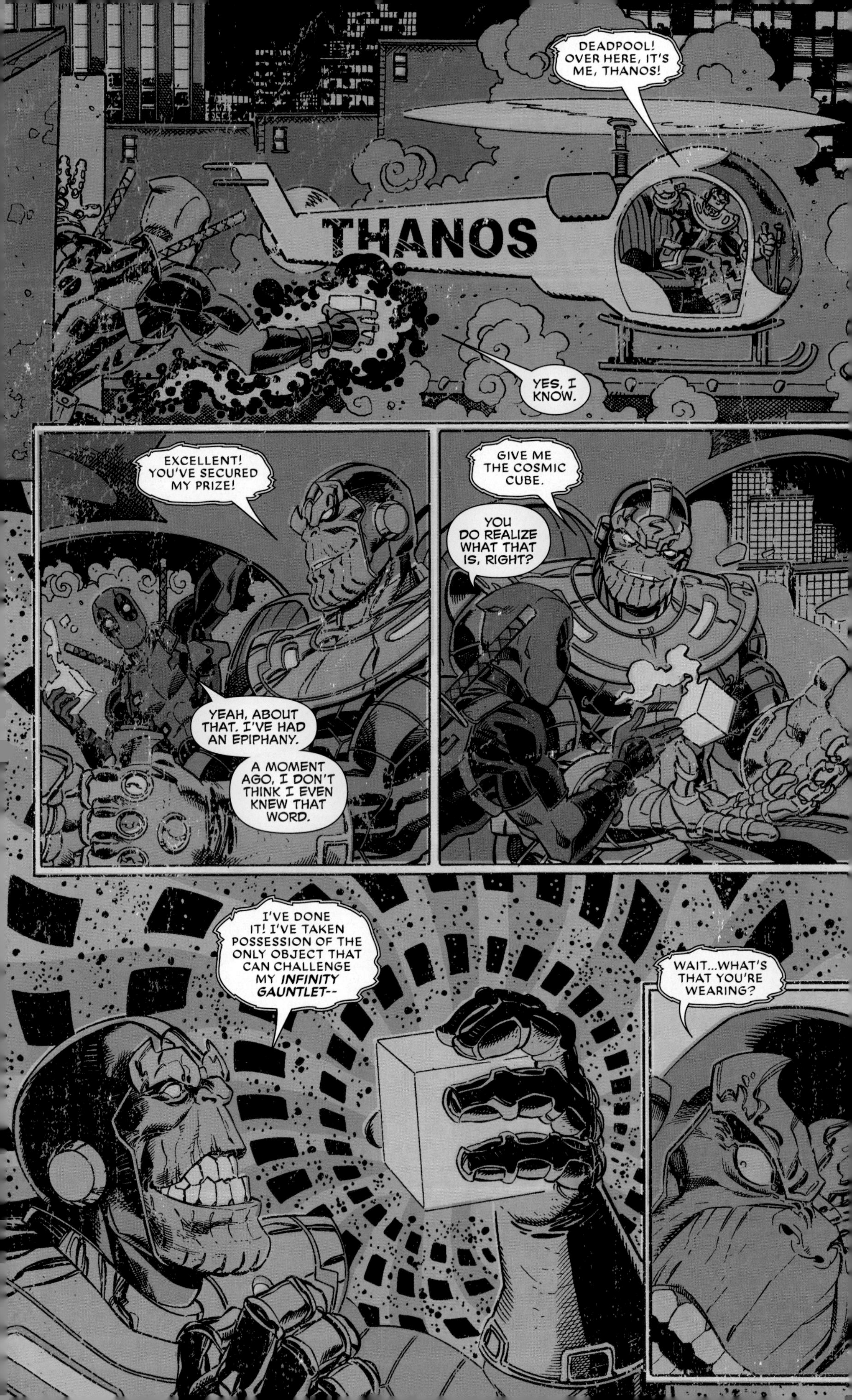
DEADPOOL! OVER HERE, IT'S ME, THANOS!
THANOS
YES, I KNOW.
EXCELLENT! YOU'VE SECURED MY PRIZE!
YEAH, ABOUT THAT. I'VE HAD AN EPIPHANY.
A MOMENT AGO, I DON'T THINK I EVEN KNEW THAT WORD.
GIVE ME THE COSMIC CUBE.
YOU DO REALIZE WHAT THAT IS, RIGHT?
I'VE DONE IT! I'VE TAKEN POSSESSION OF THE ONLY OBJECT THAT CAN CHALLENGE MY *INFINITY GAUNTLET*--
WAIT...WHAT'S THAT YOU'RE WEARING?

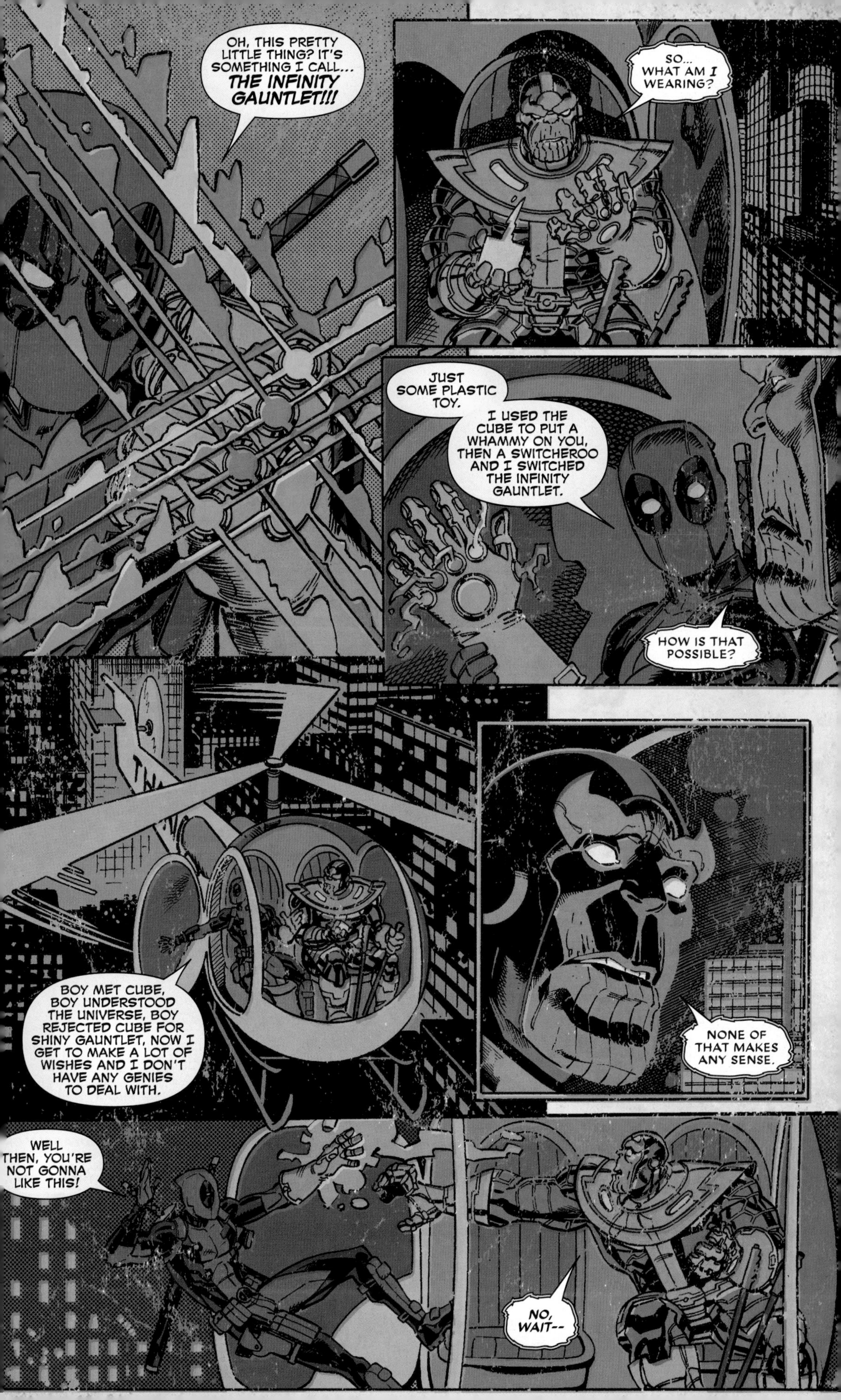
OH, THIS PRETTY LITTLE THING? IT'S SOMETHING I CALL... THE INFINITY GAUNTLET!!!
SO... WHAT AM I WEARING?
JUST SOME PLASTIC TOY.
I USED THE CUBE TO PUT A WHAMMY ON YOU, THEN A SWITCHEROO AND I SWITCHED THE INFINITY GAUNTLET.
HOW IS THAT POSSIBLE?
BOY MET CUBE, BOY UNDERSTOOD THE UNIVERSE, BOY REJECTED CUBE FOR SHINY GAUNTLET, NOW I GET TO MAKE A LOT OF WISHES AND I DON'T HAVE ANY GENIES TO DEAL WITH.
NONE OF THAT MAKES ANY SENSE.
WELL THEN, YOU'RE NOT GONNA LIKE THIS!
NO, WAIT--

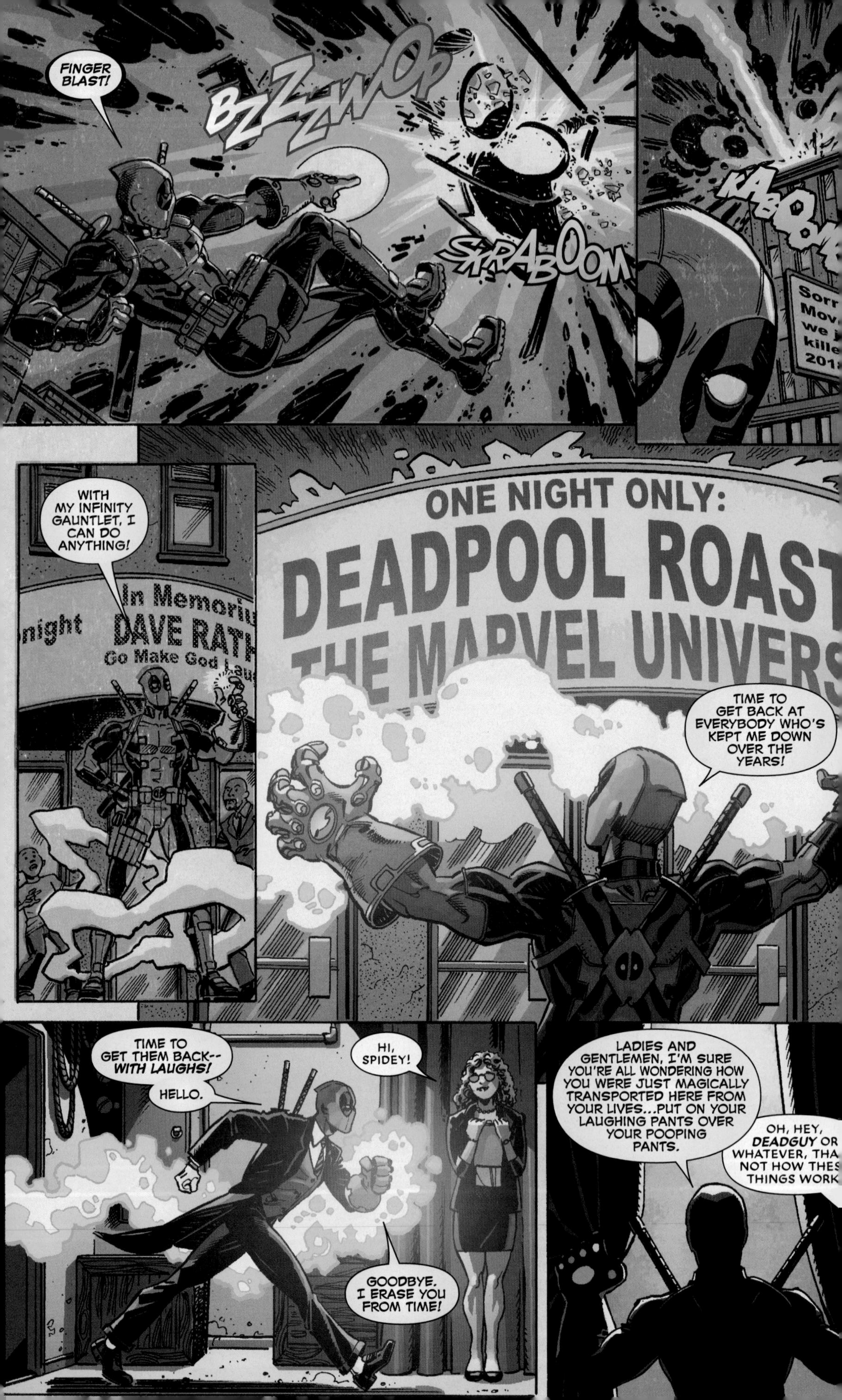
FINGER BLAST!
BZZZWOP
SKRABOOM
KABOOM
Sorr
Mov
we j
kille
201
WITH MY INFINITY GAUNTLET, I CAN DO ANYTHING!
In Memori
night
DAVE RATH
Go Make God Lau
ONE NIGHT ONLY:
DEADPOOL ROAST
THE MARVEL UNIVERS
TIME TO GET BACK AT EVERYBODY WHO'S KEPT ME DOWN OVER THE YEARS!
TIME TO GET THEM BACK-- WITH LAUGHS!
HELLO.
HI, SPIDEY!
GOODBYE. I ERASE YOU FROM TIME!
LADIES AND GENTLEMEN, I'M SURE YOU'RE ALL WONDERING HOW YOU WERE JUST MAGICALLY TRANSPORTED HERE FROM YOUR LIVES...PUT ON YOUR LAUGHING PANTS OVER YOUR POOPING PANTS.
OH, HEY, DEADGUY OR WHATEVER, THA NOT HOW THES THINGS WORK

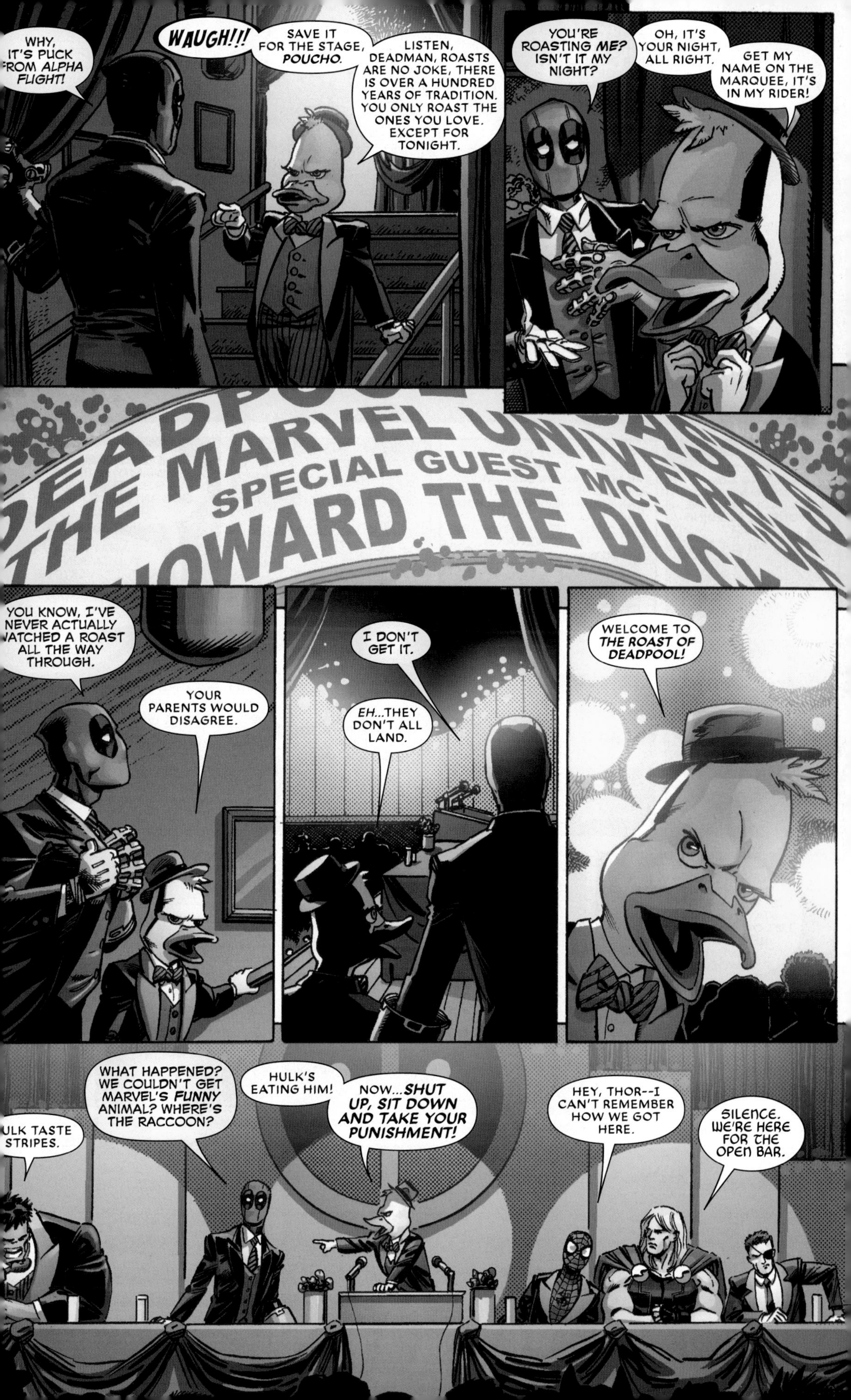

WHY, IT'S PUCK FROM ALPHA FLIGHT!
WAUGH!!!
SAVE IT FOR THE STAGE, POUCHO.
LISTEN, DEADMAN, ROASTS ARE NO JOKE, THERE IS OVER A HUNDRED YEARS OF TRADITION. YOU ONLY ROAST THE ONES YOU LOVE. EXCEPT FOR TONIGHT.
YOU'RE ROASTING ME? ISN'T IT MY NIGHT?
OH, IT'S YOUR NIGHT, ALL RIGHT.
GET MY NAME ON THE MARQUEE, IT'S IN MY RIDER!
THE MARVEL UNIVERSE
SPECIAL GUEST MC:
HOWARD THE DUCK
YOU KNOW, I'VE NEVER ACTUALLY WATCHED A ROAST ALL THE WAY THROUGH.
YOUR PARENTS WOULD DISAGREE.
I DON'T GET IT.
EH...THEY DON'T ALL LAND.
WELCOME TO THE ROAST OF DEADPOOL!
ULK TASTE STRIPES.
WHAT HAPPENED? WE COULDN'T GET MARVEL'S FUNNY ANIMAL? WHERE'S THE RACCOON?
HULK'S EATING HIM!
NOW...SHUT UP, SIT DOWN AND TAKE YOUR PUNISHMENT!
HEY, THOR--I CAN'T REMEMBER HOW WE GOT HERE.
SILENCE. WE'RE HERE FOR THE OPEN BAR.

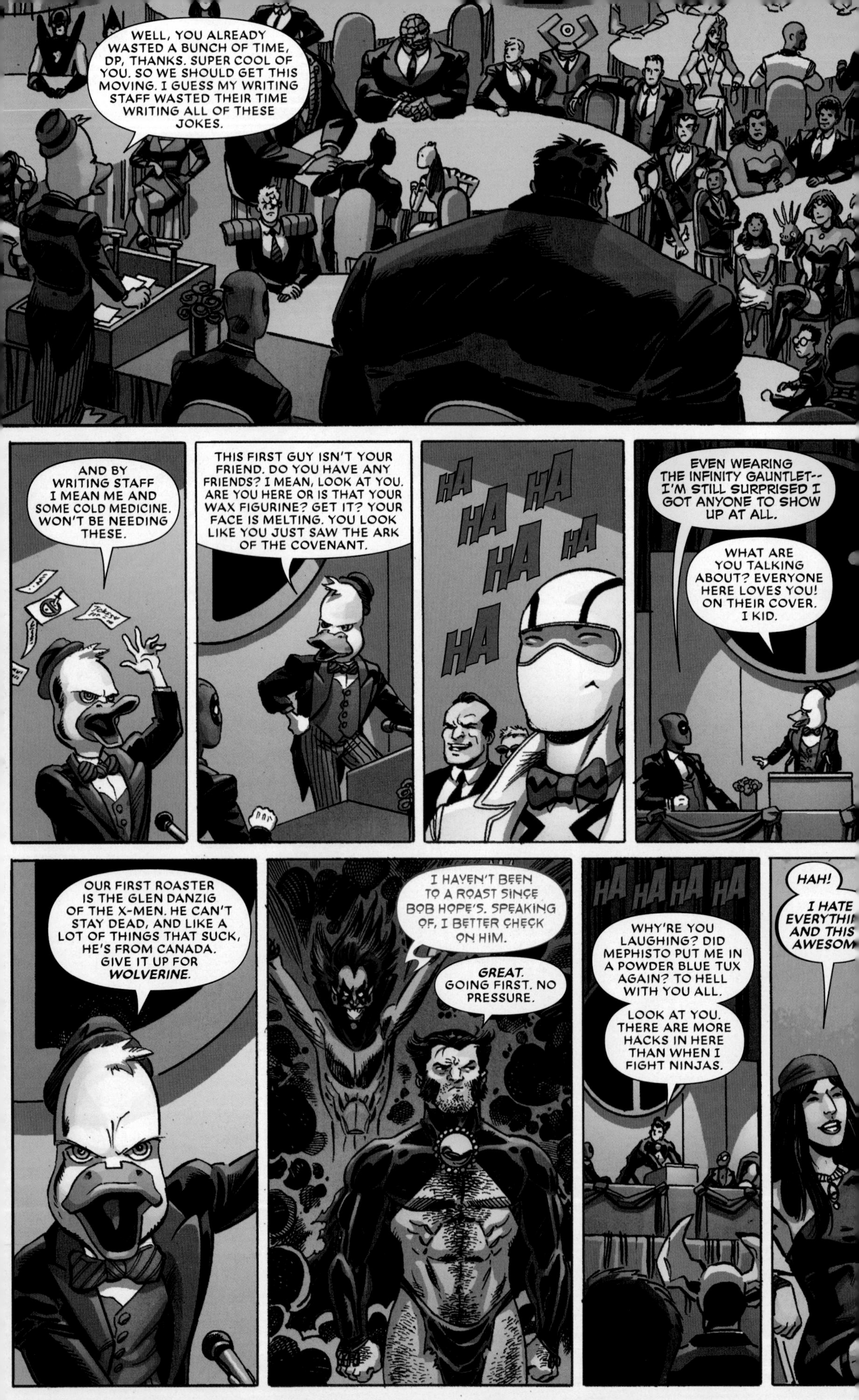
WELL, YOU ALREADY WASTED A BUNCH OF TIME, DP, THANKS. SUPER COOL OF YOU. SO WE SHOULD GET THIS MOVING. I GUESS MY WRITING STAFF WASTED THEIR TIME WRITING ALL OF THESE JOKES.
AND BY WRITING STAFF I MEAN ME AND SOME COLD MEDICINE. WON'T BE NEEDING THESE.
THIS FIRST GUY ISN'T YOUR FRIEND. DO YOU HAVE ANY FRIENDS? I MEAN, LOOK AT YOU. ARE YOU HERE OR IS THAT YOUR WAX FIGURINE? GET IT? YOUR FACE IS MELTING. YOU LOOK LIKE YOU JUST SAW THE ARK OF THE COVENANT.
HA HA HA HA HA HA HA
EVEN WEARING THE INFINITY GAUNTLET-- I'M STILL SURPRISED I GOT ANYONE TO SHOW UP AT ALL.
WHAT ARE YOU TALKING ABOUT? EVERYONE HERE LOVES YOU! ON THEIR COVER. I KID.
OUR FIRST ROASTER IS THE GLEN DANZIG OF THE X-MEN. HE CAN'T STAY DEAD, AND LIKE A LOT OF THINGS THAT SUCK, HE'S FROM CANADA. GIVE IT UP FOR ***WOLVERINE***.
I HAVEN'T BEEN TO A ROAST SINCE BOB HOPE'S. SPEAKING OF, I BETTER CHECK ON HIM.
GREAT. GOING FIRST. NO PRESSURE.
HA HA HA HA HA
WHY'RE YOU LAUGHING? DID MEPHISTO PUT ME IN A POWDER BLUE TUX AGAIN? TO HELL WITH YOU ALL.
LOOK AT YOU. THERE ARE MORE HACKS IN HERE THAN WHEN I FIGHT NINJAS.
HAH!
I HATE EVERYTHI AND THIS AWESOM

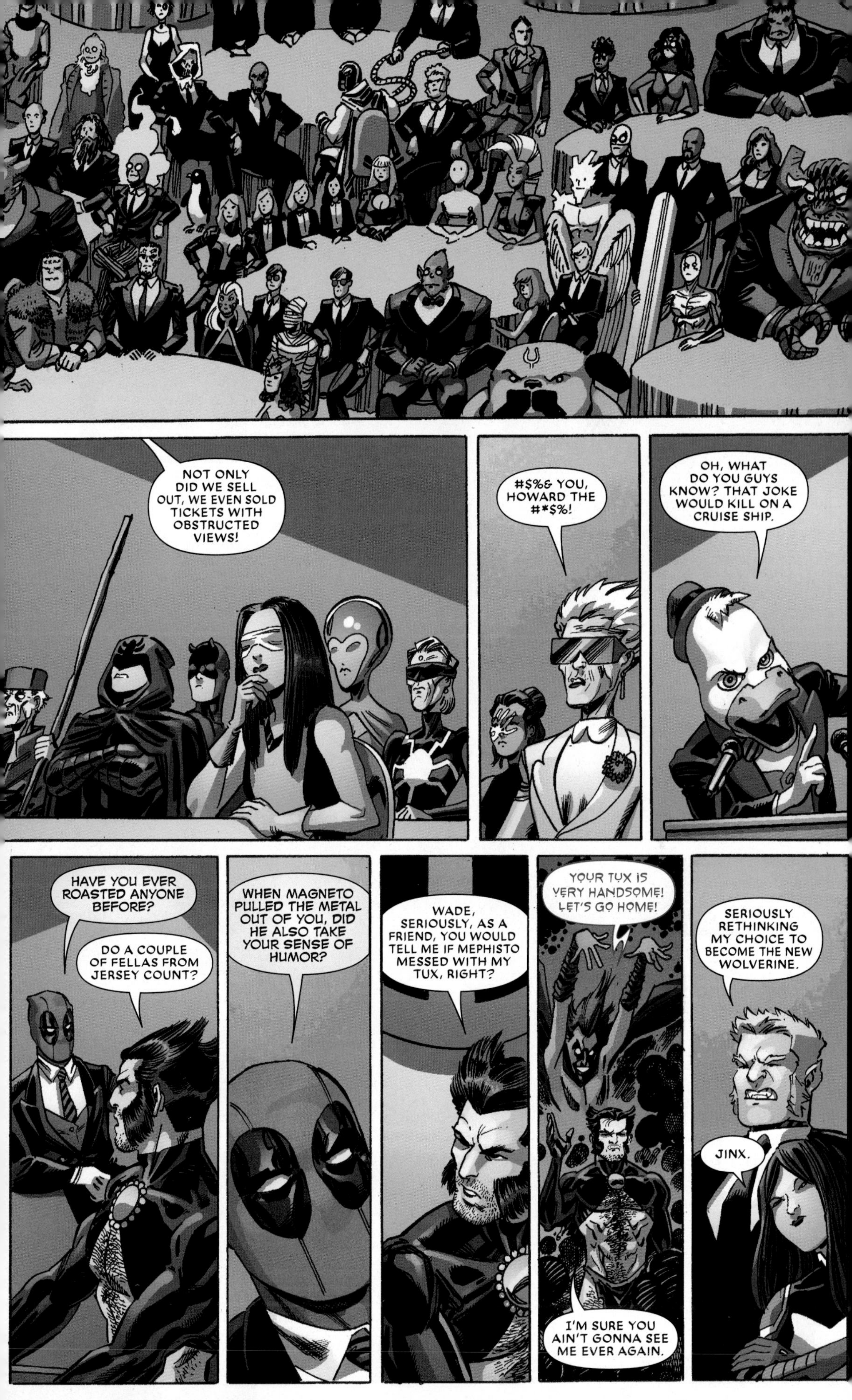
NOT ONLY DID WE SELL OUT, WE EVEN SOLD TICKETS WITH OBSTRUCTED VIEWS!
#$%& YOU, HOWARD THE #*$%!
OH, WHAT DO YOU GUYS KNOW? THAT JOKE WOULD KILL ON A CRUISE SHIP.
HAVE YOU EVER ROASTED ANYONE BEFORE?
DO A COUPLE OF FELLAS FROM JERSEY COUNT?
WHEN MAGNETO PULLED THE METAL OUT OF YOU, DID HE ALSO TAKE YOUR SENSE OF HUMOR?
WADE, SERIOUSLY, AS A FRIEND, YOU WOULD TELL ME IF MEPHISTO MESSED WITH MY TUX, RIGHT?
YOUR TUX IS VERY HANDSOME! LET'S GO HOME!
I'M SURE YOU AIN'T GONNA SEE ME EVER AGAIN.
SERIOUSLY RETHINKING MY CHOICE TO BECOME THE NEW WOLVERINE.
JINX.

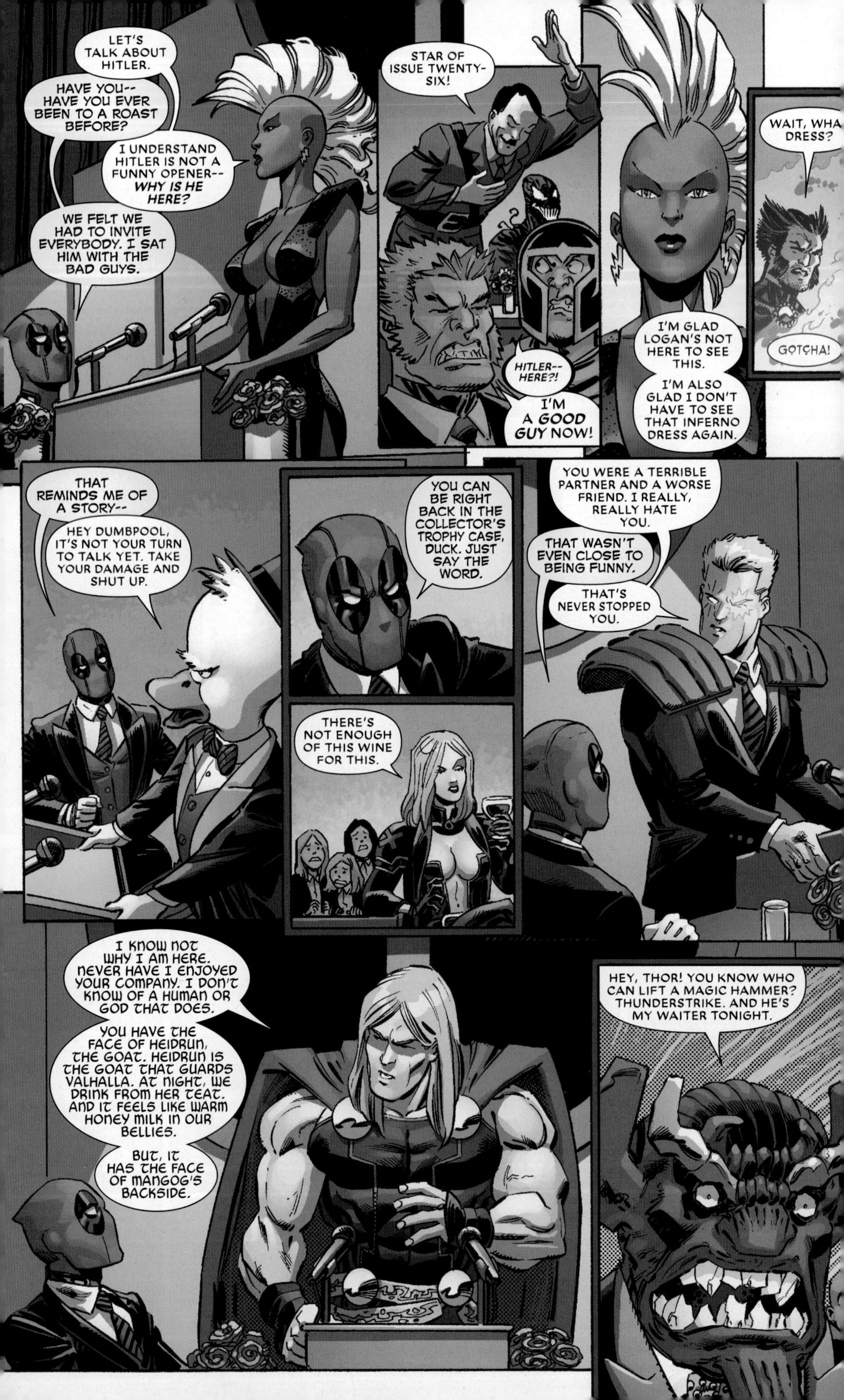
LET'S TALK ABOUT HITLER.
HAVE YOU-- HAVE YOU EVER BEEN TO A ROAST BEFORE?
I UNDERSTAND HITLER IS NOT A FUNNY OPENER-- WHY IS HE HERE?
WE FELT WE HAD TO INVITE EVERYBODY. I SAT HIM WITH THE BAD GUYS.
STAR OF ISSUE TWENTY-SIX!
HITLER-- HERE?!
I'M A GOOD GUY NOW!
I'M GLAD LOGAN'S NOT HERE TO SEE THIS.
I'M ALSO GLAD I DON'T HAVE TO SEE THAT INFERNO DRESS AGAIN.
WAIT, WHA DRESS?
GOTCHA!
THAT REMINDS ME OF A STORY--
HEY DUMBPOOL, IT'S NOT YOUR TURN TO TALK YET. TAKE YOUR DAMAGE AND SHUT UP.
YOU CAN BE RIGHT BACK IN THE COLLECTOR'S TROPHY CASE, DUCK. JUST SAY THE WORD.
THERE'S NOT ENOUGH OF THIS WINE FOR THIS.
YOU WERE A TERRIBLE PARTNER AND A WORSE FRIEND. I REALLY, REALLY HATE YOU.
THAT WASN'T EVEN CLOSE TO BEING FUNNY.
THAT'S NEVER STOPPED YOU.
I KNOW NOT WHY I AM HERE. NEVER HAVE I ENJOYED YOUR COMPANY. I DON'T KNOW OF A HUMAN OR GOD THAT DOES.
YOU HAVE THE FACE OF HEIDRUN, THE GOAT. HEIDRUN IS THE GOAT THAT GUARDS VALHALLA. AT NIGHT, WE DRINK FROM HER TEAT. AND IT FEELS LIKE WARM HONEY MILK IN OUR BELLIES.
BUT, IT HAS THE FACE OF MANGOG'S BACKSIDE.
HEY, THOR! YOU KNOW WHO CAN LIFT A MAGIC HAMMER? THUNDERSTRIKE. AND HE'S MY WAITER TONIGHT.

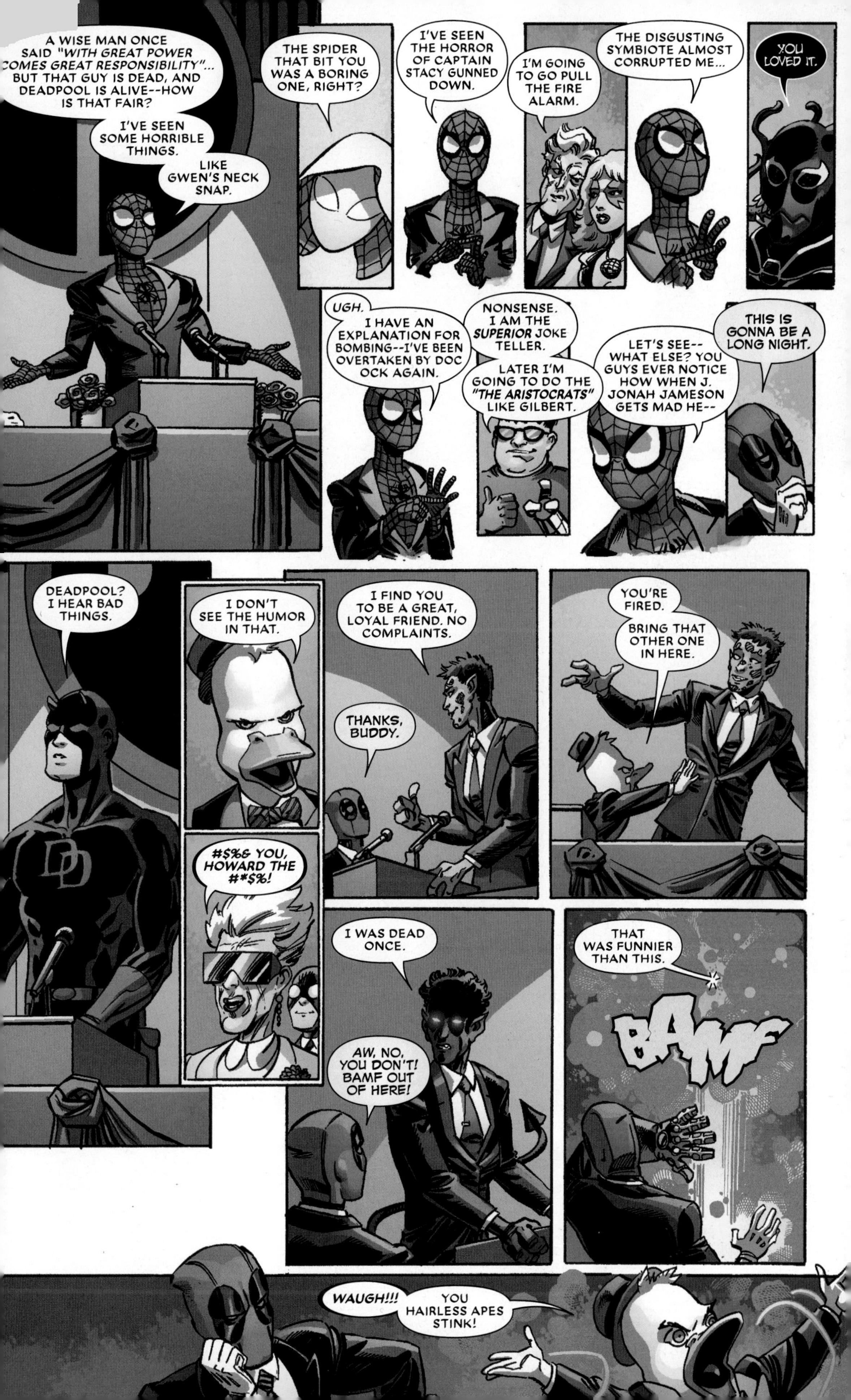

A WISE MAN ONCE SAID "WITH GREAT POWER COMES GREAT RESPONSIBILITY"... BUT THAT GUY IS DEAD, AND DEADPOOL IS ALIVE--HOW IS THAT FAIR?
I'VE SEEN SOME HORRIBLE THINGS.
LIKE GWEN'S NECK SNAP.
THE SPIDER THAT BIT YOU WAS A BORING ONE, RIGHT?
I'VE SEEN THE HORROR OF CAPTAIN STACY GUNNED DOWN.
I'M GOING TO GO PULL THE FIRE ALARM.
THE DISGUSTING SYMBIOTE ALMOST CORRUPTED ME...
YOU LOVED IT.
UGH.
I HAVE AN EXPLANATION FOR BOMBING--I'VE BEEN OVERTAKEN BY DOC OCK AGAIN.
NONSENSE. I AM THE SUPERIOR JOKE TELLER.
LATER I'M GOING TO DO THE "THE ARISTOCRATS" LIKE GILBERT.
LET'S SEE--WHAT ELSE? YOU GUYS EVER NOTICE HOW WHEN J. JONAH JAMESON GETS MAD HE--
THIS IS GONNA BE A LONG NIGHT.
DEADPOOL? I HEAR BAD THINGS.
I DON'T SEE THE HUMOR IN THAT.
#$%& YOU, HOWARD THE #*$%!
I FIND YOU TO BE A GREAT, LOYAL FRIEND. NO COMPLAINTS.
THANKS, BUDDY.
YOU'RE FIRED.
BRING THAT OTHER ONE IN HERE.
I WAS DEAD ONCE.
AW, NO, YOU DON'T! BAMF OUT OF HERE!
THAT WAS FUNNIER THAN THIS.
BAMF
WAUGH!!!
YOU HAIRLESS APES STINK!

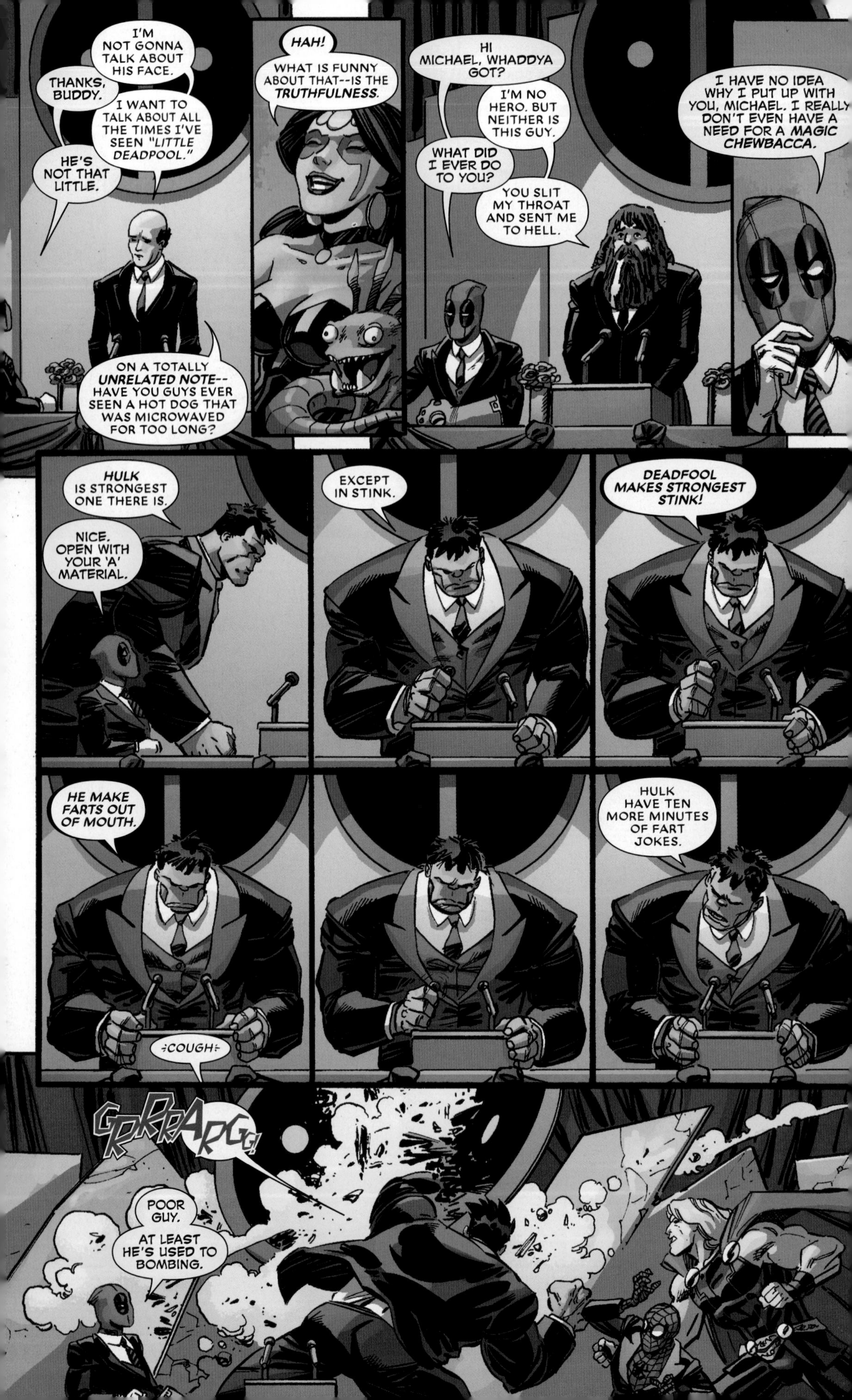
I'M NOT GONNA TALK ABOUT HIS FACE.
THANKS, BUDDY.
I WANT TO TALK ABOUT ALL THE TIMES I'VE SEEN "LITTLE DEADPOOL."
HE'S NOT THAT LITTLE.
ON A TOTALLY UNRELATED NOTE-- HAVE YOU GUYS EVER SEEN A HOT DOG THAT WAS MICROWAVED FOR TOO LONG?
HAH!
WHAT IS FUNNY ABOUT THAT--IS THE TRUTHFULNESS.
HI MICHAEL, WHADDYA GOT?
I'M NO HERO. BUT NEITHER IS THIS GUY.
WHAT DID I EVER DO TO YOU?
YOU SLIT MY THROAT AND SENT ME TO HELL.
I HAVE NO IDEA WHY I PUT UP WITH YOU, MICHAEL. I REALLY DON'T EVEN HAVE A NEED FOR A MAGIC CHEWBACCA.
HULK IS STRONGEST ONE THERE IS.
NICE. OPEN WITH YOUR 'A' MATERIAL.
EXCEPT IN STINK.
DEADFOOL MAKES STRONGEST STINK!
HE MAKE FARTS OUT OF MOUTH.
HULK HAVE TEN MORE MINUTES OF FART JOKES.
COUGH
GRRRARGG!
POOR GUY.
AT LEAST HE'S USED TO BOMBING.

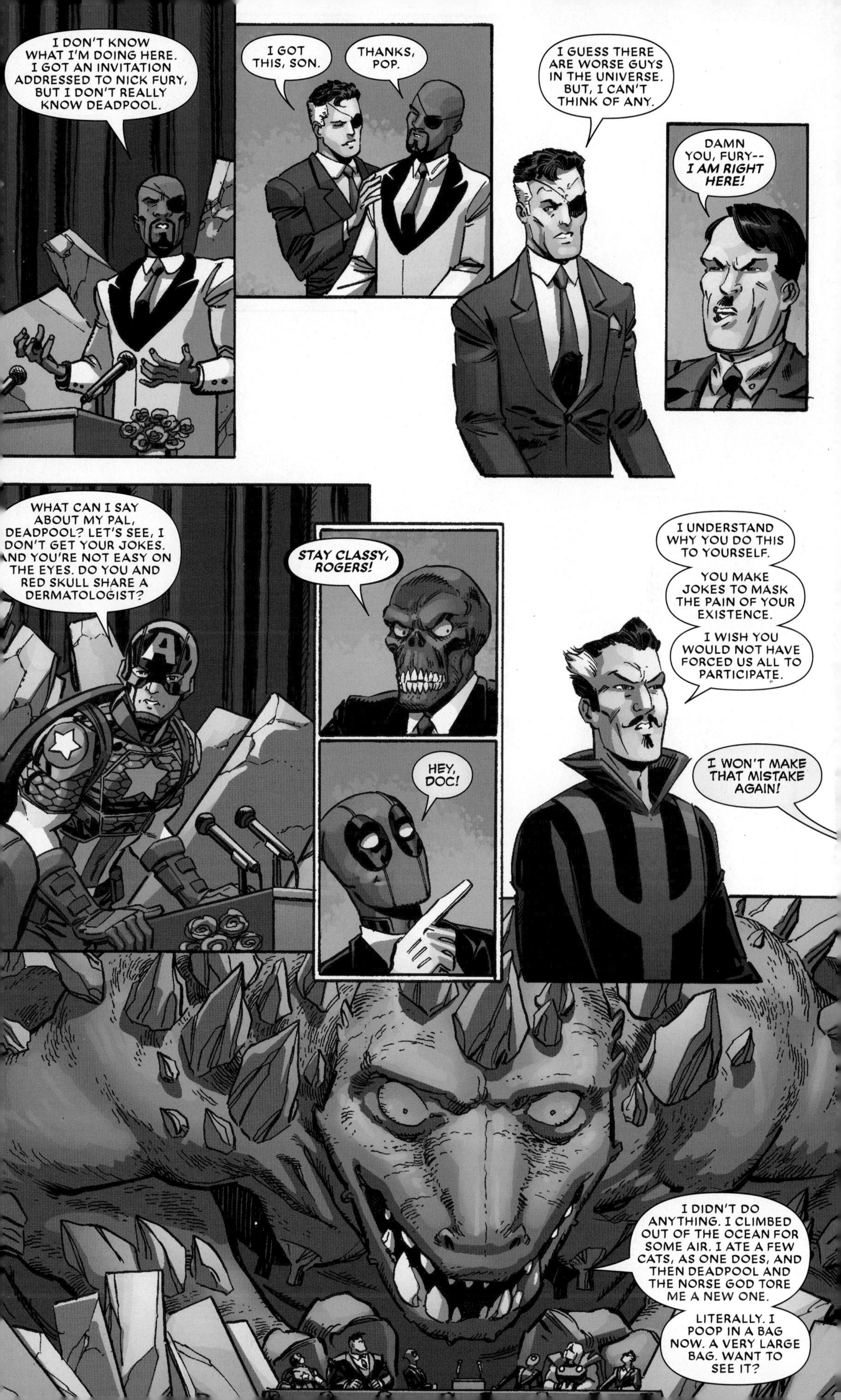
I DON'T KNOW WHAT I'M DOING HERE. I GOT AN INVITATION ADDRESSED TO NICK FURY, BUT I DON'T REALLY KNOW DEADPOOL.
I GOT THIS, SON.
THANKS, POP.
I GUESS THERE ARE WORSE GUYS IN THE UNIVERSE. BUT, I CAN'T THINK OF ANY.
DAMN YOU, FURY-- I AM RIGHT HERE!
WHAT CAN I SAY ABOUT MY PAL, DEADPOOL? LET'S SEE, I DON'T GET YOUR JOKES. AND YOU'RE NOT EASY ON THE EYES. DO YOU AND RED SKULL SHARE A DERMATOLOGIST?
STAY CLASSY, ROGERS!
HEY, DOC!
I UNDERSTAND WHY YOU DO THIS TO YOURSELF.
YOU MAKE JOKES TO MASK THE PAIN OF YOUR EXISTENCE.
I WISH YOU WOULD NOT HAVE FORCED US ALL TO PARTICIPATE.
I WON'T MAKE THAT MISTAKE AGAIN!
I DIDN'T DO ANYTHING. I CLIMBED OUT OF THE OCEAN FOR SOME AIR. I ATE A FEW CATS, AS ONE DOES, AND THEN DEADPOOL AND THE NORSE GOD TORE ME A NEW ONE.
LITERALLY. I POOP IN A BAG NOW. A VERY LARGE BAG. WANT TO SEE IT?

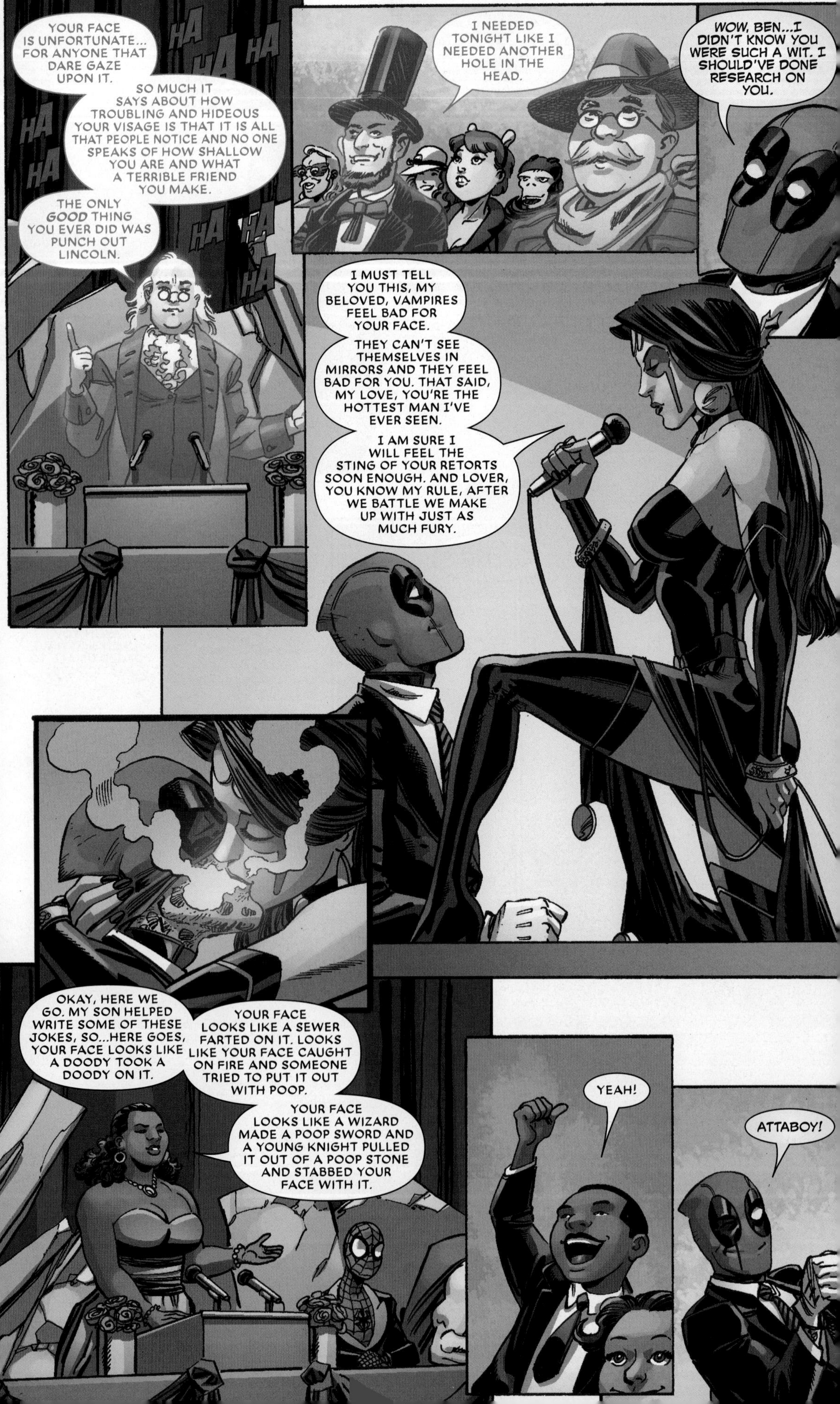

YOUR FACE IS UNFORTUNATE... FOR ANYONE THAT DARE GAZE UPON IT.
SO MUCH IT SAYS ABOUT HOW TROUBLING AND HIDEOUS YOUR VISAGE IS THAT IT IS ALL THAT PEOPLE NOTICE AND NO ONE SPEAKS OF HOW SHALLOW YOU ARE AND WHAT A TERRIBLE FRIEND YOU MAKE.
THE ONLY *GOOD* THING YOU EVER DID WAS PUNCH OUT LINCOLN.
HA HA HA HA HA HA HA HA HA HA
I NEEDED TONIGHT LIKE I NEEDED ANOTHER HOLE IN THE HEAD.
WOW, BEN...I DIDN'T KNOW YOU WERE SUCH A WIT. I SHOULD'VE DONE RESEARCH ON YOU.
I MUST TELL YOU THIS, MY BELOVED, VAMPIRES FEEL BAD FOR YOUR FACE.
THEY CAN'T SEE THEMSELVES IN MIRRORS AND THEY FEEL BAD FOR YOU. THAT SAID, MY LOVE, YOU'RE THE HOTTEST MAN I'VE EVER SEEN.
I AM SURE I WILL FEEL THE STING OF YOUR RETORTS SOON ENOUGH. AND LOVER, YOU KNOW MY RULE, AFTER WE BATTLE WE MAKE UP WITH JUST AS MUCH FURY.
OKAY, HERE WE GO. MY SON HELPED WRITE SOME OF THESE JOKES, SO...HERE GOES, YOUR FACE LOOKS LIKE A DOODY TOOK A DOODY ON IT.
YOUR FACE LOOKS LIKE A SEWER FARTED ON IT. LOOKS LIKE YOUR FACE CAUGHT ON FIRE AND SOMEONE TRIED TO PUT IT OUT WITH POOP.
YOUR FACE LOOKS LIKE A WIZARD MADE A POOP SWORD AND A YOUNG KNIGHT PULLED IT OUT OF A POOP STONE AND STABBED YOUR FACE WITH IT.
YEAH!
ATTABOY!

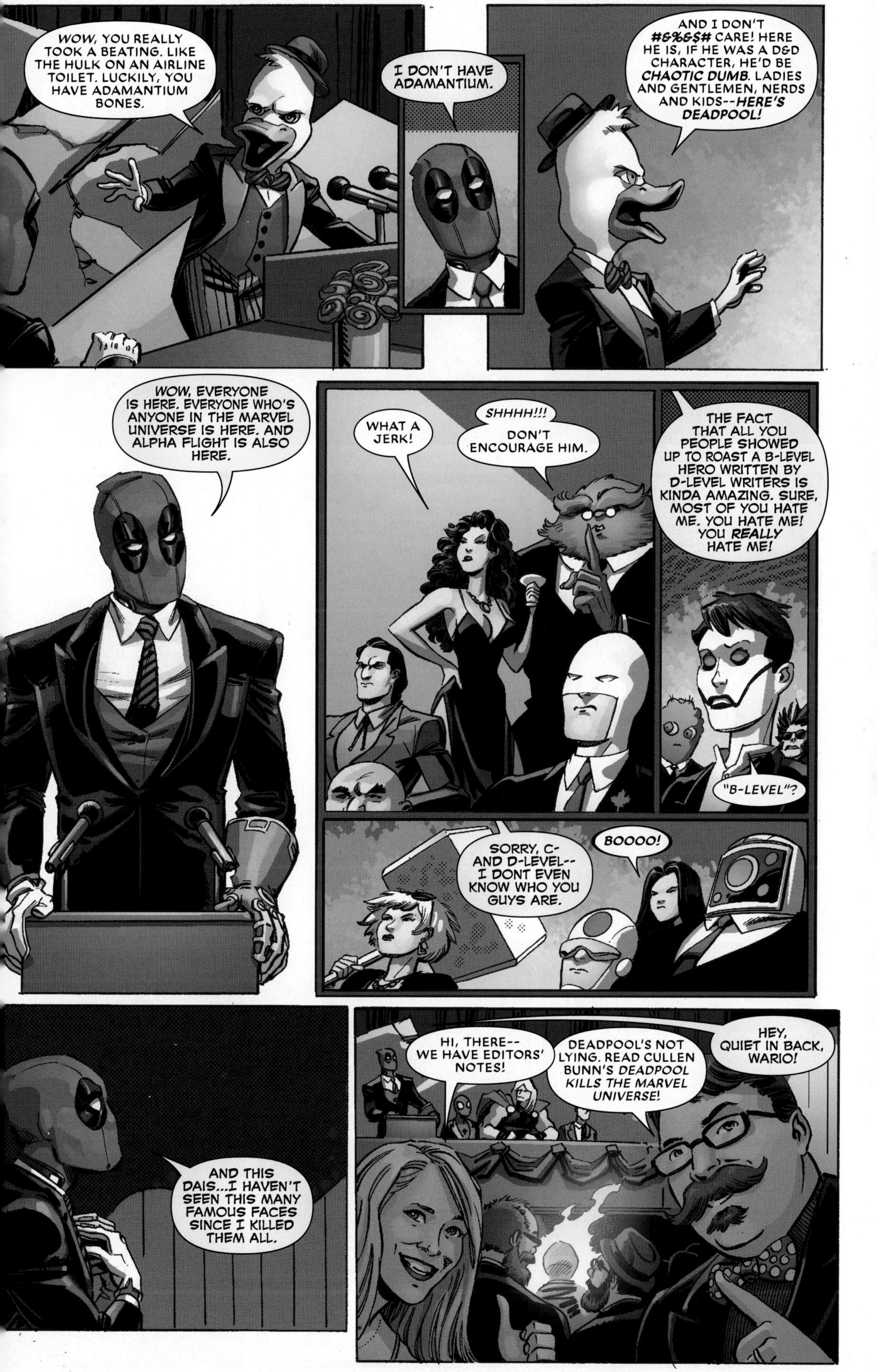
WOW, YOU REALLY TOOK A BEATING. LIKE THE HULK ON AN AIRLINE TOILET. LUCKILY, YOU HAVE ADAMANTIUM BONES.
I DON'T HAVE ADAMANTIUM.
AND I DON'T #&%&$# CARE! HERE HE IS, IF HE WAS A D&D CHARACTER, HE'D BE CHAOTIC DUMB. LADIES AND GENTLEMEN, NERDS AND KIDS--HERE'S DEADPOOL!
WOW, EVERYONE IS HERE. EVERYONE WHO'S ANYONE IN THE MARVEL UNIVERSE IS HERE. AND ALPHA FLIGHT IS ALSO HERE.
WHAT A JERK!
SHHHH!!! DON'T ENCOURAGE HIM.
THE FACT THAT ALL YOU PEOPLE SHOWED UP TO ROAST A B-LEVEL HERO WRITTEN BY D-LEVEL WRITERS IS KINDA AMAZING. SURE, MOST OF YOU HATE ME. YOU HATE ME! YOU REALLY HATE ME!
"B-LEVEL"?
SORRY, C- AND D-LEVEL-- I DONT EVEN KNOW WHO YOU GUYS ARE.
BOOOO!
AND THIS DAIS...I HAVEN'T SEEN THIS MANY FAMOUS FACES SINCE I KILLED THEM ALL.
HI, THERE-- WE HAVE EDITORS' NOTES!
DEADPOOL'S NOT LYING. READ CULLEN BUNN'S DEADPOOL KILLS THE MARVEL UNIVERSE!
HEY, QUIET IN BACK, WARIO!

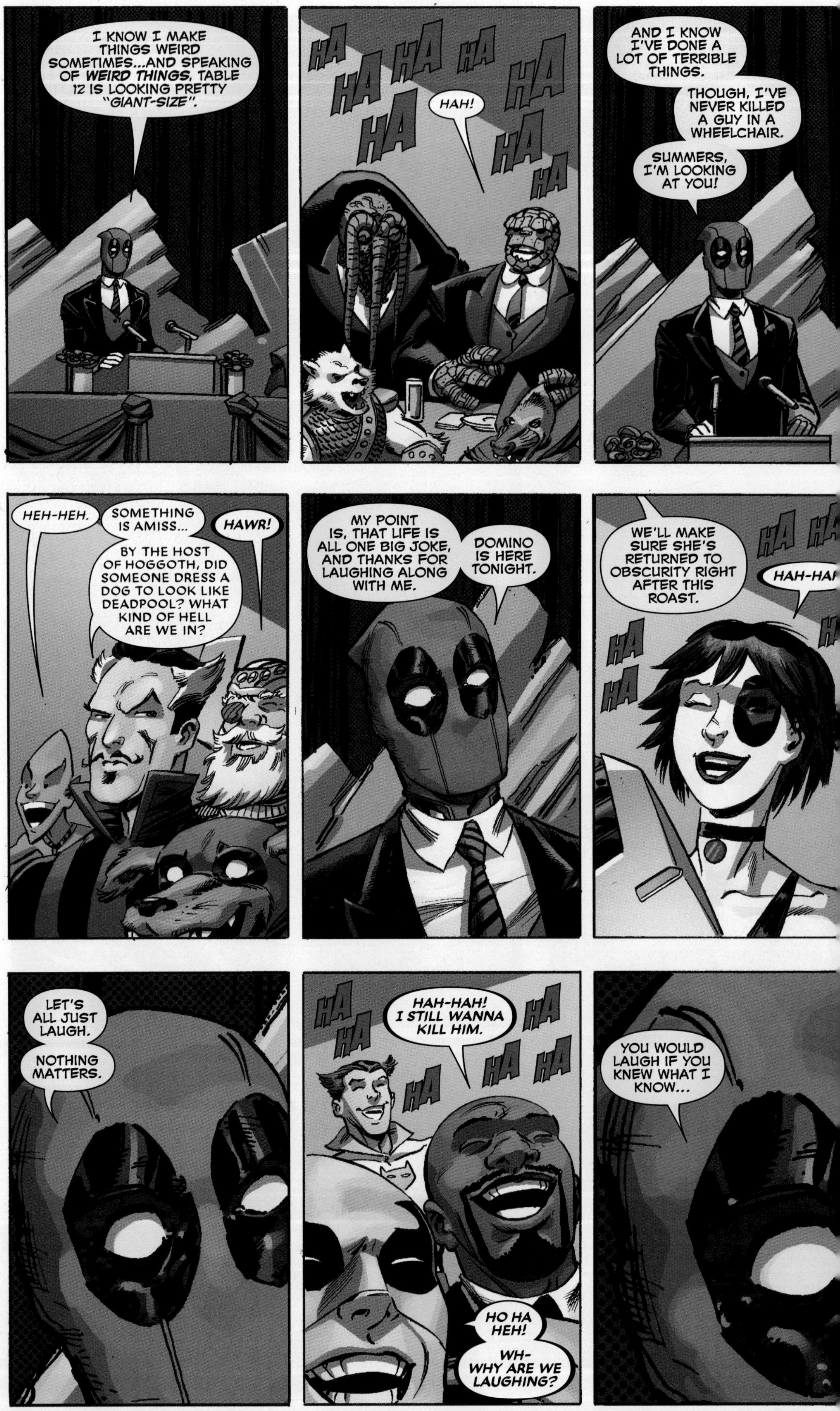
I KNOW I MAKE THINGS WEIRD SOMETIMES...AND SPEAKING OF WEIRD THINGS, TABLE 12 IS LOOKING PRETTY "GIANT-SIZE".
HA HA HA HA HA HA HA HA HA HA
HAH!
AND I KNOW I'VE DONE A LOT OF TERRIBLE THINGS.
THOUGH, I'VE NEVER KILLED A GUY IN A WHEELCHAIR.
SUMMERS, I'M LOOKING AT YOU!
HEH-HEH.
SOMETHING IS AMISS...
BY THE HOST OF HOGGOTH, DID SOMEONE DRESS A DOG TO LOOK LIKE DEADPOOL? WHAT KIND OF HELL ARE WE IN?
HAWR!
MY POINT IS, THAT LIFE IS ALL ONE BIG JOKE, AND THANKS FOR LAUGHING ALONG WITH ME.
DOMINO IS HERE TONIGHT.
WE'LL MAKE SURE SHE'S RETURNED TO OBSCURITY RIGHT AFTER THIS ROAST.
HA HA HA HA
LET'S ALL JUST LAUGH.
NOTHING MATTERS.
HA HA
HAH-HAH! I STILL WANNA KILL HIM.
HA HA HA HA
HO HA HEH!
WH- WHY ARE WE LAUGHING?
YOU WOULD LAUGH IF YOU KNEW WHAT I KNOW...

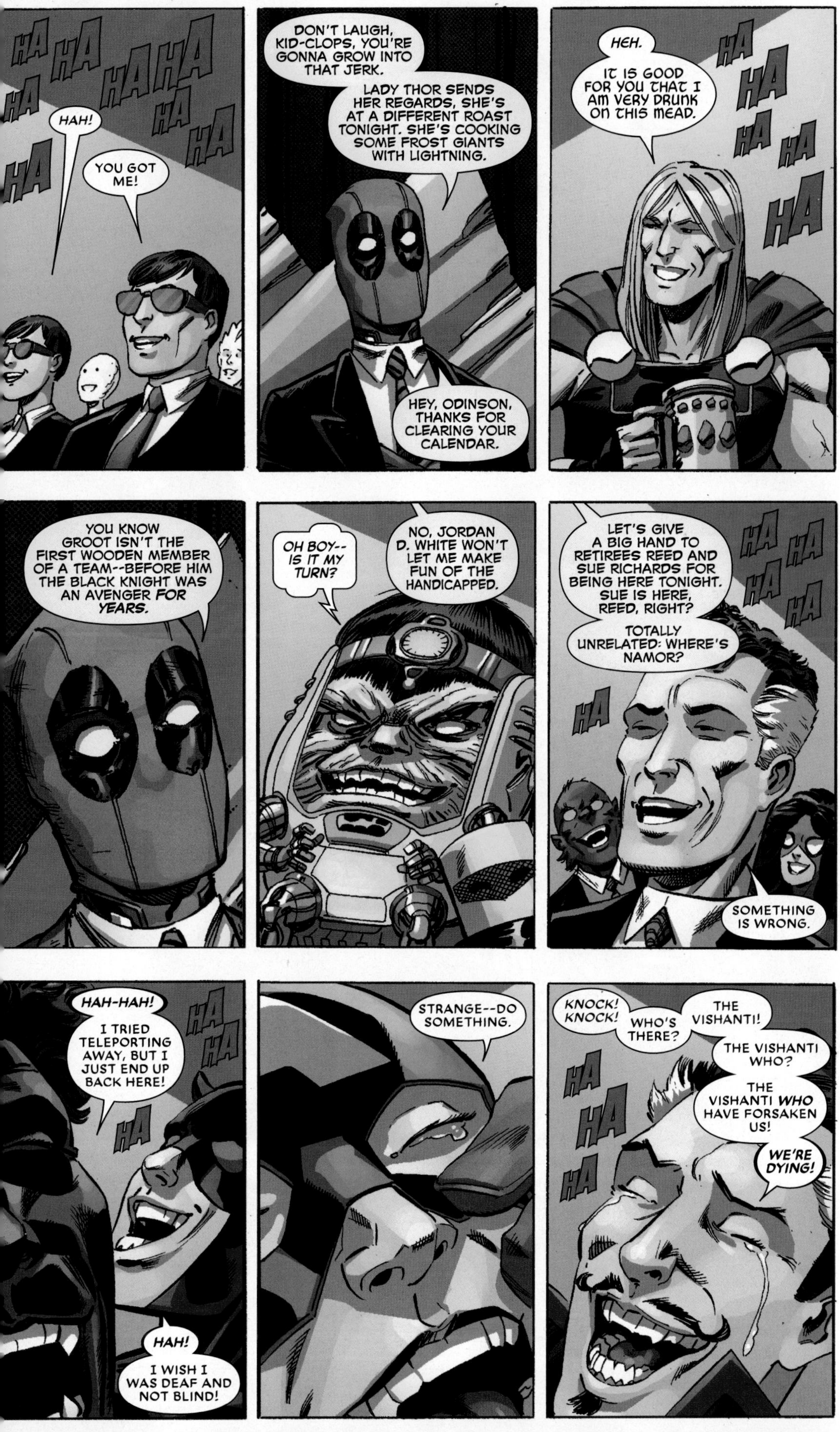
HA HA HA HA HA HA HA HA HA
HAH!
YOU GOT ME!
DON'T LAUGH, KID-CLOPS, YOU'RE GONNA GROW INTO THAT JERK.
LADY THOR SENDS HER REGARDS, SHE'S AT A DIFFERENT ROAST TONIGHT. SHE'S COOKING SOME FROST GIANTS WITH LIGHTNING.
HEY, ODINSON, THANKS FOR CLEARING YOUR CALENDAR.
HEH.
IT IS GOOD FOR YOU THAT I AM VERY DRUNK ON THIS MEAD.
HA HA HA HA HA
YOU KNOW GROOT ISN'T THE FIRST WOODEN MEMBER OF A TEAM--BEFORE HIM THE BLACK KNIGHT WAS AN AVENGER FOR YEARS.
OH BOY-- IS IT MY TURN?
NO, JORDAN D. WHITE WON'T LET ME MAKE FUN OF THE HANDICAPPED.
LET'S GIVE A BIG HAND TO RETIREES REED AND SUE RICHARDS FOR BEING HERE TONIGHT. SUE IS HERE, REED, RIGHT?
TOTALLY UNRELATED: WHERE'S NAMOR?
HA HA HA HA HA
SOMETHING IS WRONG.
HAH-HAH!
I TRIED TELEPORTING AWAY, BUT I JUST END UP BACK HERE!
HA HA HA
HAH!
I WISH I WAS DEAF AND NOT BLIND!
STRANGE--DO SOMETHING.
KNOCK! KNOCK!
WHO'S THERE?
THE VISHANTI!
THE VISHANTI WHO?
THE VISHANTI WHO HAVE FORSAKEN US!
WE'RE DYING!
HA HA HA HA

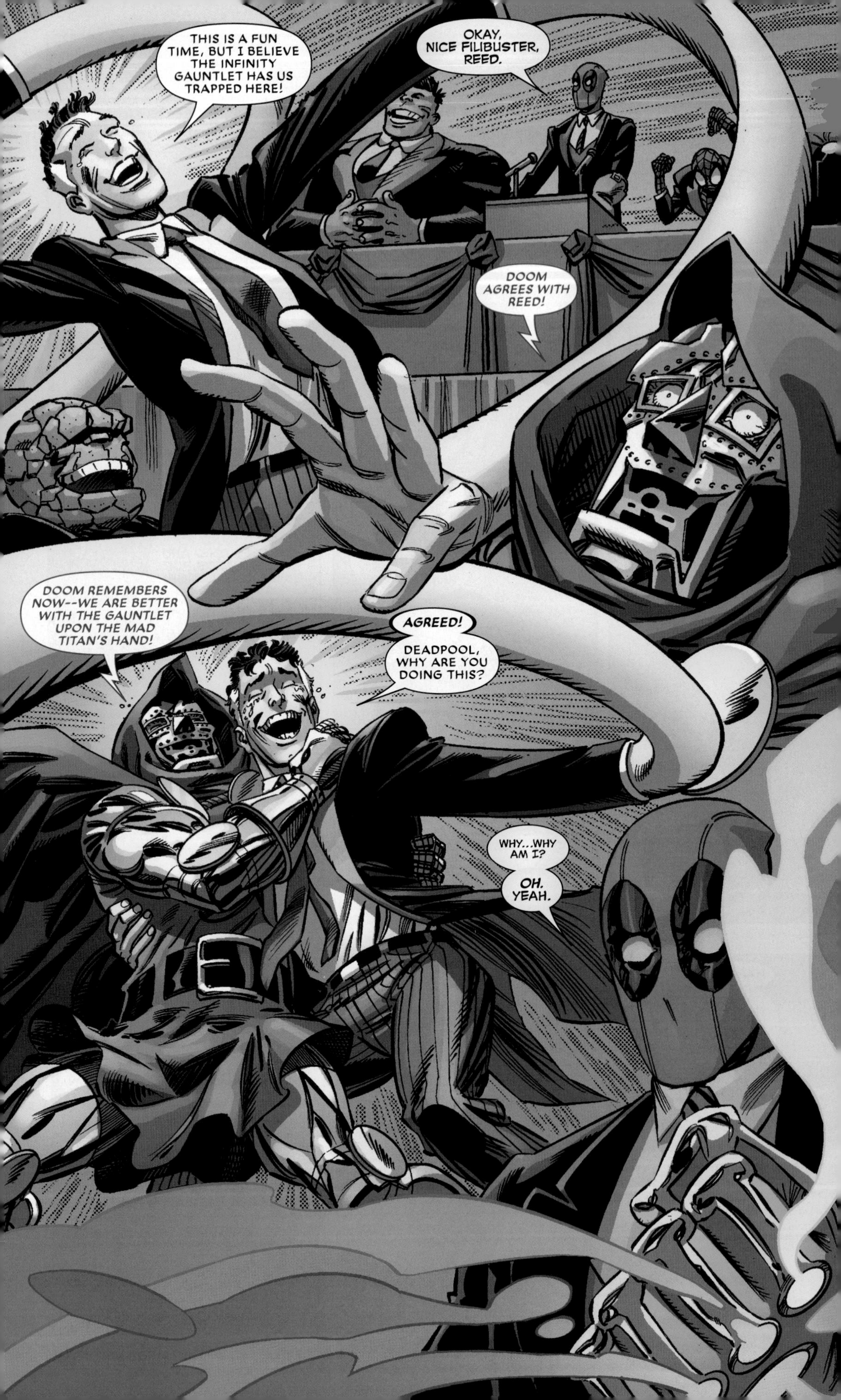
THIS IS A FUN TIME, BUT I BELIEVE THE INFINITY GAUNTLET HAS US TRAPPED HERE!
OKAY, NICE FILIBUSTER, REED.
DOOM AGREES WITH REED!
DOOM REMEMBERS NOW--WE ARE BETTER WITH THE GAUNTLET UPON THE MAD TITAN'S HAND!
AGREED!
DEADPOOL, WHY ARE YOU DOING THIS?
WHY...WHY AM I?
OH. YEAH.

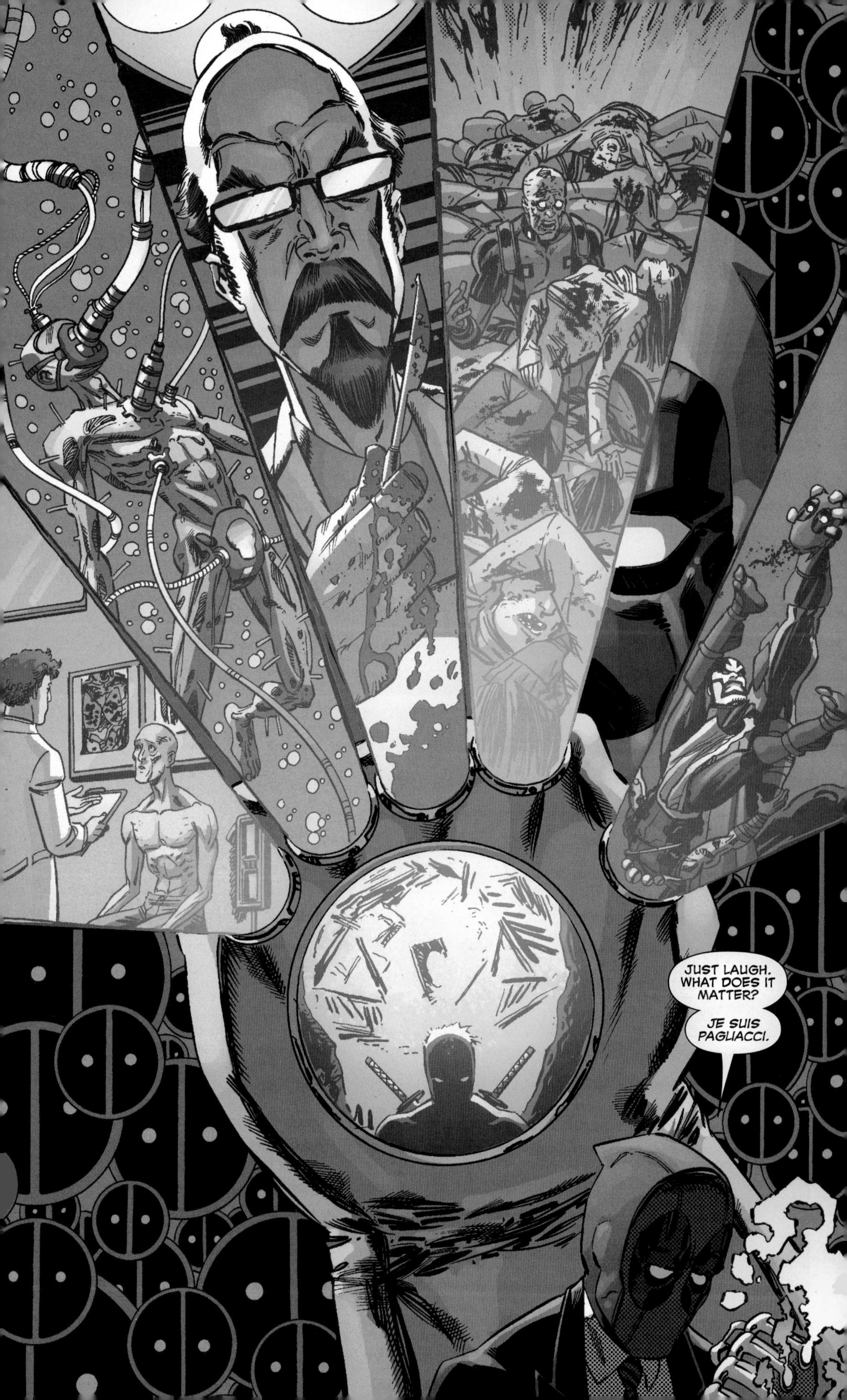
JUST LAUGH. WHAT DOES IT MATTER?
JE SUIS PAGLIACCI.

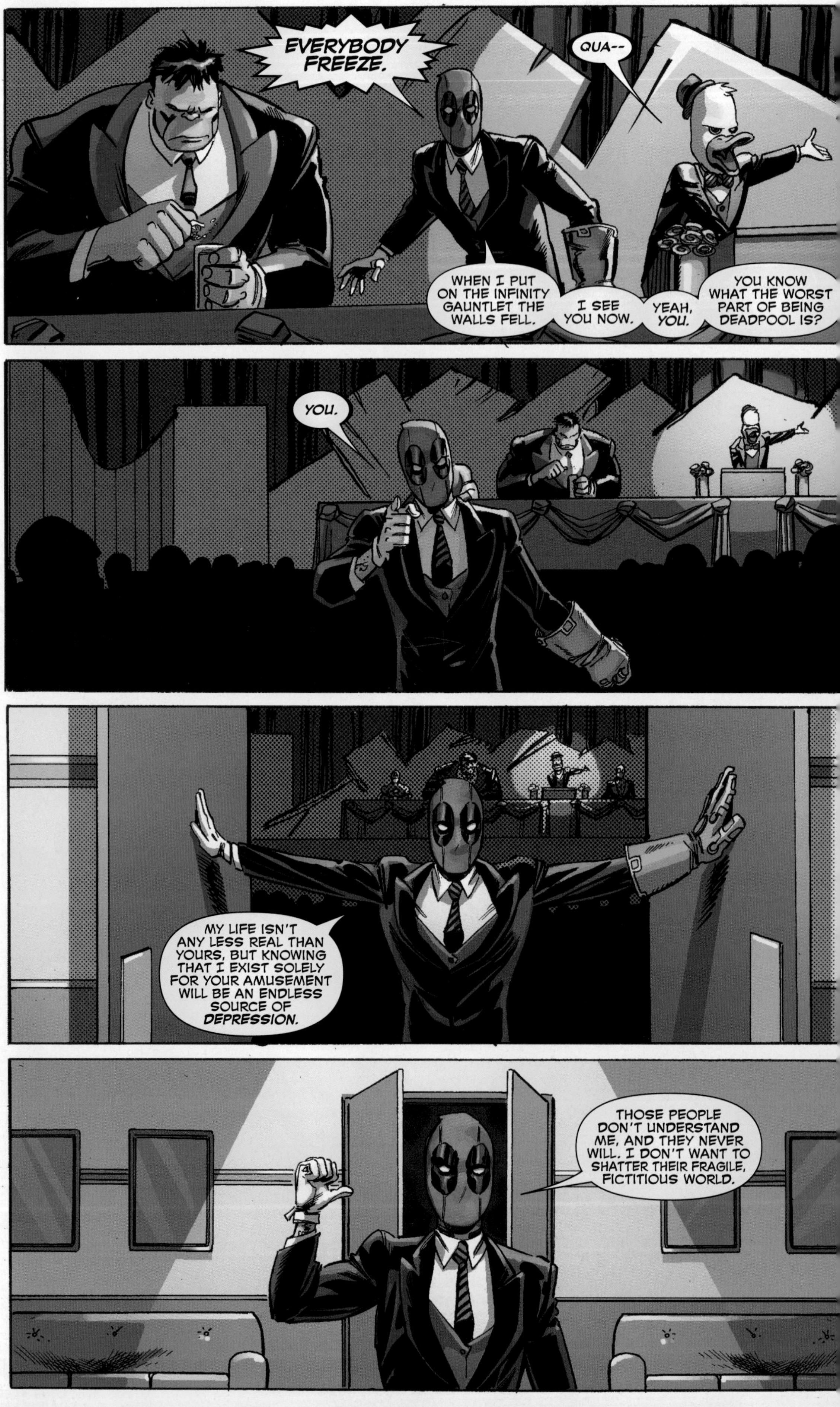
EVERYBODY FREEZE.
QUA--
WHEN I PUT ON THE INFINITY GAUNTLET THE WALLS FELL.
I SEE YOU NOW.
YEAH, *YOU.*
YOU KNOW WHAT THE WORST PART OF BEING DEADPOOL IS?
YOU.
MY LIFE ISN'T ANY LESS REAL THAN YOURS, BUT KNOWING THAT I EXIST SOLELY FOR YOUR AMUSEMENT WILL BE AN ENDLESS SOURCE OF ***DEPRESSION.***
THOSE PEOPLE DON'T UNDERSTAND ME, AND THEY NEVER WILL. I DON'T WANT TO SHATTER THEIR FRAGILE, FICTITIOUS WORLD.

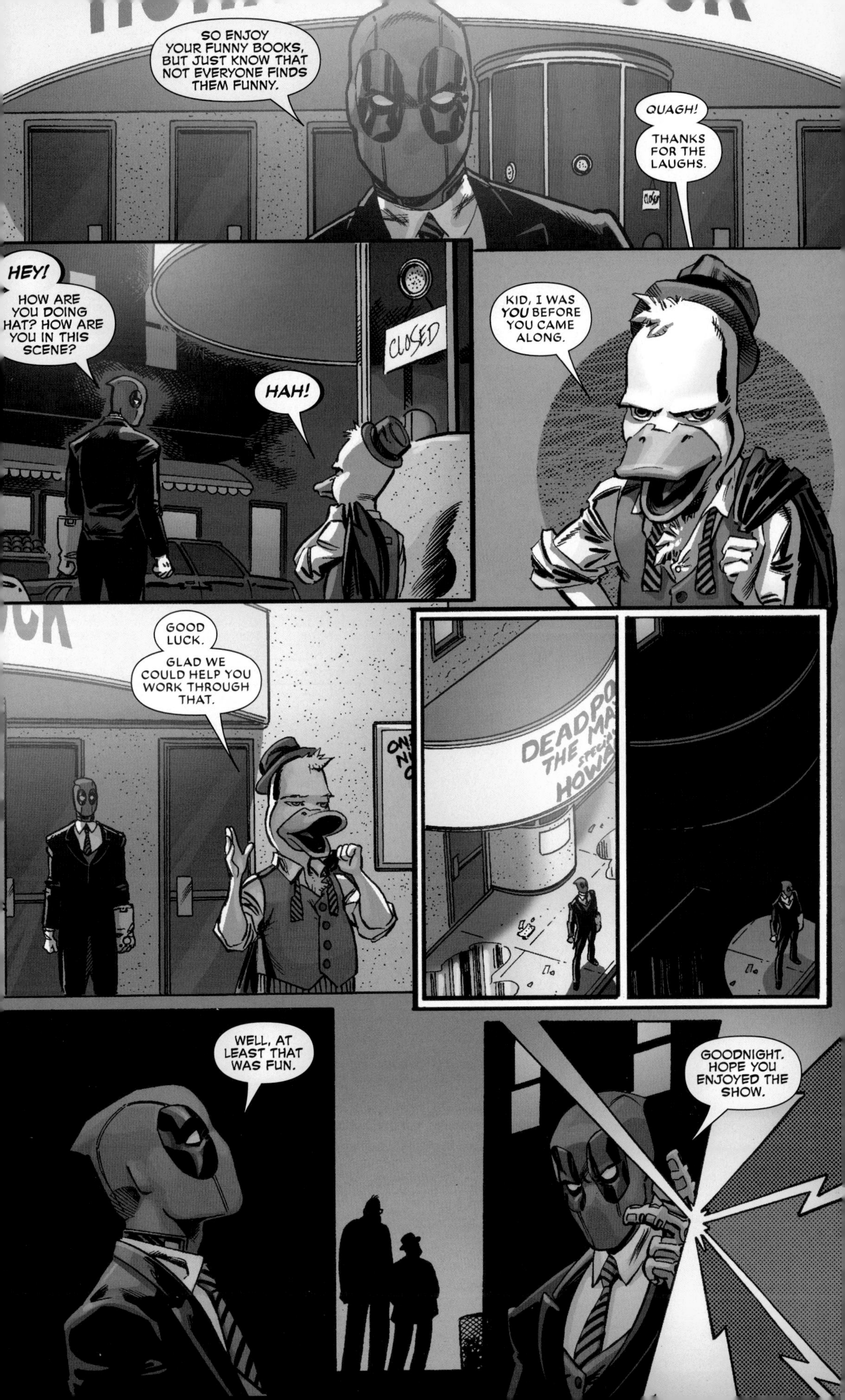
SO ENJOY YOUR FUNNY BOOKS, BUT JUST KNOW THAT NOT EVERYONE FINDS THEM FUNNY.
QUAGH!
THANKS FOR THE LAUGHS.
HEY!
HOW ARE YOU DOING HAT? HOW ARE YOU IN THIS SCENE?
CLOSED
HAH!
KID, I WAS YOU BEFORE YOU CAME ALONG.
GOOD LUCK.
GLAD WE COULD HELP YOU WORK THROUGH THAT.
WELL, AT LEAST THAT WAS FUN.
GOODNIGHT. HOPE YOU ENJOYED THE SHOW.

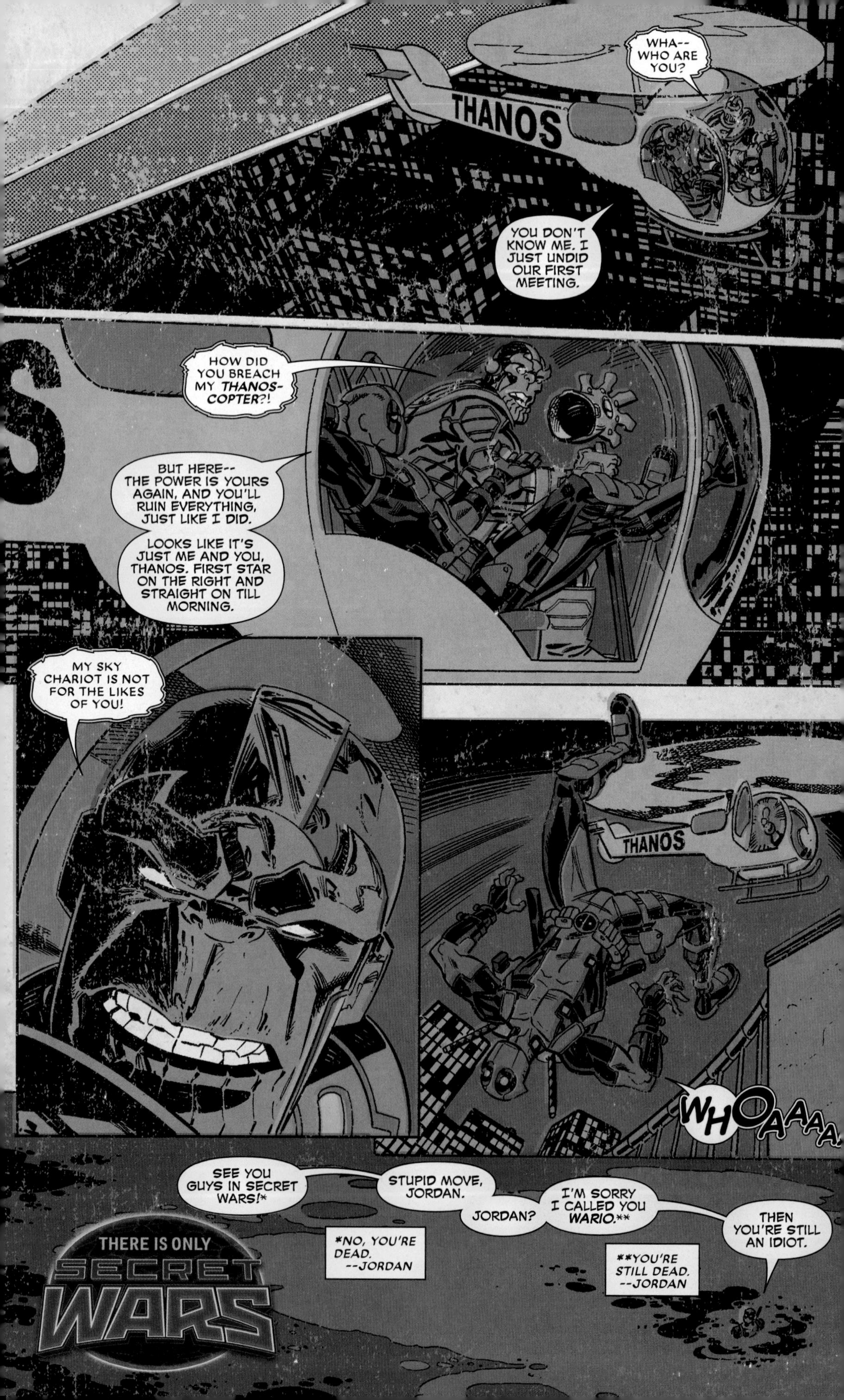
WHA-- WHO ARE YOU?
THANOS
YOU DON'T KNOW ME. I JUST UNDID OUR FIRST MEETING.
HOW DID YOU BREACH MY THANOS-COPTER?!
BUT HERE-- THE POWER IS YOURS AGAIN, AND YOU'LL RUIN EVERYTHING, JUST LIKE I DID.
LOOKS LIKE IT'S JUST ME AND YOU, THANOS. FIRST STAR ON THE RIGHT AND STRAIGHT ON TILL MORNING.
MY SKY CHARIOT IS NOT FOR THE LIKES OF YOU!
THANOS
WHOAAAA
SEE YOU GUYS IN SECRET WARS!*
STUPID MOVE, JORDAN.
JORDAN?
I'M SORRY I CALLED YOU WARIO.**
THEN YOU'RE STILL AN IDIOT.
*NO, YOU'RE DEAD. --JORDAN
**YOU'RE STILL DEAD. --JORDAN
THERE IS ONLY SECRET WARS

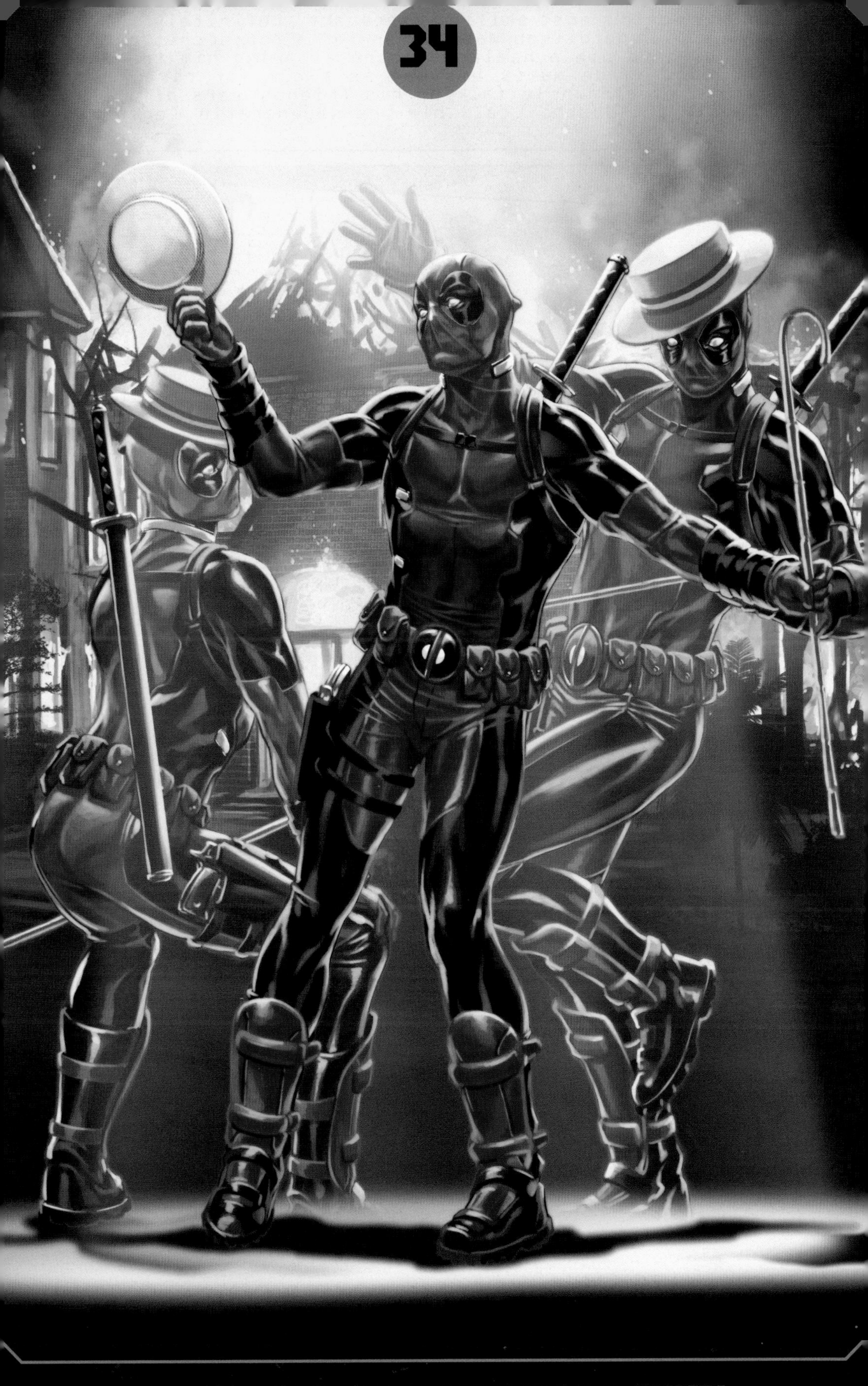
34

THE ONE WITH THE SUPER-RARE 3-D COVER!

Possibly the world's most skilled mercenary, definitely the world's most annoying, Wade Wilson was chosen for a top-secret government program that gave him a healing factor allowing him to heal from any wound. Now, Wade makes his way as a gun for hire, shooting his prey's faces off while talking his friends' ears off. Call him the Merc with the Mouth...call him the Regeneratin' Degenerate... call him...**DEADPOOL**.

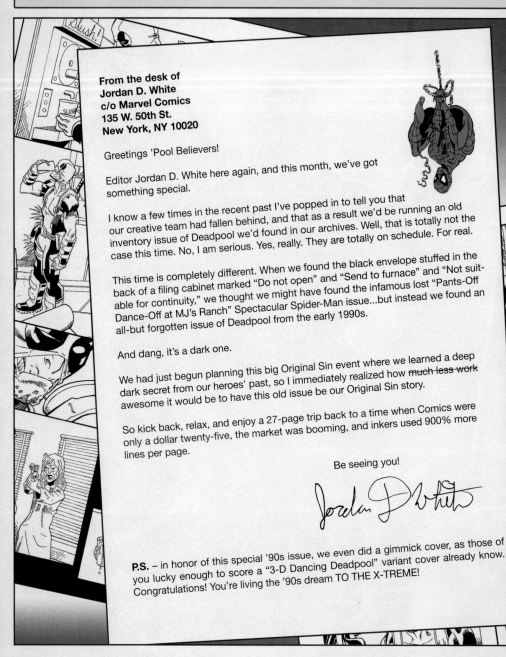

From the desk of
Jordan D. White
c/o Marvel Comics
135 W. 50th St.
New York, NY 10020

Greetings 'Pool Believers!

Editor Jordan D. White here again, and this month, we've got something special.

I know a few times in the recent past I've popped in to tell you that our creative team had fallen behind, and that as a result we'd be running an old inventory issue of Deadpool we'd found in our archives. Well, that is totally not the case this time. No, I am serious. Yes, really. They are totally on schedule. For real.

This time is completely different. When we found the black envelope stuffed in the back of a filing cabinet marked "Do not open" and "Send to furnace" and "Not suitable for continuity," we thought we might have found the infamous lost "Pants-Off Dance-Off at MJ's Ranch" Spectacular Spider-Man issue...but instead we found an all-but forgotten issue of Deadpool from the early 1990s.

And dang, it's a dark one.

We had just begun planning this big Original Sin event where we learned a deep dark secret from our heroes' past, so I immediately realized how ~~much less work~~ awesome it would be to have this old issue be our Original Sin story.

So kick back, relax, and enjoy a 27-page trip back to a time when Comics were only a dollar twenty-five, the market was booming, and inkers used 900% more lines per page.

Be seeing you!

Jordan D. White

P.S. – in honor of this special '90s issue, we even did a gimmick cover, as those of you lucky enough to score a "3-D Dancing Deadpool" variant cover already know. Congratulations! You're living the '90s dream TO THE X-TREME!

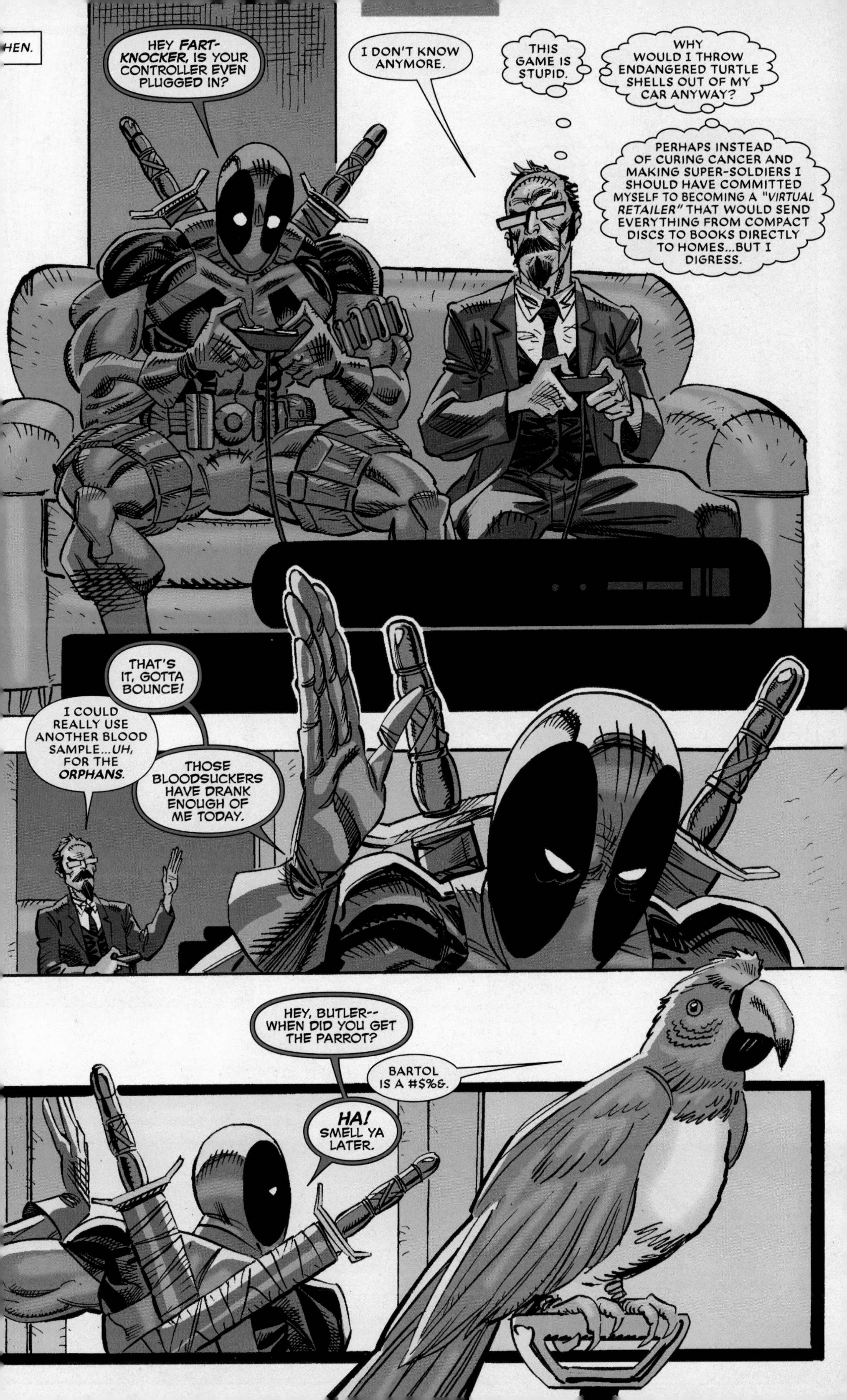
HEN.
HEY FART-KNOCKER, IS YOUR CONTROLLER EVEN PLUGGED IN?
I DON'T KNOW ANYMORE.
THIS GAME IS STUPID.
WHY WOULD I THROW ENDANGERED TURTLE SHELLS OUT OF MY CAR ANYWAY?
PERHAPS INSTEAD OF CURING CANCER AND MAKING SUPER-SOLDIERS I SHOULD HAVE COMMITTED MYSELF TO BECOMING A "VIRTUAL RETAILER" THAT WOULD SEND EVERYTHING FROM COMPACT DISCS TO BOOKS DIRECTLY TO HOMES...BUT I DIGRESS.
THAT'S IT, GOTTA BOUNCE!
I COULD REALLY USE ANOTHER BLOOD SAMPLE...UH, FOR THE ORPHANS.
THOSE BLOODSUCKERS HAVE DRANK ENOUGH OF ME TODAY.
HEY, BUTLER-- WHEN DID YOU GET THE PARROT?
BARTOL IS A #$%&.
HA! SMELL YA LATER.

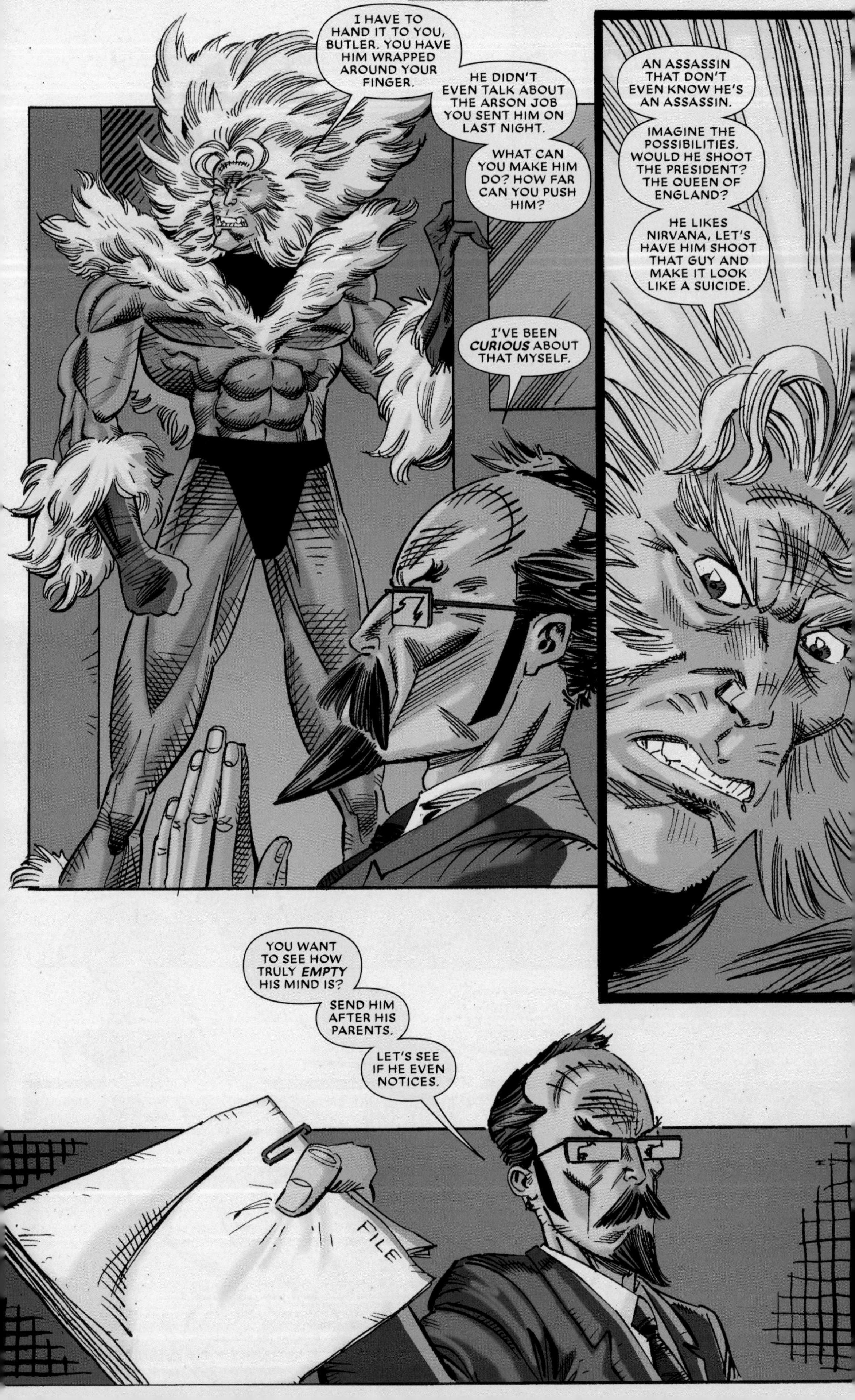
I HAVE TO HAND IT TO YOU, BUTLER. YOU HAVE HIM WRAPPED AROUND YOUR FINGER.
HE DIDN'T EVEN TALK ABOUT THE ARSON JOB YOU SENT HIM ON LAST NIGHT.
WHAT CAN YOU MAKE HIM DO? HOW FAR CAN YOU PUSH HIM?
I'VE BEEN *CURIOUS* ABOUT THAT MYSELF.
AN ASSASSIN THAT DON'T EVEN KNOW HE'S AN ASSASSIN.
IMAGINE THE POSSIBILITIES. WOULD HE SHOOT THE PRESIDENT? THE QUEEN OF ENGLAND?
HE LIKES NIRVANA, LET'S HAVE HIM SHOOT THAT GUY AND MAKE IT LOOK LIKE A SUICIDE.
YOU WANT TO SEE HOW TRULY *EMPTY* HIS MIND IS?
SEND HIM AFTER HIS PARENTS.
LET'S SEE IF HE EVEN NOTICES.
FILE

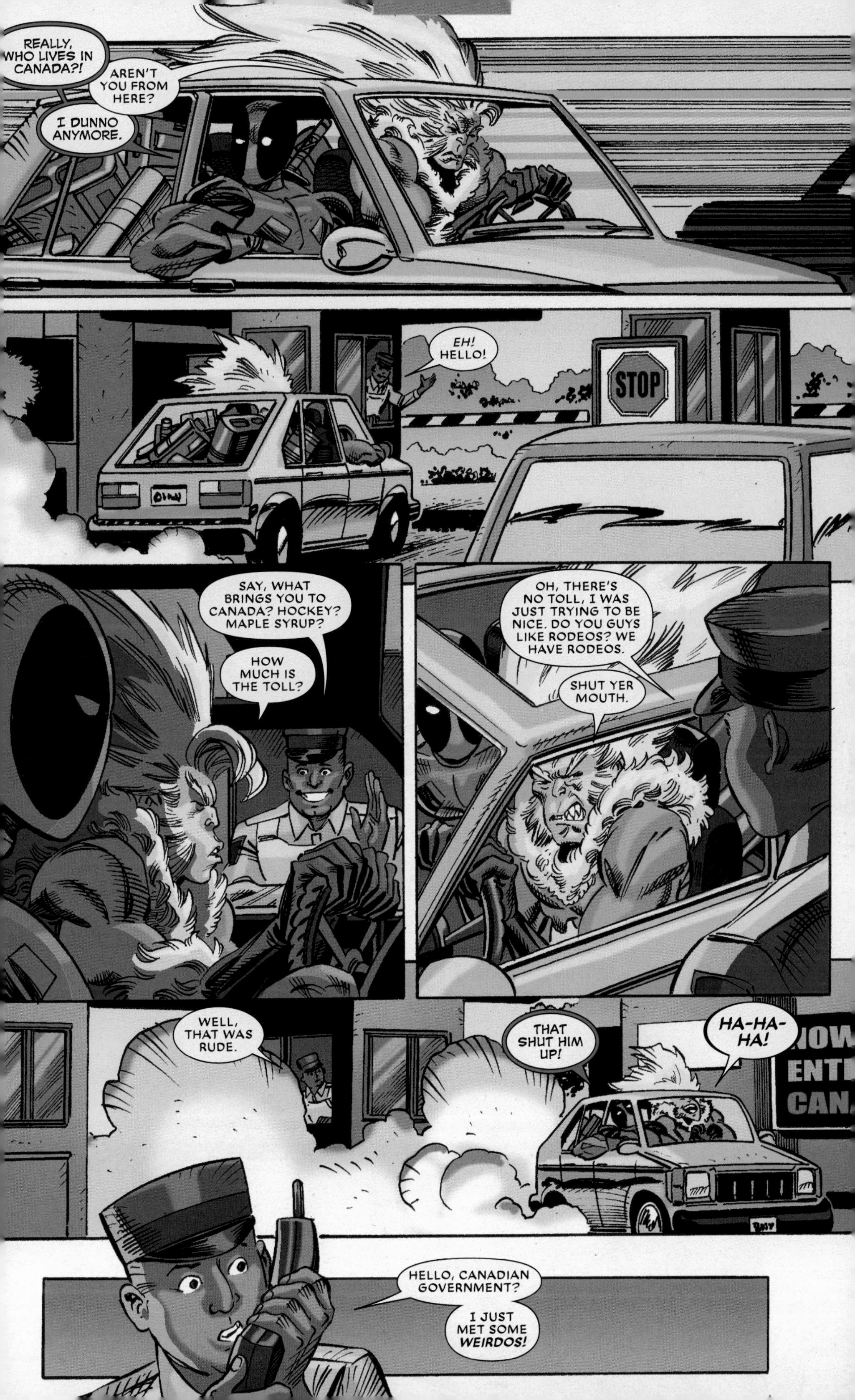
REALLY, WHO LIVES IN CANADA?!
AREN'T YOU FROM HERE?
I DUNNO ANYMORE.
EH! HELLO!
STOP
SAY, WHAT BRINGS YOU TO CANADA? HOCKEY? MAPLE SYRUP?
HOW MUCH IS THE TOLL?
OH, THERE'S NO TOLL, I WAS JUST TRYING TO BE NICE. DO YOU GUYS LIKE RODEOS? WE HAVE RODEOS.
SHUT YER MOUTH.
WELL, THAT WAS RUDE.
THAT SHUT HIM UP!
HA-HA-HA!
HELLO, CANADIAN GOVERNMENT?
I JUST MET SOME *WEIRDOS!*

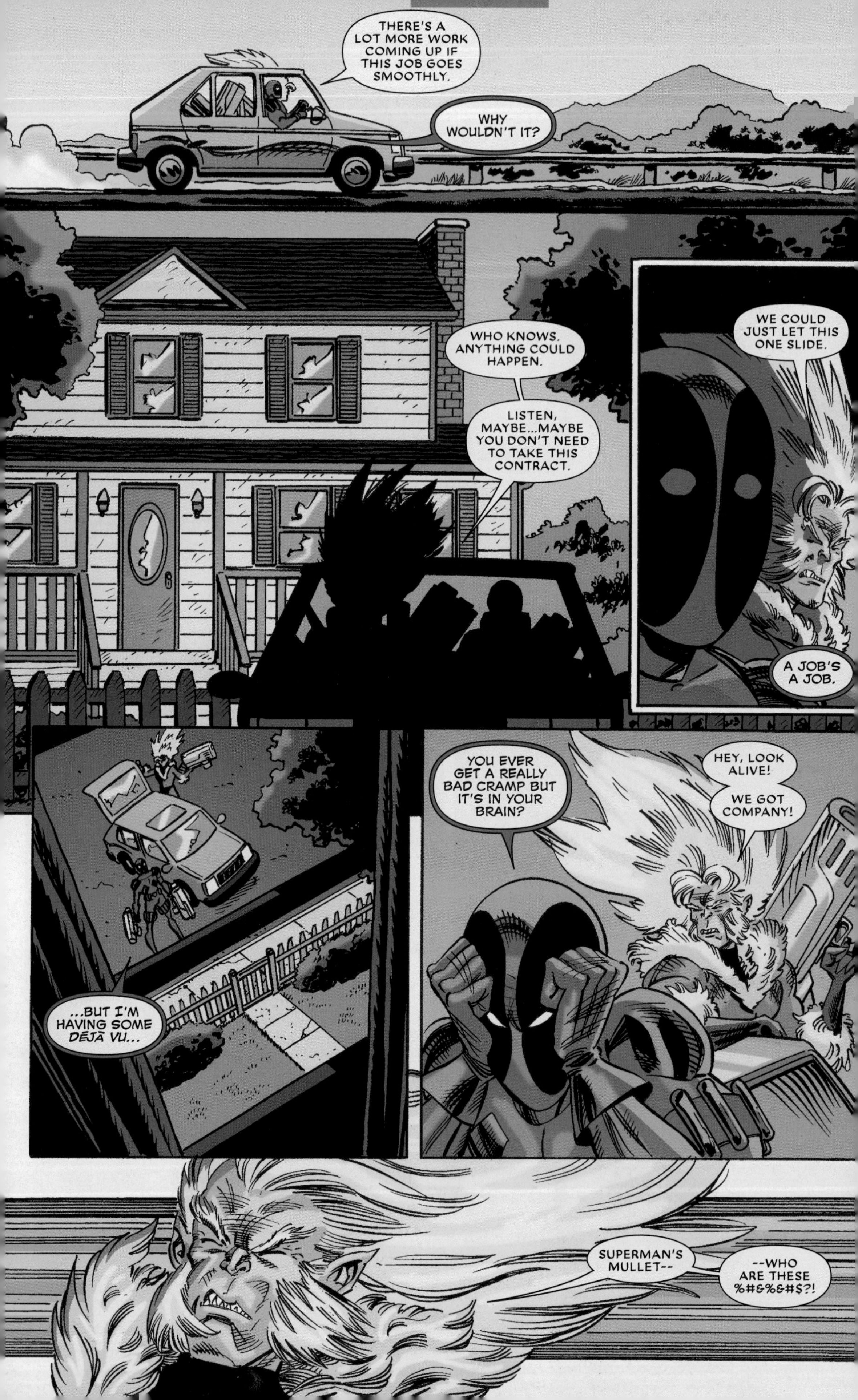
THERE'S A LOT MORE WORK COMING UP IF THIS JOB GOES SMOOTHLY.
WHY WOULDN'T IT?
WHO KNOWS. ANYTHING COULD HAPPEN.
LISTEN, MAYBE...MAYBE YOU DON'T NEED TO TAKE THIS CONTRACT.
WE COULD JUST LET THIS ONE SLIDE.
A JOB'S A JOB.
...BUT I'M HAVING SOME DÉJÀ VU...
YOU EVER GET A REALLY BAD CRAMP BUT IT'S IN YOUR BRAIN?
HEY, LOOK ALIVE!
WE GOT COMPANY!
SUPERMAN'S MULLET--
--WHO ARE THESE %#&%&#$?!

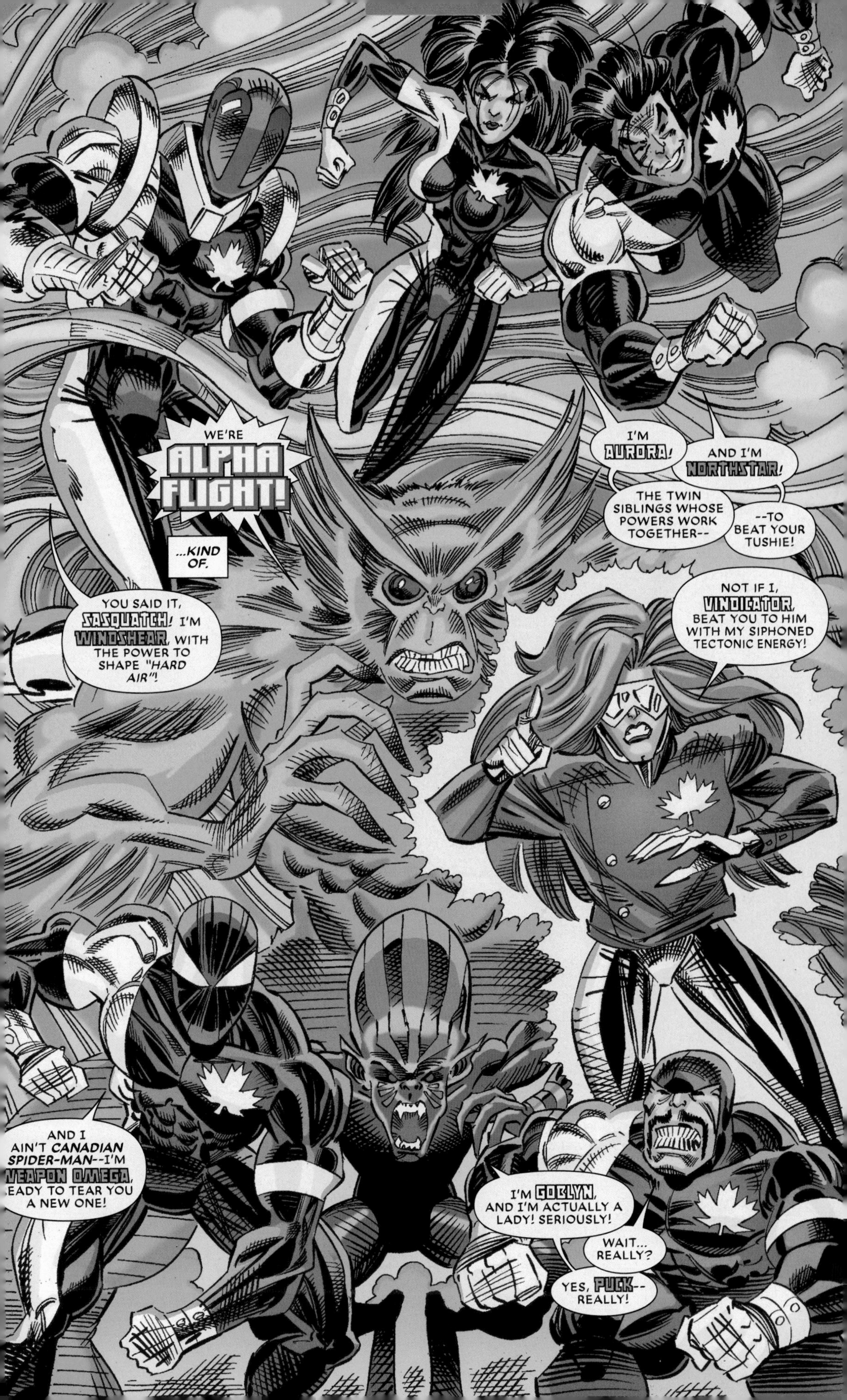
WE'RE ALPHA FLIGHT!
...KIND OF.
YOU SAID IT, SASQUATCH! I'M WINDSHEAR, WITH THE POWER TO SHAPE "HARD AIR"!
I'M AURORA!
AND I'M NORTHSTAR!
THE TWIN SIBLINGS WHOSE POWERS WORK TOGETHER--
--TO BEAT YOUR TUSHIE!
NOT IF I, VINDICATOR, BEAT YOU TO HIM WITH MY SIPHONED TECTONIC ENERGY!
AND I AIN'T CANADIAN SPIDER-MAN--I'M WEAPON OMEGA, READY TO TEAR YOU A NEW ONE!
I'M GOBLYN, AND I'M ACTUALLY A LADY! SERIOUSLY!
WAIT... REALLY?
YES, PUCK-- REALLY!

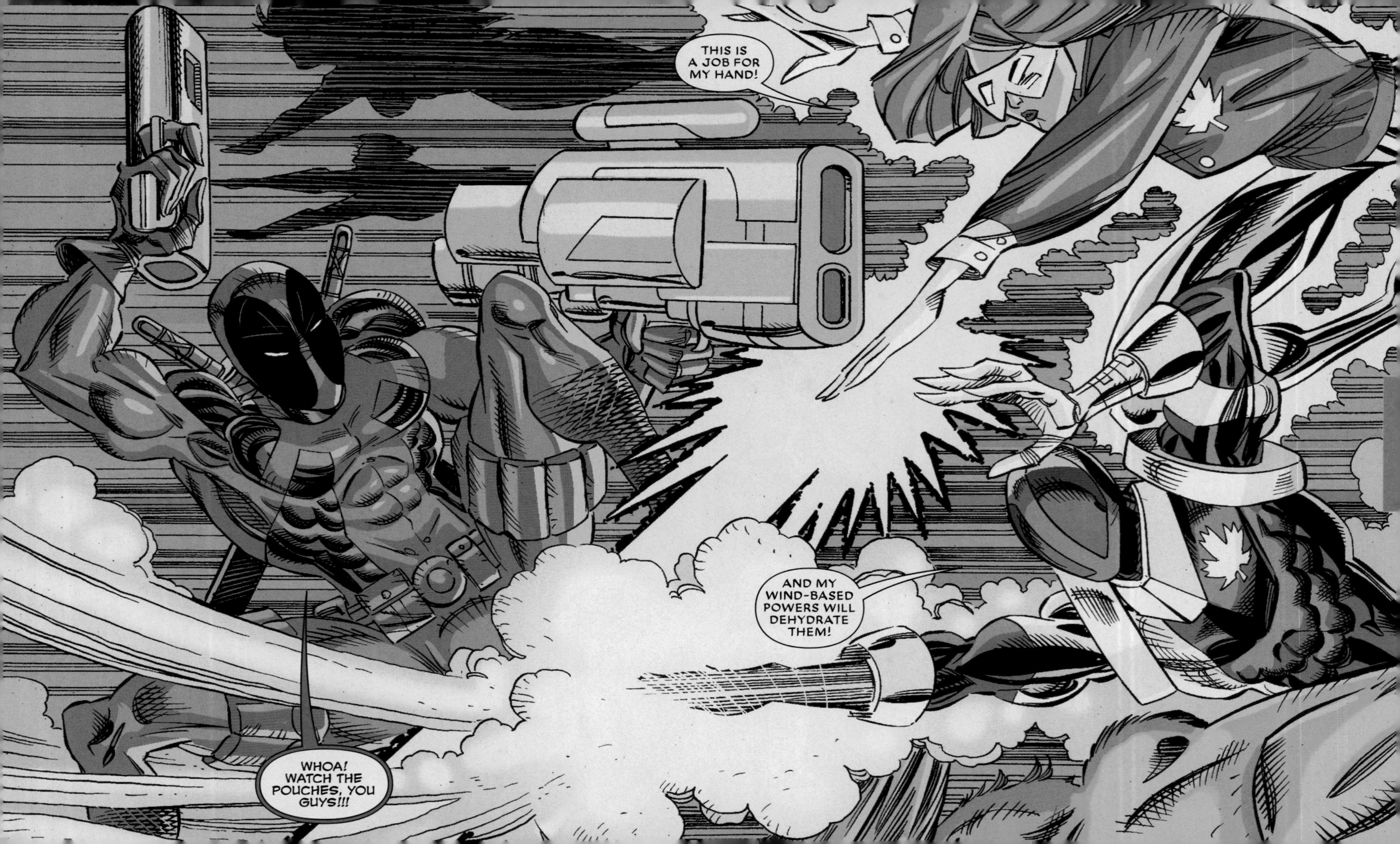
THIS IS A JOB FOR MY HAND!
AND MY WIND-BASED POWERS WILL DEHYDRATE THEM!
WHOA! WATCH THE POUCHES, YOU GUYS!!!

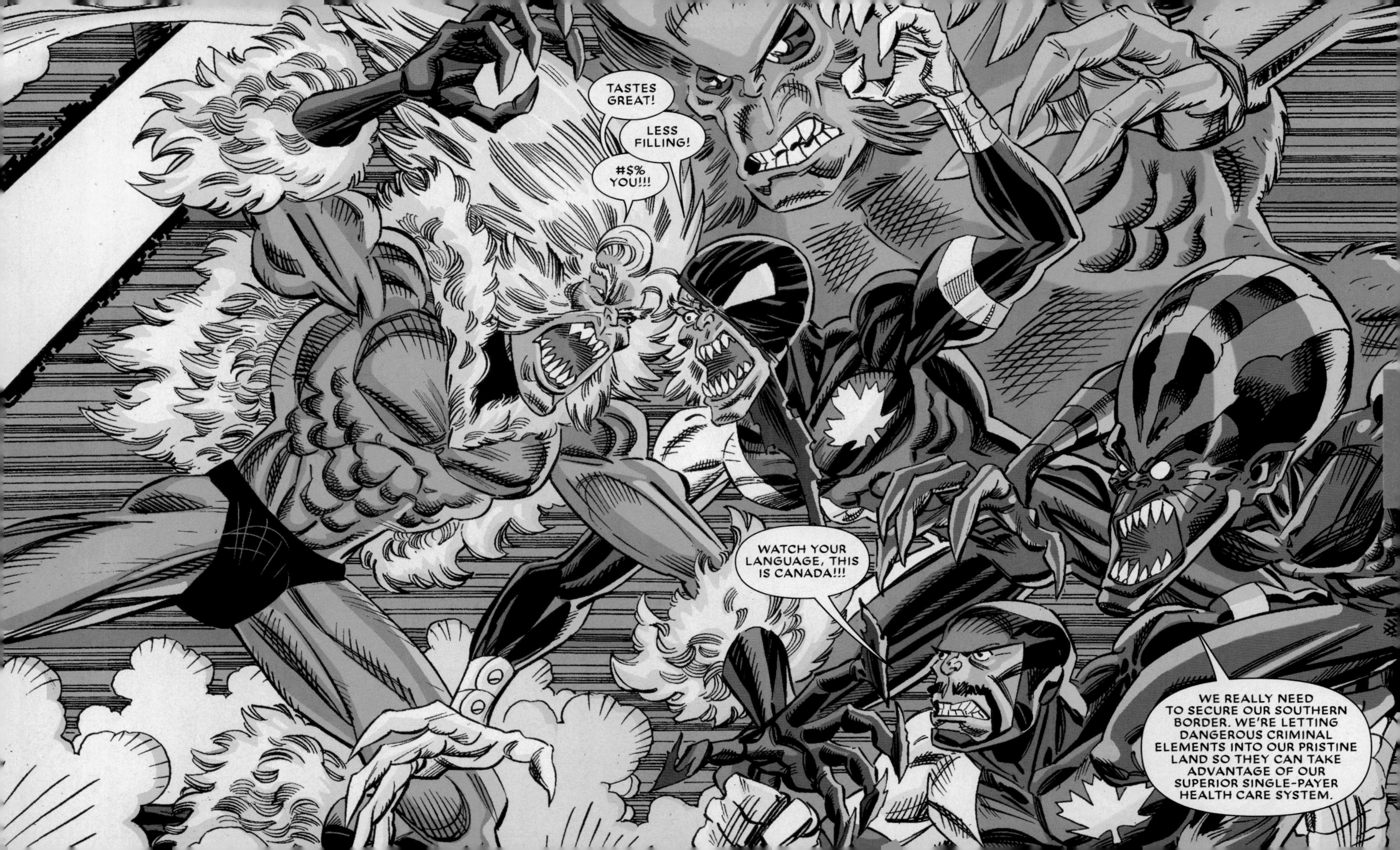
TASTES GREAT!
LESS FILLING!
#$% YOU!!!
WATCH YOUR LANGUAGE, THIS IS CANADA!!!
WE REALLY NEED TO SECURE OUR SOUTHERN BORDER. WE'RE LETTING DANGEROUS CRIMINAL ELEMENTS INTO OUR PRISTINE LAND SO THEY CAN TAKE ADVANTAGE OF OUR SUPERIOR SINGLE-PAYER HEALTH CARE SYSTEM.

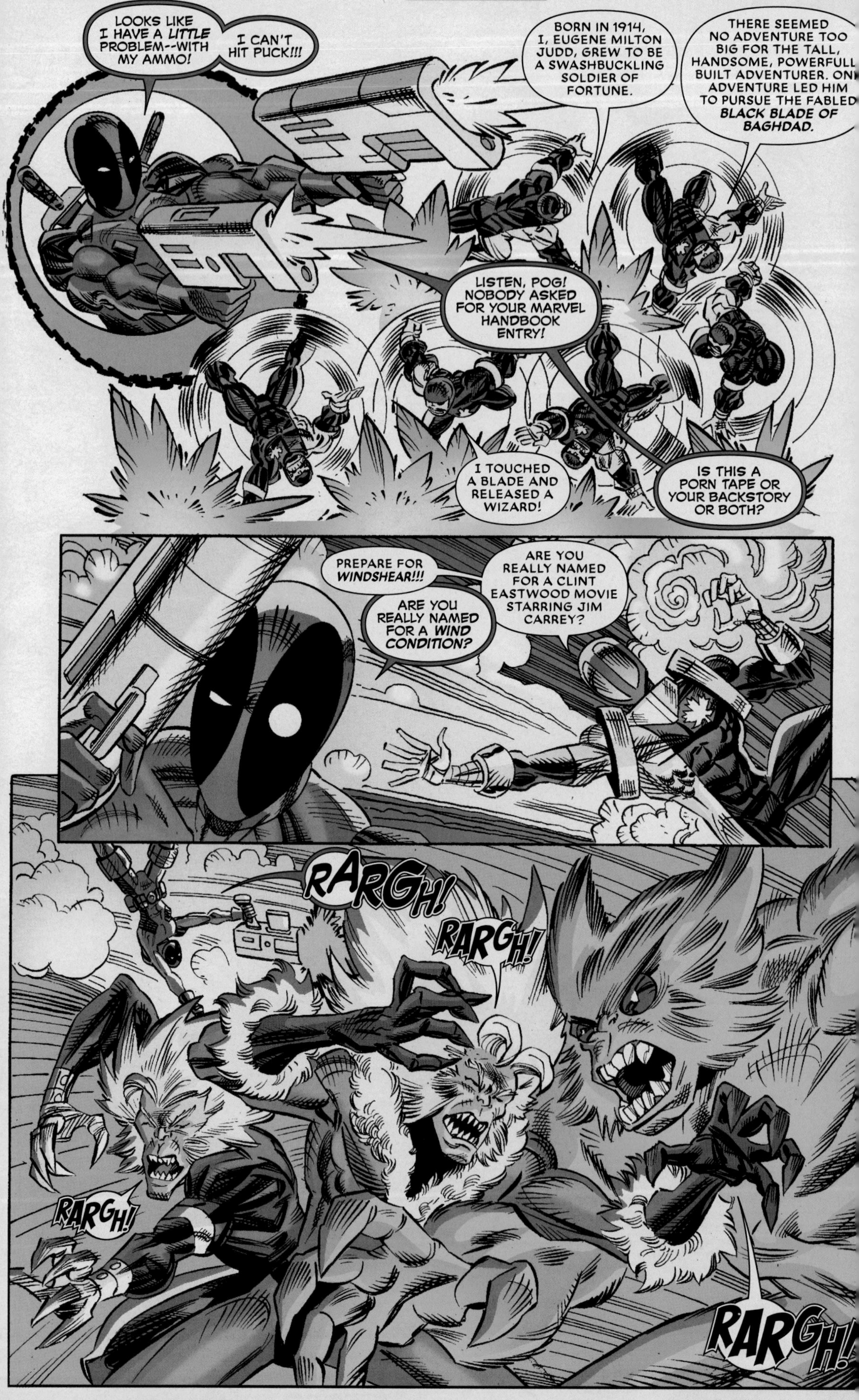

LOOKS LIKE I HAVE A *LITTLE* PROBLEM--WITH MY AMMO!
I CAN'T HIT PUCK!!!
BORN IN 1914, I, EUGENE MILTON JUDD, GREW TO BE A SWASHBUCKLING SOLDIER OF FORTUNE.
THERE SEEMED NO ADVENTURE TOO BIG FOR THE TALL, HANDSOME, POWERFULL BUILT ADVENTURER. ON ADVENTURE LED HIM TO PURSUE THE FABLED ***BLACK BLADE OF BAGHDAD.***
LISTEN, POG! NOBODY ASKED FOR YOUR MARVEL HANDBOOK ENTRY!
I TOUCHED A BLADE AND RELEASED A WIZARD!
IS THIS A PORN TAPE OR YOUR BACKSTORY OR BOTH?
PREPARE FOR *WINDSHEAR!!!*
ARE YOU REALLY NAMED FOR A *WIND CONDITION?*
ARE YOU REALLY NAMED FOR A CLINT EASTWOOD MOVIE STARRING JIM CARREY?
RARGH!
RARGH!
RARGH!
RARGH!

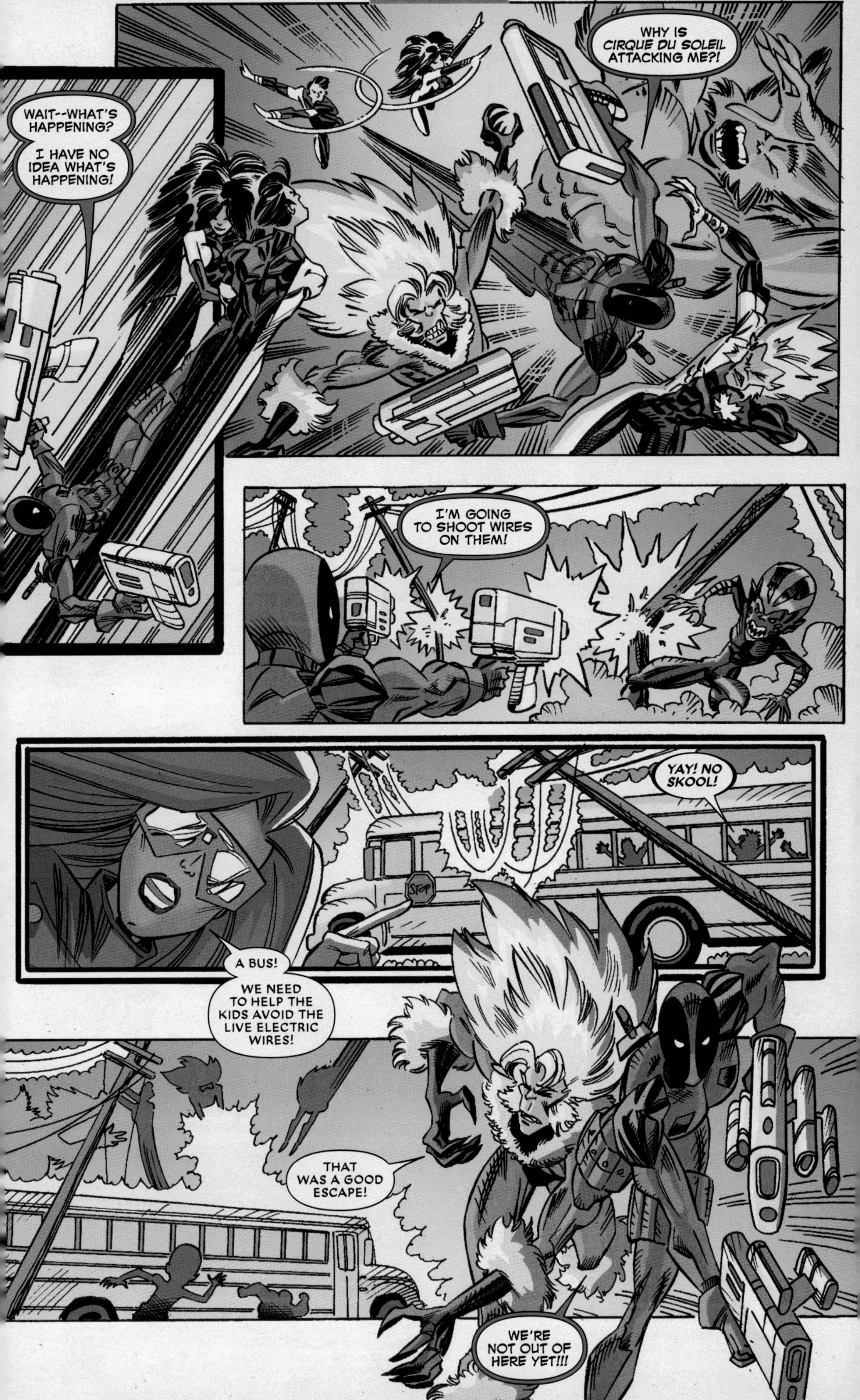
WHY IS CIRQUE DU SOLEIL ATTACKING ME?!
WAIT--WHAT'S HAPPENING?
I HAVE NO IDEA WHAT'S HAPPENING!
I'M GOING TO SHOOT WIRES ON THEM!
YAY! NO SKOOL!
STOP
A BUS!
WE NEED TO HELP THE KIDS AVOID THE LIVE ELECTRIC WIRES!
THAT WAS A GOOD ESCAPE!
WE'RE NOT OUT OF HERE YET!!!

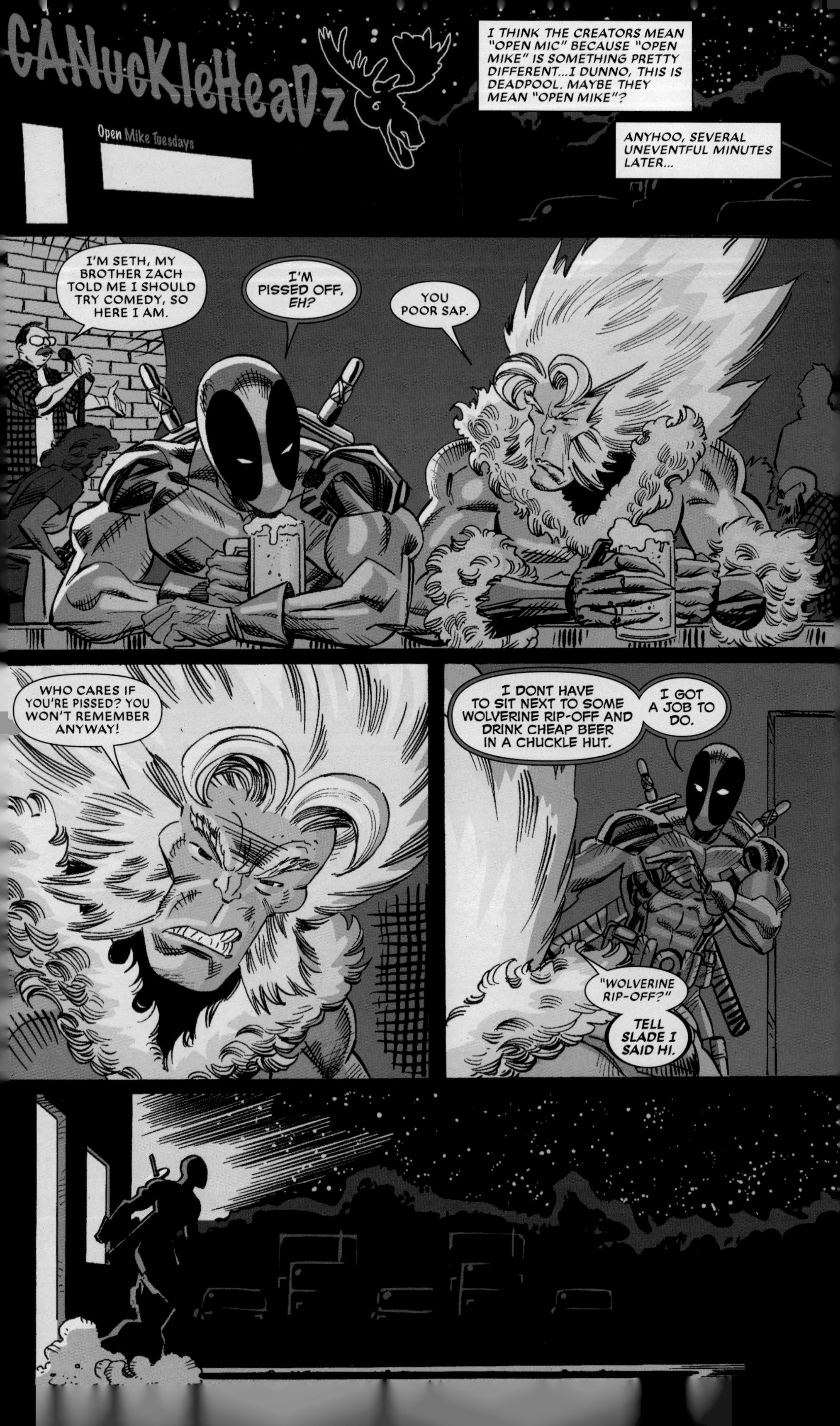
CANucKleHeaDz
Open Mike Tuesdays
I THINK THE CREATORS MEAN "OPEN MIC" BECAUSE "OPEN MIKE" IS SOMETHING PRETTY DIFFERENT...I DUNNO, THIS IS DEADPOOL. MAYBE THEY MEAN "OPEN MIKE"?
ANYHOO, SEVERAL UNEVENTFUL MINUTES LATER...
I'M SETH, MY BROTHER ZACH TOLD ME I SHOULD TRY COMEDY, SO HERE I AM.
I'M PISSED OFF, EH?
YOU POOR SAP.
WHO CARES IF YOU'RE PISSED? YOU WON'T REMEMBER ANYWAY!
I DONT HAVE TO SIT NEXT TO SOME WOLVERINE RIP-OFF AND DRINK CHEAP BEER IN A CHUCKLE HUT.
I GOT A JOB TO DO.
"WOLVERINE RIP-OFF?"
TELL SLADE I SAID HI.

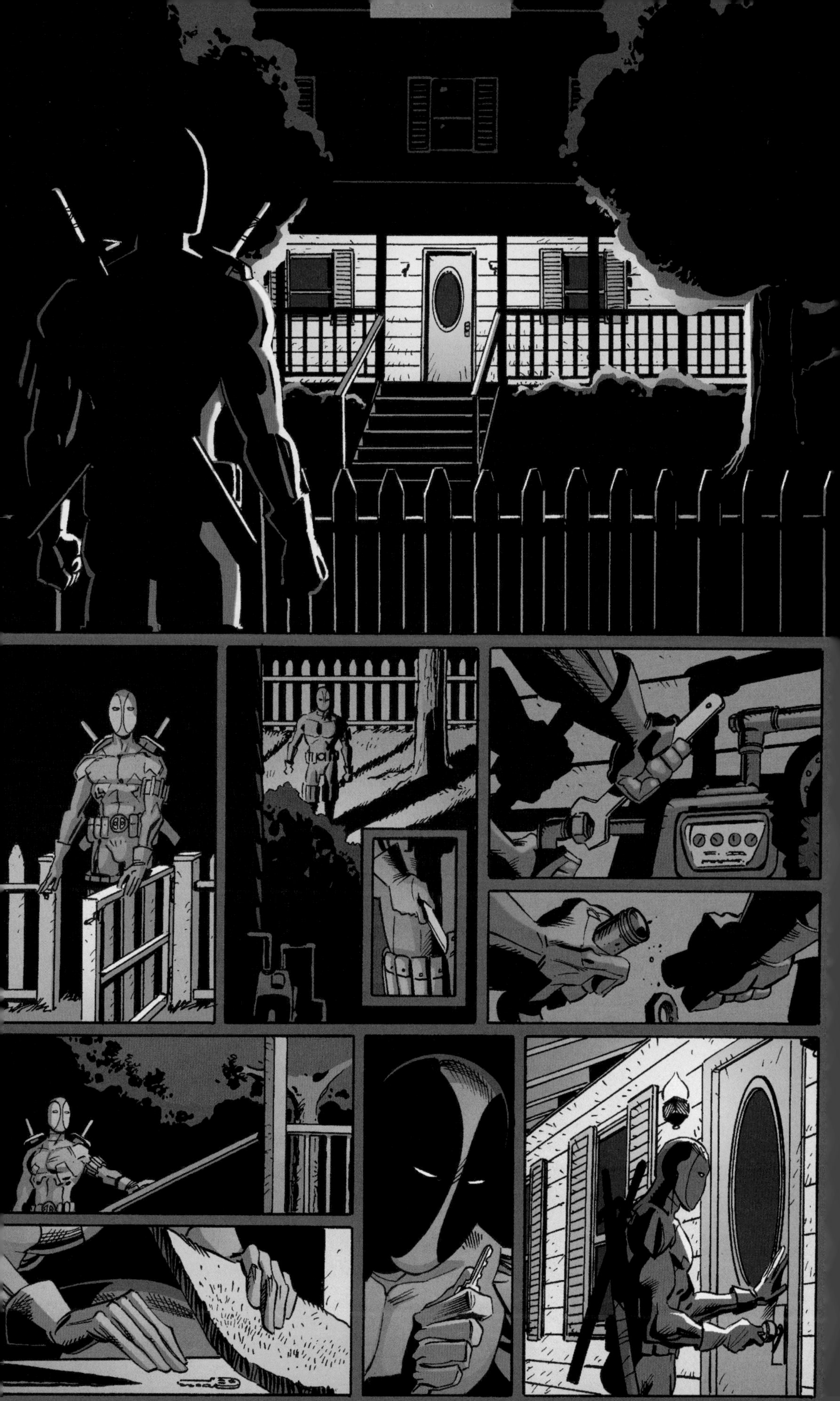

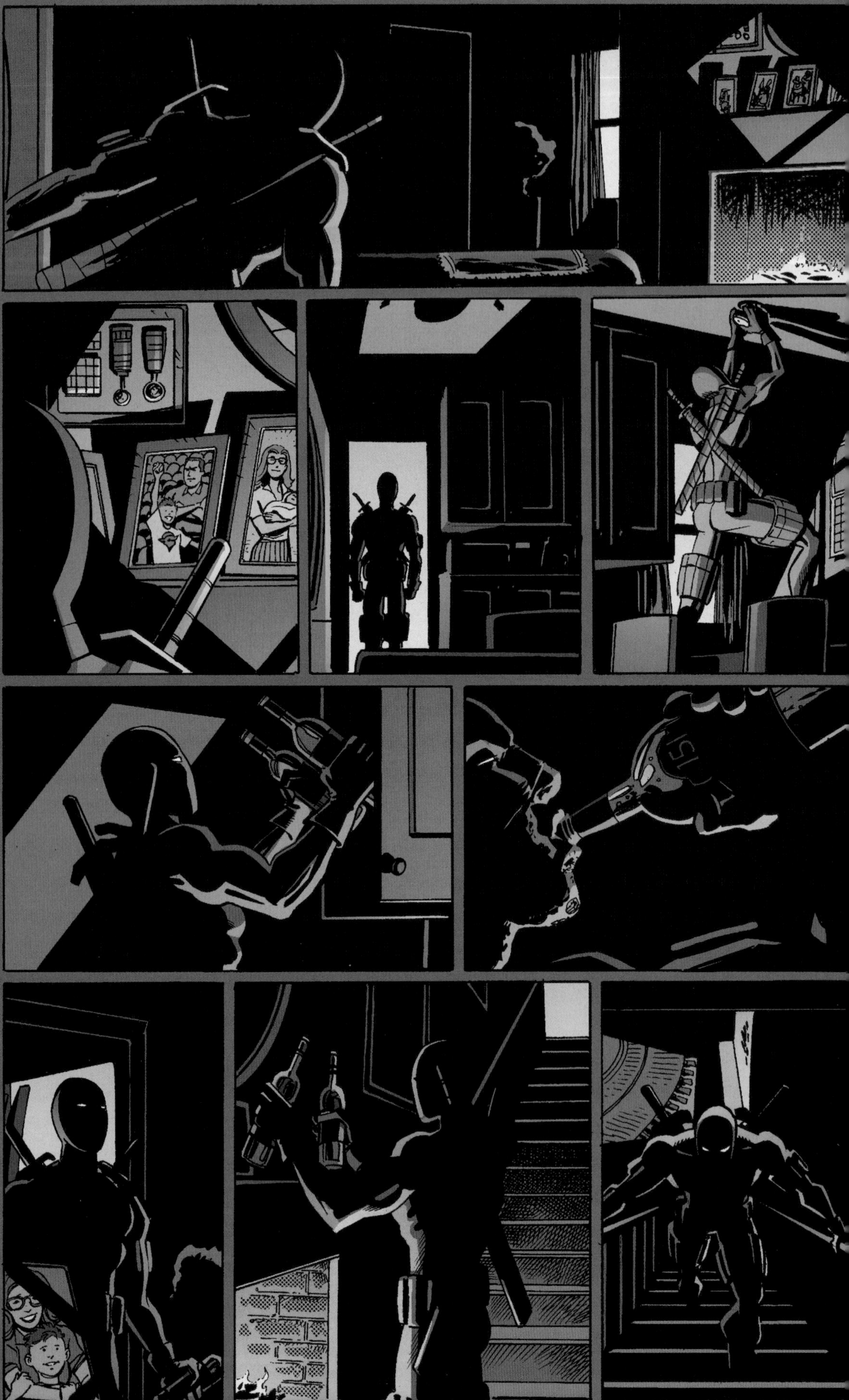

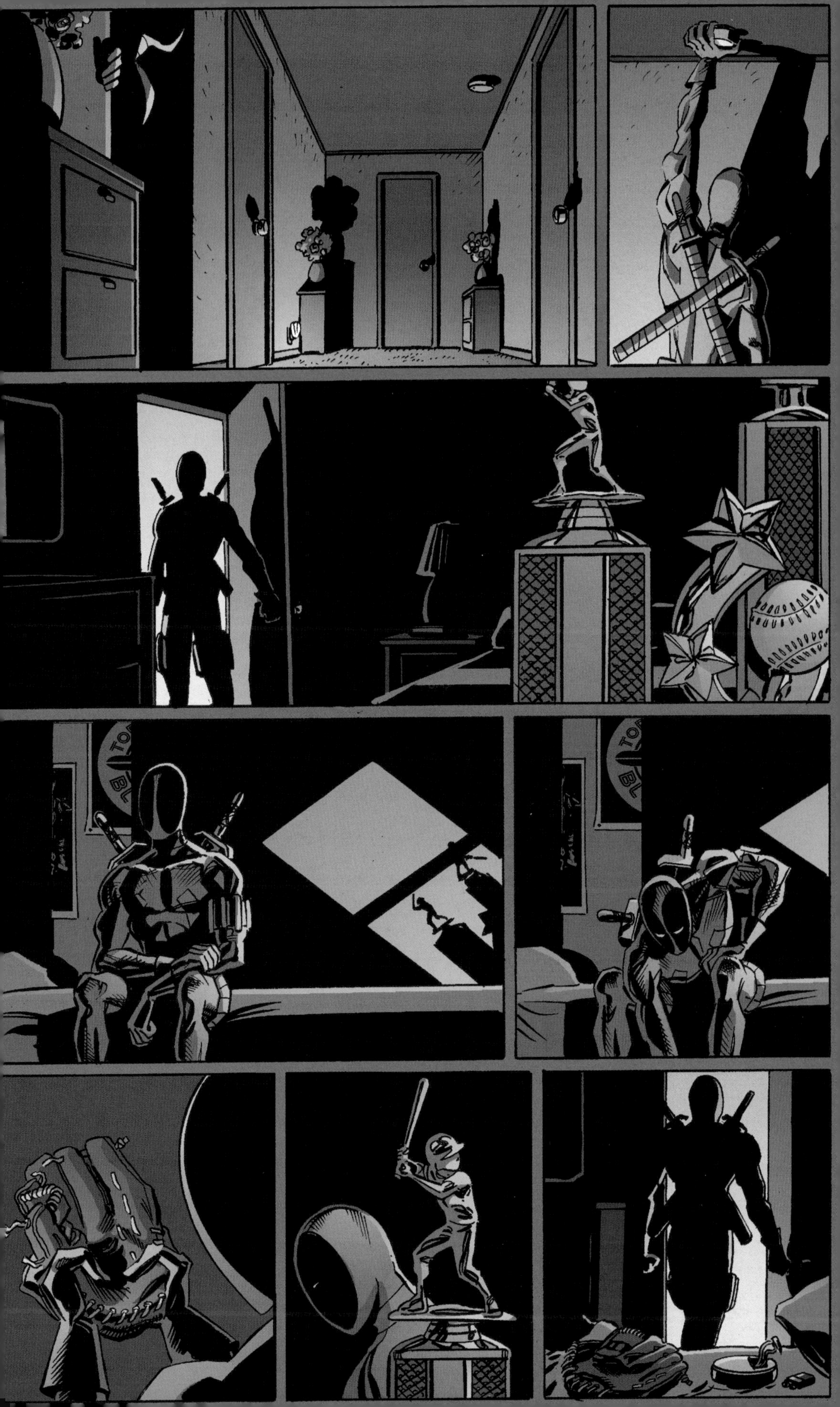

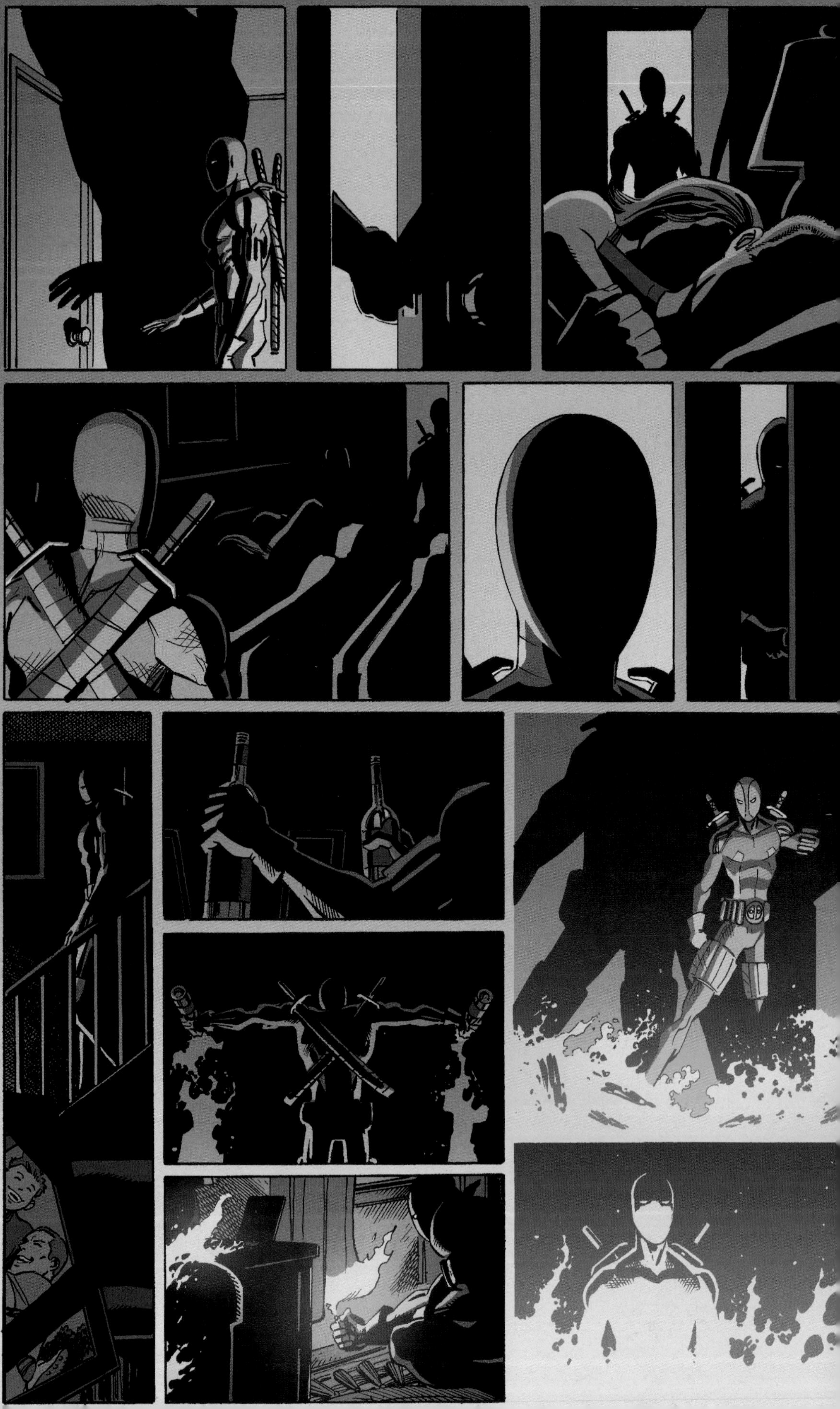

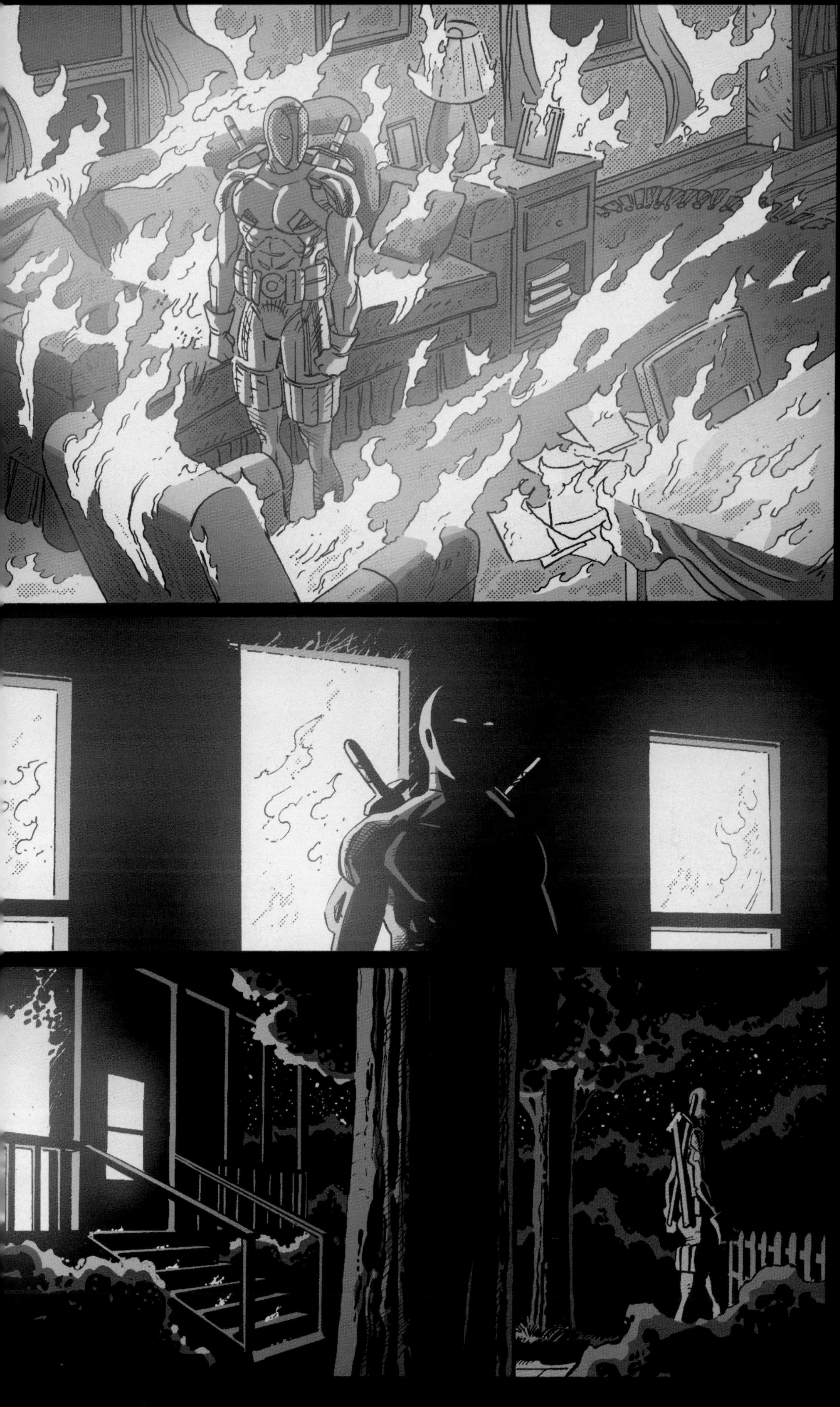

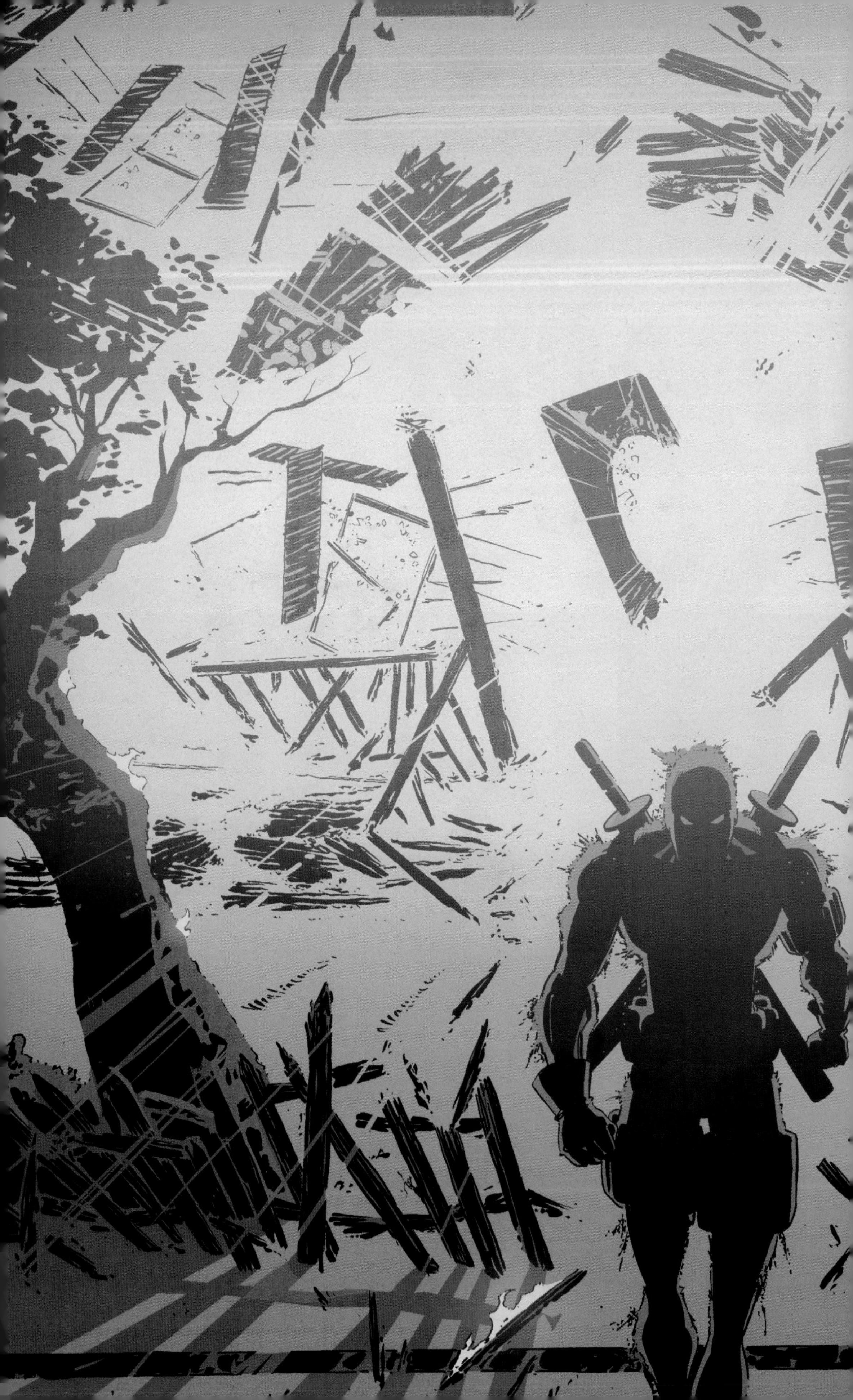

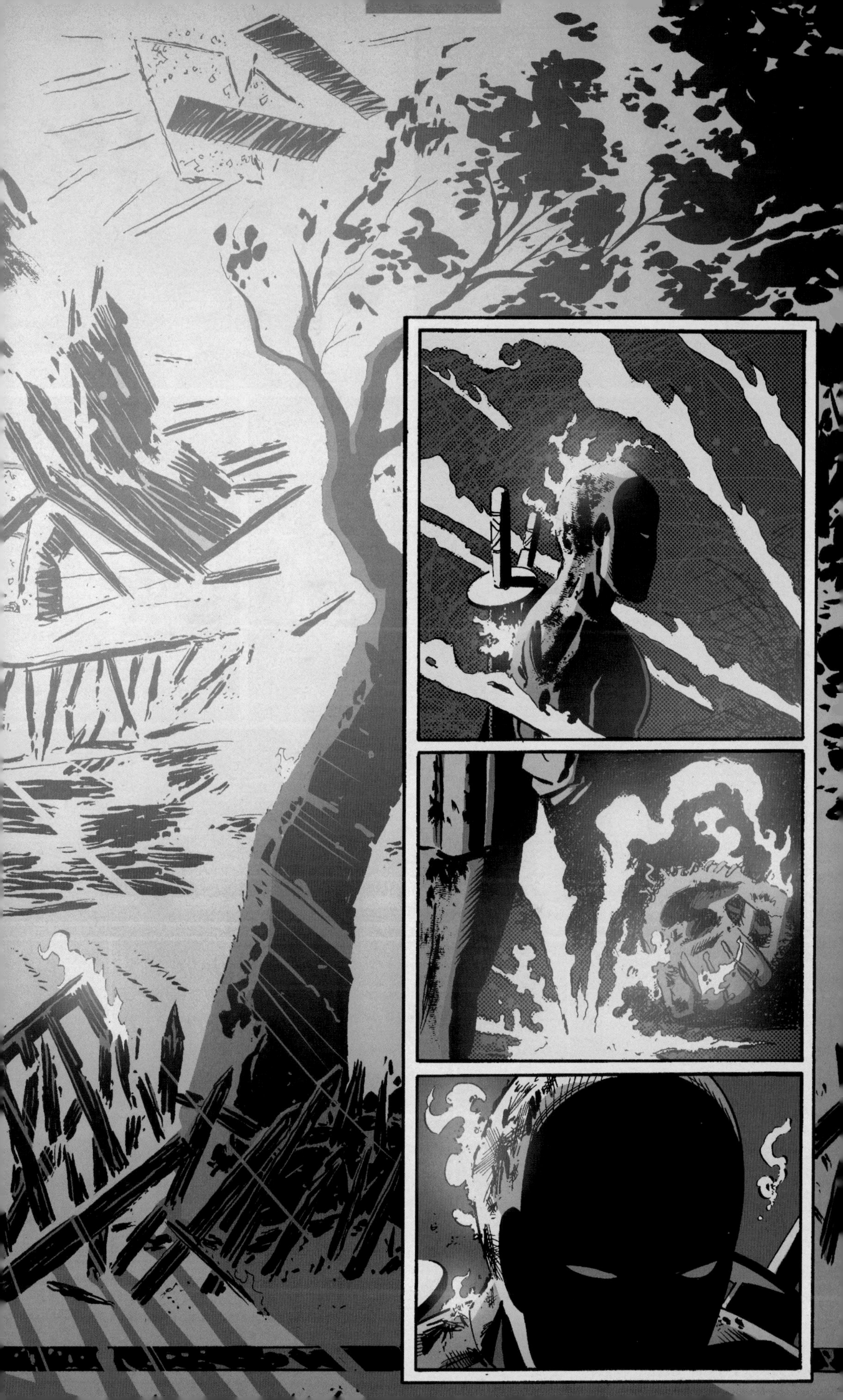

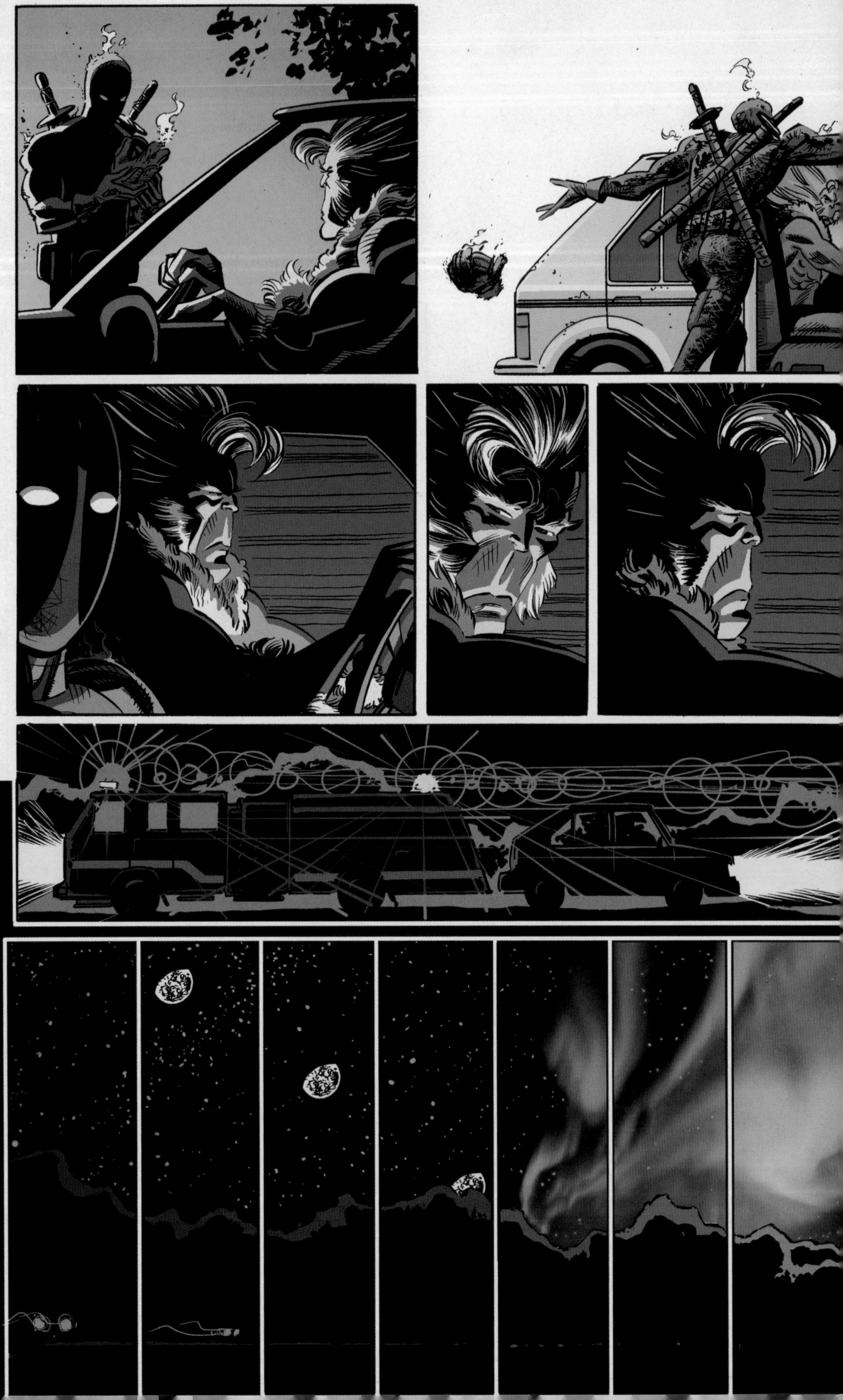

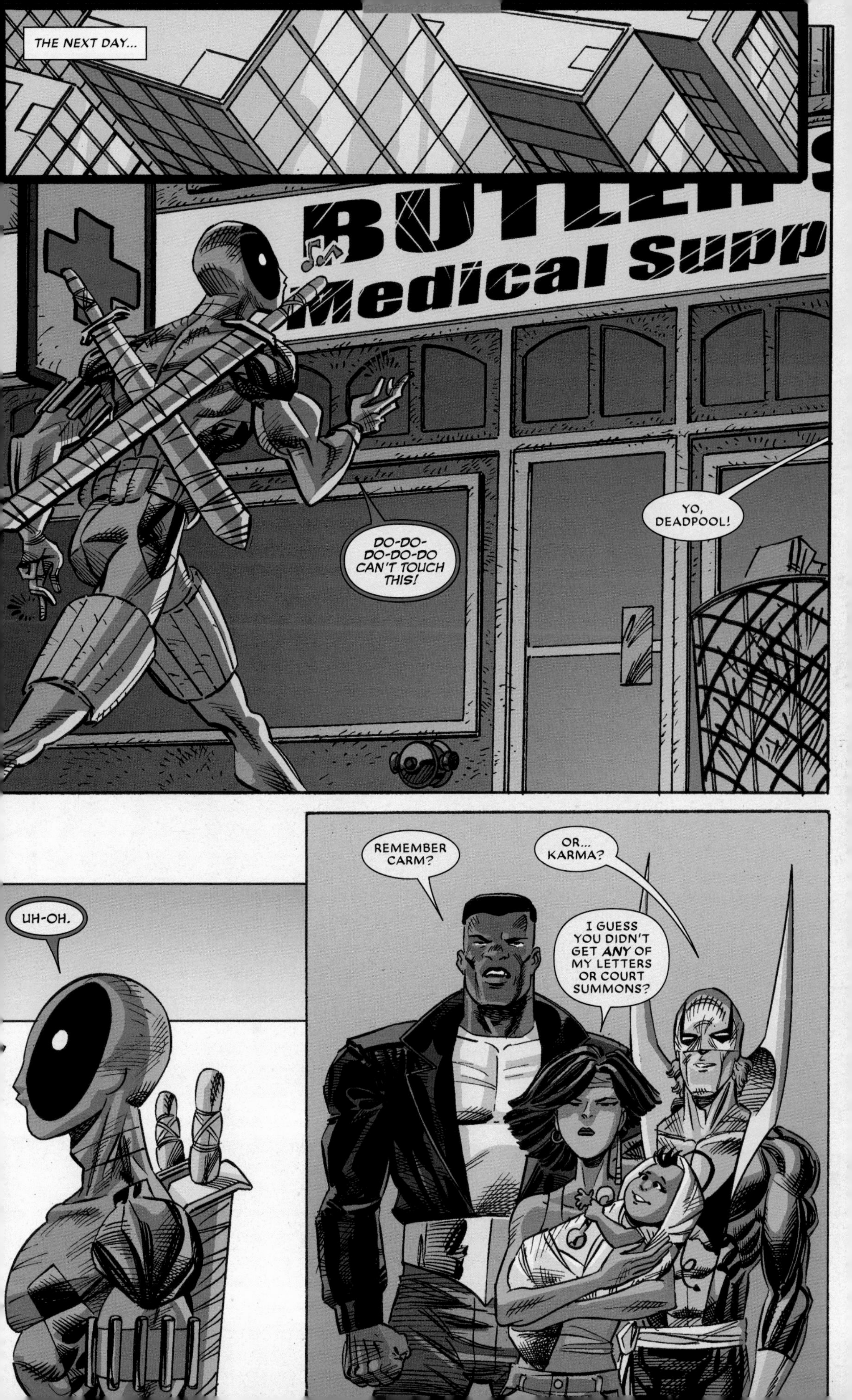
THE NEXT DAY...
BUTLER'S
Medical Supp
DO-DO-DO-DO-DO CAN'T TOUCH THIS!
YO, DEADPOOL!
REMEMBER CARM?
OR... KARMA?
UH-OH.
I GUESS YOU DIDN'T GET ANY OF MY LETTERS OR COURT SUMMONS?

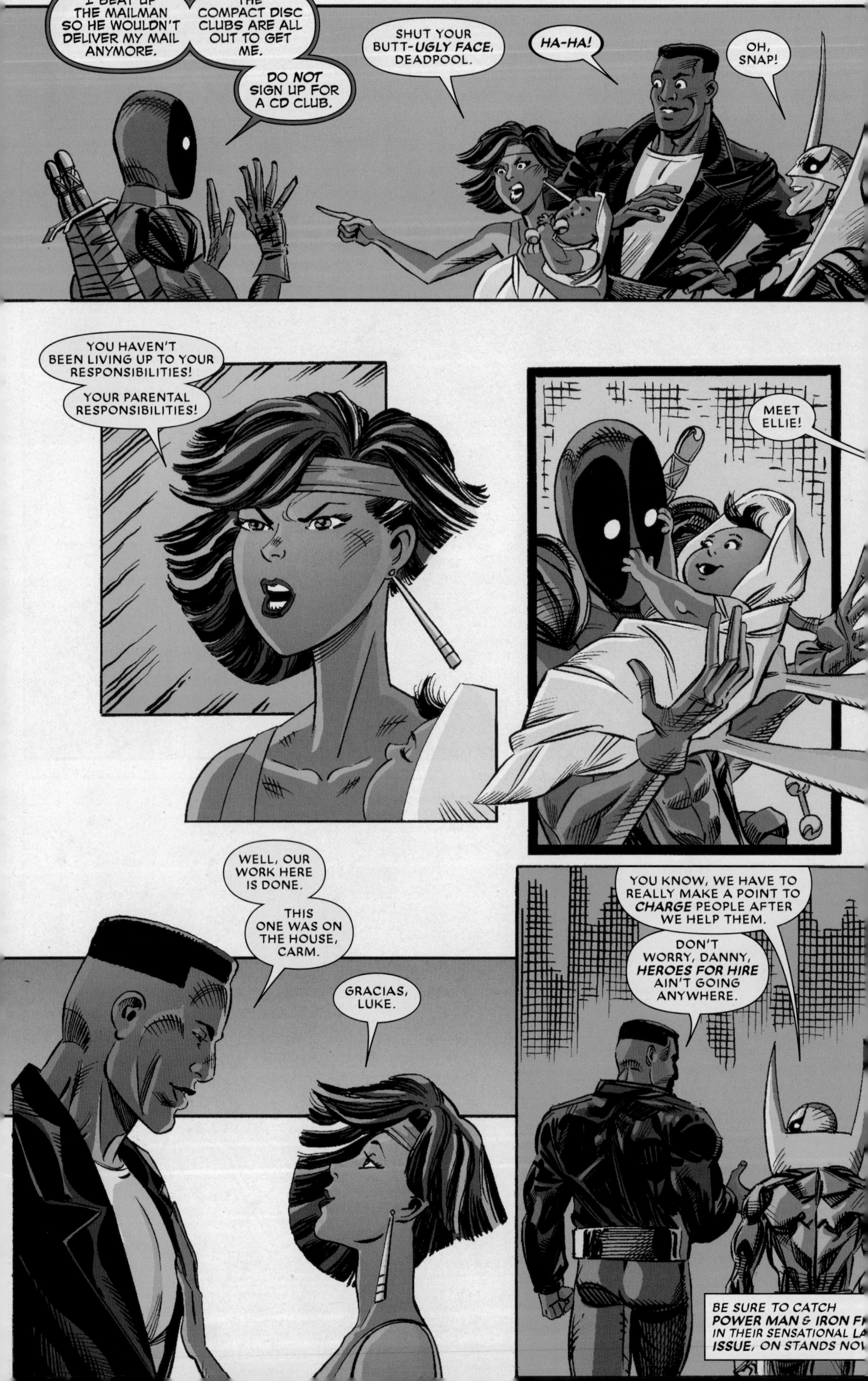

I BEAT UP THE MAILMAN SO HE WOULDN'T DELIVER MY MAIL ANYMORE.
THE COMPACT DISC CLUBS ARE ALL OUT TO GET ME.
DO NOT SIGN UP FOR A CD CLUB.
SHUT YOUR BUTT-UGLY FACE, DEADPOOL.
HA-HA!
OH, SNAP!
YOU HAVEN'T BEEN LIVING UP TO YOUR RESPONSIBILITIES!
YOUR PARENTAL RESPONSIBILITIES!
MEET ELLIE!
WELL, OUR WORK HERE IS DONE.
THIS ONE WAS ON THE HOUSE, CARM.
GRACIAS, LUKE.
YOU KNOW, WE HAVE TO REALLY MAKE A POINT TO CHARGE PEOPLE AFTER WE HELP THEM.
DON'T WORRY, DANNY, HEROES FOR HIRE AIN'T GOING ANYWHERE.

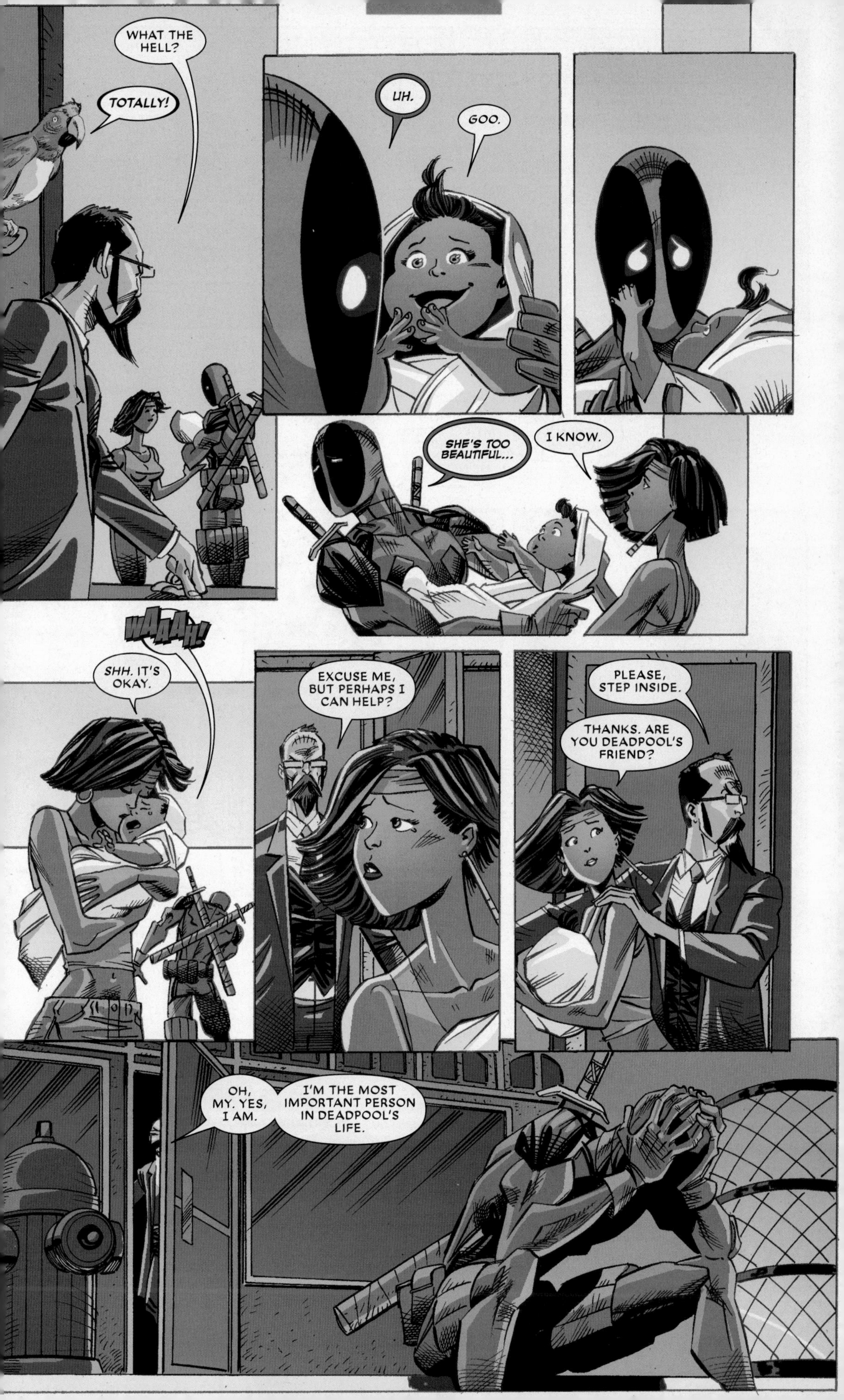
WHAT THE HELL?
TOTALLY!
UH.
GOO.
SHE'S TOO BEAUTIFUL...
I KNOW.
WAAAH!
SHH. IT'S OKAY.
EXCUSE ME, BUT PERHAPS I CAN HELP?
PLEASE, STEP INSIDE.
THANKS. ARE YOU DEADPOOL'S FRIEND?
OH, MY. YES, I AM.
I'M THE MOST IMPORTANT PERSON IN DEADPOOL'S LIFE.

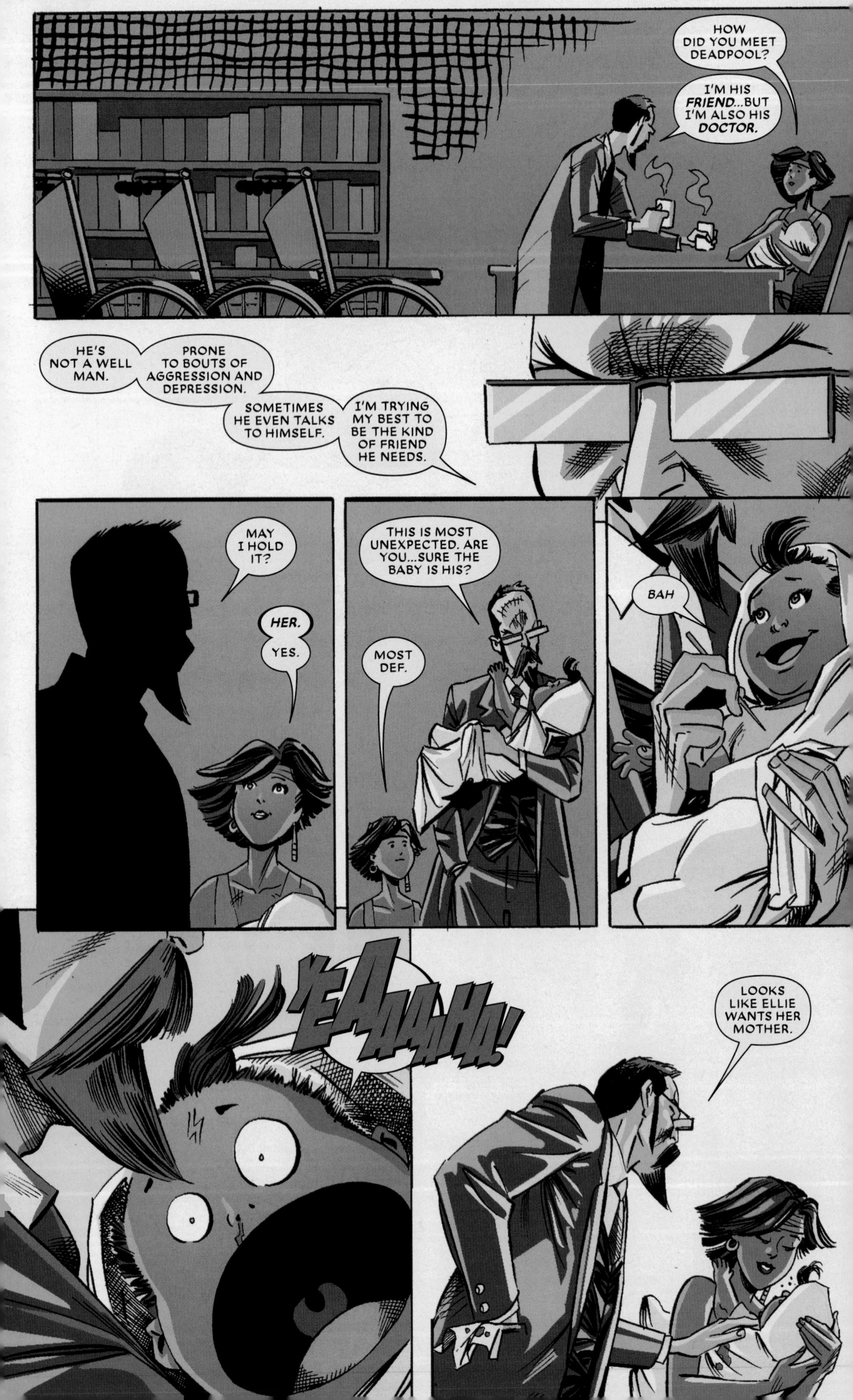

HOW DID YOU MEET DEADPOOL?
I'M HIS FRIEND...BUT I'M ALSO HIS DOCTOR.
HE'S NOT A WELL MAN.
PRONE TO BOUTS OF AGGRESSION AND DEPRESSION.
SOMETIMES HE EVEN TALKS TO HIMSELF.
I'M TRYING MY BEST TO BE THE KIND OF FRIEND HE NEEDS.
MAY I HOLD IT?
HER.
YES.
THIS IS MOST UNEXPECTED. ARE YOU...SURE THE BABY IS HIS?
MOST DEF.
BAH
YEAAAAHA!
LOOKS LIKE ELLIE WANTS HER MOTHER.

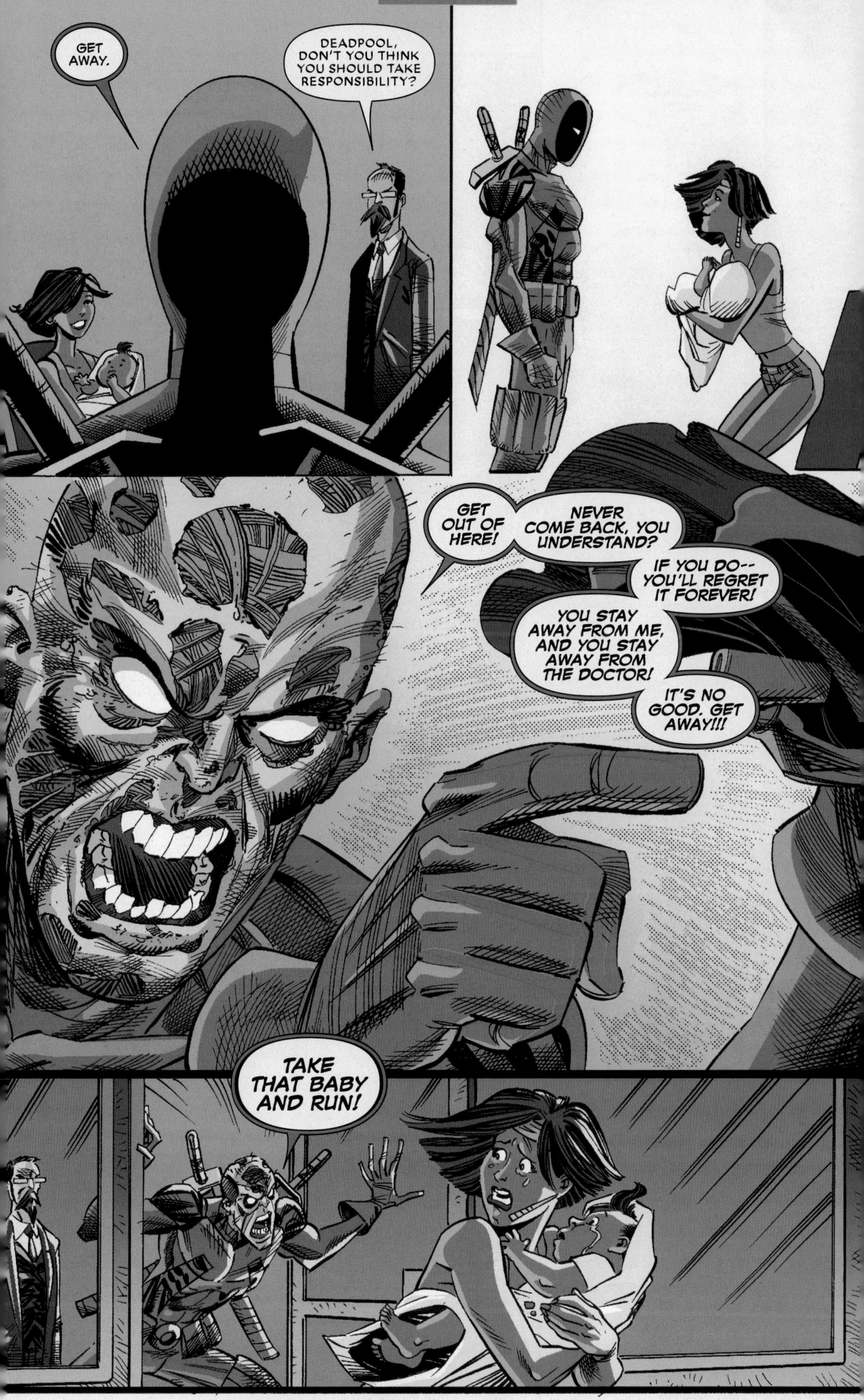
GET AWAY.
DEADPOOL, DON'T YOU THINK YOU SHOULD TAKE RESPONSIBILITY?
GET OUT OF HERE!
NEVER COME BACK, YOU UNDERSTAND?
IF YOU DO-- YOU'LL REGRET IT FOREVER!
YOU STAY AWAY FROM ME, AND YOU STAY AWAY FROM THE DOCTOR!
IT'S NO GOOD. GET AWAY!!!
TAKE THAT BABY AND RUN!

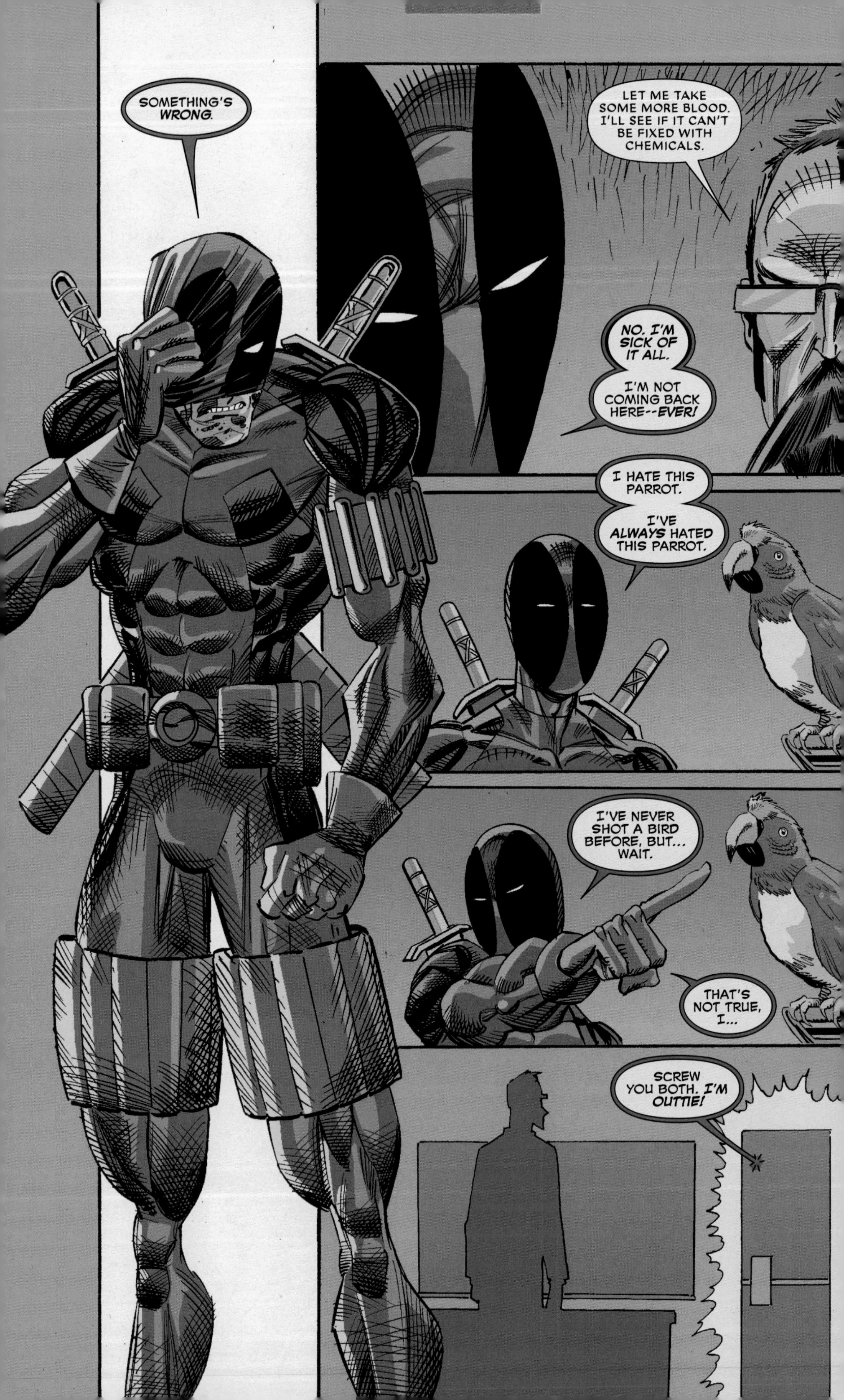
SOMETHING'S WRONG.
LET ME TAKE SOME MORE BLOOD. I'LL SEE IF IT CAN'T BE FIXED WITH CHEMICALS.
NO. I'M SICK OF IT ALL.
I'M NOT COMING BACK HERE--EVER!
I HATE THIS PARROT.
I'VE ALWAYS HATED THIS PARROT.
I'VE NEVER SHOT A BIRD BEFORE, BUT... WAIT.
THAT'S NOT TRUE, I...
SCREW YOU BOTH. I'M OUTTIE!

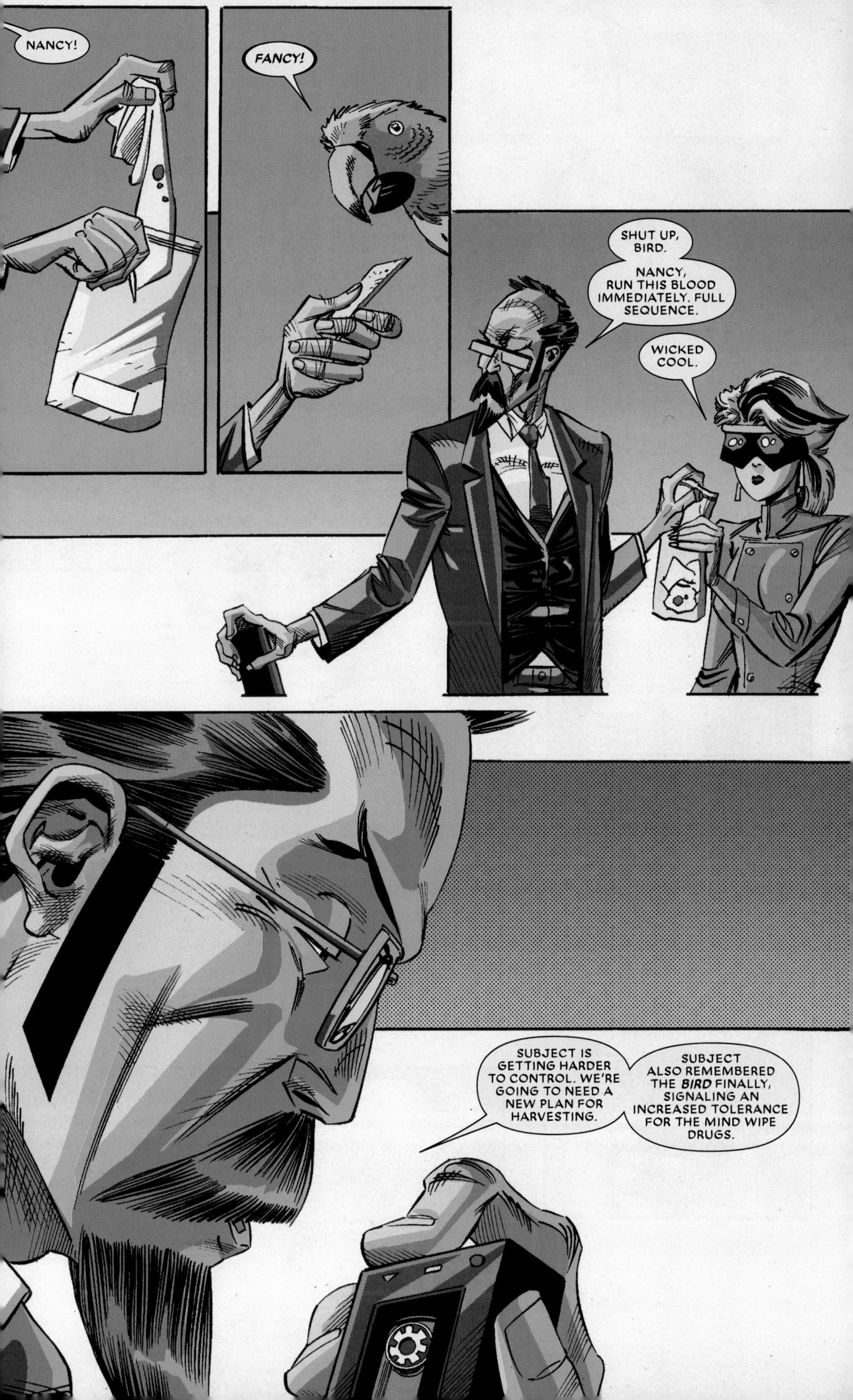
NANCY!
FANCY!
SHUT UP, BIRD.
NANCY, RUN THIS BLOOD IMMEDIATELY. FULL SEQUENCE.
WICKED COOL.
SUBJECT IS GETTING HARDER TO CONTROL. WE'RE GOING TO NEED A NEW PLAN FOR HARVESTING.
SUBJECT ALSO REMEMBERED THE BIRD FINALLY, SIGNALING AN INCREASED TOLERANCE FOR THE MIND WIPE DRUGS.

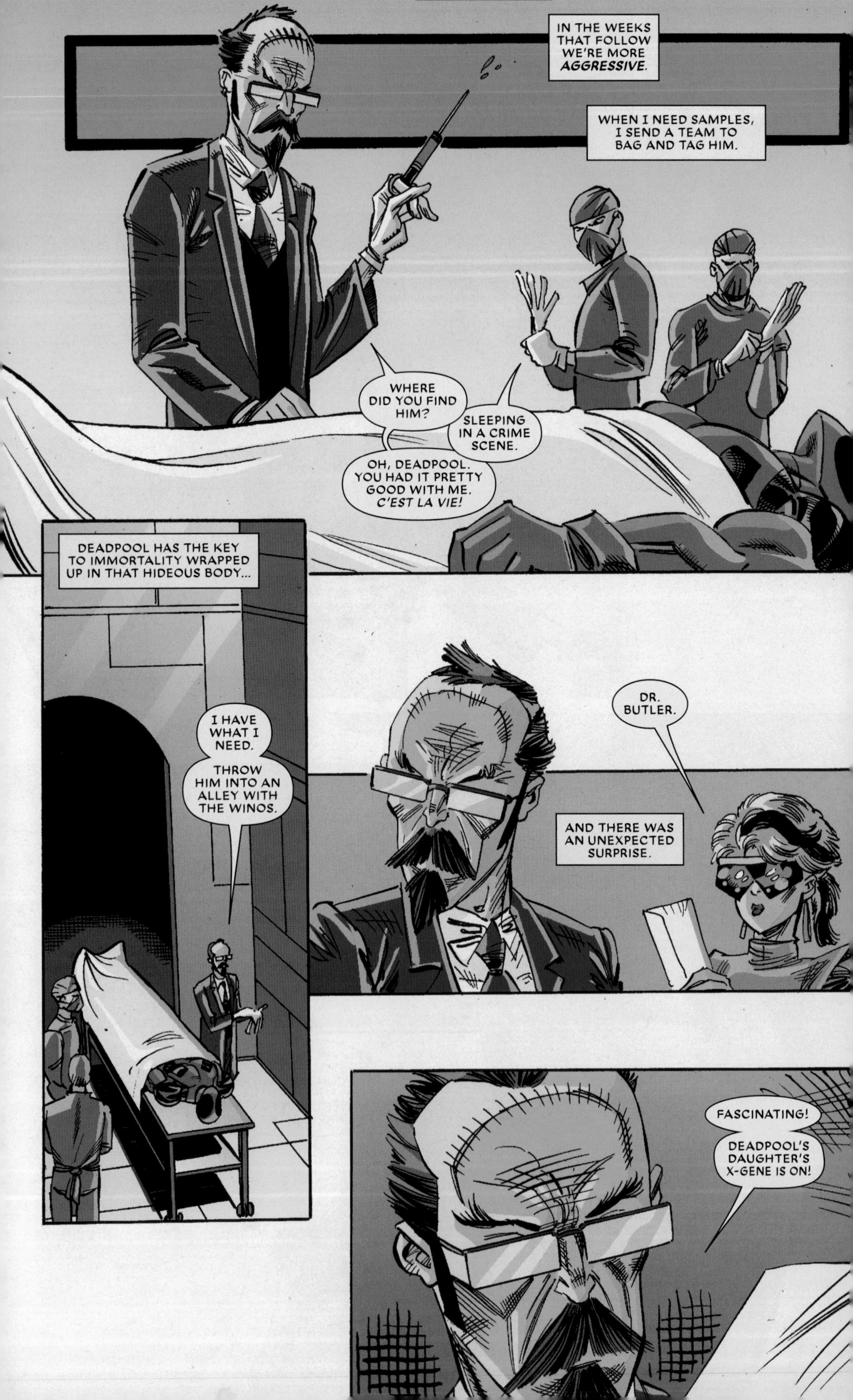
IN THE WEEKS THAT FOLLOW WE'RE MORE *AGGRESSIVE*.
WHEN I NEED SAMPLES, I SEND A TEAM TO BAG AND TAG HIM.
WHERE DID YOU FIND HIM?
SLEEPING IN A CRIME SCENE.
OH, DEADPOOL. YOU HAD IT PRETTY GOOD WITH ME. *C'EST LA VIE!*
DEADPOOL HAS THE KEY TO IMMORTALITY WRAPPED UP IN THAT HIDEOUS BODY...
I HAVE WHAT I NEED.
THROW HIM INTO AN ALLEY WITH THE WINOS.
DR. BUTLER.
AND THERE WAS AN UNEXPECTED SURPRISE.
FASCINATING!
DEADPOOL'S DAUGHTER'S X-GENE IS ON!

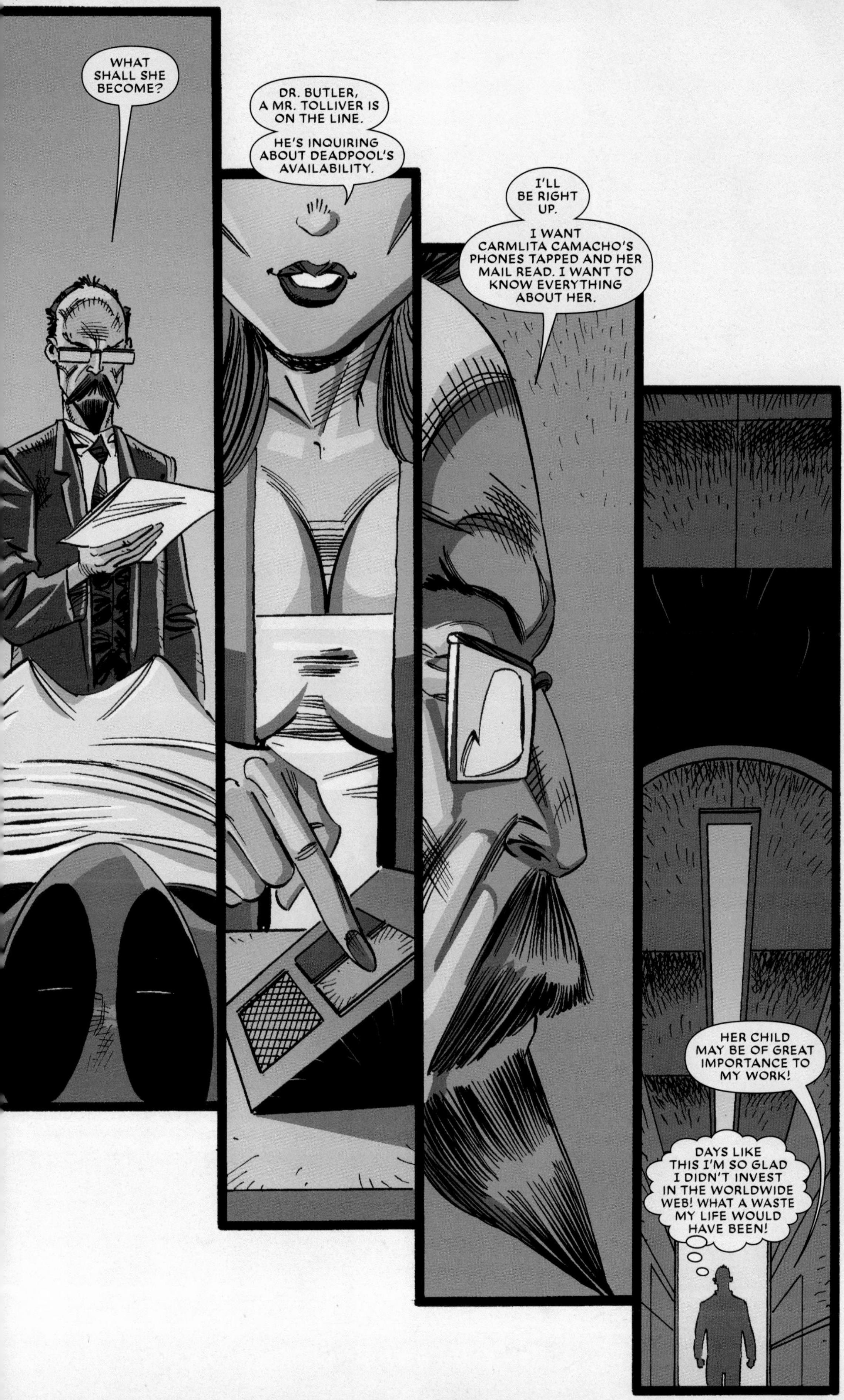
WHAT SHALL SHE BECOME?
DR. BUTLER, A MR. TOLLIVER IS ON THE LINE.
HE'S INQUIRING ABOUT DEADPOOL'S AVAILABILITY.
I'LL BE RIGHT UP.
I WANT CARMLITA CAMACHO'S PHONES TAPPED AND HER MAIL READ. I WANT TO KNOW EVERYTHING ABOUT HER.
HER CHILD MAY BE OF GREAT IMPORTANCE TO MY WORK!
DAYS LIKE THIS I'M SO GLAD I DIDN'T INVEST IN THE WORLDWIDE WEB! WHAT A WASTE MY LIFE WOULD HAVE BEEN!

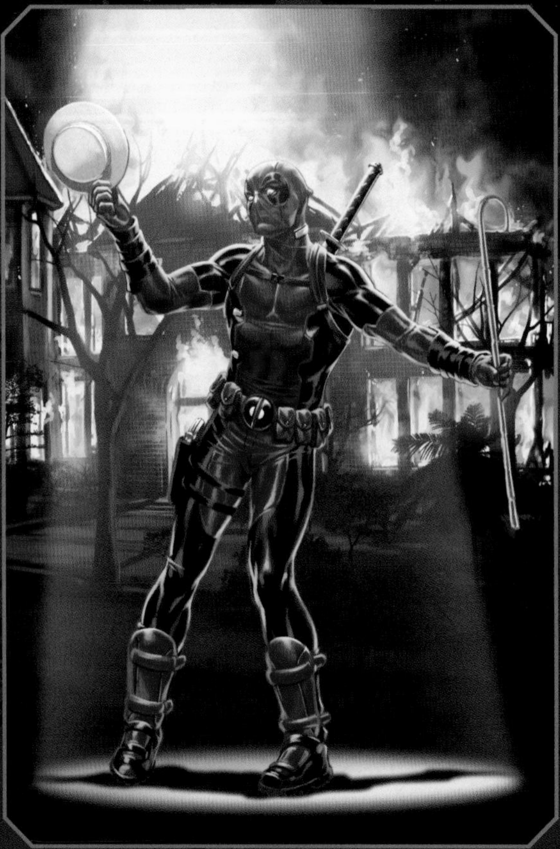

#34 STANDARD COVER ART

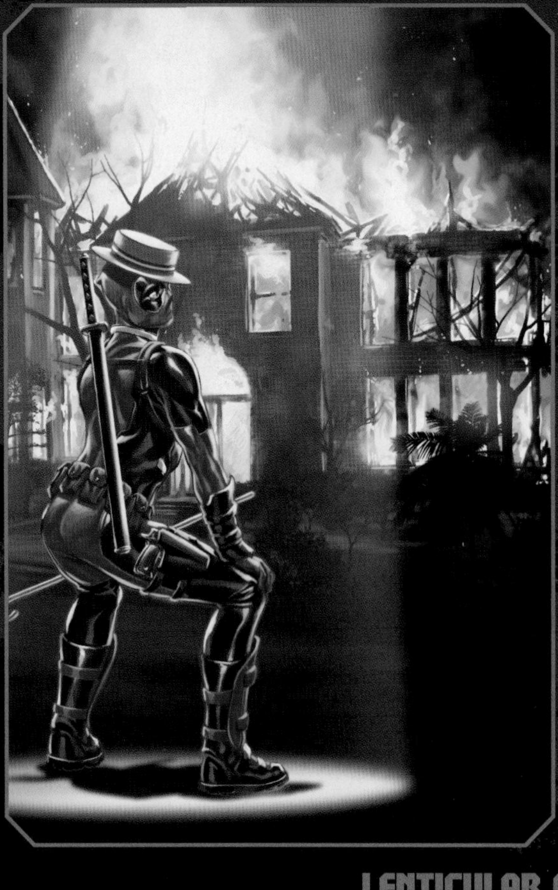

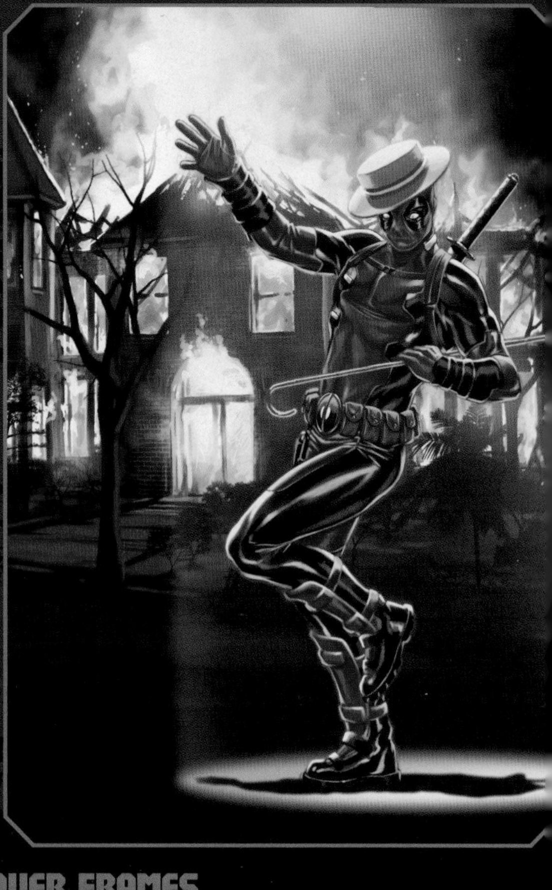

LENTICULAR COVER FRAMES

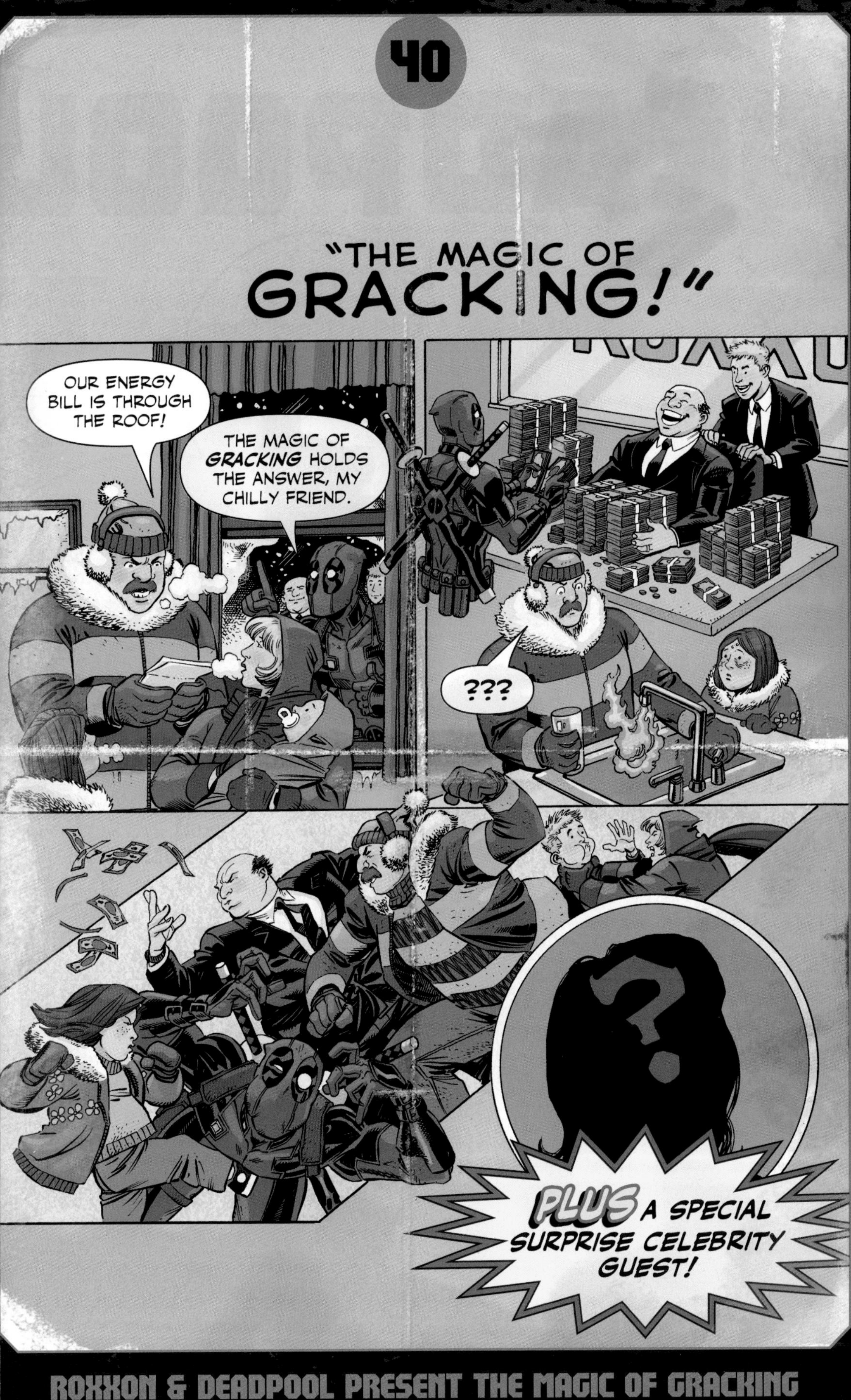
40
"THE MAGIC OF GRACKING!"
OUR ENERGY BILL IS THROUGH THE ROOF!
THE MAGIC OF GRACKING HOLDS THE ANSWER, MY CHILLY FRIEND.
???
PLUS A SPECIAL SURPRISE CELEBRITY GUEST!
ROXXON & DEADPOOL PRESENT THE MAGIC OF GRACKING

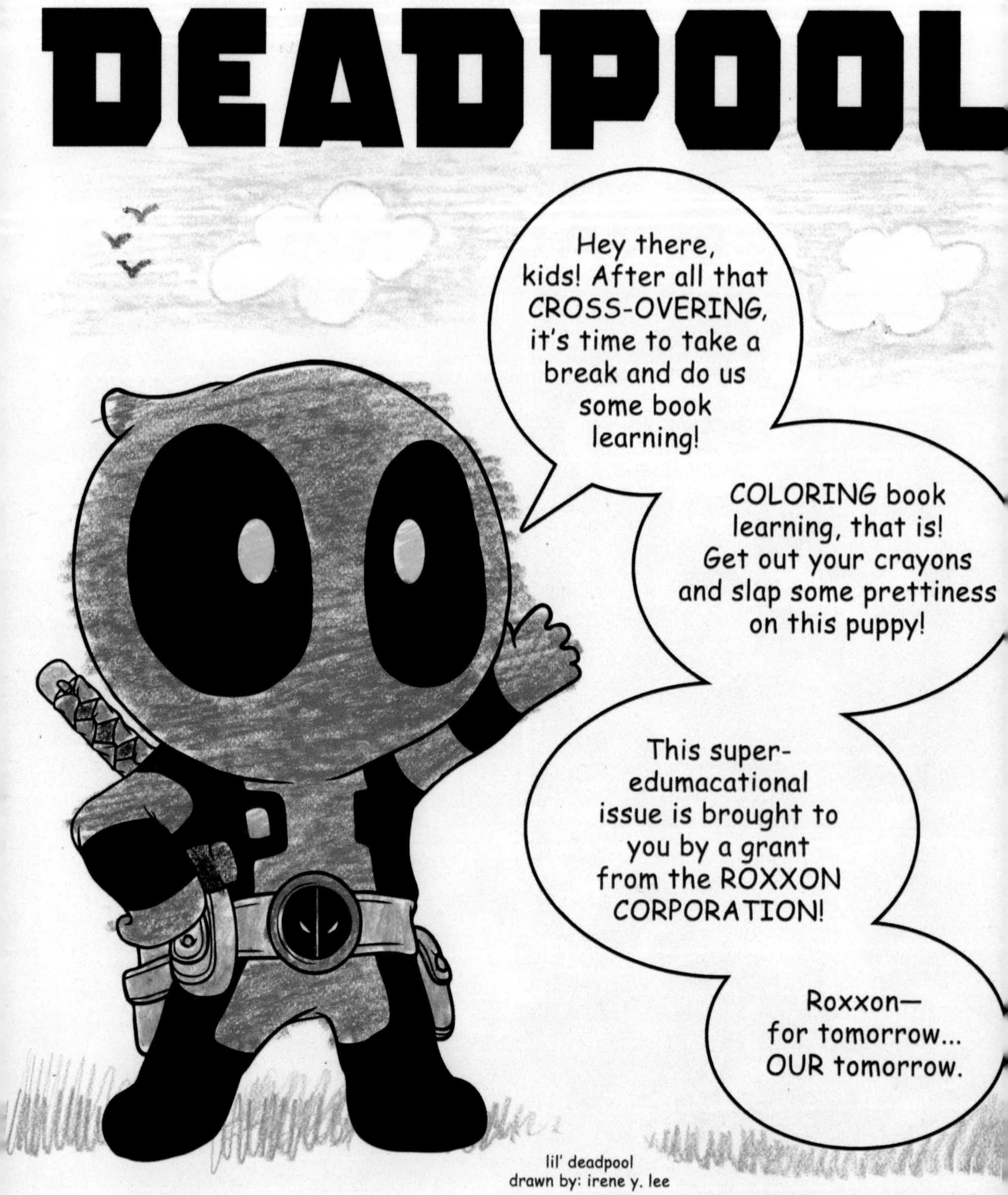
DEADPOOL
Hey there, kids! After all that CROSS-OVERING, it's time to take a break and do us some book learning!
COLORING book learning, that is! Get out your crayons and slap some prettiness on this puppy!
This super-edumacational issue is brought to you by a grant from the ROXXON CORPORATION!
Roxxon— for tomorrow... OUR tomorrow.
lil' deadpool
drawn by: irene y. lee

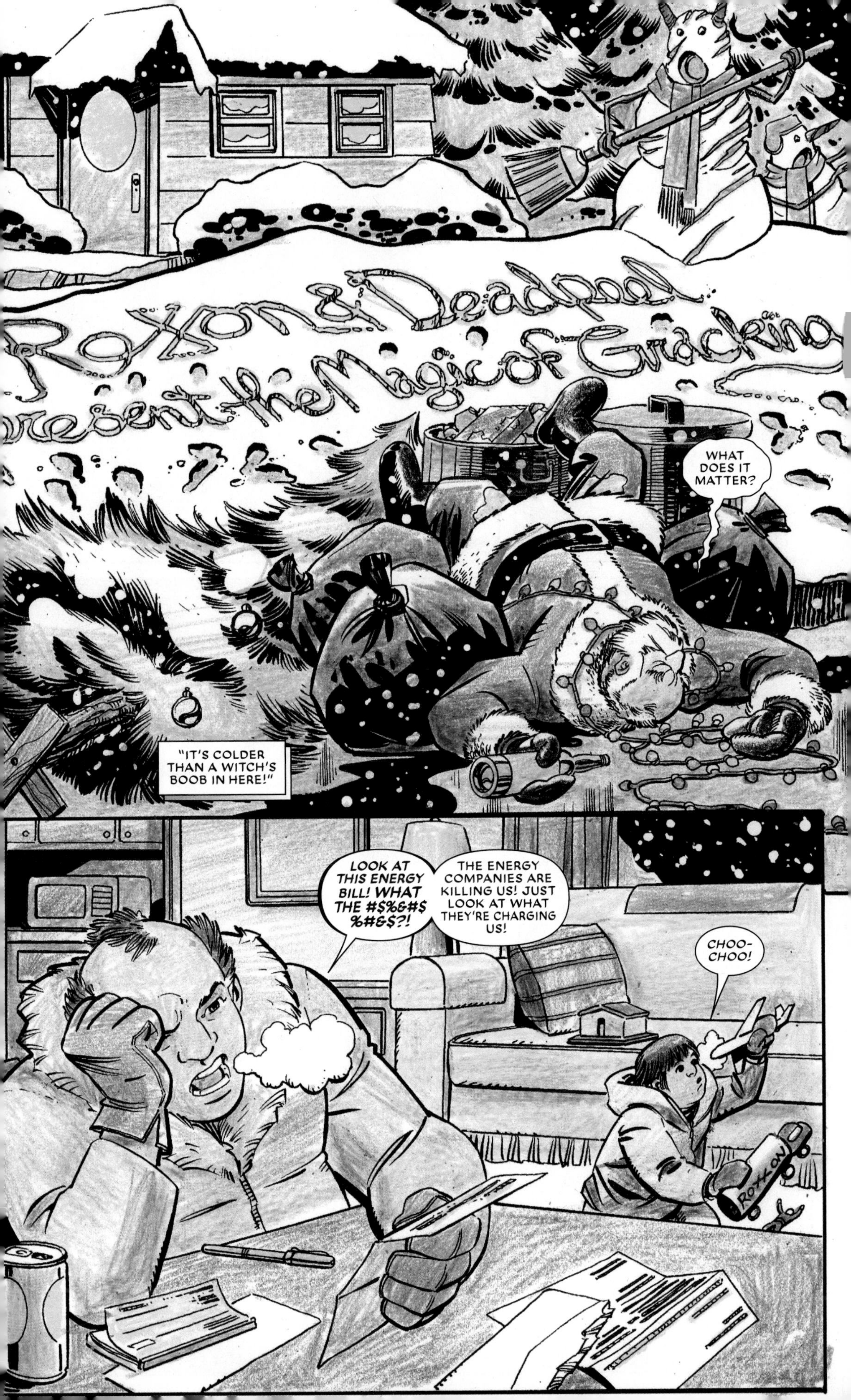
Roxxon & Deadpool
resent the Magic of Fracking
WHAT DOES IT MATTER?
"IT'S COLDER THAN A WITCH'S BOOB IN HERE!"
LOOK AT THIS ENERGY BILL! WHAT THE #$%&#$ %#&$?!
THE ENERGY COMPANIES ARE KILLING US! JUST LOOK AT WHAT THEY'RE CHARGING US!
CHOO-CHOO!
ROXXON

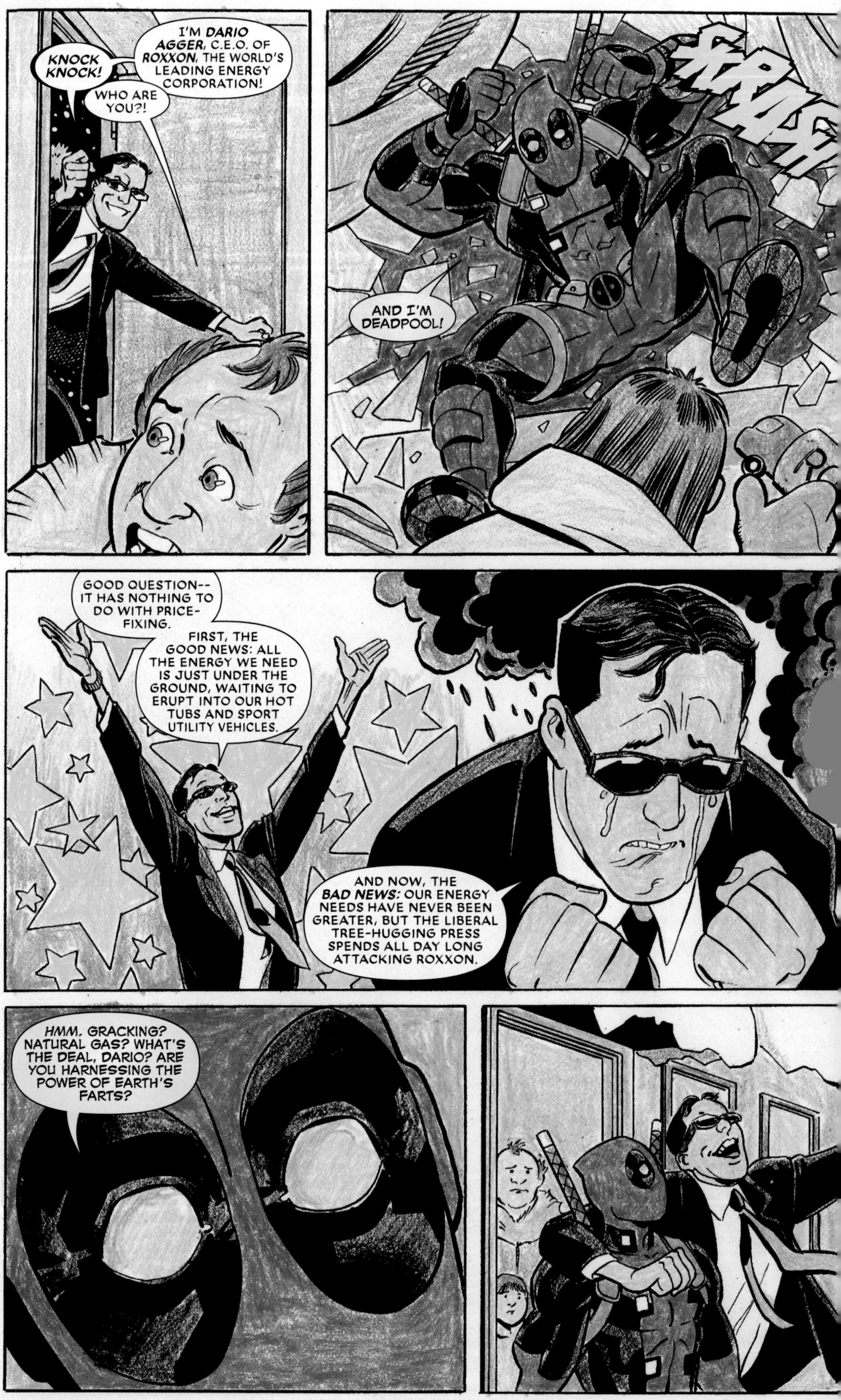
KNOCK KNOCK!
I'M DARIO AGGER, C.E.O. OF ROXXON, THE WORLD'S LEADING ENERGY CORPORATION!
WHO ARE YOU?!
SKRASH
AND I'M DEADPOOL!
GOOD QUESTION-- IT HAS NOTHING TO DO WITH PRICE-FIXING.
FIRST, THE GOOD NEWS: ALL THE ENERGY WE NEED IS JUST UNDER THE GROUND, WAITING TO ERUPT INTO OUR HOT TUBS AND SPORT UTILITY VEHICLES.
AND NOW, THE BAD NEWS: OUR ENERGY NEEDS HAVE NEVER BEEN GREATER, BUT THE LIBERAL TREE-HUGGING PRESS SPENDS ALL DAY LONG ATTACKING ROXXON.
HMM. GRACKING? NATURAL GAS? WHAT'S THE DEAL, DARIO? ARE YOU HARNESSING THE POWER OF EARTH'S FARTS?

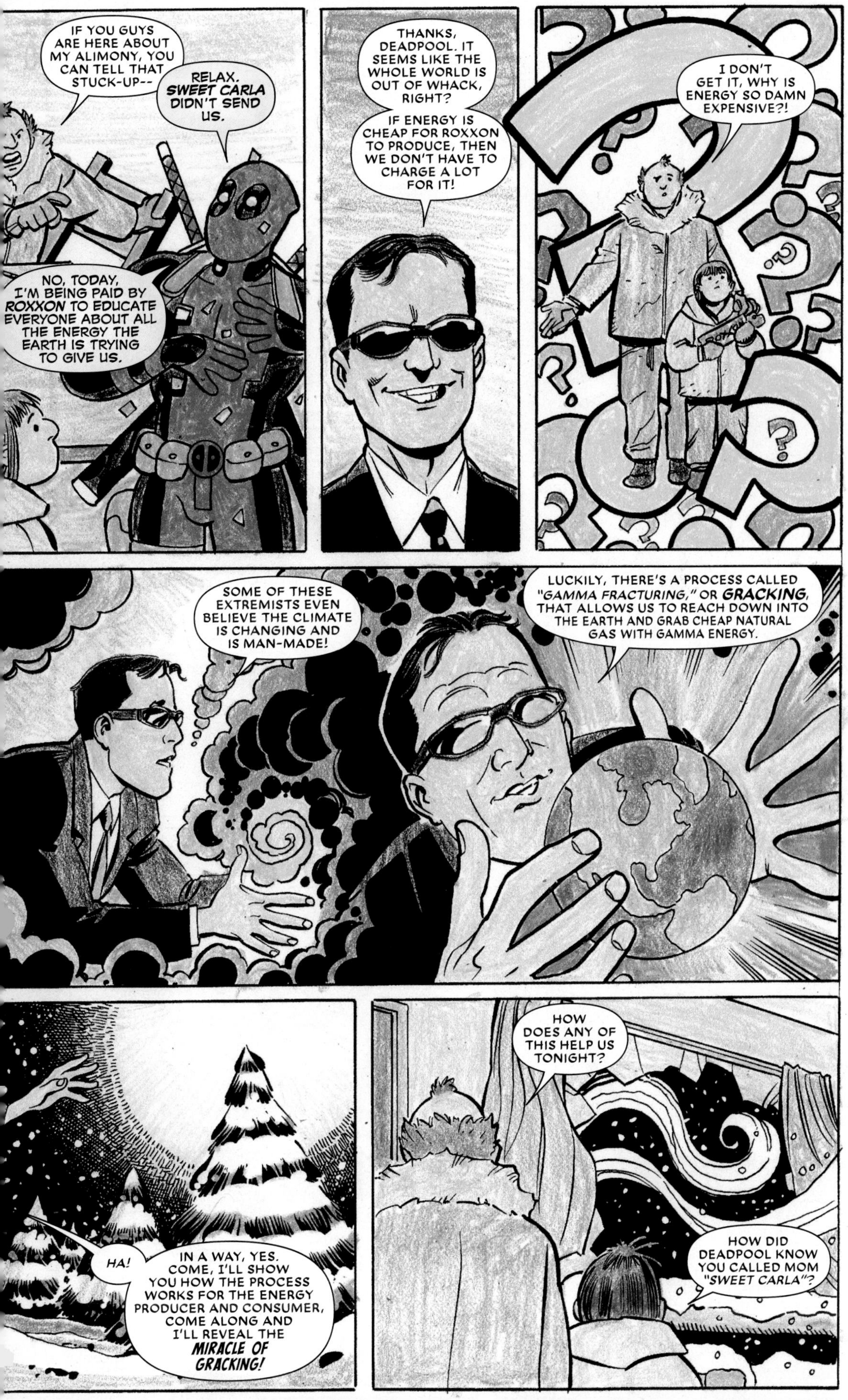
IF YOU GUYS ARE HERE ABOUT MY ALIMONY, YOU CAN TELL THAT STUCK-UP--
RELAX. SWEET CARLA DIDN'T SEND US.
NO, TODAY, I'M BEING PAID BY ROXXON TO EDUCATE EVERYONE ABOUT ALL THE ENERGY THE EARTH IS TRYING TO GIVE US.
THANKS, DEADPOOL. IT SEEMS LIKE THE WHOLE WORLD IS OUT OF WHACK, RIGHT?
IF ENERGY IS CHEAP FOR ROXXON TO PRODUCE, THEN WE DON'T HAVE TO CHARGE A LOT FOR IT!
I DON'T GET IT, WHY IS ENERGY SO DAMN EXPENSIVE?!
SOME OF THESE EXTREMISTS EVEN BELIEVE THE CLIMATE IS CHANGING AND IS MAN-MADE!
LUCKILY, THERE'S A PROCESS CALLED "GAMMA FRACTURING," OR GRACKING, THAT ALLOWS US TO REACH DOWN INTO THE EARTH AND GRAB CHEAP NATURAL GAS WITH GAMMA ENERGY.
HOW DOES ANY OF THIS HELP US TONIGHT?
HA!
IN A WAY, YES. COME, I'LL SHOW YOU HOW THE PROCESS WORKS FOR THE ENERGY PRODUCER AND CONSUMER, COME ALONG AND I'LL REVEAL THE MIRACLE OF GRACKING!
HOW DID DEADPOOL KNOW YOU CALLED MOM "SWEET CARLA"?

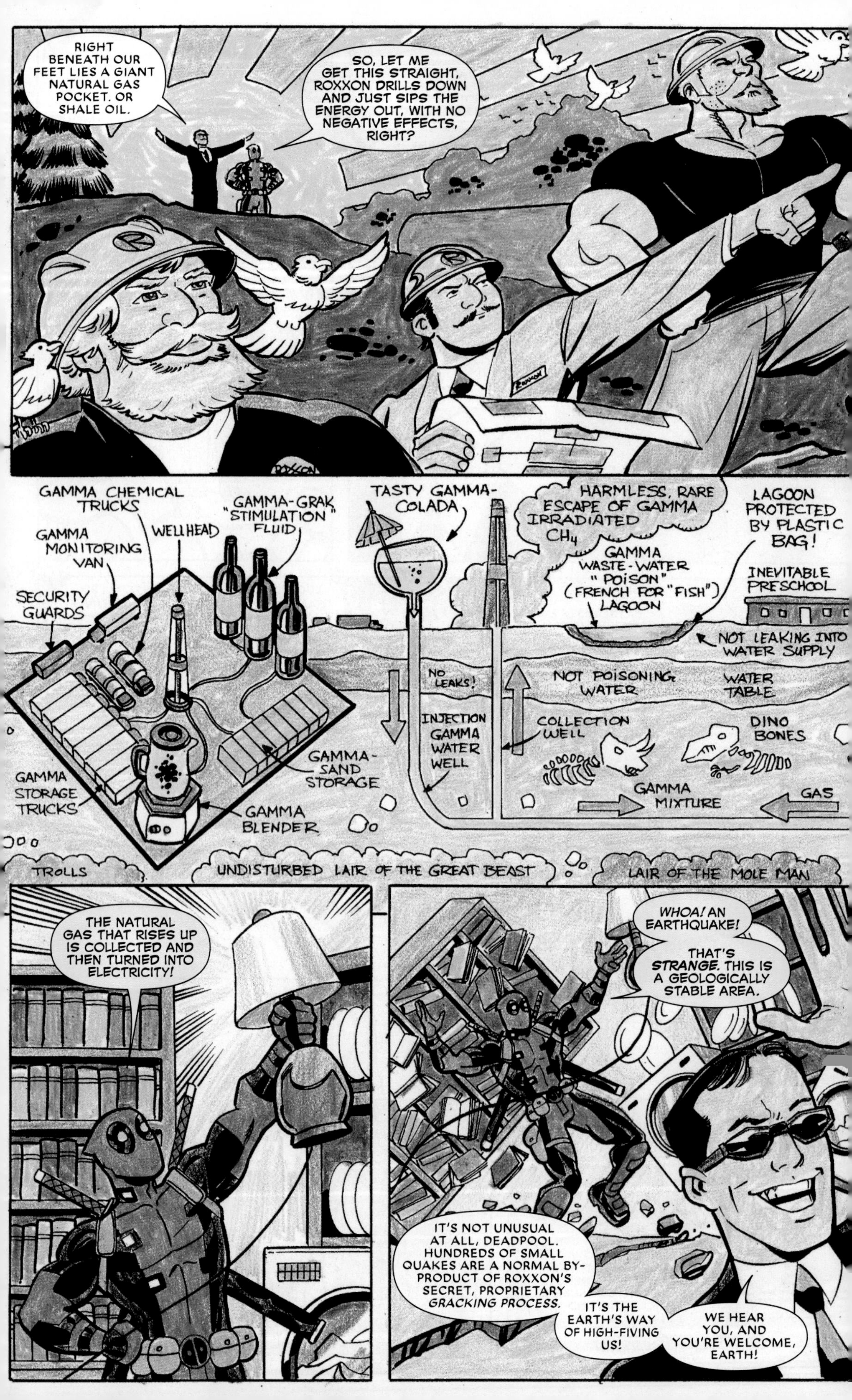
RIGHT BENEATH OUR FEET LIES A GIANT NATURAL GAS POCKET. OR SHALE OIL.
SO, LET ME GET THIS STRAIGHT, ROXXON DRILLS DOWN AND JUST SIPS THE ENERGY OUT, WITH NO NEGATIVE EFFECTS, RIGHT?
GAMMA CHEMICAL TRUCKS
GAMMA MONITORING VAN
SECURITY GUARDS
WELLHEAD
GAMMA-GRAK "STIMULATION" FLUID
TASTY GAMMA-COLADA
HARMLESS, RARE ESCAPE OF GAMMA IRRADIATED CH_4
LAGOON PROTECTED BY PLASTIC BAG!
GAMMA WASTE-WATER "POISON" (FRENCH FOR "FISH") LAGOON
INEVITABLE PRESCHOOL
NOT LEAKING INTO WATER SUPPLY
NO LEAKS!
NOT POISONING WATER
WATER TABLE
INJECTION GAMMA WATER WELL
COLLECTION WELL
DINO BONES
GAMMA-SAND STORAGE
GAMMA STORAGE TRUCKS
GAMMA BLENDER
GAMMA MIXTURE
GAS
TROLLS
UNDISTURBED LAIR OF THE GREAT BEAST
LAIR OF THE MOLE MAN
THE NATURAL GAS THAT RISES UP IS COLLECTED AND THEN TURNED INTO ELECTRICITY!
WHOA! AN EARTHQUAKE!
THAT'S STRANGE. THIS IS A GEOLOGICALLY STABLE AREA.
IT'S NOT UNUSUAL AT ALL, DEADPOOL. HUNDREDS OF SMALL QUAKES ARE A NORMAL BY-PRODUCT OF ROXXON'S SECRET, PROPRIETARY GRACKING PROCESS.
IT'S THE EARTH'S WAY OF HIGH-FIVING US!
WE HEAR YOU, AND YOU'RE WELCOME, EARTH!

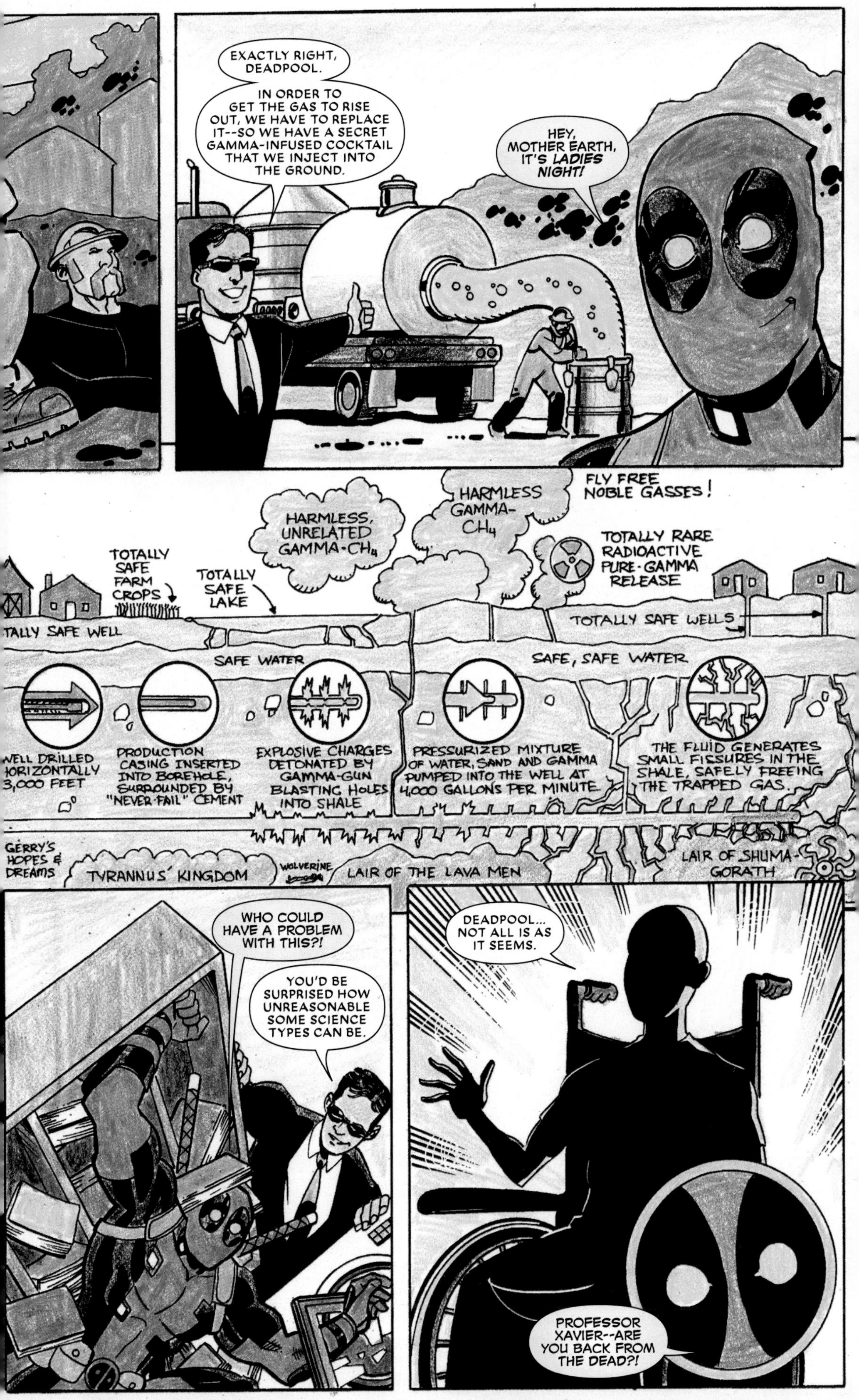
EXACTLY RIGHT, DEADPOOL.
IN ORDER TO GET THE GAS TO RISE OUT, WE HAVE TO REPLACE IT--SO WE HAVE A SECRET GAMMA-INFUSED COCKTAIL THAT WE INJECT INTO THE GROUND.
HEY, MOTHER EARTH, IT'S *LADIES NIGHT!*
FLY FREE NOBLE GASSES!
HARMLESS GAMMA-CH_4
HARMLESS, UNRELATED GAMMA-CH_4
TOTALLY RARE RADIOACTIVE PURE-GAMMA RELEASE
TOTALLY SAFE FARM CROPS
TOTALLY SAFE LAKE
TALLY SAFE WELL
TOTALLY SAFE WELLS
SAFE WATER
SAFE, SAFE WATER
WELL DRILLED HORIZONTALLY 3,000 FEET
PRODUCTION CASING INSERTED INTO BOREHOLE, SURROUNDED BY "NEVER-FAIL" CEMENT
EXPLOSIVE CHARGES DETONATED BY GAMMA-GUN BLASTING HOLES INTO SHALE
PRESSURIZED MIXTURE OF WATER, SAND AND GAMMA PUMPED INTO THE WELL AT 4,000 GALLONS PER MINUTE.
THE FLUID GENERATES SMALL FISSURES IN THE SHALE, SAFELY FREEING THE TRAPPED GAS.
GERRY'S HOPES & DREAMS
TYRANNUS' KINGDOM
WOLVERINE
LAIR OF THE LAVA MEN
LAIR OF SHUMA-GORATH
WHO COULD HAVE A PROBLEM WITH THIS?!
YOU'D BE SURPRISED HOW UNREASONABLE SOME SCIENCE TYPES CAN BE.
DEADPOOL... NOT ALL IS AS IT SEEMS.
PROFESSOR XAVIER--ARE YOU BACK FROM THE DEAD?!

NO, DEADPOOL. MY NAME IS TIM.

OH. WELL, COOL PROFESSOR X COSPLAY!

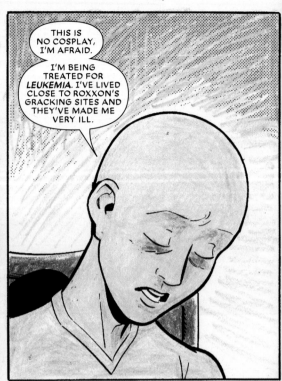

THIS IS NO COSPLAY, I'M AFRAID.

I'M BEING TREATED FOR *LEUKEMIA*. I'VE LIVED CLOSE TO ROXXON'S GRACKING SITES AND THEY'VE MADE ME VERY ILL.

SORRY TO HEAR ABOUT YOUR CANCER, BUT *UH*... MAYBE YOU'LL GROW UP...BIG AND DEADPOOL, LIKE ME?

UH, HEY, DARIO. IS THIS *TRUE?!* DOES GRACKING MAKE PEOPLE SICK?

I'M NOT A SCIENTIST, BUT-- I DO KNOW THERE'S NO PROOF OUR CHEMICALS ARE ANYTHING OTHER THAN A WONDERFUL, PROPRIETARY SECRET USED IN THE COLLECTION OF NATURAL GAS.

WOW, WHAT AN *$&#&&#.*

COME VISIT MY HOME.

THERE'S MORE BAD NEWS, I'M AFRAID.

COOL. SPEAKING OF POLLUTION, YOU COOL WITH ME DROPPING A DEUCE AT YOUR PAD?

HEY! WHOSE PROPAGANDA COMIC IS THIS?!

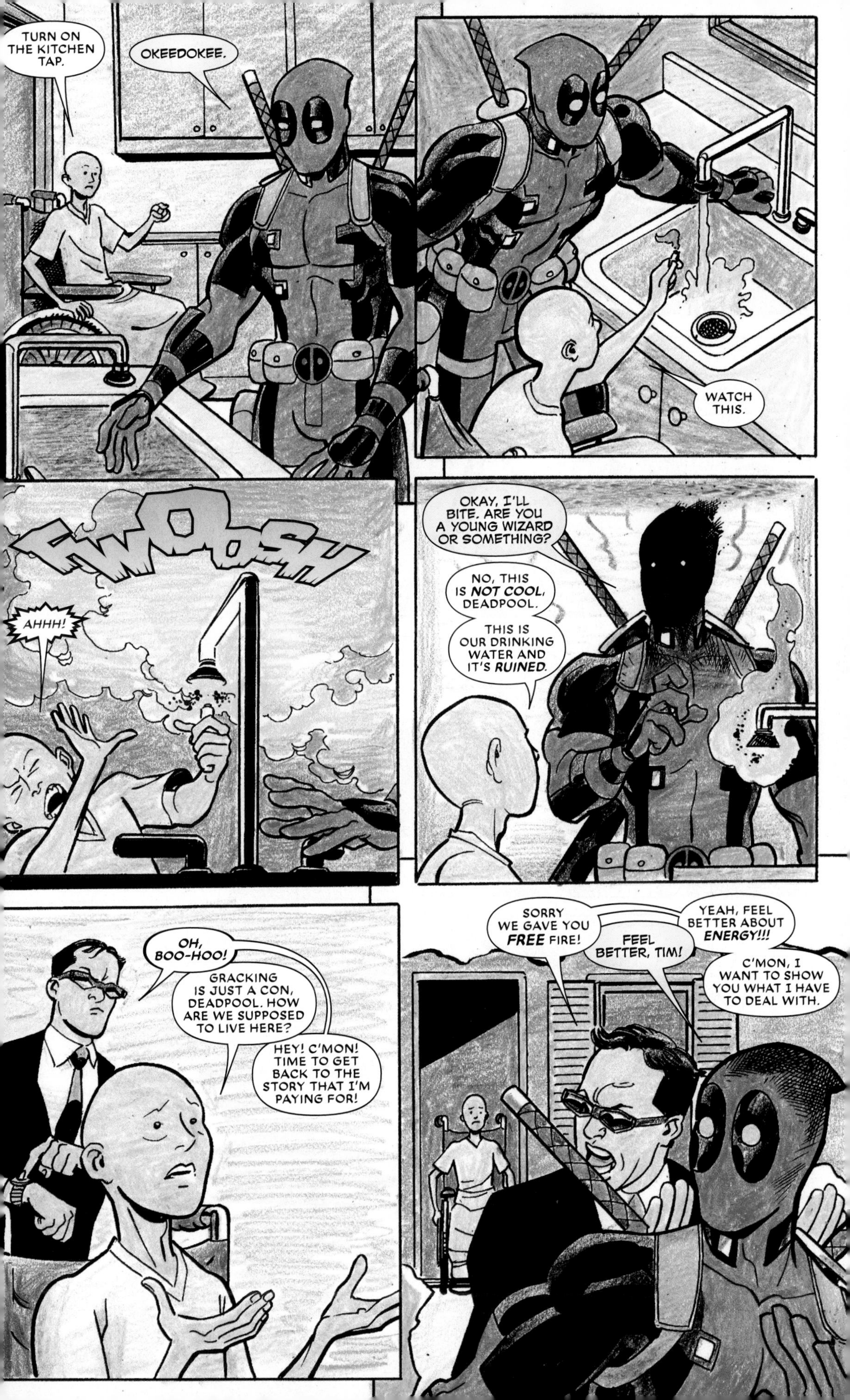

TURN ON THE KITCHEN TAP.
OKEEDOKEE.
WATCH THIS.
FWOOSH
AHHH!
OKAY, I'LL BITE. ARE YOU A YOUNG WIZARD OR SOMETHING?
NO, THIS IS NOT COOL, DEADPOOL.
THIS IS OUR DRINKING WATER AND IT'S RUINED.
OH, BOO-HOO!
GRACKING IS JUST A CON, DEADPOOL. HOW ARE WE SUPPOSED TO LIVE HERE?
HEY! C'MON! TIME TO GET BACK TO THE STORY THAT I'M PAYING FOR!
SORRY WE GAVE YOU FREE FIRE!
FEEL BETTER, TIM!
YEAH, FEEL BETTER ABOUT ENERGY!!!
C'MON, I WANT TO SHOW YOU WHAT I HAVE TO DEAL WITH.

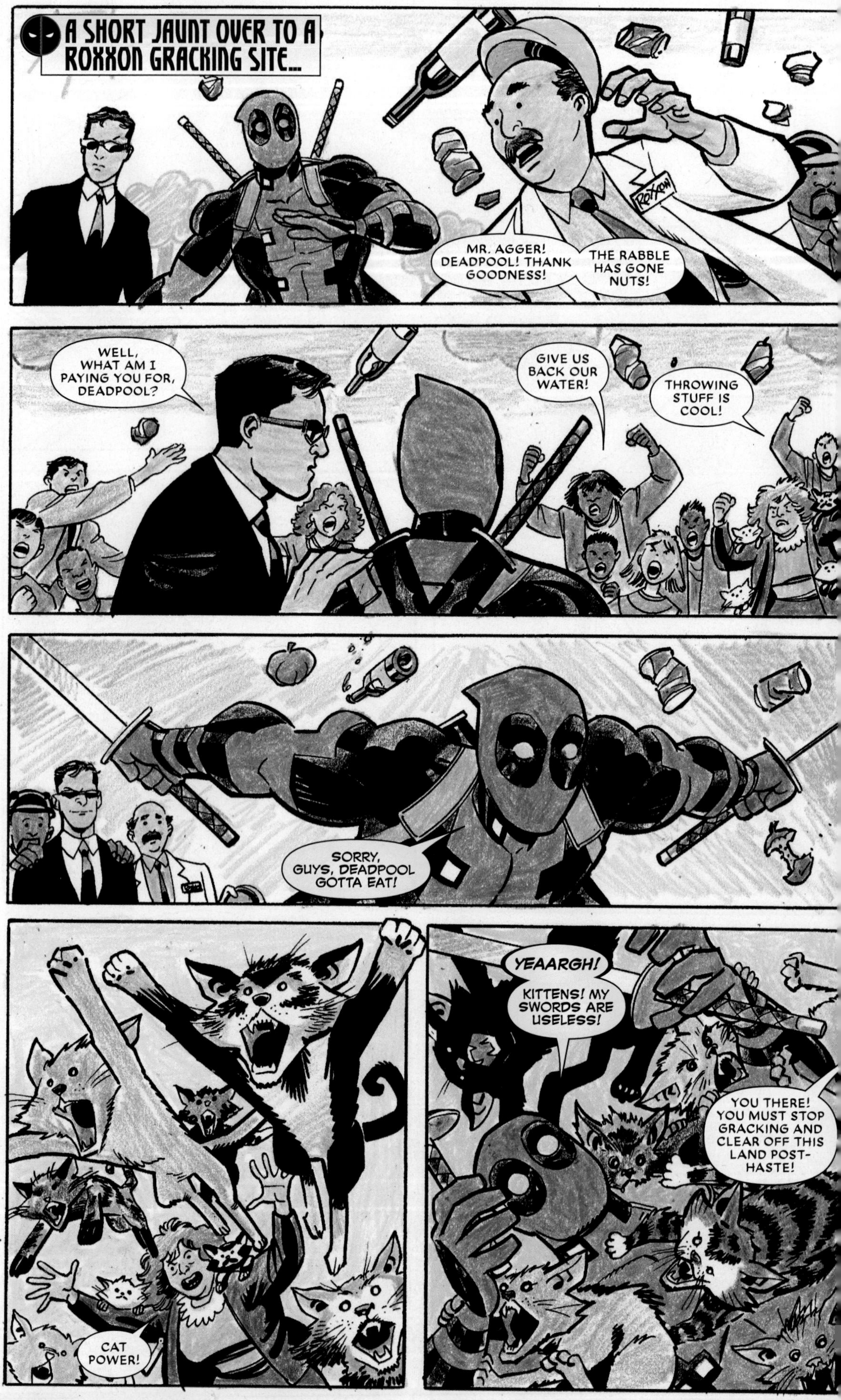
A SHORT JAUNT OVER TO A ROXXON GRACKING SITE...
ROXXON
MR. AGGER! DEADPOOL! THANK GOODNESS!
THE RABBLE HAS GONE NUTS!
WELL, WHAT AM I PAYING YOU FOR, DEADPOOL?
GIVE US BACK OUR WATER!
THROWING STUFF IS COOL!
SORRY, GUYS, DEADPOOL GOTTA EAT!
CAT POWER!
YEAARGH!
KITTENS! MY SWORDS ARE USELESS!
YOU THERE! YOU MUST STOP GRACKING AND CLEAR OFF THIS LAND POST-HASTE!

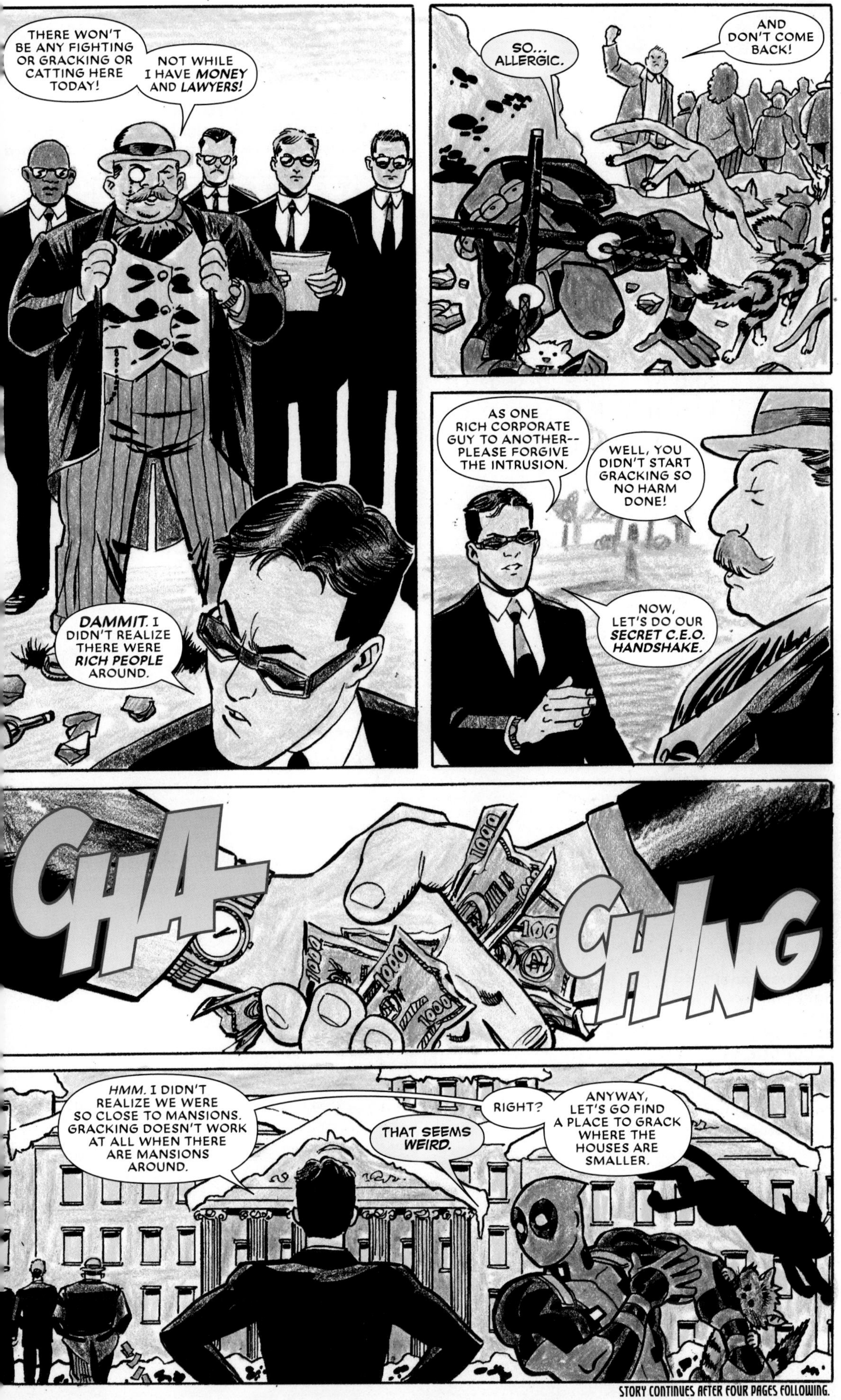
THERE WON'T BE ANY FIGHTING OR GRACKING OR CATTING HERE TODAY!
NOT WHILE I HAVE *MONEY* AND *LAWYERS!*
DAMMIT. I DIDN'T REALIZE THERE WERE *RICH PEOPLE* AROUND.
SO... ALLERGIC.
AND DON'T COME BACK!
AS ONE RICH CORPORATE GUY TO ANOTHER-- PLEASE FORGIVE THE INTRUSION.
WELL, YOU DIDN'T START GRACKING SO NO HARM DONE!
NOW, LET'S DO OUR *SECRET C.E.O. HANDSHAKE.*
CHA CHING
HMM. I DIDN'T REALIZE WE WERE SO CLOSE TO MANSIONS. GRACKING DOESN'T WORK AT ALL WHEN THERE ARE MANSIONS AROUND.
THAT SEEMS *WEIRD.*
RIGHT?
ANYWAY, LET'S GO FIND A PLACE TO GRACK WHERE THE HOUSES ARE SMALLER.

STORY CONTINUES AFTER FOUR PAGES FOLLOWING.

Word Search!
Find these words:
Deadpool, Squirrel Girl, Tolliver, Sledpool, Domino, Shuma-Gorath, Dormammu and Fin Fang Foom!

```
O M W S E D U I J S K K S H S
S N R O R L E M Y A V I L A H
E C O R Q E L A M E U W E D U
L O U T X H W I D A U Q D O M
P S E S R O H T E P M N P O A
M S A N S E L L E D O R O D G
I B L I N D E L O R Q O O Y O
N Z X D O M I N O H C Z L D R
R O T C A F G N I L A E H E A
S Q U I R R E L G I R L S P T
R E V I L L O T T U P K O P H
M O O F G N A F N I F U N I X
P P W S G S M H O V D Q A Z Y
W Y A U O G T L A X F J H Z F
U J Z R Q L B Q F O M J T G U
```

Word Scramble!
Unscramble these eight jumbles, one letter to each square, to form eight ordinary words

T S E R C E   R A W S

O H R E S S

B N D I L   L A

E C C D L A E L N

L E I E L

G E A N I H L   O C F A R T

O L A P E D O D

N P S L E I P

Now plug in the circled letters to form the name of an evil villain!

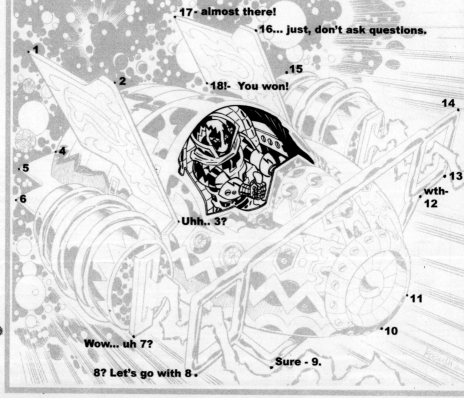

Connect the Dots!

Help Deadpool fight crime in his AWESOME SLEDPOOL by connecting the dots and completing this picture!

·17- almost there!

·16... just, don't ask questions.

·1

·15

·2

·18!- You won!

14·

·4

·13

·5

wth-
12

·6

·Uhh.. 3?

·11

·10

Wow... uh 7?

·Sure - 9.

8? Let's go with 8 ·

ACTIVITY FUN PAGES!

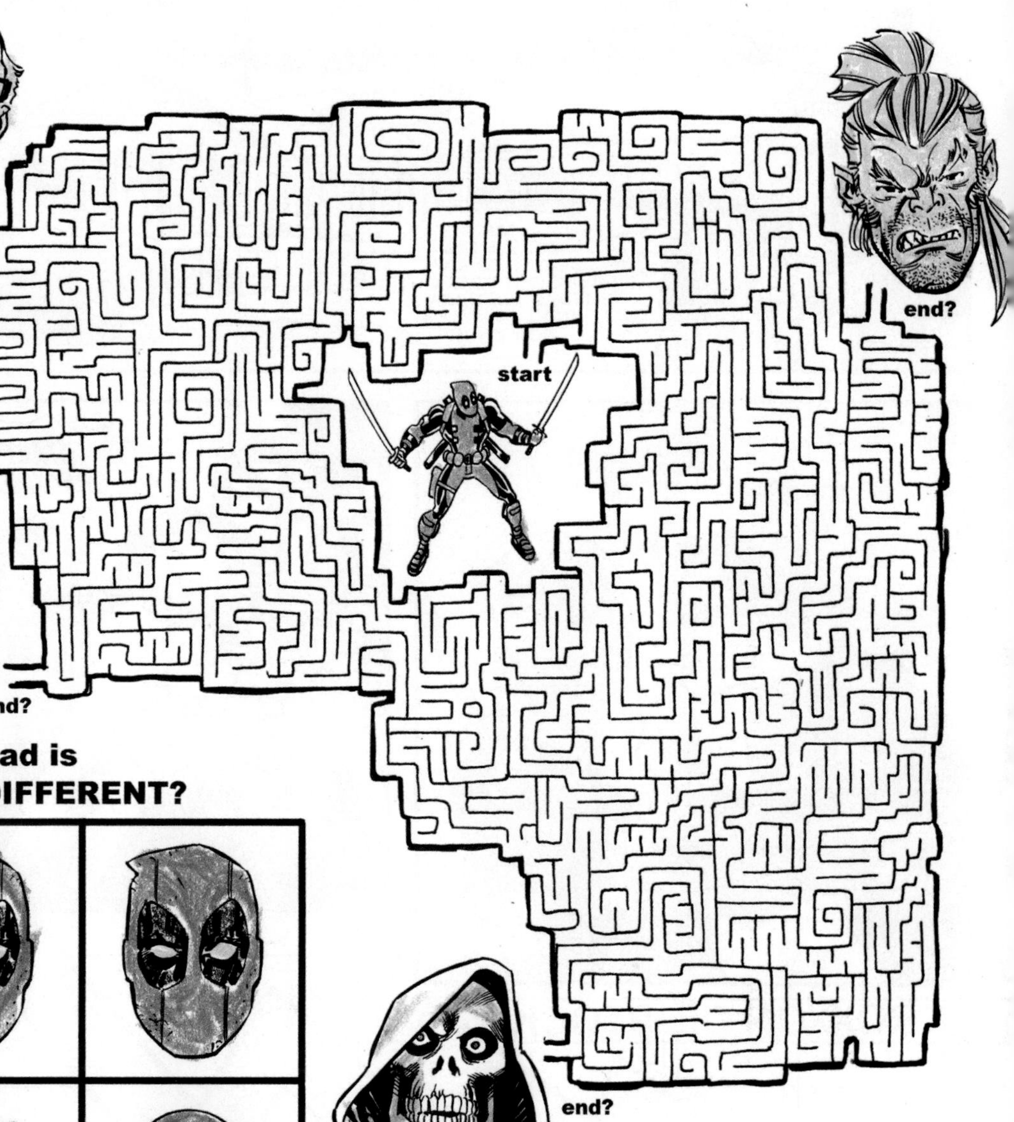
end?
start
end?
end?

hich head is slightly DIFFERENT?

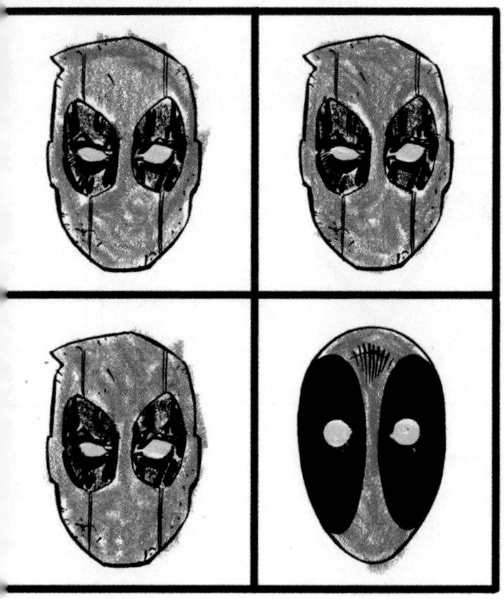

rossword!

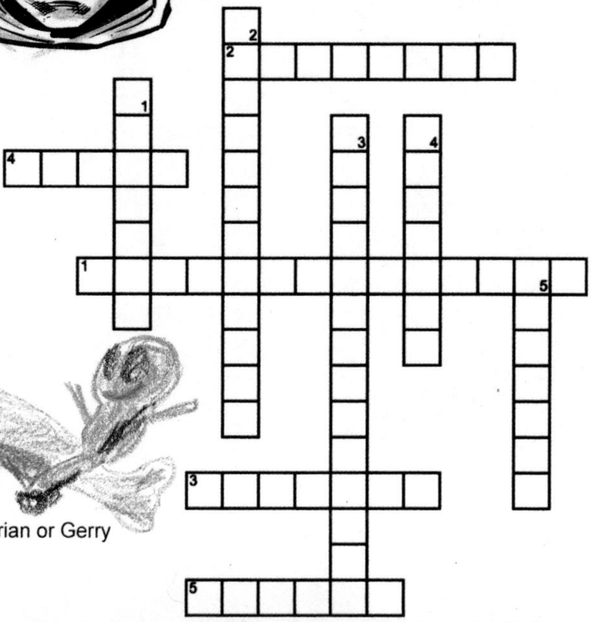

Across:

1. Someone Deadpool has never slept with
2. Deadpool never kills on this holiday
3. Hero of Deadpool NOW
4. Guy we haven't gotten around to killing yet
5. Description of Ellie

Down:

1. Wife of Deadpool
2. A word never written into our volume by Brian or Gerry
3. Hoping it's good
4. Father of Deadpool
5. An unfortunate young woman

Answers to puzzles found on final page!

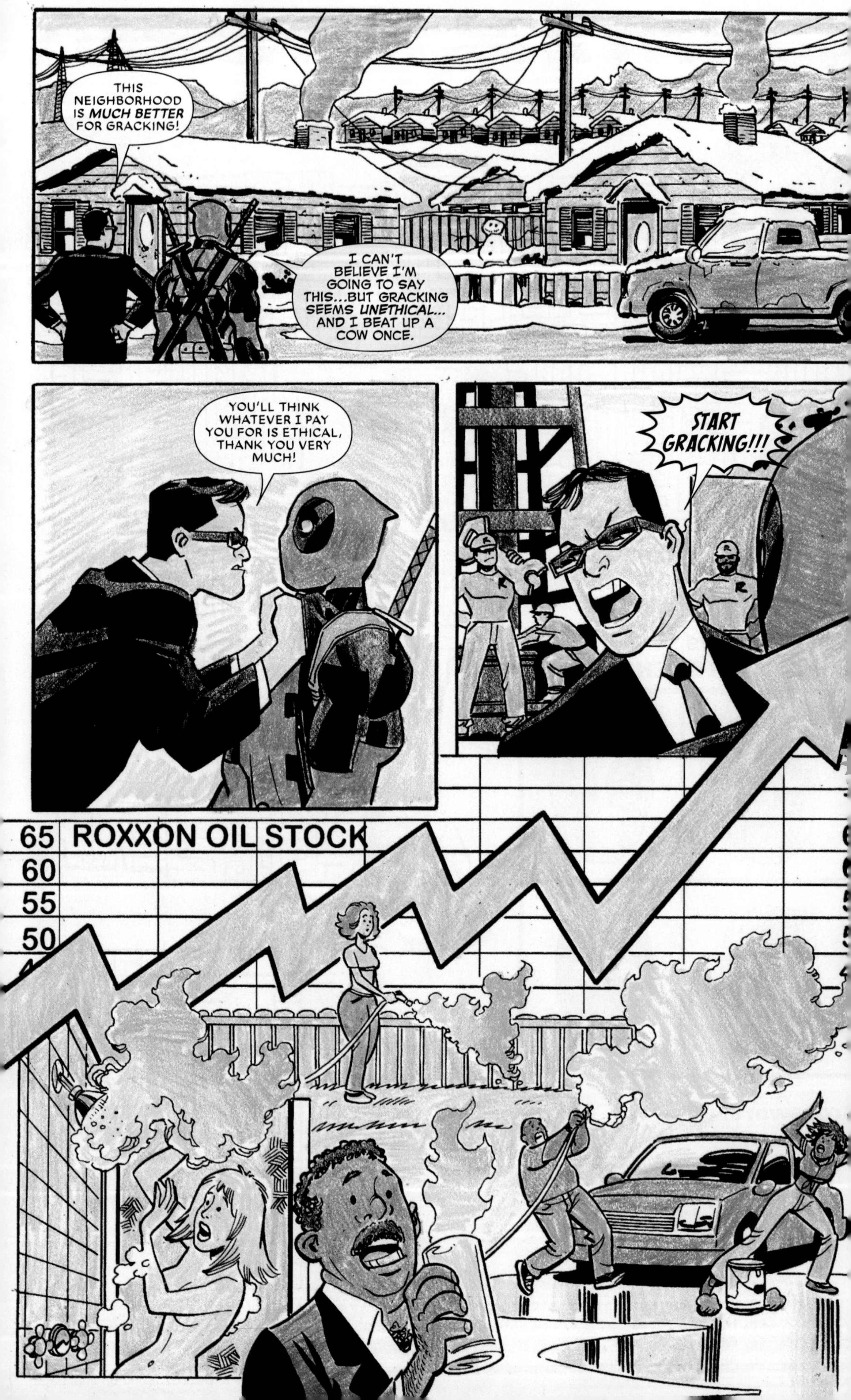
THIS NEIGHBORHOOD IS *MUCH BETTER* FOR GRACKING!
I CAN'T BELIEVE I'M GOING TO SAY THIS...BUT GRACKING SEEMS *UNETHICAL*... AND I BEAT UP A COW ONCE.
YOU'LL THINK WHATEVER I PAY YOU FOR IS ETHICAL, THANK YOU VERY MUCH!
START GRACKING!!!
65
60
55
50
ROXXON OIL STOCK

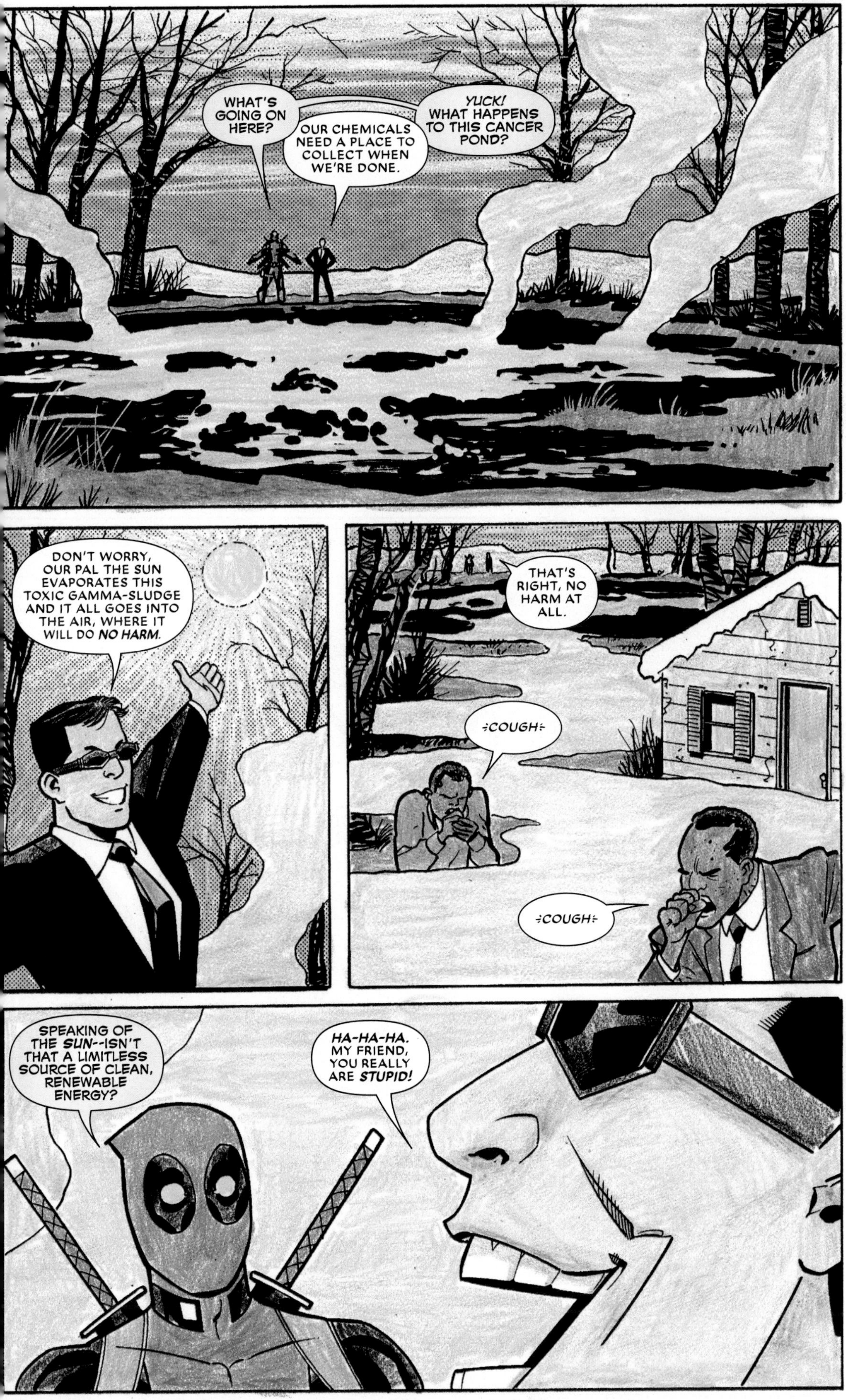
WHAT'S GOING ON HERE?
OUR CHEMICALS NEED A PLACE TO COLLECT WHEN WE'RE DONE.
YUCK! WHAT HAPPENS TO THIS CANCER POND?
DON'T WORRY, OUR PAL THE SUN EVAPORATES THIS TOXIC GAMMA-SLUDGE AND IT ALL GOES INTO THE AIR, WHERE IT WILL DO NO HARM.
THAT'S RIGHT, NO HARM AT ALL.
-COUGH-
-COUGH-
SPEAKING OF THE SUN--ISN'T THAT A LIMITLESS SOURCE OF CLEAN, RENEWABLE ENERGY?
HA-HA-HA. MY FRIEND, YOU REALLY ARE STUPID!

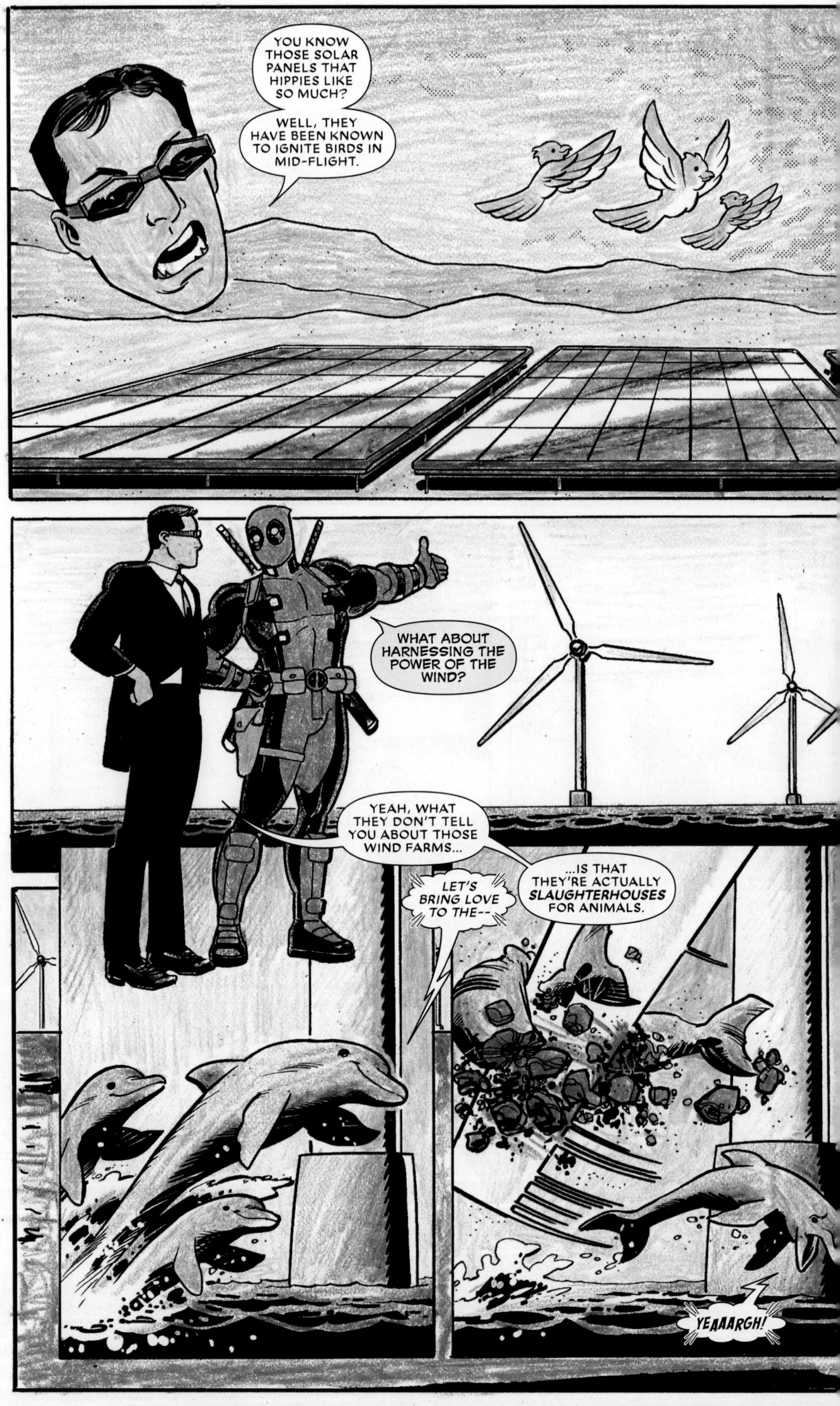
YOU KNOW THOSE SOLAR PANELS THAT HIPPIES LIKE SO MUCH?
WELL, THEY HAVE BEEN KNOWN TO IGNITE BIRDS IN MID-FLIGHT.
WHAT ABOUT HARNESSING THE POWER OF THE WIND?
YEAH, WHAT THEY DON'T TELL YOU ABOUT THOSE WIND FARMS...
...IS THAT THEY'RE ACTUALLY *SLAUGHTERHOUSES* FOR ANIMALS.
LET'S BRING LOVE TO THE--
YEAAARGH!

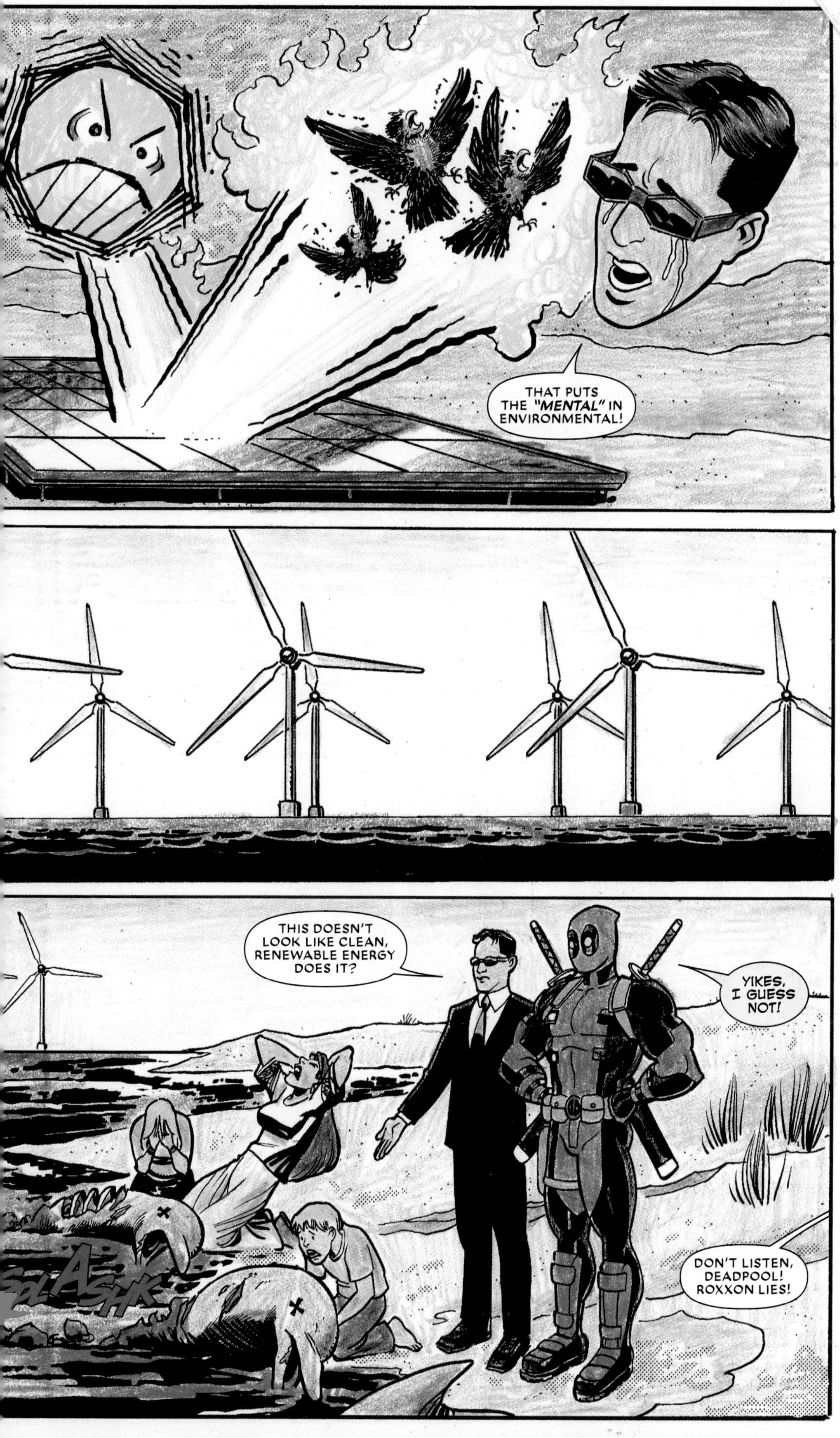
THAT PUTS THE "MENTAL" IN ENVIRONMENTAL!
THIS DOESN'T LOOK LIKE CLEAN, RENEWABLE ENERGY DOES IT?
YIKES, I GUESS NOT!
SPLASHK
DON'T LISTEN, DEADPOOL! ROXXON LIES!

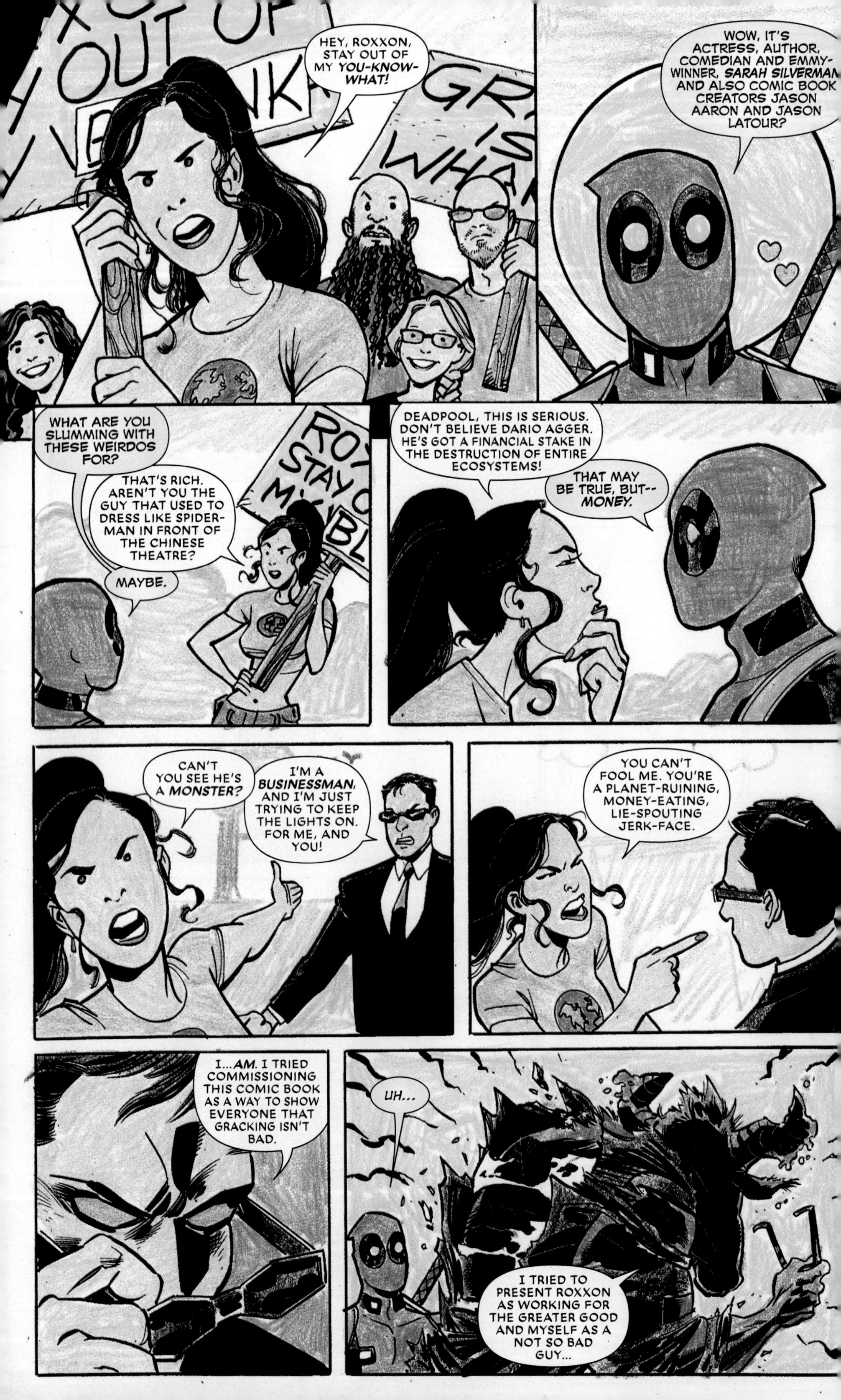
HEY, ROXXON, STAY OUT OF MY *YOU-KNOW-WHAT!*
WOW, IT'S ACTRESS, AUTHOR, COMEDIAN AND EMMY-WINNER, *SARAH SILVERMAN* AND ALSO COMIC BOOK CREATORS JASON AARON AND JASON LATOUR?
WHAT ARE YOU SLUMMING WITH THESE WEIRDOS FOR?
THAT'S RICH. AREN'T YOU THE GUY THAT USED TO DRESS LIKE SPIDER-MAN IN FRONT OF THE CHINESE THEATRE?
MAYBE.
DEADPOOL, THIS IS SERIOUS. DON'T BELIEVE DARIO AGGER. HE'S GOT A FINANCIAL STAKE IN THE DESTRUCTION OF ENTIRE ECOSYSTEMS!
THAT MAY BE TRUE, BUT-- *MONEY.*
CAN'T YOU SEE HE'S A *MONSTER?*
I'M A *BUSINESSMAN*, AND I'M JUST TRYING TO KEEP THE LIGHTS ON. FOR ME, AND YOU!
YOU CAN'T FOOL ME. YOU'RE A PLANET-RUINING, MONEY-EATING, LIE-SPOUTING JERK-FACE.
I...*AM.* I TRIED COMMISSIONING THIS COMIC BOOK AS A WAY TO SHOW EVERYONE THAT GRACKING ISN'T BAD.
UH...
I TRIED TO PRESENT ROXXON AS WORKING FOR THE GREATER GOOD AND MYSELF AS A NOT SO BAD GUY...

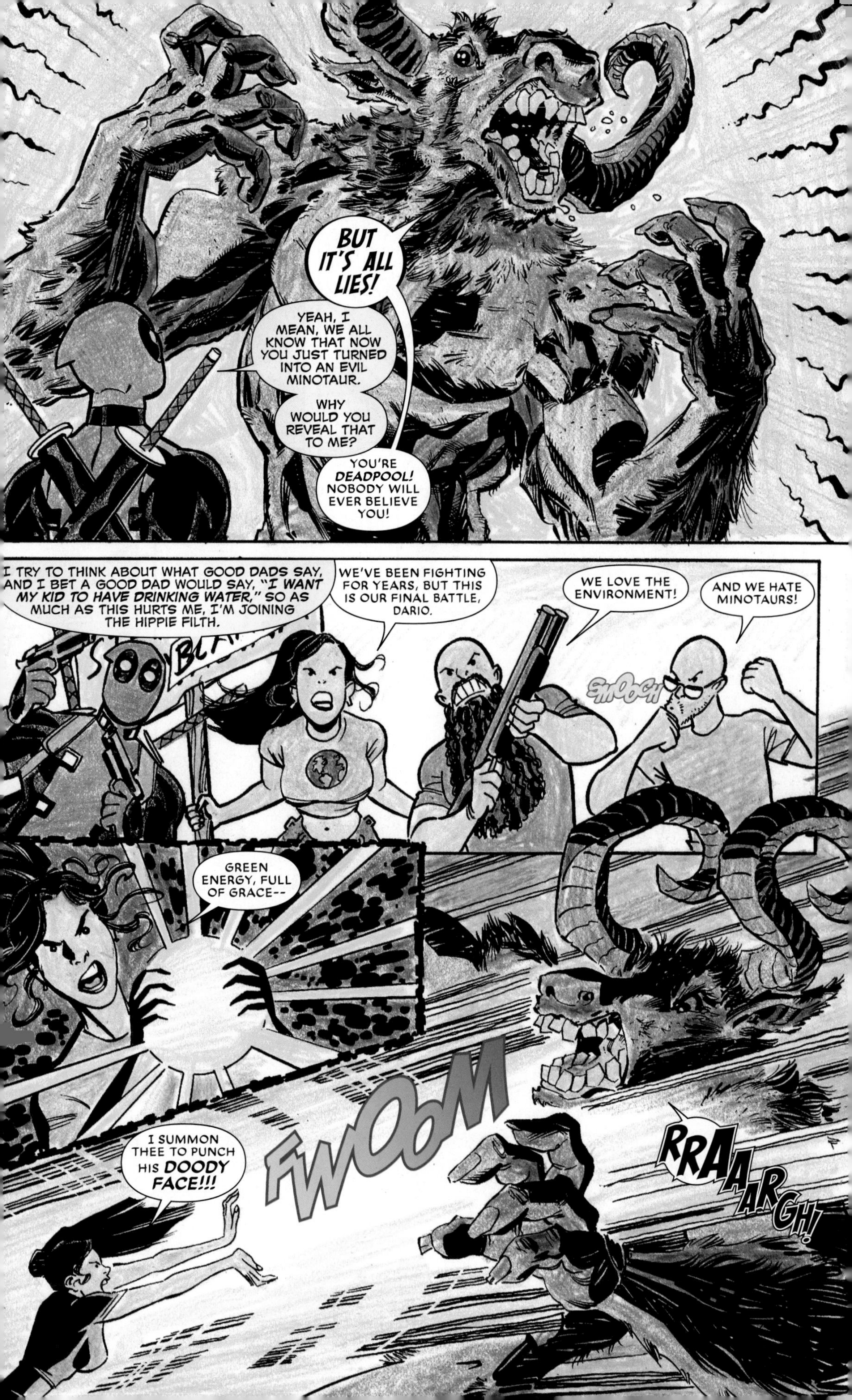
BUT IT'S ALL LIES!
YEAH, I MEAN, WE ALL KNOW THAT NOW YOU JUST TURNED INTO AN EVIL MINOTAUR.
WHY WOULD YOU REVEAL THAT TO ME?
YOU'RE *DEADPOOL!* NOBODY WILL EVER BELIEVE YOU!
I TRY TO THINK ABOUT WHAT GOOD DADS SAY, AND I BET A GOOD DAD WOULD SAY, *"I WANT MY KID TO HAVE DRINKING WATER,"* SO AS MUCH AS THIS HURTS ME, I'M JOINING THE HIPPIE FILTH.
WE'VE BEEN FIGHTING FOR YEARS, BUT THIS IS OUR FINAL BATTLE, DARIO.
WE LOVE THE ENVIRONMENT!
AND WE HATE MINOTAURS!
SHOOCH
GREEN ENERGY, FULL OF GRACE--
I SUMMON THEE TO PUNCH HIS **DOODY FACE!!!**
FWOOOM
RRAAAARGH!

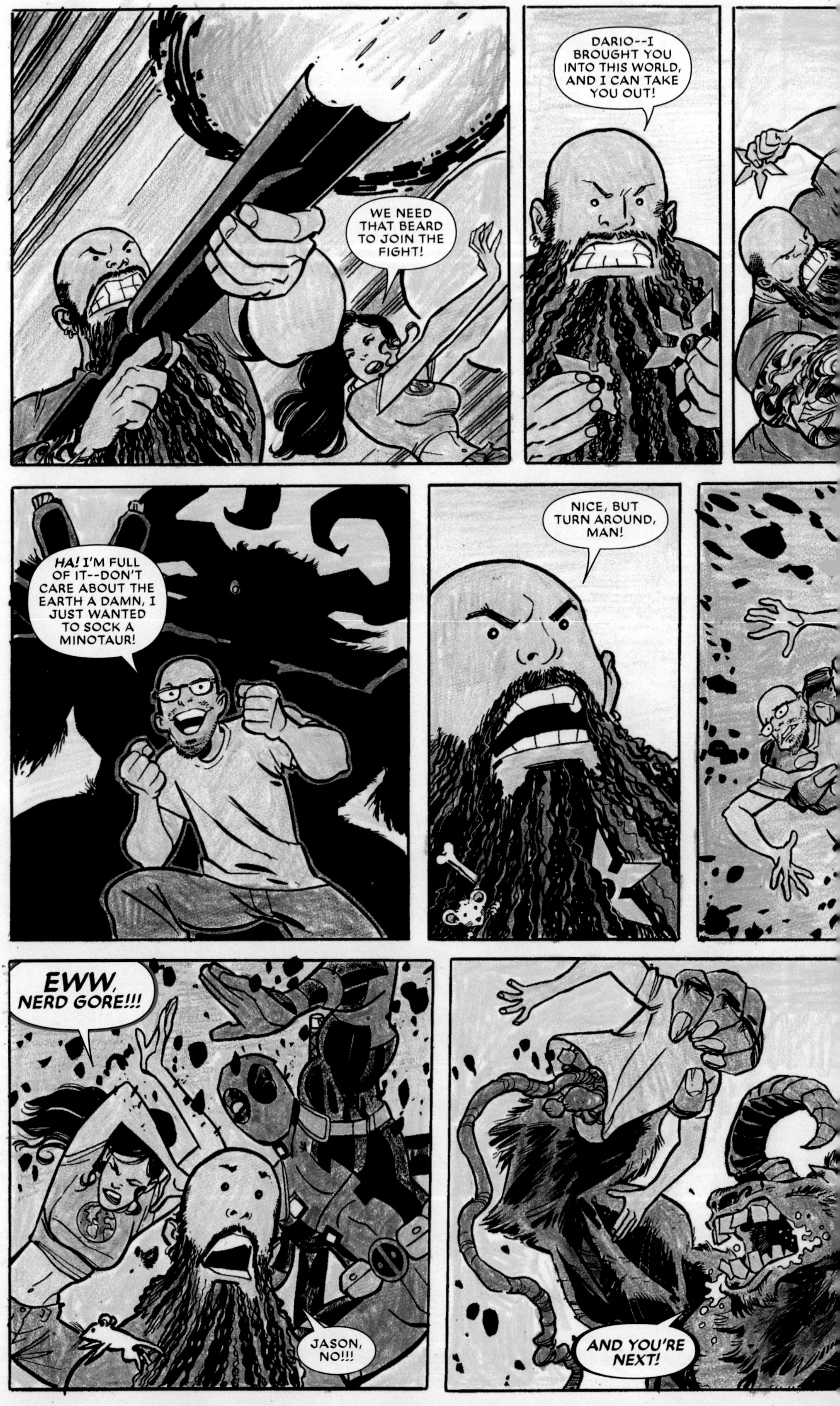
WE NEED THAT BEARD TO JOIN THE FIGHT!
DARIO--I BROUGHT YOU INTO THIS WORLD, AND I CAN TAKE YOU OUT!
HA! I'M FULL OF IT--DON'T CARE ABOUT THE EARTH A DAMN, I JUST WANTED TO SOCK A MINOTAUR!
NICE, BUT TURN AROUND, MAN!
EWW, NERD GORE!!!
JASON, NO!!!
AND YOU'RE NEXT!

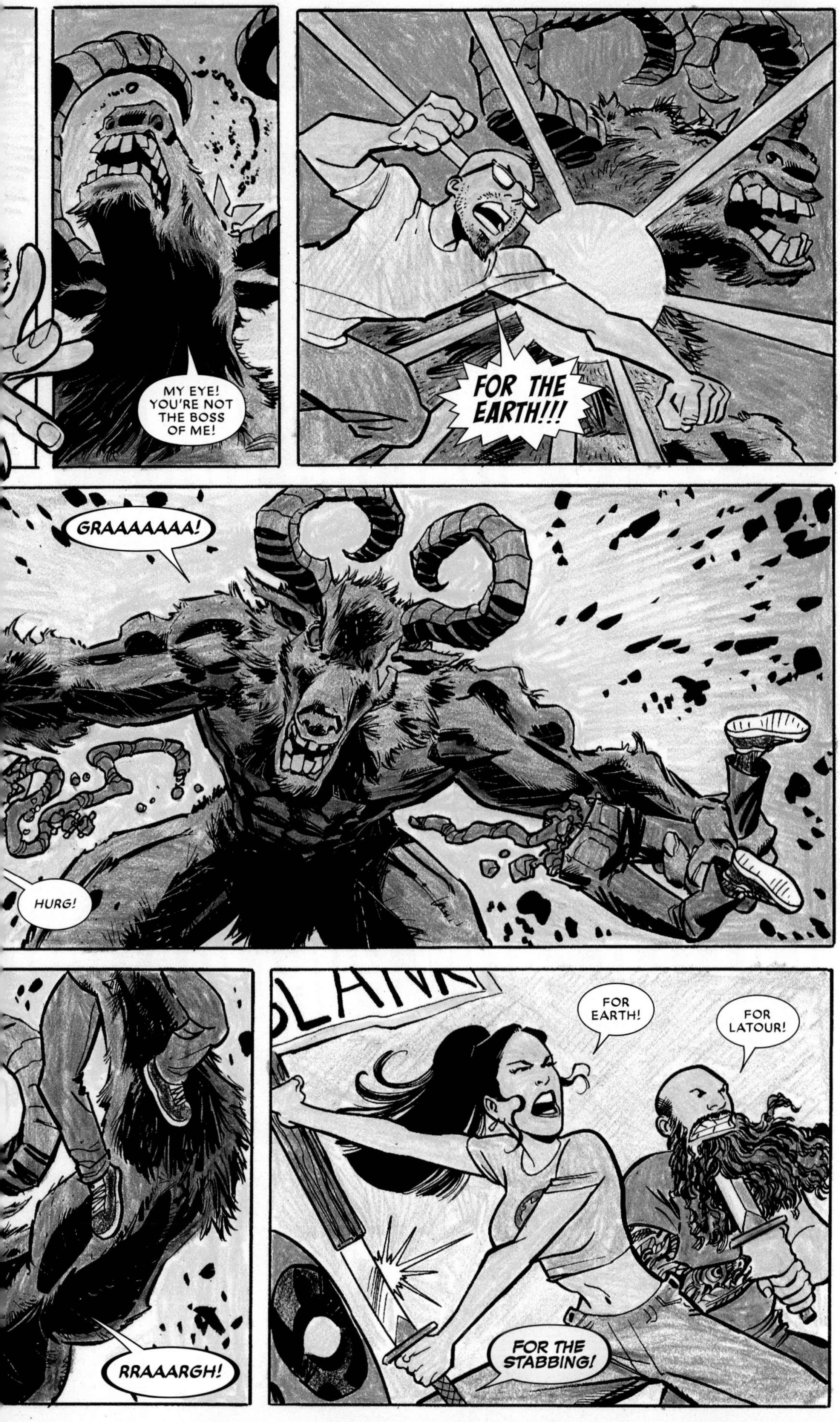
MY EYE! YOU'RE NOT THE BOSS OF ME!
FOR THE EARTH!!!
GRAAAAAAA!
HURG!
RRAAARGH!
FOR EARTH!
FOR LATOUR!
FOR THE STABBING!

DUE TO GRAPHIC VIOLENCE AND OBSCENE CONTENT, THIS SCENE HAS BEEN OMITTED FROM PUBLICATION.

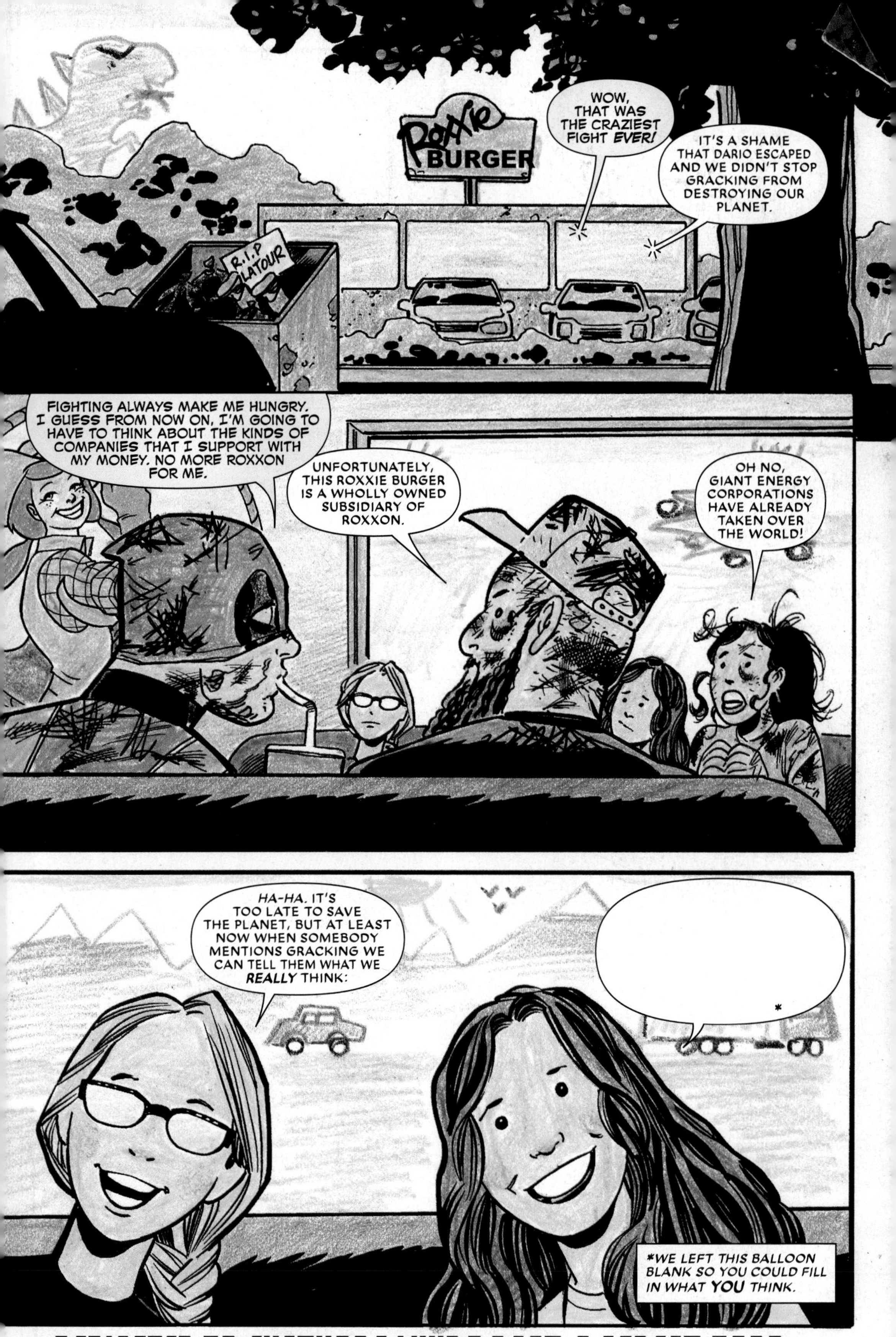
ROXXIE BURGER
R.I.P LATOUR
WOW, THAT WAS THE CRAZIEST FIGHT *EVER!*
IT'S A SHAME THAT DARIO ESCAPED AND WE DIDN'T STOP GRACKING FROM DESTROYING OUR PLANET.
FIGHTING ALWAYS MAKE ME HUNGRY. I GUESS FROM NOW ON, I'M GOING TO HAVE TO THINK ABOUT THE KINDS OF COMPANIES THAT I SUPPORT WITH MY MONEY. NO MORE ROXXON FOR ME.
UNFORTUNATELY, THIS ROXXIE BURGER IS A WHOLLY OWNED SUBSIDIARY OF ROXXON.
OH NO, GIANT ENERGY CORPORATIONS HAVE ALREADY TAKEN OVER THE WORLD!
HA-HA. IT'S TOO LATE TO SAVE THE PLANET, BUT AT LEAST NOW WHEN SOMEBODY MENTIONS GRACKING WE CAN TELL THEM WHAT WE *REALLY* THINK:
*
*WE LEFT THIS BALLOON BLANK SO YOU COULD FILL IN WHAT **YOU** THINK.

DEDICATED TO EVERYONE LIVING NEAR A CANCER POND.
AND JASON LATOUR. REST IN PEACE,
MY SOUTHERN BRO-STARD.

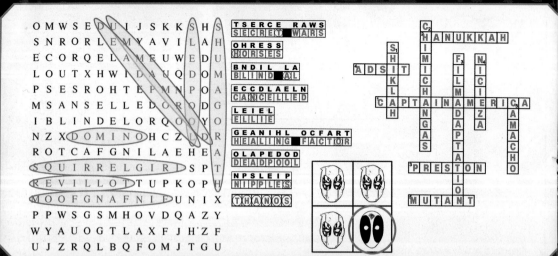

DEADPOOL #40
ACTIVITY BOOK ANSWER KEY

TO ACCESS THE FREE *MARVEL AUGMENTED REALITY APP* THAT ENHANCES AND CHANGES THE WAY YOU EXPERIENCE COMICS:

1. Download the app for free via
   marvel.com/ARapp
2. Launch the app on your camera-enabled Apple iOS® or Android™ device*

3. Hold your mobile device's camera over any cover or panel with the **AR** graphic.
4. Sit back and see the future of comics in action!

*Available on most camera-enabled Apple iOS® and Android™ devices. Content subject to change and availability.

AR

INDEX

Issue #20
New Villains .... Page 3, Panel 1
As the Page Turns episode 5 .... Page 16, Panel 1

Issue #13
Scapie White explains the ten rings of the Mandarin .... Page 11, Panel 4
The Official Handbook of the Marvel Universe: The White Man .... Page 20, Panel 8

Issue #7
Anti-drinking PSA video .... Page 10, Panel 1
1980s usenet version of Marvel AR .... Page 18, Panel 4